The Biographical Dictionary
of Greater India

Also by Henry Scholberg

Reference
    The District Gazetteers of British India : a Bibliography (1970)
    Bibliographie des Français dans l'Inde (1973)
    Catalog of the Ames Library of South Asia (16 Vols.) (1980)
    Bibliography of Goa and the Portuguese in India (1982)
    The Encyclopedias of India (1986)
    South Asia Biographical Dictionary Index (2 Vols.) (1987)

History
    Windsor Green! Twenty-Five Years of Town House Living (1990)
    The Indian Literature of the Great Rebellion (1992)
    Fortress Portugal in India : a Photographic History of the Portuguese Forts of India (1995)
    Windsor Green : a Five-year Supplement (1996)
    The French Pioneers of Minnesota : Les Pionniers Français du Minnesota (1997)

Drama
    The Boy King : a Play for Children of All Countries (1964)
    Calcutta 1851 (1976)
    Saroja : a Play in Three Countries (1977)
    Lakshmibai & the Captain (1985)
    Chandragupta Larka Raja (Hindi translation by P.N. Shastri of 'The Boy King') (1986)
    Balak Raja (Bengali translation by Dilip Chakraborty of 'The Boy King') (1986)
    Golden Bells : Two Plays for Advent (1992)
        CONTENTS: The Bells of Christmas Eve and The Golden Gift
    In The Time of Trial : Two Plays for Good Friday (1993)
        CONTENTS: The Face of Jesus and Pontius Pilate And The Dreams Of Claudia
    Katie Luther : a One-Act Play About Luther's Wife (1993)

Novels
    The Return of the Raj (American edition) (1993)
    A Hindi Movie (1994)
    The Return of the Raj (Indian edition) (1995)
    Tibet! (1995)

... and in the Works
    The Lonely Chipmunk : a Children's Story (1997)

The Biographical Dictionary of Greater India

Edited by
HENRY SCHOLBERG

"No one rises so high as he who knows not
whither he is going."

— Oliver Cromwell

Promilla & Co., Publishers
NEW DELHI

First published 1998 in India by Promilla & Co., Publishers
'Sonali', C-127, Sarvodaya Enclave, New Delhi 110 017

ISBN 81-85002-23-1
Library of Congress Card No. 97-905544

The biographical dictionary of greater India / edited by Henry Scholberg. —
New Delhi : Promilla & Co., 1998.

406 p. ; 25 cm.
Includes bibliographical references and index.
ISBN 81-85002-23-1

1. India—Biography—Dictionaries.   2. South Asia—
Biography—Dictionaries.   I. Scholberg, Henry, 1921-

Printed in India at Rakmo Press Pvt. Ltd.,
C-95, Okhla Industrial Area, Phase I, New Delhi 110 020
Typesetting and page-makeup at Alpha Graphics,
6A/1, Ganga Chambers, W.E.A., Karol Bagh, New Delhi 110 005

This volume is dedicated to

Mother Teresa

In her wise, devoted and humble way
this great lady personified
the best that abides in all of us.

TABLE OF CONTENTS

12.   THE RELIGIOUS LEADERS 257

13.   THE WRITERS 295

INTRODUCTION

"Let us now praise famous men."
— Ecclesiasticus 44:1

The purpose of the present work is to bring together into a single volume persons of note who have contributed to the history and culture of South Asia from the beginning of recorded history until the twentieth century.

The expression "Greater India" is intended to include the countries of Afghanistan, Bangladesh, India, Nepal, Pakistan and Sri Lanka.

About 60 years ago Rushbrook Williams published a book entitled *Great Men of India*. It is a fine work, devoted as it is to men of distinction from ancient, medieval and modern times: political leaders, scientists, reformers, educators and writers. There are just over 50 sketches, and it is not the intention here to level criticism on the book. Contributors included distinguished names like C.F. Andrews, Charles Kincaid, H.G. Rawlinson, H.H. Dodwell, Mrs. Rhys Davids, K.M. Panikkar and Naoroji Dumasia.

However, the implication of the book was that the only people of note who contributed to Indian history and culture were Indians. The statement our present work makes is that South Asia was influenced by persons from both within and without.

Therefore, along with Gautama Buddha, Asoka, Chandragupta Maurya, Krishnadevaraya, Rammohun Roy, Rani Lakshmibai, Nehru and Gandhi are Alexander the Great, St. Thomas, Vasco da Gama, Clive, Dupleix, Kipling and Lord Mountbatten.

This book is more than a biographical dictionary. It is a history book, relating the panorama of a great sub-continent as mirrored in the lives of the men and women who have made it what it is today.

There will be complaints for which the editor make no apologies. The view of history is necessarily subjective. Even a cell of history cannot be put on a slide and examined objectively under a microscope.

If you, the reader, were to compile a list of 150 or so famous people of South Asia, you would no doubt include many of the names we have listed here. By the same token you would eliminate some of our names and include some of your own.

There is no way that our choice of 157 names is going to please everyone. There are bound to be names whose inclusion will be questioned by some, and there are undoubtedly names whose exclusion will be questioned by others. And there will be some people who will question why more words were devoted to this one than to that one.

It is a sad fact of life that there are sometimes questions for which there are no answers.

We have tried, and we are sanguine enough to believe we succeeded, to make the sketches factual, accurate and readable. As a former librarian, this editor can affirm that reference books can be crushingly dull. One does not normally curl up with a book from the reference shelf and read it in front of the fire place. It is our hope that one might do so with this volume.

Nor should one read this book with the notion that it will impart a complete understanding of India. No book does that. However, this book will put the reader on the road to comprehending a region of the world which mystifies those who have never been there almost as much as it mystifies those who have lived there all their lives.

Names and Place Names

One of the problems confronting people who write about or study South Asia, is that of Romanization of the words and names of the region. Because the original words and names are in any of the several scripts, there are different ways of transliterating them into the Roman alphabet. Fortunately, there are a few names about which there is general agreement: Gandhi, Ranade, Gokhale, Akbar, Iqbal, Ramanuja — to name a few.

The many cause problems: Banerjee can be Bandopadhyay, Nehru Neharu, Premchand Premacanda, Tagore Thakura, Aurangzeb Aurangzib, Babur Babar — to name a few of the many.

In our work we have been guided for the most part by "popular usage." But what does one do when there is no recognisable popular usage ? One makes up one's own rules and tries to obey them.

Muslim names, or names originating in the Arabic, Persian or Urdu scripts, cause the most difficulty because there is so little general agreement there. For the sake of consistency R.C. Majumdar's *Advanced History of India* has usually been our guide, particularly for names of the Delhi Sultanate and Mughal (not Moghul or Mogal) periods.

As for place names, there are those of the pre-British period, the British period and the post-British period. Originally it was the Ganga river. Then the Greeks and the British came along, and it became Ganges. Now it is Ganga again. The same can be said of Banaras, Benaras and Varanasi.

What we have tried to do in the sketches is use the spelling in use at the time the subject was living. Thus, Nana Sahib was at Cawnpore in 1857. Today he would be at Kanpur.

As for English words, we are staying with English English as opposed to American English; so we have labour, connexion, sceptic and civilisation.

For doing this, can anyone put us in gaol?

Our thanks go to our many contributors, most of whom are historians. We have also heard from a political scientist, a geologist, professors of religion, librarians and not a few free lance writers.

Words can also cause confusion. "Sati" can be spelled "suttee" and "Brahman" "Brahmin." "Brahman" is the preferred spelling of the word which signifies the highest caste of the Hindus. "Brahmin" usually refers to a rich, snooty person, like a Boston Brahmin. Read on!

— **Henry Scholberg**
January 1996

THE CONTRIBUTORS

Glenn Ames — Assistant Professor, Department of History, University of Toledo, Toledo, OH (La Bourdonnais, La Haye, François Martin)

Subir K. Banerjee — Professor, Department of Geology, University of Minnesota (João de Castro)

Usha T. Bhasker — Head, South Asia Section, Oriental Division, New York Public Library (Andal)

Swami Chetanananda — Head, Vedanta Society of St. Louis and monk of the Ramakrishna Order (Ramakrishna, Vivekananda)

P. N. Chopra — Secretary and Chief Editor, Sardar Patel Society (Sardar Patel)

Diane Clayton — Librarian, Hamline University, St. Paul, Minnesota (Indira Gandhi, Sarojini Naidu, Nur Jahan, Mother Teresa)

Frank F. Conlon — Professor of History, University of Washington (Mountstuart Elphinstone, Govind Mahadev Ranade, Lokamanya Tilak)

John Correia-Afonso S.J. — Former Director, Heras Institute of Indian History and Culture, Bombay (Vasco da Gama)

James F. Fisher — Professor of Sociology and Anthropology, Carleton College, Northfield, Minnesota (Mahendra Bir Bikram Shah, Prithvinarayan Shah)

James D. Hunt — Professor of History, Shaw University, Raleigh, North Carolina (Mahatma Gandhi)

Mohd. Ikram — Professor Emeritus of History, Punjab University, Lahore (Ayub Khan, Zia-ul-Haq)

Milton Israel — Professor of History, University of Toronto (Ramananda Chatterjee)

Donald C. Johnson — Librarian, Ames Library of South Asia, University of Minnesota (Johann Buehler)

Blair B. Kling — Professor of History, University of Illinois (Dwarkanath Tagore, Jamsetji Nusserwanji Tata)

David Kopf — Professor of History, University of Minnesota (Bankim Chandra Chatterjee)

Gregory C. Kozlowski — Professor of History, DePaul University, Chicago (Jawaharlal Nehru)

James W. Laine — Professor of Religious Studies, Macalester College, St. Paul, Minnesota (Shivaji)

Joyce C. Lebra — Professor Emeritus of History, University of Colorado, Boulder, Colorado (Rani of Jhansi, Netaji Bose)

Roger Loug — Professor Emeritus of History, University of Delaware (Zulfiqar Ali Bhutto)

Niharkana Majumdar — Professor Emeritus of History, Lady Brabourne College, Calcutta (Robert Lord Clive)

George M. Moraes — Editor, *India : Past and Present* (St. Francisco Xavier)

K.A. Nizami — Professor of History, Aligarh Muslim University (Abul Fazl, Akbar the Great)

Pravrajika Atmaprana — Ramakrishna Sarada Mission, New Delhi (Sister Nivedita)

S. Ramakrishnan — Executive Director, Bharatiya Vidya Bhavan (Ramanuja)

Henry Scholberg — Professor Emeritus and Former Librarian, Ames Library of South Asia (Alexander the Great, James Skinner, Muhammad Ali Jinnah, Muhammad Iqbal, V.K. Krishna Menon, Francisco Luís Gomes)

Sergei Serebriany — Senior Research Fellow, Gorky Institute of World Literature, Moscow, U.S.S.R. (Chaitanya, Kabir, Kalidas, Raja Rammohun Roy, Rabindranath Tagore, Tulsi Das, Vidyasagar)

Om P. Sharma — Head, South Asia Section, University of Michigan Library (Warris Shah)

B.S. Shastry — Head & Professor, Department of History, Goa University, Bambolim, Goa (Krishnadeva Raya)

Gopal Singh — Governor of Goa (Guru Nanak, Guru Gobind Singh)

Michael W. Sonnleitner — Professor of Political Science, University of Northern Iowa (Vinoba Bhave)

Teotonio R. de Souza — Xavier Centre of Historical Research (Affonso de Albuquerque)

Eleanor Zelliot — Professor of History, Carleton College, Northfield, Minnesota (Bhimrao Ramji Ambedkar, Gopal Krishna Gokhale)

Publisher's Note: We thank the named contributors listed above for their sketches and for their forbearance and patience. We also thank the unnamed contributors who submitted their works anonymously.

GLOSSARY

Advaita	non-dualism
Ahimsa	non-killing
Atma	soul
Ayurveda	ancient Hindu medicine
Bhakti	religious devotion, or piety
Brahmacharya	life-long chastity
Brahman	a member of the highest Hindu caste
Brahmin	a rich American, usually from Boston
Chaddar	shawl
Chakra	spinning wheel
Feringhi	European (a pejorative term)
Guru	teacher
Hartal	labour strike
Jagir	estate
Jagirdar	ruler of an estate
Jauhar	group self-immolation
Kafir	infidel; a term used by Muslims for non-Muslims
Karma	fate; destiny
Khadi	hand-woven cloth
Kotwal	chief of police
Kshatriya	the second highest Hindu caste
Maharajadhiraja	supreme king of great kings
Masnavi	a poem in rhymed couplets
Mujahid	freedom fighter
Nautch	dance, performed usually by women
Nawab	governor; ruler
Nirvana	the state of a snuffed out candle
Nyaya	the problem of knowledge
Pandal	a shed or arbour constructed for temporary use
Pargana	district

Sadhana	search for complete meditation
Samadhi	complete meditation
Sannyasa	monastic vows
Sannyasi	ascetic
Sati	self-immolation of a widow on the pyre of her husband
Satyagraha	truth force
Sudra	the lowest Hindu caste
Swadeshi	indigenous
Swaraj	self-rule
Tathagata	the Enlightened One
Tirthankara	prophet; in Jainism
Ulema	Muslim theologian
Upasaka	lay Buddhist
Vaishya	the third highest Hindu caste
Vakil	lawyer
Vedanta	a system of idealistic monism
Vikramaditya	Sun of valour
Vizir	prime minister
Yoga	the union of the human soul with the Universal Spirit
Zilla	district

Note : It is worth mentioning that some of these terms have been taken into the English language.

CHAPTER 1

ANCIENT PERIOD

Alexander the Great	Kanishka
Chandragupta Maurya	Samudra Gupta
Chanakya	Chandra Gupta II
Asoka the Great	Harshavardhana

$\mathcal{T}$he ancient period of Indian history produced kings, writers, religious innovators and scientists who left their footprints. This chapter is concerned with the rulers — the *Maharajadhirajas* (supreme kings of great kings) — of the early days of India's recorded history.

Their lives are revealed in inscriptions, coins, traditions, and observations made by foreign visitors. The Asokan pillar tells about Samudra Gupta (*maharajadhiraja*), the greatest of the Gupta kings. The Chinese pilgrims, Fa Hsien and Hsuan Tsang, wrote of Chandra Gupta II (Vikramaditya) and Harshavardhana. Kanishka is found in the Chinese historical records. The mighty deeds of Chandragupta Maurya are reported by the historians, Greek and Roman, who copied from the writings of Megasthenes, a Greek ambassador to the court at Pataliputra.

The great historian of the period was Bana whose *Harsha Charita* records the life of Harshavardhana.

Each king who built his empire did so with conquest followed by conquest. However, once these kings gained control of their kingdoms, they generally ruled them with wisdom and compassion. Asoka stands above the others as one who learned most to abhor violence and to promote genuine peace.

All of the persons sketched in this chapter were kings, with the exception of Chanakya. He might more appropriately belong to the section which features great writers. However, his close association with his king and with the founding of the Maurya Dynasty argues forcibly for his being listed in Chapter 1.

ALEXANDER THE GREAT
(356-323 B.C.)

Alexander III, king of Macedonia, was born in 356 B.C. at Pella in Macedonia. He died thirty-three years later (13 June 323 B.C.) in Persia and is known to history as Alexander the Great.

As a teenager his tutor was Aristotle who imbued in him with a love of Greek culture which never left him. He won his first battle at the age of 14, and when 16, he victoriously commanded forces of his father's army at the Battle of Chaeronea which was won by Macedonia.

His father, Philip II, was assassinated in 336, and Alexander succeeded to the throne with the support of the army. He then embarked on a career of conquests which took him through Persia, to Egypt and ultimately to India. For the purposes here, the concern is with his activities in India.

Alexander fought four great battles. At Granicus (334 B.C.) he defeated the Persians, at Issus (333 B.C.) he defeated Darius and his Persian army, at Gaugamela (331 B.C.) he defeated them again, and finally at the Jhelum River (326 B.C.) he defeated King Porus and his Indian army in what is known as the Battle of the Hydaspes.

Alexander had left Bactria in 327 and proceeded through what is present day Afghanistan. He crossed the Hindu Kush and invaded India, but to secure his lines of communication he had established garrisons near modern Kabul. He spent the winter of 327-326 fighting tribes in the Kunar and Swat valleys and eventually conquered the city of Nyasa.

At Taxila he met Raja Ambhi with whom he arranged for support in the form of elephants and troops in return for aid against Taxila's enemy Porus.

Prior to the battle, Alexander was on the east bank of Jhelum and Porus on the west. The monsoon had begun, and Porus did not believe Alexander would attack till the monsoon wash over because he thought the river was unfordable, which it was. However, Alexander found a place about twenty-two kilometres north, and crossed at that point. He then attacked Porus in a ferocious battle during which Porus' elephants panicked and trampled friend and foe alike.

According to Plutarch, after the battle, Alexander asked Porus how he wished to be treated; and Porus answered: "As a king." This so impressed Alexander that he made Porus satrap of his Indian conquests.

Alexander wished to push farther east at this point, but his troops, who were weary of battle and not a little homesick, came close to mutiny. He decided to return to Persia. He went by land with part of his army while his admiral, Nearchus, went by sea with the remainder of the army.

Alexander's last years were spent consolidating his empire and trying to solve problems which had remained unsolved while he was busy fighting battles. That he cried because he had no more worlds to conquer is probably more apocryphal than true.

Alexander's influence on world history can not be underestimated. The period which followed his death is known as the Hellenistic Age.

When it was over, the Age of Rome took its place. Greek had become the lingua franca of the Mediterranean region, and this facilitated the spread of Christianity there.

It cannot be said Alexander the Great's influence in India was great. The extent to which he may have influenced Indian political and social institutions is negligible, and the same can probably be said of Greek influence on Indian learning. To quote the French scholar Sylvain Levy, "The name of Alexander the Great which has maintained the same prestige in the traditions of the Near East as in those of the West, has not yet been discovered even in a single Indian text."

However, in Gandhara and Taxila are found works which combine the best of Indian art with the best of Greek art.

Can this be the only legacy of Alexander in Greater India ?

— **Henry Scholberg**

Suggested Further Readings

McCrindle, John Watson, 1825-1913.
The invasion of India by Alexander the Great ... — New York : Barnes & Noble, [1969]
xxxix, 432 p. : ill., maps ; 23 cm. Reprint of 1896 ed.

Tarn, William Woodthorpe, Sir, 1869-1957.
Alexander the Great. — Cambridge (England) : University Press, 1948-50.
2 v. : fold. map ; 23 cm.

CHANDRAGUPTA MAURYA

The origin of Chandragupta is obscure, and documentation on it comes from varied sources: Greek and Roman historians, the *Puranas*, Pali chronicles from Sri Lanka, and Jain and Buddhist tradition.

Even the Sanskrit play *Mudrarakshasa* contains reference to him as being *vrishala* (of low birth, a Sudra); however, this term can also mean a Kshatriya who broke away from Brahmanical traditions.

Justin describes Sandracottus (Chandragupta) as being of "low origin," and both he and Plutarch claim he had an ecounter with Alexander. According to Jain tradition, Chandragupta was born of a family which raised peacocks. On the other hand, Buddhist tradition says, he came from a Kshatriya clan called Moriyas, derived from the word for peacock.*

This tradition says, his father, chief of his tribe, died in a border skirmish, after which the widow sought refuge in Pataliputra, where she gave birth to Chandragupta. In his childhood he was abducted by a cowherd who later sold him to a hunter. In turn he was purchased by Chanakya (also known as Kautilya), a political adviser, for 1,000 karshapanas.

---

* It is noteworthy that the family crest of Asoka, Chandragupta's grandson, contains a peacock.

The story goes that Chanakya had offered his services to the Nanda King of Magadha but had been rudely and summarily turned down. One day he happened upon some children who were playing a game in which one of them (Chandragupta) pretended to be the king. Chanakya saw potential in the young "king," bought him from the hunter, took him to Taxila and taught him the art of kingship. As a child, then, Chandragupta could have been in Taxila at the time Alexander passed through; so it is entirely possible that he may have seen him, if not have actually had a personal encounter with him. One version of the encounter is that he offended Alexander and was sentenced to die, but he escaped. (Chanakya would later be remembered in history as an early day Machiavelli and the author of the *Arthashastra*, a treatise on statecraft.)

In the Buddhist text, *Mahavatsa-tika*, Chanakya, following the completion of Chandragupta's education, raised an army and put Chandragupta in command of it. Justin's version has it that his army was a band of robbers. It is more likely that Arrian's description is correct of the recruits as persons from republican, or kingless tribes (known as *Arashtrakas*), then found in the Punjab.

Chandragupta, with his new-found army, fought against the Greeks following the departure of Alexander. To quote Justin:

> India, after Alexander's death, as if the yoke of servitude had been shaken off her neck, had put this Prefect (Philip) to death. Sandracottus was the leader who achieved this freedom .... He was born in humble life .... Having collected a band of robbers, he instigated the Indians to overthrow the existing government ... He was thereafter prepared to attack Alexander's Prefects, mounted on an elephant which fought vigorously in front of the army.

Following his success in the Punjab against foreign rule, Chandragupta turned his attention to Magadha which was under the corrupt rule of the Nandas.

He marched on the capital, Pataliputra, but in doing so, committed serious errors. In the Buddhist version:

> In his ambition to be a monarch, without beginning at the frontier and taking towns as he passed, he invaded the heart of the country and found his army surrounded by people on all sides and routed like a child eating the middle part of a cake and not eating from the edges, which were thrown away.

He tried a second time and made a second mistake. He began operations from the frontiers and conquered several states, but neglected to post garrisons to hold his conquests.

On his third try he succeeded, posting garrisons along the way. He conquered Pataliputra in a great battle, seized the government of Magadha and put its king, Dhanananda, to death.

The Jain version of this campaign reads:

Like a child burning his finger which he greedily puts in the middle of a dish, instead of eating from the outer part which was cool, Chanakya had been defeated because he had not secured the surrounding country before attacking the stronghold of the enemy. Profiting by this advice, Chanakya went to Himatvatuka and entered into an alliance with Parvataka, the king of the place .... They opened the campaign by reducing the provinces.

The kingdom of Magadha, now ruled by Chandragupta, extended roughly from the Punjab to Bihar and as far south as the Tinnevelli district. Tamil tradition speaks of a "Mauryan upstart" who advanced that far.

In 304 B.C. Seleukos, one of Alexander's generals, tried to reconquer India. Chandragupta defeated him in battle and in the treaty of peace acquired Parapondisadae (Kabul), Aria (Herat), Arachosia (Kandahar) and Gedrosia (part of Afghanistan and modern Baluchistan). For his part, Seleukos acquired 500 elephants and was authorised to place a Greek ambassador named Megasthenes in the court of Chandragupta.

Between the writings of Chanakya and Megasthenes, we are given a fairly clear picture of India during the early years of the Mauryan Empire. (Only fragments of Megasthenes' writings are extant, but he was widely quoted by later writers.) The kingdom was divided into provinces, each with its own *adhipati* (governor). The smallest unit of government was the *grama* (village) ruled by a *gramani* and groups of 10, 20, 100, and 1,000 villages were ruled by *dasi, vimsi, satesa* and *sahasresa*.

These officials collected revenue and enforced the laws. The villages were largely self-governing and functioned like republics. Every ten villages were served by a market town called a *samgrahana*, and every 300 or 400 villages had their county towns called *kharvataka* and *dronamukha*.

Megasthenes gave a vivid description of the city of Pataliputra and said that the king was carried in a golden palanquin adorned with tassels of pearls. He was protected by armed female guards.

The principal royal sport was the hunt, and popular sports consisted of fights of bulls, rams, elephants, rhinos and ox races.

The reign of Chandragupta lasted about twenty four years.

According to Jain tradition, towards the end Chandragupta abdicated, converted to the religion of Mahavira and lived out his last days in Sravana Belgola in Karnataka. This tradition is contradicted by Greek writers who say he never lost his taste for the hunt.

He died in 296 B.C. and was succeeded by his son, Bindusara, known to the Greeks as *Amitraghata*, "the Slayer of Foes".

Chandragupta was the first ruler to bring much of India into one kingdom, but his mighty empire would last only a few generations.

Suggested Further Readings

McCrindle, John Watson, 1825-1913.
    Ancient India as described in the classical literature. — Westminster : Constable, 1901.
    xxi, 226 p. ; 21 cm.

Nilakanta Sastri, Kallidaikurichi Aiyah Aiyar.
    The age of the Nandas and the Mauryas. — Banaras : Motilal Banarsidas, 1952.
    xxi, 438 p. : plates, fold. maps ; 22 cm.

CHANAKYA

The story of Chanakya (or Kautilya or Vishnugupta), the author of the
Arthashastra might more appropriately belong to the part which contains
sketches of illustrious writers, both ancient and modern. However, his life
and work is so closely identified with that of Chandragupta Maurya that it
may fit better here.

His origin, like that of the king he so nobly served, is obscure. It is
unanimously conceded, however, that he was a Brahman. It is not known
where or when he was born or where he acquired his understanding of
statecraft, which is the subject of his great work; but at some point he is
supposed to have offered his services to Dhanananda, the king of Magadha,
the capital of which was Pataliputra.

(Pataliputra was the Sanskrit name of the present city of Patna, the
capital of Bihar. In Chanakya's time it was known by the Greeks as Palibotra.
This name survived several centuries, and early Ptolemaic maps of India
show a city called Palibotra on the Ganga River, which the Greeks called
Ganges River.)

Dhanananda rejected Chanakya's offer of service, and the next we learn
of Chanakya is that he is in the area of the Vindhya Hills. He is in a village
common when he notices some children playing a game in which one of
them (Chandragupta) plays the part of a king.

Chanakya saw something in the character of this make-believe king,
bought him from his owner, who was a hunter, for 1,000 karshapanas and
took him to Taxila for his education.

The education lasted seven or eight years, after which Chanakya gathered an army to fight the Greeks who were left to rule the country on the
departure of Alexander. The army was financed, according to legend, by a
conveniently-found buried treasure.

Chandragupta defeated Greek rulers in the Punjab and then turned his
attention to Magadha where Chanakya had a score to settle. Chanakya made
an alliance with Parvataka, the king of the Himalayan kingdom,
Himatvatuka, and marched on Pataliputra, defeated Dhanananda, whose
armies were led by Bhadrasala.

With Chandragupta on the throne, Chanakya served as his adviser and
chief minister. Like many ancient manuscripts, the date of its writing is not
certain, and even its authorship is in dispute. The German school (Jolly,
Winternitz, Schmidt) puts the date of the *Arthashastra* to the fourth century
A.D.

That Chanakya (Kautilya) was responsible for defeating the Nanda king and enthroning Chandragupta is found in this passage from the *Vishnupurana*:

(First) Mahapadma, then his sons, only nine in number, will be lords of the earth for a hundred years. Those Nandas Kautilya, a Brahman, will slay. On their death, the Mauryas will enjoy the earth. Kautilya himself will install Chandragupta on their throne. His son will be Bindusara, and his son Ashokavardhana.

It is deduced from epigraphical evidence that Chandragupta became king in 321 B.C. and that Asoka ascended the throne around 273 B.C.; so it can therefore be reckoned that the *Arthashastra* was written some time during that interval.

The *Arthashastra* was not the only work on ancient Indian polity. In the concluding verse are these words:

Drshtva vipratipattim bahudha sastreshu bhashya-karanam,
Svayameva Vishnuguptas cakara sutram ca bhashyam ca.*

The *Arthashastra* is divided into 15 books:

Book   I   :   Concerning Discipline
Book   II   :   The Duties of Government Superintendents
Book   III :   Concerning Law
Book   IV   :   Removal of Thorns
Book   V   :   Conduct of Courtiers
Book   VI   :   The Source of Sovereign States
Book   VII :   The End of Sixfold Policy
Book   VIII :   Concerning Vices and Calamities
Book   IX   :   The Work of an Invader
Book   X   :   Relating to War
Book   XI   :   The Conduct of Corporation
Book   XII :   Concerning a Powerful Enemy
Book   XIII :   Strategic Means to Capture a Fortress
Book   XIV :   Secret Means
Book   XV   :   The Plan of a Treatise

Book I is a table of contents, explaining what is going to be in the subsequent books. Book XV explains how a treatise should be written. It should consist of 15 Books, 150 chapters, 180 sections and 6,000 *shlokas*, each *shloka* having 32 syllables.

Some of the chapters contain a code of laws, laying down appropriate punishments, such as fines, mutilation and torture, for malefactors. Other portions are concerned with protocol, conduct and administrative duties of government servants.

---

*   (Having seen discrepancies in many ways on the part of the writers of commentaries on the *Sastras*, Vishnugupta himself has made this *Sutra* and commentary.)

Books VI-X and XII-XIV have to do with sovereignty, diplomacy and military strategy. "Whatever pleases himself the king shall not consider as good," says Chanakya, "but whatever pleases his subjects he shall consider as good."

Book VI says a good king should be "born of high family, godly, possessed of valour, seeing through the medium of aged persons, virtuous, truthful, not of a contradictory nature, grateful, having large aims, highly enthusiastic, not addicted to procrastination, powerful to control his neighbouring kings, of resolute mind, having an assembly of ministers of no mean quality, and possessed of a taste for discipline — these are the qualities of an inviting nature."

Chanakya has advice which should be taken seriously by rulers even in this century:

A wise king can make even the poor and miserable elements of his sovereignty happy and prosperous; but a wicked king will surely destroy the most prosperous and loyal elements of his kingdom.

Hence a king of unrighteous character and of vicious habits will, though he is an emperor, fall prey either to the fury of his own subjects or to that of his enemies.

But a wise king, trained in politics, will, though he possesses a small territory, conquer the whole earth with the help of the beautiful elements of his sovereignty, and will never be defeated.

Suggested Further Readings

Kautilya.
Kautilya's Arthasastra / tr. by R. Shamasastry. — 7th ed. — Mysore : Mysore Printing and Publishing House, [1961]
xxxix, 484, iii p. ; 22 cm.
[1st ed. 1909]

Law, Narendra Nath.
Aspects of ancient Indian polity. — Oxford : Clarendon, 1921.
xx, 228 p. ; 23 cm.

ASOKA THE GREAT

The date of Asoka's birth is not known, and not many historians are brave enough to hazard a guess. What is known is that he was the grandson of Chandragupta who founded the Mauryan Dynasty in approximately 324 B.C. (not long after Alexander left India) and the son of Bindusara, the second in the Mauryan lineage.

On the death of Bindusara in circa 273 B.C., Asoka became ruler of the Mauryan kingdom for a reign of about 40 years. He was officially enthroned at Pataliputra (modern Patna) about four years after Bindusara's death.

What we know of his life and works is gleaned from his inscriptions, edicts and literary tradition. In the inscriptions he is often referred to as Devanampiya ("Beloved of the Gods") or Priyadarsin ("Of Benevolent Appearance").

During his father's lifetime, Asoka is believed to have been viceroy of the northwestern region which included Kashmir and the Punjab with its capital in Taxila. After that he was viceroy of the western region with its capital at Ujjain. According to a Sinhala legend, Asoka was in Ujjain at the time of his father's death.

In the first eight years of his reign he continued the aggressive policies of his father — who was called "Slayer of Foes" by Greek historians — and grandfather, under whom the Mauryan Empire had grown to include most of both Afghanistan and India. His first major action was that of putting down a revolt in Taxila.

But his war with the Kalingas in southern Orissa changed him forever. It is said that after a great victory he surveyed the battlefield and was appalled by the death and suffering he witnessed there; whereupon, he gave up his violent ways and adopted a policy of peace.

An edict recording this event reads in part:

His Majesty King Priyadarsin in the ninth year of his reign conquered the Kalingas.

One hundred and fifty thousand were thence carried away captive, one hundred thousand were slain, and many times that number perished.

Ever since the annexation of the Kalingas, His Majesty has zealously protected the Law of Piety, has been devoted to that law, and has proclaimed its precepts.

His Majesty feels remorse on account of the conquest of the Kalingas, because, during the subjugation of a previously unconquered country, slaughter, death and taking occur, whereat His Majesty feels profound sorrow and regret ....

After the Kalinga War, Asoka became an *upasaka* (lay Buddhist), steeped himself in Buddhist teachings and altered his policies radically. Instead of conquest by armed force, there would be "conquest by morality." The "reverberation of the war drum" would be replaced by the "reverberation of the law."

Not content with the peaceful policies within his own empire, Asoka sent forth missionaries to neighbouring kingdoms. However, he never tried to force his beliefs on others, and he maintained tolerant, if not friendly, relations with Hindu communities within his realm and with nearby kingdoms.

He opposed animal slaughter, whether for providing food or for sacrificial purposes, and he discouraged the royal hunt. In one of his edicts he states:

Obedience must be rendered to mother and father, likewise to elders; firmness (of compassion) must be shown towards animals; truth must be spoken: these same moral virtues must be practised.

In the same way the pupil must show reverence to the master, and one must behave in a suitable manner towards relatives.

During the 13th year after his coronation, Asoka began a programme of circuits by which, every five years his officials would proclaim the moral law throughout the land.

There is no record of the last eight years of his life, except that he died in 232 B.C. and that he was succeeded by two of his grandsons: Dasaratha, who ruled the eastern and Samprati, the western parts of his empire. His empire survived him, but not for long.

Asoka was one of those rare phenomena in Indian history, and indeed in the history of the world, who combined in one person the qualities of both greatness and goodness.

Suggested Further Readings

Bhandarkar, Devadatta Ramkrishna, 1875-1950.
    Asoka. — 4th ed. — [Calcutta] : University of Calcutta, 1969.
    xxx, 366 p. ; 23 cm. — (Carmichael lectures ; 1923)

Gokhale, Balkrishna Govind.
    Asoka Maurya. — New York : Twayne, [1966]
    194 p. : map ; 21 cm. — (Twayne's rulers and statesmen of the world series ; 3)

Smith, Vincent Arthur, 1848-1920.
    Asoka : the Buddhist emperor of India. — Oxford : Clarendon, 1901.
    204 p. : port. ; 18.5 cm. — (Rulers of India ; v. 28)

KANISHKA

The life of Kanishka, one of the great kings of ancient India, is documented by Chinese sources, inscriptions and coins.

The date of Kanishka was the subject of a two-day seminar in 1913 which fixed it at 58 A.D., but the debate among historians may never cease. The traditional date of Kanishka, 78 A.D., is the beginning of the Saka era. *Britannica* has him flourishing circa 120 A.D. Other scholars have his reign starting as late as 140 A.D. Whatever the date of Kanishka, it is agreed that he ruled twenty-three years and that his realm included Kashmir and Afghanistan. He was a Kushan (Kuie-Shuang), belonging to one of the five tribes into which the Yue-Chi (Indo-Scythians) were divided after their occupation of Bactria.

Kanishka is thought to have been the successor of Kadphises II, the Kushan ruler who conquered parts of the Indian interior, set up a governor to rule in his name and then became a convert to Saivism. In his time Kanishka increased his domain so that ultimately it extended from Bukhara on the west to Pataliputra on the east and the Pamirs in the north to central India in the south. His capital was at Purushapura (Peshawar).

He was a patron of the arts, as were many of the great kings of ancient India, but his fame rests chiefly on his patronage of Buddhism. He expended large sums towards the construction of Buddhist monuments and convened the fourth Buddhist council at Jullundur under the leadership of his teacher, Vasumitra. The beginning of Mahayana Buddhism is thought to date from this council. The council was called because Kanishka was confused by the many different views expressed by monks who visited him daily. In the Chinese historical records this account is given :

> In the 400th year after the *Nirvana* of Tathagata, Kanishka, king of Gandhara, at the proper time having fulfilled his destiny, his royal influence reached far, so that distant peoples adhered to him. In his spare moments amidst the affairs of government he always studied the Buddhist *sutras*, and daily invited one monk to enter the palace and to expound the doctrine. But because different explanations of the doctrine were held by the various sects, the king was filled with doubt, and he had no way to remove his uncertainty ....
>
> The king then issued an edict to assemble saintly and wise men from far and near. Thereupon people from the four quarters came together like the spoke at the hub ...
>
> The proceedings of the council were engraved on copper plates.

Kanishka was tolerant of all religions because his coins honoured Brahmanic, Zoroastrian and Greek gods — and of course, the Buddha.

Suggested Further Reading

Narain, A.K.
   From Alexander to Kanishka. — Varanasi : Banaras Hindu University, 1967.
   vi, 117 p., plates ; 26 cm. — (Department of Ancient Indian Culture & Archaeology.
   Monographs ; No. 1)

SAMUDRA GUPTA

The Gupta Age began with the founding of the Gupta Dynasty by Chandra Gupta I. He was not the first of the family to rule, but the first to assume the title *Maharajadhiraja* (supreme king of great kings) and make it stick. This was around 320 A.D., when he formed a matrimonial alliance with a Lichchavi princess, Kumara Devi. The Lichchavis at that time ruled parts of Bihar and possibly, portions of Nepal as well.

Chandra was the son of Ghatotkacha and the grandson of Sri Gupta. He conquered most of the Gangetic Plain from Prayaga (Allahabad) to northern Bengal.

Towards the end of his reign, circa 335, he held an assembly of councillors during which his successor, Samudra, was nominated.

Samudra, the greatest of the Gupta rulers, was well-known outside his kingdom as is indicated by the *Tantrikamandaka*, a Javanese manuscript, and by the action of Sri Meghavarna of Ceylon in sending an ambassador to him to obtain permission to build a monastery for Ceylonese pilgrims at Bodh Gaya.

However, most of the information about him comes from an inscription engraved on the Asokan pillar at Allahabad. It is a eulogy composed by Harisena, and there is also an epigraph which was found in central India. Numerous coins issued during the reign of Samudra tell of his conquests.

Samudra conquered many kingdoms during his reign, the first two being Ahichchhatra in Rohilkhand and Padmavati in central India, ruled by Achutya and Nagasena respectively. Other kings in north and central India defeated by Samudra were Rudradeva, Matila, Nagadatta, Chandravarman, Ganapatinaga, Nandin and Balavarman.

Samudra also invaded the Deccan, defeating Mahendra of Kosala in the Upper Mahanadi Valley, Vraghra Raja (the tiger king of the wilderness of Mahakantara), Mantaraja of Kurala, Mahendragiri of Pishtapura in the Godavari district, Svamidatta of Kottura in the north of the Tamil country, Damana of Erindapapa, Nilaraja of Avamukta, Hastivarman (the Salankayana king of Vengi which is located between the Godavari and Krishna rivers), Ugrasena of Pulakka thought to be in the Nellore district, Kubera of Devarashtra in the Vizagapatam district, Dhananjaya of Kusthalapur around North Arcot and Vishnugopa of the Palava kingdom of Kanchipuram in the Chingleput district.

He restored the Deccan kings to their thrones and extracted tribute from them, but in the north he totally uprooted many kings and ruled their lands directly.

It is not only his military conquests for which Samudra Gupta is famous. He was a patron of the arts and a scholar, poet and musician in his own right. One of his coins shows him playing a musical instrument, a harp or lyre.

At his death in about 380, Samudra Gupta was succeeded by his son Chandra Gupta II, called Vikramaditya.

Suggested Further Readings

A list of books on Samudra and all the Guptas will be found following the sketch of Chandra Gupta II.

CHANDRA GUPTA II, VIKRAMADITYA

Chandra Gupta II succeeded to the throne of his father, Samudra Gupta, in about 380 A.D. Whether this was in the natural progression of things, or, as some scholars believe, that it occurred in a more dramatic fashion, is a matter of conjecture.

The story goes that the prince who inherited the throne was a weak prince named Rama Gupta. He agreed to surrender his wife, Dhruvadevi, to a Saka tyrant. His younger brother, Chandra Gupta, saved the family honour by slaying the tyrant, after which he murdered his brother and married his grieving widow.

Once on the throne, he continued his father's aggressive policies by conquering the Saka rulers of Ujjain, but he also strengthened his empire by matrimonial alliances. He married his daughter Prabhavati to the Vataka king, Rudrasena II. When the king died at an early age, she served as regent for the heirs to his throne, thereby increasing Gupta power in that part of the country. Chandra Gupta also consolidated his influence with the Naga rulers by accepting the hand of princess Kuberanaga.

Chandra took the title *Vikramaditya*, meaning "Sun of Valour," and surrounded himself in his court with the *Navaratna* ("nine gems"). These were the great writers who produced lasting works of Sanskrit literature that sparkled in the Golden Age of India. Chief of these was Kalidasa, "India's Shakespeare."

One of the celebrated events of the reign of Chandra II was the arrival of Fa-Hsien, a pilgrim from China. In his journal he spoke highly of conditions in the Ganges Valley:

> The people are numerous and happy .... The king governs without decapitation or other corporal punishment; criminals are simply fined, lightly or heavily according to the circumstances. Even in repeated attempts at wicked rebellion, they only have their right hands cut off.

On the death of Chandra in 413, Kumara Gupta I succeeded to the throne, followed in 455 by Skanda Gupta who repelled the Huns and took the *Vikramaditya* title. After his death in 467, the Gupta Empire went into decline, the last of the line being Vainya Gupta who reigned around 510.

Suggested Further Readings

Banerjee, Rakhal Das, 1885-1930.
    The age of the imperial Guptas. — New Delhi : Ramanand Vidya Bhawan, 1981.
    250 p., [16] p. of plates : ill. ; 22 cm.

Dandekar, R.N.
    The age of the Guptas and other essays. — Delhi : Ajanta, 1982.
    viii, 391 p. ; 23 cm. — (Select writings ; 4)

Ganguly, Dilip Kumar, 1939–
    The imperial Guptas and their times. — New Delhi : Abhinav, 1987.
    xii, 184 p. ; 23 cm.

HARSHAVARDHANA,
KING OF THANESAR & KANAUJ
(c.590-c.647)

Harshavardhana was born circa 590, the son of King Prabhakara Vardhana of Thanesar (in the Punjab) and Queen Yasovati "in the month Jyaistha, on the twelfth day of the dark fortnight, the Pleiads being in the ascendant, just after the twilight time."

For an ancient Indian king, his life is well documented. There are inscriptions, travel records of Hsuan Tsang, a Chinese pilgrim, and *Harsha Charita* by Bana, the court chronicler. Most of the quotations in this sketch are from the *Harsha Charita*.

Harsha's family background is also well documented. He was of the Maukhari Dynasty of Kanauj. His father is thought to have been the son of a Gupta princess. He was a petty chief in a district called Sthanvisvara in the land of Srikantha. He fought against the Huns who were invading India around this time, and he conquered much of north India. In the inscriptions it is recorded that he was the "one whose fame spread beyond the four seas, and to whom submitted other kings in power or love." He called himself *Maharajadhiraja* (supreme king of great kings) and was the son of Aditya Vardhana and grandson of Rajya Vardhana I who were merely Maharajas.

Harsha had a brother, Rajya, and a sister, Rajyasri, both of whom were older than he. The sister was married off to Prince Graha Varman, the son of Avanti Varman, king of Kanauj. Shortly after that, Rajya Vardhana, the elder brother, was fighting the Huns because the king was too old and feeble to do so himself. During this time young Harsha, aged about 16, was hunting lions, tigers and boars in the foot hills. When he learned that his father, the king was dying, he hurried to his side. The king's last words to Harsha were:

> Succeed to this world, appropriate my treasury, make prize of the feudatory kings, support the burden of royalty, protect the people, guard well your dependents, practise well your arms, annihilate your foes.

When Rajya arrived on the scene, bandages covering arrow wounds suffered from Hun arrows, he was so saddened by his father's death that he resolved to renounce the world and become an ascetic, leaving his throne to his younger brother, Prince Harsha. But Prince Harsha persuaded him to remain on the throne.

Rajya did not remain on the throne for long. A servant of Rajyasri, brought word that Rajyasri's husband, Graha Varman, had been killed by Deva Gupta, the "wicked lord of Malwa", and that Rajyasri "has been confined like a brigand's wife with a pair of iron fetters kissing her feet and cast into prison."

As if that was not enough, the servant reported that Deva Gupta was planning to attack Thanesar. Rajya immediately mounted a campaign against Malwa, was victorious in short order but afterwards was killed by Sasanka, the king of Gauda. The situation that confronted the 16-year-old Harsha was that both Kanauj and Thanesar had been deprived of their kings. At this point in his life, Harsha had been contemplating entering a Buddhist monastery, and when the ministers of Kanauj requested him to assume the throne of Kanauj, he was reluctant to accept it.

This point has been disputed by historians. According to Hsuan Tsang, however, he went to consult a statue of Buddha. When he approached it, the statue came to life and asked him what he wanted. He replied that he was troubled over the deaths of his father and his brother and that he was hesitant to accept the "royal dignity" that was being offered to him. Buddha informed him that he had been a hermit in his previous life and that because of his meritorious conduct, he had been born a prince in this life. Therefore, he should accept the kingship and "if you give your mind to compassion the condition of the distressed and cherish them, then before long you shall rule over the five Indies."

Harshavardhana, king of Thanesar and Kanauj, on accepting the "royal dignity," was first confronted with two tasks: to rescue his sister and to punish his brother's murderer.

Rajyasri had managed to escape from her captivity and hide out in the Vindhya Forest. When Harsha found her, it was not a moment too soon. In despair, she was about to throw herself on a funeral pyre. Harsha saved her in the nick of time.

During the next six years (606-612) Harsha waged wars against his enemies and established an empire that extended more or less from Gujarat to Assam. Gauda was not subdued until 619.

There is considerable difference of opinion among historians as to the exact dimension of Harsha's kingdom. It was not a tightly knit empire. Conquered kings remained on their thrones but were required to pay tribute and homage to Harsha. The area directly under his control consisted of modern Uttar Pradesh and parts of Rajasthan and the Punjab.

Around 620 he attempted an invasion of the Deccan, and after his death in about 647, his kingdom disintegrated.

He was a patron of the arts and religion, both Buddhist and Hindu, and he gave a gift of a temple, about 35 metres in height made of brass or bronze, to the famous university at Nalanda.

According to R.C. Majumdar, Harsha "was undoubtedly one of the greatest rulers of ancient India." Bana, his biographer, paid the greatest tribute:

Through him the earth does, indeed, possess a true king! Wonderful is his royalty, surpassing the gods!

Suggested Further Readings

Bana.
>   Harsa-charita tr. by E.B. Cowell and F.W.Thomas. — London : Royal Asiatic Society,
>   1897.
>   xiv, 284 p. ; 22 cm. — (Oriental Translation Fund new series)

Hsuan Tsang.
>   Si-yu-ki. Buddhist records of the western world. — New York : Paragon, 1968.
>   2 v. in 1 ; 23 cm.

Mukherjee, Radha Kumud.
>   Harsha. — London : Oxford University Press, 1926.
>   201 p. : ill., facsims., fold. map ; 17.5 cm. — [Rulers of India series] Calcutta Univer-
>   sity Readership lectures, 1925.

CHAPTER 2

THE DELHI SULTANATE PERIOD

Qutb-ud-Din Aibak 1206-1210   Ala-ud-Din Khilji 1296-1316
Iltutmish 1210-1236   Ghiyas-ud-Din Tughluq 1320-1325
Sultana Raziyyah 1236-1240   Muhammad Bin Tughluq 1325-1351
Balban 1266-1287   Sikandar Lodi 1489-1517

*T*he Delhi Sultanate is one of the most intriguing periods of Indian history. It was a dramatic time. There was violence, but the period also produced great literature and art. It is well-documented by Muslim chroniclers and poets: Ibn Batutah, Amir Khusrau, Barani, Ferishta.

But the most fascinating aspect of the drama was its cast of characters. Many were weak, but some were strong; they had to be strong to survive. It is the strong ones who make up Chapter 2. The five dynasties of the Delhi Sultanate were so structured that they would function properly only if there was a strong ruler at the top. As soon as the strong ruler died, the kingdom fell apart unless it was headed by another strong ruler.

The Sultanate lasted 320 years, from 1206 to 1526. This may not seem like a long time, but consider that the Mughul Empire lasted only 171 years (1526-1707) and British India only 190 (1757-1947) and the U.S.A. at this writing is only 223 years old.

There were five dynasties during the Sultanate: Slave (1206-1296), Khilji (1296-1320), Tughluq (1320-1414), Sayyid (1414-1451) and Lodi (1451-1526).

We have chosen to feature seven Sultans and one Sultana in this chapter. Because of the shortness of her reign and her inability to survive, perhaps the Sultana should not have been included in the dramatis personae. However, she was a strong, resourceful woman and would have made her mark had she not been cut down by the meanness and bigotry of the time. She deserves a supporting role.

Suggested Further Readings

Basu, Syama Prasad.
  The Tughluqs : years of experiments. — Calcutta : U.N. Dhur, [197-]
  178 p. ; 20 cm.

Cambridge history of India. — Cambridge (Eng.) : University Press, 1922-.
  vol. : ill., fold. maps ; 25 cm
  Contents: v. 3. Turks and Afghans. – ed. by Wolseley Haig.

The history and culture of the Indian people. — Bombay : Bharatiya Vidya Bhavan, [1951-]
    v. : ill., plates, ports. ; 24 cm.
    Contents: v. 6. The Delhi Sultanate.

Saran, Parmatma, 1943–
    Studies in the medieval Indian history — Delhi : Ranjit, [c1952]
    225 p. ; 19 cm.

QUTB-UD-DIN AIBAK

Qutb-ud-Din Aibak's life began in Turkestan in slavery. The date of his birth is not known, but at some point during his childhood he was taken to Nishapur where he was bought by its Qazi, Fakhr-ud-Din Abdul Aziz Kufi, who arranged for his military and religious training.

After the Qazi died, Qutb-ud-Din Aibak was sold by the Qazi's sons to a merchant who took him to Ghazni where he was bought by Muiz-ud-Din Muhammad of Ghur (sometimes known as Muhammad Ghori). This was the turning point of his life.

Muhammad was impressed with his qualities and made him *Amir-i-Akhur**. He served his master well and was taken along on some of the Indian campaigns.

After the second battle of Tarain in 1192 he was placed in charge of the Indian conquests. He strengthened his position by marrying the daughter of Taj-ud-Din Yildiz, governor of Kirman, and marrying his own daughter off to Iltutmish. He strengthened his position further in 1192 with the capture of Hansi, Meerut, Delhi, Ranthambhor and Koil. He established headquarters in Delhi in 1193 and in the following year, together with Muhammad, he defeated the Gahadavala ruler, Jaichand, at Chandawar, and acquired the kingdoms of Kanauj and Benares.

This victory was followed by victories over Ajmer (1195), Anhilwara (1197), Badaun (1197-98), Kanauj (1198-99) and Kalinjar (1202-03).

On the assassination in 1206 of Muiz-ud-Din Muhammad of Ghur (who had no male heirs), Qutb-ud-Din Aibak moved to Lahore and assumed control of the conquered territories there. Ghiyas-ud-Din Mahmud, the nephew and new ruler of Ghur, conferred on Qutb-ud-Din Aibak all the insignia of royalty: a canopy, a crown and a throne, and gave him the title of Sultan.

However, Taj-ud-Din Yildiz challenged his authority. Fighting broke out between them in 1208, and Qutb-ud-Din Aibak defeated Yildiz, and occupied Ghazni for 40 days. The people urged Yildiz to return, which he did. Instead of staying to fight, Qutb-ud-Din Aibak returned to Lahore.

After ruling for four years, he died in 1210 in Lahore when he fell off his horse while playing *chaugan***.

---

 * Lord of the stables.
 ** A form of polo.

During his short reign he built the Jama Masjid over what was once a Hindu temple. The Qutb Minar which graces the landscape of Delhi is not a monument devoted to him, as some think, but to Khwaja Qutb-ud-Din of Ush near Baghdad.

Qutb-ud-Din Aibak is sometimes called the founder of the Slave Dynasty of India. That he established Muslim rule in India is true enough, but the description of his dynasty as "Slave" is not entirely accurate, inasmuch as only three of its rulers were ever slaves (Qutb-ud-Din Aibak, Ala-ud-Din Khilji and Balban) and all three of these were manumitted by their masters before they came to the throne. Qutb-ud-Din Aibak established Muslim rule in India which lasted nearly 500 years. That is his legacy to Hindustan.

ILTUTMISH

Iltutmish was, according to the noted historian, R.C. Majumdar, "the greatest ruler of the early Turkish Sultanate of Delhi." This Sultanate is commonly known as the Slave Dynasty.

His name has several spellings. Beale's *Oriental Biographical Dictionary* has it "Altimsh". Dr. Majumdar, quoted above, and *Britannica* both approve the rendition used in this sketch.

Iltutmish came from the tribe of Ilbari in Turkestan. He was a handsome lad, and his brothers, in their jealousy, deprived him of his heritage. Like Joseph of Biblical times, he was sold into slavery, but it was his good fortune eventually to be purchased by the viceroy of Delhi, Qutb-ud-Din Aibak, whom he served well and under whom he became governor of Badaun. Later he married Qutb-ud-Din Aibak's daughter.

When Qutb-ud-Din Aibak fell off his horse and died in 1210, the throne went to Aram Baksh about whom little is known. He was either the son or brother of Qutb-ud-Din Aibak or someone who happened to be in the right place at the right time. At that time there was no set rule, like primogeniture, to determine succession; so it fell to the Amirs and Maliks of Lahore to choose a new Sultan.

The Amirs and Maliks of Lahore were not happy with their first choice; so they turned to Iltutmish, who by this time had the title Malik Shams-ud-Din, and called him to Lahore. He answered the call and defeated the army of Aram Baksh in the plains of Jud near Delhi.

This was either in 1210 or 1211, and the Slave Dynasty is generally said to have begun at that date. Iltutmish established his capital at Delhi, and his Dynasty would last until 1290.

The death of Qutb-ud-Din Aibak seemed to have been a signal for general secessionism. In Bengal, Ali Mardan, who had been appointed governor by Qutb-ud-Din Aibak, declared himself Sultan and refused to pay allegiance to Delhi. Gwalior and Ranthambhor, ruled by Hindu princes, broke away, and the Amirs of Delhi rebelled. Iltutmish faced these adversities with resolution. He first put down the Amirs and then the smaller principalities in north India.

In 1215, Taj-ud-Din Yildiz, who had declared himself Sultan of Ghazni, had been expelled from his capital by Sultan Muhammad, the Shah of Khwarazm, and had fled to and conquered much of the Punjab. Iltutmish met him in battle at Tarain and took him prisoner to Badaun. In the meantime Nasir-ud-Din Qabacha, governor of Multan and Ush had advanced to Lahore, but was expelled from Lahore by Iltutmish in 1217.

Iltutmish spent much of his reign in military activity: putting down revolts and conquering new territories. But he found time to be a patron of the arts and built the famous Qutb Minar as a memorial to Khwaja Qutb-ud-Din of Ush near Baghdad.

In about 1229 he received a robe of honour from the Khalifah of Baghdad and was declared *Sultan-i-Azam* (Great Sultan). On his coins he had described himself as the lieutenant of the Khalifah. He died in battle in 1236 after a reign of 26 years.

SULTANA RAZIYYAH

The Sultana Raziyyah is one of the tragic figures of Indian history. She had the advantage of being nominated to the throne by her father, Iltutmish, when he was on his death bed. She was a gifted and strong-willed woman. Her downfall was caused by the prejudice of the powerful Turkish nobles who could not accept the rule of a woman — however devout, able and courageous she may have been.

Though Iltutmish had nominated Raziyyah to succeed him in 1236, the nobles elevated her eldest brother, Rukn-ud-Din Firuz, to the throne. He was an incompetent king who preferred to enjoy the material benefits of the Sultanate while he left the management of the affairs of the state to his mother. This was too much for the nobles; so they threw Firuz and the queen-mother in prison and placed Raziyyah on the throne. Firuz met his untimely end shortly after that.

Trouble started when the nobles perceived that Raziyyah was favouring her Abyssinian slave, Jalal-ud-Din Yaqut. Some contemporaneous historians claimed that her relationship bordered on the criminal, but Ferishta was more charitable. He noted that "a very great degree of familiarity was observed to exist between the Abyssinian and the Queen, so much so, that when she rode, he always lifted her on to her horse by raising her up under her arms."

Ikhtiyar-ud-Din Altuniyah, the governor of Sarhind, was the first to rebel. Raziyyah marched against him, but in the battle that followed, Yaqut was slain and Raziyyah imprisoned.

Not one to admit defeat, Raziyyah decided that her only course of action then was to marry her enemy; which she did. She and her newly-acquired husband marched towards Delhi but were defeated in a battle near Kaithal 13 October 1240 by Muiz-ud-Din Bahram. She and Altuniya were put to death the next day.

She had been Sultana for a little over three-and-half years, but they were not happy ones. She did everything in her power to maintain the dignity of her high office. According to Ferishta, "she read the Koran with correct pronunciation, and in father's lifetime employed herself in the affairs of Government."

Minhaj-ud-Siraj, another historian, wrote even more glowingly of her:

> She was a great sovereign, sagacious, just, beneficient, the patron of the learned, a dispenser of justice, the cherisher of her subjects, and of warlike talent, and was endowed with all the qualifications necessary for Kings.

The years that followed the downfall of Raziyyah were dismal ones. Bahram was totally unfit to rule, and his successor, Ala-ud-Din Masud, was no better.

They were followed in 1246 by Nasir-ud-Din Mahmud, a God-fearing man whose passion was calligraphy. He spent many happy hours copying the Koran and left the affairs of the government to his *vizir*, Balban.

His reign finally ended in 1266.

Raziyyah is buried in Old Delhi. Her tomb is not too far from Delhi Gate. It takes a bit of luck to find it, but if one is persistent enough, one can find it.

BALBAN

Ghiyas-ud-Din Balban, like two of his predecessors (Qutb-ud-Din Aibak and Iltutmish), was a former slave. Like them, he hailed from the Ibari tribe of Turkestan. He was born around 1207, and as a boy he was taken captive by the Mongols and sold into slavery in Baghdad. His master brought him to Delhi in 1232 where he was purchased by Iltutmish.

He thus became one of the Turkish slaves known as "The Forty" (*Chahelgan*). Because he showed extraordinary intelligence and ability, he soon became the *Khasdar* (or personal attendant) of Iltutmish. He rose even higher under Sultan Nasir-ud-Din Mahmud, becoming his *vizir* (prime minister). In 1266, with the death of Mahmud, who made a better calligrapher than ruler, Balban became Sultan.

Since the death of Iltutmish in 1236, the Sultanate had fallen into disrepair. The Muslims at this point constituted a small minority in India, surrounded as they were by an overwhelming Hindu majority. The Sultanate was a military occupation which had to depend on the loyalty of Hindu *rajas* and its own, sometimes rebellious, Muslim nobles for its existence.

Balban at once began the process, which would occupy most of his 21-year reign, of engaging in one military campaign after another. Barani, the historian, summed up the situation that existed during the years that followed the death of Iltutmish and preceded Balban's rise to power:

Fear of the governing power, which is the basis of all good government, and the source of the glory and splendour of all States, had departed from the hearts of all men, and the country had fallen into a wretched condition.

Not only was the government being threatened by Mongol incursions, but the roads were unsafe because of robber bands that roamed unchecked about the countryside.

Balban's first order of business was to reform the army and clear the Doab of the bandits (today they would be called *dacoits*) who disrupted life and commerce in and around Delhi. He built or repaired forts at strategic locations (Patiali, Bhojpur, Kampil, Jalili, etc.) so that at a later time Barani could write that "the roads have ever since been free from robbers."

From 1271 until 1279 Balban had to contend with a Mongol invasion that advanced into the Punjab and Sind and at one point even crossed the Sutlej. Finally three of his generals, two of whom were his sons, beat them off, and the Mongol threat was temporarily alleviated.

The next trouble spot for Balban occurred in Bengal where Tughril Khan, Balban's deputy, rose in revolt. Balban sent two of his generals to Bengal to put down the insurrection, but both failed. Finally, he went himself and restored order.

Balban's final crisis occurred towards the end of his reign. In 1285, the Mongols once again invaded the Punjab. This time, Balban's son, Muhammad, in fighting them off was killed in ambush. He earned the posthumous title, *Khan-i-Shahid* (Martyr Prince), but his death so affected Balban, now about 80, that his health failed. He died in 1287, and the Slave Dynasty too died soon after.

ALA-UD-DIN KHILJI

The Slave Dynasty came to an end in 1290, three years after the death of Balban. Balban had been succeeded, against his last will and testament, by his fun-loving teenage son, Muiz-ud-Din Kaiqubad, who was done in by a Khilji nobleman whose father had been executed at Kaiqubad's order. Kaiqubad's body was unceremoniously tossed into the Jumna, and the Khilji faction of the court took over the government with Jalal-ud-Din Firuz as Sultan.

Firuz was an old man at the time (70 years old) and could not control the Khilji nobles who vied with each other for power. Shortly after becoming Sultan, he appointed his nephew and son-in-law, Ala-ud-Din Khilji, governor of Kara in the region of Allahabad.

In 1292, Ala-ud-Din conducted a successful raid in Malwa and captured Bhilsa, for which he was rewarded with the governorship of Avadh, to add to that of Kara. He then turned his attention to the south and conquered Devagiri (present Daulatabad), acquiring a large amount of gold.

On his return to the north in July 1296, he was met by Firuz who, on a pre-arranged signal, was attacked. Firuz's last words were:

"Ah, you wretch, Ala-ud-Din! What have you done?"

At this, a second attacker cut off his head and presented it to Ala-ud-Din who wasted little time proclaiming himself Sultan.

Like Balban before him, Ala-ud-Din, upon assuming the throne, had to put down revolts and fight off Mongol incursions.

First, he conquered Multan which was ruled by two of his cousins, sons of the late Sultan. Next, in February 1298, two of his generals defeated the Mongols who had reached Lahore.

Later that year, Ala-ud-Din sent Ulugh Khan and Nusrat Khan on a successful invasion of Gujarat. It was at this juncture that Ala-ud-Din assumed the title *Sikandar Sana**.

He also thought of starting a new religion. Like Muhammad, who had four companions, he, Ala-ud-Din, had four: Ulugh Khan, Zafar Khan, Nusrat Khan and Alp Khan. Fortunately for Ala-ud-Din, he was persuaded by the *kotwal*** of Delhi that religion stemmed from divine inspiration, not from political ambition.

Shortly after that, in 1299, a horde of 200,000 Mongols under the leadership of Qutlugh Khwajah, a descendant of Genghis Khan, attacked Delhi and surrounded and blockaded it. The city was saved by Zafar Khan who charged the enemy and lost his life in the battle. That night, under cover of darkness, the Mongols folded their tents and quietly crept away.

Following the defeat of the Mongols, Ala-ud-Din undertook the siege of the virtually impregnable fortress of Ranthambhor in Rajputana. During the siege he was informed of insurrections by his nephews, Umar Khan, governor of Budaun, and Mangu Khan, governor of Oudh. Ala-ud-Din put down these revolts, punished the offenders and was then in a position to continue the siege of Ranthambhor which was finally captured. The women of the fort performed *jauhar*** rather than submitting to the enemy.

The reign of Ala-ud-Din, which lasted about 20 years, is remembered largely for the Muslim conquest of south India. Prior to becoming Sultan, Ala-ud-Din had conquered Devagiri, but after coming to power, he extended his kingdom all the way to Madurai. He was the first Muslim ruler to conquer the southern territories.

Unfortunately, the administration of the kingdom required a strong ruler at its head. At the death of Ala-ud-Din in 1313, there was no such person at hand, and the Dynasty soon fell to the Tughluqs.

The reign of Ala-ud-Din was a veritable golden age of the Delhi Sultanate period. The arts flourished, and mosques, mausolea, forts and universities sprang up. One of the greatest poets of medieval India, Amir

---

* Alexander the Second.
** Chief of Police.
*** Self-immolation.

Khusrau, lived and wrote during this period. There were other poets (Khwaja Hasan, Sadr-ud-Din Ali, Fakhr-ud-Din Khawas, Hamid-ud-Din Raja, Maulana Arif, Abdul-Hakim and Shibab-ud-Din Sadr-Nishin) as well as religious leaders and philosophers of note.

There is a memorial to Ala-ud-Din which stands in the compound of the Kutb Minar. It has a larger base than the Kutb Minar, but does not go up very high. It was to have been a minar to overshadow the Qutb Minar.

Ala-ud-Din began constructing it in honour of himself, but it was never finished. He died too soon.

Suggested Further Readings

Lal, Kishori Saran, 1920–
    History of the Khiljis (1290-1320). — Allahabad : Indian Press, 1950.
    xvi, 416 p. : ill. ; 20 cm.

Ziya al-Din Barani.
    The reign of Alauddin Khilji / translated from Zia-ud-Din Barani's Tarikh-i-Firuz
    Shahi by A.R. Fuller and A.Kallaque. — Calcutta : Pilgrim, [1967]
    162 p. ; 24 cm.

GHIYAS-UD-DIN TUGHLUQ

Ghazi Malik was the founder of the Tughluq Dynasty. According to Ferishta, Ghazi's father, Malik Tughluq, was a Turkish slave of Balban and married a Jat lady from Punjab. Their son, Ghazi Malik, was born towards the beginning of the reign of Balban (1266). In Amir Khusrau's *Tughluq Namah*, Ghazi Malik, known in history as Ghiyas-ud-Din Tughluq, makes the following statement about his early life:

> I was a man unknown to fame, experiencing the coldness and bitterness of life. It was the late Sultan, Jalal-ud-Din Firuz who showed me favour and drew me near. I became a personal attendant of his. After his death [in 1296], I was much depressed and eaten up with anxiety as to my future. At last Ala-ud-Din ascended the throne, and because of his kindness, I began to make gradual progress. I sought service under Ulugh Khan, the Sultan's brother. After his death I was again cast a drift. Before long, however, I entered the service of Sultan Ala-ud-Din. It is by his favour that I have attained the position you see me in.

These words were delivered in 1320 to the assembly in the Siri palace where the nobles chose him to be their Sultan. He had made a name for himself fighting off repeated Mongol incursions in the Punjab when he was governor of the Punjab.

It was a time of total disaster, typical of the situation that would prevail whenever a strong ruler was followed by a weak one. Malik Kafur succeeded Ala-ud-Din and lasted about three years. He was duly assassinated and replaced by Khusrau Khan, the chief conspirator against him. After four months in office, Khusrau Khan was beheaded by nobles because he showed too much favour to the Hindus.

On his accession Ghiyas-ud-Din had two tasks which needed attention: one, the empire built by Ala-ud-Din was breaking up under the incompetence of his successors, and two, the administration was in a state of total disorder. He did his best to solve both problems.

In the Deccan, the Kakatiya ruler of Warangal not only refused to pay tribute to Delhi but engaged in some military campaigns of his own. Ghiyas-ud-Din dispatched his son, Prince Jauna, to deal with the errant ruler. The first attempt failed, but the second, four months later, succeeded when the Warangal fort was taken and the country renamed Sultanpur.

Ghiyas-ud-Din also saw to civil matters: stemming corruption, promoting agriculture and digging canals.

In Bengal, civil war had broken out in 1318 between two brothers whose father, the ruler, Shams-ud-Din Firuz Shah, had died. Ghiyas-ud-Din went to Bengal himself, captured one of the brothers, Ghiyas-ud-Din Bahadur, and put the other brother, Nasir-ud-Din, on the throne as a vassal.

On his return from the Bengal campaign in 1325, Ghiyas-ud-Din died when a wooden structure Prince Jauna had built for him collapsed and killed him. There is disagreement among historians, both ancient and modern, as to whether this was murder or accidental. Whichever it was, Prince Jauna soon after became Sultan and took the name, Muhammad bin Tughluq.

MUHAMMAD BIN TUGHLUQ

Muhammad bin Tughluq, the son of Ghiyas-ud-Din Tughluq, was born around 1290. He was known by several names: Ulugh Khan, Malik Fakhr-ud-Din Junan and Jauna, to name a few. For purposes of brevity, Jauna will be used here. Jauna appears to have been a precocious child. It is said, he "loved to associate with the *'ulema*, the *mashaikh* (saints), the *sufis* and the philosophers."

He was proficient in theology, philosophy, medicine, history and astronomy. He also must have been athletic, for "he was also an expert at archery, tilting, riding, and in the use of the javelin."

His rise to power began after the death of Ala-ud-Din and during the brief, undistinguished reign of Qutb-ud-Din Mubarak (Malik Kafur). According to the historian Ziya-al-Din Barani, he "held a high position in the court of, and enjoyed close access to, Sultan Qutb-ud-Din."

One "high position" was that of superintendent of the royal stable, another was that of postal superintendent.

Sultan Mubarak was killed at the instigation of Khusrau Khan who then became Sultan in his stead with the name Nasir-ud-Din Khusrau Shah. Neither Jauna nor his father, Ghazi Malik, the future Sultan Ghiyas-ud-Din, who at that time was governor of the Punjab and the most powerful and popular of the nobles, were looked upon with favour by the new

Sultan. Since the new Sultan was murdering all members of the lineage of Ghazi Malik, Jauna left Delhi for safety and to join his father.

Following the defeat of the new Sultan and the enthronement of Ghiyas-ud-Din in 1320, Jauna served as a general under his father and conducted an unsuccessful campaign against Warangal. During this campaign, rumours spread that Jauna was plotting against his father. Whether there was any truth or not in these rumours, Ghiyas-ud-Din four months later sent his son on a second expedition against Warangal; this one was successful.

During Ghiyas-ud-Din's campaign in Bengal, Prince Jauna was made regent in Delhi. In preparation for his father's return he built a wooden structure in Afghanpur, not far from Delhi, at which there was to be a ceremony to honour his father. As luck (or conspiracy) would have it, the structure collapsed when his father was on it, and his father was killed.

Three days later, Prince Jauna had himself declared Sultan with the title Muhammad bin Tughluq. Forty days later he ascended the throne in Delhi. This was in the year 1325.

What Muhammad bin Tughluq possessed in genius, he apparently lacked in common sense. He knew what should be done for the good of the empire, but he appears to have overlooked the element of human nature.

The most famous example of this was his moving the capital from Delhi to Devagiri which he renamed Daulatabad, a name which has stuck. He decided that the empire needed a more centrally-located capital; so he moved, not only the court, but the entire population of Delhi to Daulatabad, 1100 kilometres away. Horror stories abound concerning the transmigration. If one is to believe Ibn Batutah, a bed-ridden cripple was shot from Delhi to Daulatabad by a ballista, and a blind man was dragged all the way behind an ox cart. When he arrived, all that remained of him was one leg. Shortly after this, the capital was returned to Delhi. Muhammad bin Tughluq was right in identifying Daulatabad as a more central location for a capital than Delhi, but he was wrong to attempt moving the entire population of the city there.

Another scheme of Muhammad bin Tughluq that failed was the issuance of copper coins in 1329-30 with no safeguard to verify their authenticity. The result was wholesale counterfeiting on the part of the populace. The problem was endemic because people were using funny money for everything from buying vegetables in the bazaar to paying taxes. The result was a financial catastrophe. Ultimately, Muhammad bin Tughluq had to repeal his edict and buy back all the copper coins, the good ones along with the bad ones, at their face value in gold and silver.

Yet another disastrous scheme of Muhammad bin Tughluq was that of attempting to put the agriculture of the Doab on a paying basis. He needed revenue to maintain his military; so he increased taxes, according to some sources, by 50 percent, but according to others, by 100 percent. The scheme might have wrought better results had not a famine struck the land around this time. The final result was chaos.

While all this was going on, Muhammad bin Tughluq was beset with other crises: the Mongols were again threatening Delhi, and Bengal was in the process of seceding.

The Mongols were either beaten off or bought off, but the Bengal situation was not as easily solved. Bengal broke away and in 1341 was soon followed by Telingana. Madura had already been lost in 1334. It was while trying to put down rebellion in Sind that Muhammad bin Tughluq fell ill and died 20 March 1351 at Tattah after a reign of 26 years.

Muhammad bin Tughluq was followed by his cousin, Firuz Shah Tughluq, who was proclaimed Sultan 23 March 1351. He remained on the throne until his death in 1388. But the empire of the Tughluqs never regained its territory and its prestige.

In 1389 Timur made his celebrated raid into India, and the Tughluq Dynasty finally died a natural death with the coming of the Sayyids in 1414.

The late R.C. Majumdar summed up the problem of evaluating Muhammad bin Tughluq by admitting that he was "indeed an extraordinary personality, and to determine his place in history is a difficult task. Was he a genius or a lunatic? An idealist or a visionary? A bloodthirsty tyrant or a benevolent king? A heretic or a devout Mussalman? There is no doubt that he was one of the most learned and accomplished scholars of his time ...."

Suggested Further Readings

Husain, Agha Mahdi.
    The rise and fall of Muhammad bin Tughluq. — London : Luzac, 1938.
    274 p. : ill. ; 22 cm.

Husain, Agha Mahdi.
    Tughluq Dynasty. — [Calcutta] : Thacker Spink, 1963.
    xl, 675 p. : ill., maps, facsims. ; 22 cm.

SIKANDAR LODI

The last family to rule in Delhi before the advent of the Mughuls was the Lodi Dynasty. It began when Buhlul Lodi, an Afghan, took over the throne of Delhi 19 April 1451. Buhlul was from the Shahu Khel clan of the tribe of Lodi, and, considering the times in which he lived, he remained on the Delhi throne for a surprisingly long time — 38 years.

A horse trader in his youth, he had distinguished himself during the reign of the Sayyid Sultan, Muhammad Shah. As chief of Sirhind, he had defended the kingdom against an invasion from Malwa, and when the last of the Sayyids, Ala-ud-Din Alam Shah, retired to a life of pleasure in Budaun, Buhlul assumed control of what was left of the Delhi Kingdom, taking the name Buhlul Shah Ghazi.

However, his reign was not a particularly memorable one. He did manage to bring into the Delhi sphere some of the chieftans of the Doab who had basked in freedom during the Sayyid period. His most memorable accomplishment was the conquest and annexation of Jaunpur, the ruler of which, Mahmud Shah Sharqi, had threatened Delhi.

Buhlul died in July 1489 at Jalali and was succeeded by his son, Nizam Khan, who took the name Sikandar Shah. He was the ablest of the three sovereigns of the Lodi Dynasty, extending the borders of the kingdom all the way to Bihar and Tirhut.

Sikandar had to contend with numerous rebellions, one of the most serious of which was provided by Husain Sharqi, the last of the Jaunpur kings, who was anxious to recover the kingdom he had lost to Buhlul. He was defeated twice in battle by Sikandar, and after the second defeat, he fled to Bengal. Sikandar pursued him to the border of Bengal where he met Husain Shah, the ruler of Bengal. Being in no position to fight him, he concluded a non-aggression pact with him.

Delhi during this period had not only lost its past glory, but had become run down and dilapidated. Sikandar decided Agra would be a more strategic place from which to govern; so he moved his capital there.

The administration of the kingdom was reformed and improved under Sikandar, and his reign was one of relative prosperity. He was a benevolent ruler who showed genuine concern for the welfare of his subjects. His main fault lay in his intolerance of faiths other than Islam. Although he destroyed many Hindu temples and built mosques over their ruins, in his administrative dealings with people, he showed no religious favouritism.

He died 21 November 1517 from a throat disease.

He was succeeded by his eldest son, Ibrahim. An attempt was made by some nobles to split the kingdom, putting Ibrahim's brother on the throne in Jaunpur. Ibrahim at first agreed to this dual monarchy arrangement, but soon recanted.

Ibrahim spent almost all of his time in suppressing revolts, most of which had been instigated by Afghan nobles.

Finally, Babar, the ruler of Kabul, put an end to his troubles and defeated him in battle at Panipat 20 April 1526. Ibrahim died there and the Lodi Dynasty died with him.

The age of the Mughuls had dawned.

CHAPTER 3

THE MUGHUL PERIOD

Babar
Humayun
Akbar the Great
Sher Shah Suri

Jahangir
Nur Jahan
Shah Jahan
Aurangzeb

$\mathcal{T}$ he Mughul Period of India's history lasted from 1526 when Babar rose to prominence from nowhere until 1707, when Aurangzeb, the last of the Great Mughuls, died. The family remained on the throne throughout the remaining years of the eighteenth century but the once magnificent empire dwindled in power and prestige until its last remaining monarch, the poet Bahadur Shah II, "King of Delhi," became a pathetic rallying point for disgruntled sepoys in May 1857.

The word "Mughul" comes from the word "Mongol" and has crept into the English language, taking the form "mogul," meaning "a very rich or important person." For example, Andrew Carnegie, John D. Rockefeller and James J. Hill were called "American Moguls."

The Dynasty was interrupted briefly when Sher Shah Suri defeated Humayun, Babar's opium smoking son, in 1539 at the Battle of Chausa. Sher Shah died a few years later, and Humayun made a comeback in 1555 when he defeated the incompetent successors of the Suri Dynasty at the Battle of Sirhind. Seven months later Humayun, while in a drunken stupor, fell down the stairs of his library and died.

He was succeeded by Akbar, who has "the Great" attached to his name. Akbar conquered much of Hindustan and tried to solve the country's religious diversity by creating a religion which had components of many faiths and would be acceptable to all. It was called *Din-i-Ilahi* and contained elements of Islam, Hinduism and even Christianity.

After Akbar came Jahangir, best remembered for his interest in horticulture and for having a domineering wife, Nur Jahan. They produced several sons, the most prominent of whom was Shah Jahan, the great builder. His love for his wife, the Begam Arjumand Bano who is remembered in history as Mumtaz Mahal, is one of the great love stories of history.

She died in childbirth in 1631 after giving Shah Jahan 14 children. To commemorate his love he built her a tomb called the Taj Mahal. It is one of the most beautiful buildings in the world.

One of the sons of Shah Jahan and Mumtaz was the bigot Aurangzeb who overthrew his father in 1658 and conquered, or reconquered, much of

India that had been lost during the reigns of his father and grandfather. He did his best to stamp out the Hindu religion, destroying temples and erecting mosques over them.

After his death in 1707, the Mughul empire decreased in size as one ineffectual ruler followed another. The death of the empire was hastened by the ascendancy of the East India Company which by 1818 had become the paramount power in Hindustan, and the Mughul empires coffin was nailed shut with the failure of the Revolt of 1857.

BABAR
(1483-1530)

Zahir-ud-Din Muhammad, better known as Babar, the founder of the Mughul Empire in India, was one of the most refreshingly colourful, romantic, delightful, adventurous and resilient characters ever to grace the panorama of Indian history.

A Chaghatai Turk, he was born in Farghana (in Transoxiana) 14 February 1483 A.D. (8 Muharram 888 A.H.), the son of Umar Shaikh Mirza, the son of Abu Said Mirza, the son of Muhammad Mirza, the son of Miran Shah, the son of Timur Shah, better known as Tamerlane. His mother was Kutlagh Nigar Khanam, daughter of Yunas Khan, king of Mongolistan and a descendant of Genghis Khan.

When Yunas Khan arrived to celebrate the shaving of his grandson's head, he could not pronounce the boy's Arabic name; so he dubbed him "Babar," meaning "Tiger."

His father died in 1494 and Babar, aged 11, took over as ruler of Farghana. The opening lines of his memoirs tell of it:

> In the month of Ramazan in the year eight hundred and ninety-nine I became king of Farghana.

Instead of enjoying peace under a boy king, Farghana was subjected to a period of strife in which two of Babar's uncles mounted campaigns against the small kingdom. Babar retained his position, but Farghana was partitioned and very little territory was left to him. Three years later he marched on Samarkand, conquered it and, in fulfillment of a life-long dream, sat on the Timur's throne, the two-horned seat of Alexander. He did not sit for long. He tells of it in his memoirs:

> Samarkand had been taken over after a hard and trying siege of seven months. On its capture, indeed, the soldiers took plenty of spoil; but the rest of the country had joined me or Sultan Ali of its own accord, and of course had not been given over to plunder .... Samarkand was in so distressed a state when we took it that we had to supply the inhabitants with seed-corn and food to help them to carry on till the harvest.

How could one levy taxes from so exhausted a land? My troops were thus brought to much distress, and I had nothing to give them. They began to think of home; they deserted me one by one .... All the Mongols deserted, and at last Ahmad Tambal [a leading Beg who had been highly honoured and rewarded] took himself off and left me.

Babar now had only 1,000 followers, and to make matters worse, he fell ill. For four days he was not able to eat anything. In the meantime Tambal and several other deserters revolted and put Prince Jahangir on the throne of Farghana. Babar received numerous letters from his mother and grandmother who were besieged in Andijan, the capital of Farghana, begging him to rescue them. When he was finally able to come to their assistance, Sultan Ali descended on and captured Samarkand. "For the sake of Andijan," Babar wrote, "I lost Samarkand, and I found I had lost one without saving the other."

For the next several years Babar made a number of attempts to recover Samarkand — some successful, some not. Finally, he settled in Kabul and in 1511-12 made one more attempt at recovering Samarkand. Again he failed, and now he turned his eyes towards India.

He had dreamed of repeating Timur's incursion into India. During one of his periods of exile a 111-year-old woman told him of Timur's exploits there, and he was determined to emulate him.

He conquered Kandahar in 1522, and luck being on his side for a change, he was invited to India by two nobles who were dissatisfied with Ibrahim Lodi, the last of the Lodi kings of India, and who was about to be the last ruler of the Delhi Sultanate.

One of the nobles was Daulat Khan whose son had received cruel punishment from Ibrahim. The other was Ibrahim's uncle, Alam Khan who was a pretender to the throne.

Babar marched on India and occupied Lahore in 1524. Daulat Khan and Alam Khan suddenly realized they had made a terrible mistake. Babar was not paying a social call; he meant to stay. So his erstwhile confederates turned against him and forced him to go back to Kabul.

Returning to India with reinforcements the next year, Babar occupied Punjab once more, but this time was able to force Daulat Khan to submit to him.

Babar next marched Delhi and met the numerically superior forces of Ibrahim Lodi on the field of Panipat 21 April 1526 and won what came to be known as the First Battle of Panipat.

Babar was not impressed by Ibrahim's military skill. He said: "he was an inexperienced man, careless in his movements, who marched without order, halted or retired without method and engaged without foresight." Of the battle itself, he wrote:

By the grace and mercy of almighty God, this difficult affair was made easy to me, and that mighty army, in the space of half a day, was laid in the dust.

Ibrahim was killed in the battle, and Babar put himself on the throne of Delhi. It was only a kingdom then. It would be for his grandson, Akbar, to turn it into an empire.

On his death in Agra 26 December 1530 he was buried in a garden on the left bank of the Jumna River. Six months later his remains were transported to Kabul. In 1646, his great-great-grandson, Shah Jahan, built a mausoleum over them.

Babar was a poet, a soldier of fortune and a lover of wine and women. In Kabul he built a reservoir of marble which he filled with red wine. He and his friends would sit around it, drink from it and watch dancing girls. Over it were inscribed these words:

> Bright spring blooms here from day to day,
>   Young girls stand by the wine to pour;
> Enjoy them, Babar, while you may —
>   Your spring, once gone, returns no more.

Suggested Further Readings

Babar, Emperor of Hindustan, 1483-1530.
    Baburnama / tr. by A.S. Beveredge. — New Delhi : Oriental Books Reprint
    Corporation, [1970]
    vi, 880 p. : ill., maps ; 23 cm.

Lane-Poole, Stanley
    Babar. — Delhi : S. Chand, [1964]
    206 p. : ill., front. port. ; 19 cm. — (Rulers of India)

HUMAYUN
(1508-1556)

Humayun, whose surname was Nasir-ud-Din Muhammad, was born in Kabul 7 March 1508. His father, Babar, was the Chaghatai Turk from Transoxiana who defeated the last of the Lodi Sultans and assumed the throne of Delhi in 1526. Humayun's mother was Maham Begum.

The government Humayun inherited from his father was not a very stable one. Babar was a soldier and adventurer, which made him an interesting person to read about, but an organiser or administrator he was not. To conquer a country is one thing. To rule it for any length of time is another.

On the death of Babar 26 December 1530, Humayun became the second ruler of the Mughul Dynasty. His new kingdom consisted of Delhi, the Rajput state of Mewar, the area now called Uttar Pradesh, north Bihar and the Punjab.

His first blunder after taking office was that of giving away much of his kingdom to his ambitious and greedy brothers. He conferred the government of Kabul, Kandahar and Ghazni on Mirza Kamran. To Hindal he gave Alwar, and to Askari the fiefdom of Sambhal. Kamran Mirza soon acquired the Punjab; so much of what Humayun had inherited was given up without a fight.

In the early days of his reign, Humayun was forced to attend to hostile elements in Bundelkhand. After more or less settling his difficulties there, he turned his attention to Gujarat where Bahadur Shah had enlisted Portuguese aid and was making threatening advances into Rajputana. Humayun invaded Gujarat in 1535, but Bahadur Shah was getting less than the promised help from his erstwhile European allies. Finally, in 1537, Bahadur Shah was killed, either by being treacherously murdered by the Portuguese or by drowning in an unfortunate boat accident off the island of Diu. Whichever the truth, his death removed the threat from Gujarat.

In the meantime, problems for Humayun were growing in the east. Sher Shah Suri, an Afghan leader who had once been in the service of Babar, had developed a power base in Bihar. While Humayun was occupied in Gujarat, Sher Shah launched a campaign against Bengal and headed for the capital at Gaur. Humayun set forth to rescue the king of Bengal, but he was side-tracked at Chunar where Sher Shah had built a virtually impregnable fortress. Some of Humayun's advisers told him to capture the fortress first and then head for Gaur. Others told him to ignore Chunar and hasten to Gaur. Humayun took the wrong advice. He continued the siege of Chunar, eventually subduing it. While that was going on, Sher Shah was occupying Gaur.

By the time Humayun got to Gaur in 1538, Sher Shah had come and gone and was busy conquering Mughul territories in the west.

Humayun spent three months resting his troops in Gaur, and when he learned that Sher Shah was attacking his western cities, he started his return to Agra. On the way he was met by Sher Shah's troops at Chausa on the Ganges River near Buxar. In the battle, fought in June 1539, Humayun was badly beaten. He saved his life by jumping in the inflated skin of a *bisti* (water carrier) who brought him safely to shore.

(Later, when Humayun regained the throne, he invited the *bisti* to Delhi, and, as a reward, gave him full imperial power for two hours. The man made the most of it, spending two hours providing himself and his relatives with extensive *jagirs*.)

Humayun went to Lahore, hoping to persuade his brothers to help him regain his throne. They refused. Humayun raised an army without their help and met Sher Shah at Kanauj 17 May 1540, but was beaten a second time.

During the next 15 years Humayun became a wanderer, going from one kingdom to another, seeking asylum. For a time he was in Persia. He was in Umarkot, Sind, as a guest of Rana Parshad, when a son was born to his wife Hamida. Because Humayun had no money with which to celebrate the occasion, he broke open a pod of musk and distributed the seeds to his few followers, saying:

This is all the present I can afford to make to you on the birth of my son, whose fame will, I trust, one day be expanded over all the world, as the perfume of the musk now fills this tent."

He named the boy Akbar.

The Safawid Shah Tahmasp of Persia gave Humayun 14,000 troops with which to capture Kandahar on the condition that he would cede Kandahar to Persia on his success. Humayun captured Kandahar in 1545, but never got around to keeping his promise. In 1550, he captured Kabul from his unkind brother Kamran.

Humayun built up his forces during the ensuing five years, and in November 1554 he marched towards the Punjab, capturing Lahore in February of the next year. He then marched on Delhi and defeated the forces of Suri commanded by Sikandar Shah at Sirhind 22 June 1555.

Back on his throne, Humayun's reign lasted only seven months. He died 21 January 1556, possibly in a drunken state, when he tumbled down the stairs of his library in the fort known today as the Purana Qila. His tomb in Delhi is one of the marvels of the Mughul period. It was the scene of a British atrocity during the Revolt of 1857 when Major Hodson slaughtered two sons and a grandson of Bahadur Shah II, the last Mughul.

Humayun, like his father, was not an administrator, but unlike his father, he lacked perseverance, military skill and political wisdom. To quote Stanley Lane-Poole:

Humayun was incapable of sustained effort and after a moment of triumph would bury himself in his harem and dream away the precious hours in the opium-eater's paradise while his enemies were thundering at his gate. Naturally kind, he forgave when he should have punished; light-hearted and sociable, he revelled at the table when he should have been in the saddle. His character attracts but never dominates. In private life he might have been a delightful companion and a staunch friend. But as a king he was a failure. His name means fortunate, and never was an unlucky sovereign more miscalled.

Suggested Further Reading

Prasad, Ishwari, 1930–
     The life and times of Humáyún. — Allahabad : Central Book Depot, c1976.
     422 p., plates : ill., maps ; 22 cm.

SHER SHAH SURI
(1486-1545)

Sher Shah comes into Indian history as a sort of anomaly, a rebel who for 16 years interrupted Mughul supremacy in India. A member of the Afghan tribe of Suri, he was born in 1486, probably in Bajwara and given the name Farid Khan. His grandfather, Ibrahim Khan, entered the government service when Buhlul, the first of the Lodi Sultans, was on the Delhi throne. During the reign of Buhlul's son, Sikandar, the governor of Jaunpur, Jamal Khan, took Ibrahim into his service. Ibrahim's son, Hasan Khan, after some time was granted a *jagir* (estate) in Sasaram, Bihar.

Hasan Khan had eight sons, of which two were the legitimate sons of an Afghan mother. Farid was one of the legitimate ones. He did not get along with his father or step-mother; so at the age of 22 he left home and enlisted in the army of Jamal Khan, the governor of Jaunpur.

Farid's father wrote to Jamal Khan, requested that Farid return to Sasaram to be educated. Farid, who was an excellent student and had committed all of Sadi's poetry to memory, refused to return, saying he liked the schools in Jaunpur better.

Four years later, father and son were reconciled, and Farid accepted a post as manager of his father's *jagir* at Sasaram, saying that "the stability of every administration depended on justice and that it would be his greatest care not to violate it, whether by oppressing the weak, or by permitting the strong to infringe the laws with impunity."

He lived by these words as manager of the *jagir*, and he would live by them as governor of Bihar and as emperor of Delhi.

All would have been well at Sasaram, except that his step-mother stepped into the picture again. She used all her many charms in an effort to secure the *jagir* for her son, Suleiman, Farid's half-brother. In this impossible situation, Farid resigned his post to his full brother, Nizam, and left for Agra where he took service with Daulat Khan Lodi.

On the death of his father, Farid obtained the *jagir* of Sasaram from Daulat Khan. In 1522, he entered service with Bahadur Khan Lohani who had proclaimed himself king of Bihar. It was here that Farid got the name by which he is known in history. He was out hunting when a tiger charged his master. Farid bravely saved his master's life by killing the tiger with a sword; whereupon, Lohani gave him the title Sher Khan, "sher" meaning tiger. Also in recognition of Farid's gallantry, Lohani made him his deputy and tutor for his son.

However, all did not go well with Sher Khan. His enemies poisoned his master's mind, and his *jagir* was taken away from him. In the meantime, Babar had defeated Ibrahim Lodi at Panipat, and Sher, "impressed by the success of Mughul arms," joined Babar's army, serving there from April 1527 until June 1528. In recognition of his service, Babar restored the Sasaram *jagir* to him.

Sher left the Mughul service rather precipitously. During an encampment he commented to a companion that it would be easy to drive the Mughuls out of India if the Afghans could unite against them. Apparently, the companion let these words get back to Babar who said within Sher's hearing:

> This Afghan is not disconcerted by trifles; he may become a great man yet.

In the night Sher escaped and returned to Sasaram and once again went into the service of Bahadur Khan Lohani as guardian of his son, Jamal Khan, and deputy governor of Bihar. With the death of Lohani and the support of Sultana Lodi, his widow, Sher became the *de facto* ruler of Bihar.

When the new Mughul emperor, Humayun, was off in Gujarat settling matters with Bahadur Shah, Sher gathered about him a number of Afghan nobles who were anxious to throw out their Mughul overlord.

Sher, who had conquered Bengal once before and received a payment of 1,300,000 gold pieces, decided to conquer it so it would stay conquered. He invaded Bengal and besieged Gaur, its capital.

Humayun hastened eastward to meet Sher and put a stop to the uprising. On the way, he captured the fortress of Chunar, but in the meantime, Sher had captured Gaur and left it, heading westward to occupy Mughul lands in Bihar and Jaunpur.

The two, Sher Khan Suri and Humayun, met at Chausa on the Ganges River near Buxar in June 1539. Humayun was defeated and went into hiding. He gathered a force, met Sher at Kanauj 17 May 1540 and was beaten again.

Sher was now the ruler of Hindustan. His territories extended from Kanauj in the west to Assam and Chittagong in the east and from the Himalayas in the north to the Jharkhand Hills and Bay of Bengal in the south. He assumed the throne in Delhi 25 January 1542 and proclaimed himself Sher Shah. He spent the last years of his life subduing the Rajputs in Malwa, Raisin and Marwar. While storming the fort at Kalinjar 22 May 1545 Sher Shah was killed in an explosion. His last words were:

> Praise be to Almighty God!

Sher Shah is remembered as a soldier and a ruler who broke the sequence of Mughul rule in India, but he deserves to be remembered also as a ruler who enacted administrative reforms of lasting value. He divided his empire into 47 *sarkars*, each of which consisted of several *parganas*. The administrators of these units were moved around every three years, and were kept under close supervision of the emperor. He also reformed the land revenue system, instructing his officers to be lenient in assessment but strict in enforcement.

Ten years after Sher Shah's death when Hindustan was ruled by his successors, Humayun regained the throne, returning the Mughuls to power. V.A. Smith observed:

If Sher Shah had been spared, the Great Mughuls would not have appeared on the stage of history.

Suggested Further Reading

Qanungo, K.R.
Sher Shah : a critical study based on original sources. — Calcutta : Kar, Majumdar, 1921.
x, 452 p. : front. ; 19 cm.

AKBAR THE GREAT
(1542-1605)

Akbar, the greatest Mughul emperor, ruled India from 1556 to 1605. He was born 23 November 1542 at Umarkot (in Sind) where his father, Humayun, had found asylum with Rana Prasad.

He faced many vicissitudes in his early life. Though a truant boy with little interest in formal education, the theory of his illiteracy is a myth. Akbar was crowned at Kalanaur (district Gurdaspur) 14 February 1556. The Second Battle of Panipat (5 November 1556) which led to the defeat of Hemu, established his power in Delhi and Agra. Bairam Khan acted as his regent till 1560. Then the petticoat government of Maham Anga (1560-1564) held sway. From 1564, Akbar assumed direct control of the administration and was at the helm of affairs till his death.

During the next 20 years Akbar vigorously pursued a policy of conquest and annexation and gave shape to the Mughul Empire and its administrative institutions. In 1562, he occupied Chunar; in 1564 Gondwana and Malwa were conquered. In 1568, the famous fortress of Chittor was captured, followed by the conquest of Ranthambhor next year. Principalities of central India, including Kalinjar, were then annexed. In 1573, Gujarat was brought under control and the following year Bihar became a Mughul province. The independent Dynasty of Bengal fell in 1576; Kashmir was annexed in 1586-87 and Sind became part of the Mughul state in 1591-92. In 1599, the state of Ahmadnagar was captured and the conquest of Asirgarh followed soon after. Before Akbar closed his eyes in death, the major part of the country had been brought under his control and the political and administrative unity of the country had been firmly established.

Akbar's marriage with the daughter of Raja Bhari Mal of Amber (Jaipur) in 1562 opened a new chapter of Mughul-Rajput relations, and the Rajputs played a prominent role in the extension and consolidation of Mughul authority. Akbar's administrative system, which was half civil and half military, was effectively organised on the basis of *mansabs* (rank or grade), i.e. the number of troopers which an officer could have under his command. These *mansabs* were divided into 33 grades, the lowest rank being that of 10, and the highest that of 10,000. The *mansabs* were not hereditary; all the appointments, promotions, transfers and dismissals depended on the pleasure of the emperor.

Akbar reorganised the land revenue administration with the help of Todar Mal: he adopted measurement as the method of assessment, classified land according to fertility and irrigation facilities, fixed state demand on the basis of ten year's average assessment, collected the revenues directly, and abolished many vexatious cesses.

Akbar's greatness in the history of India lies in his vision of the political unity of India for which he struggled throughout his life. He gave shape to an *Indian* state in which all Indians had an equal sense of participation. Similarly, in the cultural sphere, his attempt was to draw inspiration from the totality of the Indian cultural tradition. He initiated a programme for translation of Sanskrit classics like *Mahábhárata*, *Rámáyana*, *Atharva Veda*, into Persian.

Keenly interested in the study of religions, Akbar established an *Ibadat Khanah* (prayer hall) where initially Muslim scholars assembled and discussed religious matters, but subsequently scholars of all religions — Hindus, Jains, Buddhists, Zoroastrians, Christians, etc. — gathered together. In 1579, the *ulema* issued a decree, called *Mahzar*, which empowered Akbar to accept any of the opinions given to him by the *ulema* and invested him also with a limited authority to initiate legislation for the welfare of the people.

Akbar sought to evolve a synthesis of religions which he considered necessary for the stability and consolidation of the Mughul authority. The *Din-i-Ilahi* has been differently interpreted as a brotherhood of intellectuals, a fraternity, a religious cult, etc. That it was essentially an effort to bring all religions on a common platform and control their activity is obvious from the four renunciations — readiness to surrender life, property, honour and religion — demanded from its followers. The *Din-i-Ilahi* did not appeal to the Indian mind: there were only one Hindu and seventeen Muslim adherents to the faith.

Akbar's ideals were reflected in his state policies and cultural activities. He abolished the pilgrim tax and the *jiziyah* in order to ensure equal religious freedom to all. The buildings at Fatehpur Sikri represented a synthesis of Hindu-Muslim architectural traditions. He adopted a large number of Hindu customs and ceremonials and celebrated Hindu festivals. His tomb at Sikandara symbolises the ideals he represented in his life.

Akbar took keen personal interest in all works of art and new inventions. Under him Indian industries and *karkhanas* made remarkable progress. Possessed of a charismatic personality, Akbar was bold, generous, gentle, humane and broad-minded.

He left a deep impact of his thought and personality on the canvas of Indian history.

— K.A. Nizami

Suggested Further Readings

Abul Fazl.
  Akbarnama / tr. by H. Beveridge. — Calcutta : Asiatic Society of Bengal, 1897-1921.
  3 v. ; 27 cm. — (Bibliotheca indica)

Abul Fazl.
  Ain-i-Akbari / tr. by H. Blochmann and Jarrett. — Calcutta : Royal Asiatic Society,
  1868-94.
  3 v. ; 24 cm. — (Bibliotheca indica)

Smith, Vincent Arthur.
  Akbar the Great Mogul — Oxford : Clarendon, 1917.
  xv, 504 p. : ill., map ; 23 cm.

Srivastava, A.L.
  Akbar the Great. — Agra : Shiva Lal Agarwala, 1926-67.
  2 v. : ill. ; 22 cm.

JAHANGIR
(1569-1627)

When Prince Salim succeeded to the throne of his father, Akbar, in 1605, he assumed the title *Nur-ud-Din Muhammad Jahangir Padshah Ghazi*. He is known to history, however, simply as Jahangir.

He was born at Fatehpur-Sikri 31 August 1569 to the daughter of Raja Bihari Mal of Amber. He was the only son of Akbar who survived him, and Akbar had wanted to disinherit him because he had caused Akbar's greatest friend, Abul Fazl, to be murdered.

Once on the throne, Jahangir initiated a number of measures to gain popularity for himself. He granted general amnesty to his opponents, released prisoners and instituted a series of edicts which were to serve as rules of conduct for his reign. These included prohibition of *zakat* (cesses), prevention of highway robbery and theft, prohibition of the sale of *sharab* (intoxicating beverages), building of hospitals, etc.

He also rewarded various persons who had helped him during his earlier years: Bir Singh Bundela, the murderer of Abul Fazl, Maha Singh (the son of Man Singh) and Mirza Ghiyas Beg, the father of Mehr-un-Nissa (later to be known as Nur Jahan), Jahangir's chief wife.

Jahangir was obligated to continue the wars that were in progress at the time of Akbar's death. This he did, concluding the conflict with Mewar in 1614 and carrying on the battle with Ahmadnagar, which was ended successfully by Prince Khurram (later Shah Jahan) in 1617 and 1621.

But Jahangir's immediate problem was with his son Khusrau who was both able and popular. In the revolt that ensued, Khusrau was captured while trying to cross the Chenab and get to Kabul to continue the struggle from there. He was reprimanded and humiliated publicly at a *darbar*. He was then imprisoned, and he died in 1622, poisoned, some believe, at the behest of Prince Khurram, his brother and future emperor.

In 1611, Jahangir had married Mehr-un-Nissa, the widow of Sher Afghan who had been involved in the struggle between Jahangir and

Khusrau. She was a beautiful and capable woman on whom the emperor bestowed the title *Nur Mahal* (Light of the Palace), revising it later to *Nur Jahan* (Light of the World). As empress she used her office effectively.

A greater threat to Jahangir's security than that of Prince Khusrau came from Prince Khurram. Khurram had established his credentials as a leader of armies in his campaigns in Rajasthan and the Deccan, for the latter of which Jahangir conferred on him the title *Shah Jahan* (King of the World). The break between father and son occurred when Shah Jahan was ordered to quell a rebellion in the northwest where the Persians had captured Kandahar, but Shah Jahan refused to do so. He was stripped of his rank and hunted from place to place.

He hid out in Bengal for a time, finally gained the support of the Abyassinian minister of Ahmadnagar and in 1623 attacked Agra. He was repulsed and two years later made peace with his father.

Jahangir died 28 October 1627 while travelling from Kashmir to Lahore, and Shah Jahan ascended the throne. Jahangir's tomb is located on the banks of Ravi in Lahore.

Jahangir was a man of glowing contradictions. He was capable of enormous cruelty and great kindness. He could be as forgiving as he was vindictive. His execution of Guru Arjan, the fifth Guru of the Sikhs, was for the most part a gratuitous act which inflamed Sikh passions and turned a peaceful religious community into a militant one. Jahangir, like many in the Mughul line, was an alcoholic; this problem he mentions with surprising frequency in his memoirs. However, unlike many of the other Mughul princes who were to die relatively young from alcoholism, he had the strength of character to control but not cure his disease.

For all his strengths and weaknesses and tergiversations, Jahangir is remembered for his love of flowers, for the "Mughul Gardens" he left for posterity and for his fondness for Kashmir. He was a patron of the arts and a devotee of Persian culture.

Suggested Further Readings

Guerreiro, Fernão, 1560?-1617.
> Jahangir and the Jesuits. — London : Routledge, [1930]
> xxx, 287 p. : port., maps ; 23 cm — (The Broadway travellers)

Holden, Edward Singleton, 1846-1914.
> The Mogul emperors of Hindustan ... — Delhi : Metropolitan Book Co., 1975.
> xvi, 365 p. : plates, ill. ; 22 cm.
> Reprint of 1895 edition.

Jahangir, Emperor of Hindustan, 1569-1627.
> Autobiographical memoirs of the Emperor Jahangir / translated from the Persian by David Price. — Calcutta : Editions Indians, [1972]
> xliii, 168 p. ; 22 cm.
> First published in 1827.

Kennedy, Pringle.
> History of the great Moghuls, 1398 to 1739 AD. — Calcutta : Thacker, Spink, [1968]
> ix, 556 p. ; 22 cm.
> Reprint of 1911 edition.

NUR JAHAN
(1577-1645)

Nur Jahan, Jahangir's chief queen, was a brilliant woman who acquired broad administrative and strategic power during the first part of the seventeenth century. She was born in Kandahar in 1577, while her parents were migrating from Persia to India. They named her Mehr-un-Nissa. Her father was Mirza Ghiyas Beg, later known as Itimad-ud-Daulah, and her mother was Asmat Begam. Historically, many of the family had served as court administrators under the Safavid kings and were now exporting their talents to Mughul India. Ghiyas Beg became a courtier to Akbar, and the family settled in Fatehpur-Sikri.

When Mehr-un-Nissa was 17, she was married to Ali Quli, a young Persian Turk who had been given the title of Sher Afghan because of killing a tiger single-handedly. Sher Afghan became a friend to Prince Salim, the future Jahangir, and was given a *jagir* in Bengal.

Jahangir ascended the throne in 1605 on his father Akbar's death, and Mehr-un-Nissa was drawn into the battle for succession. The threat to Jahangir came from his son Khusrau who was popular and talented. Mirza Ghiyas Beg and one of Mehr-un-Nissa's brothers were implicated in the plot, and Sher Afghan was also suspected. When the coup was put down, Jahangir killed the brother and sent a minister to question Sher Afghan. Both Sher Afghan and the minister died in the confrontation, and Mehr-un-Nissa was sent into the household of the dowager Ruqayyah Sultan Begam in 1607. She had with her a young daughter, Ladli Begam.

She was Beautiful

The widow, Mehr-un-Nissa, was beautiful and accomplished in literature and poetry. Jahangir was impressed with these qualities and married her in 1611. He was devoted to her and quickly gave her the title of *Nur Mahal* (Light of the Palace). In 1614, she was given the title of *Nur Jahan* (Light of the World). A skilled politician and administrator, she came to have unprecedented power as an empress. She held her own *darbars*, and coins were issued in her name.

Her family also rose with her. Her father, now known as Itimad-ud-Daulah, was forgiven for plotting against Jahangir and eventually given a title and a rise in rank to seven thousand. Her brother, Mirza Abul Hasan, was given the title of Asaf Khan and eventually reached the rank of nine thousand. Asaf Khan's daughter was Arjumand Bano Begam (later Mumtaz Mahal) who married Jahangir's son, Prince Khurram in 1612.

Two other brothers of Nur Jahan were also high ranking *mansabdars*. Together with Prince Khurram, this group worked harmoniously under the guidance of Nur Jahan to control state affairs until 1620. Jahangir, affected by too much wine and opium, handed over much of the administration to Nur Jahan.

By the early 1620s Jahangir was seriously ill with asthma, and he relied even more on Nur Jahan's abilities. Alarmed at his failing health, Nur Jahan knew that her power would be diminished if Prince Khurram were to succeed Jahangir. The ambitious woman now sought to ally herself with a different prince. She settled on Prince Shahryar, who was young and malleable, and married her daughter Ladli Begam to him in 1621.

This eventually alienated Khurram and Arjumand Bano Begam and Nur Jahan's own brother, Asaf Khan, who was now father-in-law to Khurram. The death of both Nur Jahan's parents in 1621-22 broke up the powerful coalition of the family, and the next few years before Jahangir's death in 1627 were full of intrigue.

On a military venture to the Deccan, Khurram insisted that his brother Khusrau accompany him. Khusrau died on the trip in 1622, supposedly of colic. The campaign was victorious, and Khurram had gathered followers to support his claim to the throne. Nur Jahan arranged for him to be called to another military front in Kandahar, where he would be unable to wrest the crown from Prince Shahryar if Jahangir should suddenly die. Khurram delayed. Nur Jahan encouraged Jahangir to think that Khurram was rebellious, and he was reprimanded.

Meanwhile, Mahabat Khan, a loyal general, was won over by Nur Jahan, and his enemy, Asaf Khan, was sent to Bengal. Khurram rebelled in 1623 and was faced by an imperial army at Bilochpur. He was defeated and pursued. He sued for pardon, sending his sons to court as hostages. Although the empire was troubled during this fight, it established Nur Jahan as a political strategist who got her enemies to fight amongst themselves.

Although Mahabat Khan had been helpful to her in putting down the rebellion, he favoured another prince, Parvez, over her son-in-law Shahryar. She sought to ruin him by insulting his honesty. Not fooled, Mahabat Khan attempted a dramatic play to speak directly with Jahangir and restore his honour.

Held Hostage

In 1626, he marched with Rajput troops to the imperial encampment on the Jhelum River in Lahore. There he captured the emperor and held him hostage. Nur Jahan escaped across the river to the bulk of the imperial forces and led the battle the next day on an elephant. Nur Jahan's forces were turned back, but she joined her husband. The royal party and the army were now controlled by Mahabat Khan, and they all marched to Kabul, the original destination. On the way back to Lahore Nur Jahan was able to rally forces loyal to herself and seize control once again.

Late in 1626 Parvez died. Mahabat Khan and Khurram quickly formed a powerful alliance which alarmed Nur Jahan. In early 1627, while the royal party was in Kashmir, Jahangir's health took a sudden turn for the worse. Shahryar also fell ill, and to Nur Jahan's distress, left for Lahore. Jahangir died in October on the road back to Lahore.

Immediately Nur Jahan called for a meeting of noblemen but was blocked by her brother Asaf Khan who was Khurram's father-in-law. After a short period of struggle in which a makeshift emperor was put on the throne and Shahryar was thwarted in his attempt at revolt, Khurram became emperor, taking the name Shah Jahan.

Nur Jahan was defeated in her attempt to retain power at the Mughul court. She was forced into retirement in Lahore and lived for 18 years there. She had a state pension, as well as considerable personal wealth and was known as a pious and generous woman. Her daughter, Ladli Begam, who was widowed when her husband Shahryar was executed, lived with her.

Nur Jahan died in Lahore in 1645 and was buried there in the tomb which she had designed for herself.

Nur Jahan was a brilliant politician, but she also shone in the arts. Throughout her reign with Jahangir she had many gardens and monuments built. One of her finest legacies is her father's tomb in Agra. This building, which has been regarded as the connecting link between Akbar's style and that of Shah Jahan, is of marble with fine marble screens and pietra dura work.

— **Diane Clayton**

Suggested Further Reading

Shujauddin, Muhammad.
    The life and times of Nur Jahan / Muhammad and Razia Shujauddin. — Lahore : Caravan Book House, 1967.
    146 p. : ill. ; 22 cm.
    Includes quotations in Urdu.

SHAH JAHAN
(1592-1666)

Shah Jahan, the great builder and fifth of the great Mughuls, was the third son of the emperor, Jahangir. He was born 5 January 1592 in Lahore. His mother was Balmati, the daughter of Rana Udai Singh of Jodhpur. He was brought up by his grandmother, Ruqayyah Sultana Begam, and was a favourite of his doting grandfather, Akbar, who gave him the name Khurram, which means "Joyous."

At the age of four years and four months, in accordance with Chaghatai Turk custom, little Prince Khurram was put in school with much pomp and ceremony, and Akbar provided the best teachers for him. He did not develop into a scholar, but he gained an appreciation of art for which posterity can be eternally grateful.

At the tender age of 15, he was betrothed to the girl for whom he would eventually build a great mausoleum, Arjumand Banu Begam, but the marriage was postponed five years. In the meantime, he was married off 28

October 1610 to the daughter of Muzaffar Husain Safavi. He did not get to marry his true love, Arjumand, known to history as Mumtaz Mahal, until March 1612. She was the niece of the empress, Nur Jahan.

Prince Khurram's third wife was the daughter of Shah Nawaz Khan, the son of the commander-in-chief, Abdur Rahim Khan-i-Khanan. This was a strictly political marriage. Prince Khurram's one and only love was his second wife, and she gave him 14 children, one of whom would one day overthrow him and force him to spend his last days under house arrest.

Prince Khurram won his spurs on the battlefield of Mewar where he succeeded in doing what no other Mughul general had done: he conquered the last Rajput state to hold out against the empire and forced the Rana, Amar Singh, and his son, Karan, to sue for peace.

From Mewar, Prince Khurram was transferred to the Deccan, which had been a problem for the emperor. He succeeded in bringing tentative peace to the region with the capture of some Ahmadnagar forts. Jahangir honoured his son for this deed by naming him Shah Jahan, which means "King of the World."

Shah Jahan dallied in the court for three years during which time relations between him and Nur Jahan cooled off considerably. Finally, he was sent to the Deccan to settle difficulties there, but problems were developing in the northwest where the Persians had captured Kandahar. Shah Jahan was ordered by Jahangir to proceed there to restore Mughul honour, but he refused.

This displeased the emperor considerably, and Shah Jahan was stripped of his rank and hunted from place to place. In Bengal, he sought the aid of the Portuguese, but they refused to give it, fearing reprisals from Jahangir. He finally found refuge with Malik Ambar, the Abyssinian minister of Ahmadnagar.

In 1623, he made an attack on Agra in alliance with his father-in-law, Khan-i-Khanan, but it was beaten back by the imperial army. Then in 1625, he made peace with his father and left two of his sons, Aurangzeb and Dara Shukoh, as hostages in the imperial court and returned to the Deccan.

Jahangir died in 1627, and Shah Jahan was summoned to Agra by his father-in-law (Mumtaz Mahal's father), Asaf Khan. The other claimant to the throne, Prince Shahryar, at the instance of Nur Jahan, had proclaimed himself emperor in Lahore.

Asaf Khan put Prince Dawar Bakhsh on the throne as a stop-gap emperor, awaiting the arrival of Shah Jahan from the Deccan. He arrived in haste and was proclaimed emperor in February 1628 with the title, Abul Muzaffar Shihab-ud-Din Muhammad Sahib-i-Qiran II, Shah Jahan Padshah Ghazi.

Once on the throne, Shah Jahan disposed of his rivals with relative ease and put down rebellions by the Bundela chief, Jujhar Singh, and the Afghan noble, Khan Jahan Lodi.

He then turned to the Portuguese in Hugli with whom he had a score to settle. They had refused him shelter during his fugitive period and had compounded their enmity by engaging in the slave trade, converting Indians to Christianity and, worst of all, kidnapping two of Mumtaz Mahal's slave girls.

Shah Jahan appointed Kasim Ali Khan governor of Bengal with instructions to punish the Portuguese. He did so by laying siege to Hugli, a city they had founded in circa 1579. The siege lasted three months, ending 24 June 1632. Many Portuguese were killed, and those who survived were brought to Agra where they were subjected to terrible conditions.

Shah Jahan's reign was one of building and is sometimes called the Golden Age of Mughul India. He is remembered mainly for the Taj Mahal, built for his beautiful wife, Mumtaz Mahal, and considered by many to be the most beautiful building in the world. He also built the Diwan-i-Am, the Diwan-i-Khas and the Red Fort of Agra, and similar structures in Delhi, which he renamed Shahjahanabad.

However, it was not all building for which Shah Jahan may be remembered. He did much to alleviate the suffering of the people during the famine of 1631-32, he proved to be an able administrator, and he annexed Ahmadnagar, reduced Bijapur and Golkunda to subjection and even recaptured Kandahar, though the last conquest was of short duration.

His last years were pitiful. He became severely ill in 1657, and this became the occasion of a fratricidal war of succession among his four eldest sons. Aurangzeb was ultimately victorious. He took over the throne in 1658 and put Shah Jahan in the Red Fort in chambers from which he could gaze across the Jumna River and see the Taj Mahal where his beloved Mumtaz slept. He died 22 January 1666 and was buried next to his favourite wife. While in captivity he wrote this quatrain to his son:

> Praised be the Hindus in all cases,
>> As they offer water to their dead.
> And thou, my son, art a marvelous Mussalman,
>> As thou causest me in life to lament for water.

Suggested Further Reading

Saksena, Banarsi Prasad.
   The history of Shahjahan of Dihli. — Allahabad : Indian Press, 1932.
   xxx, 373 p. : plates ; 23 cm.

AURANGZEB
(1618-1707)

Alamgir I, also known as Abul Zafar Muhi-ud-Din Muhammad, but better known as Aurangzeb (which means "Throne Ornament"), was born during the first week of November (new style) 1618 at Dohad in Gujarat. His father was the fifth Mughul emperor, Shah Jahan, and his mother was

Arjumand Banu Begam, better known as Mumtaz Mahal. He was their third son.

As a child he was well educated, learning Arabic and Persian and becoming knowledgeable in the Koran and Hadith literature, traditional sayings of the prophet Muhammad. His mother tongue was Urdu, but he was also conversant in Hindi and Chaghatai Turki.

When he was seven, he was sent to Agra as a hostage in the court of his grandfather, Jahangir, during the latter's conflict with Shah Jahan.

On the death of Jahangir in 1627 Shah Jahan ascended the throne and began his programme of building mosques, forts and, later, the Taj Mahal. In 1636, Aurangzeb, at the age of 18, was appointed viceroy of the Deccan provinces. In 1644, he announced his renunciation of the world. His father was outraged at this and fired him. Aurangzeb then hid out in the Western Ghats to mortify the flesh and commune with Allah.

However, in less than a year he gave up all that and began to gather an army, and in 1645, he was appointed governor of Gujarat. Then in 1647 his father sent him off to rule Balkh and Badakhshan which Ali Mardan and Aurangzeb's younger brother, Murad Bakhsh, had conquered two years earlier.

Aurangzeb believed it was useless to try to rule the far-flung provinces of Balkh and Badakhshan from Agra; so he surrendered them to the king of the Uzbegs and retreated. In 1648, he was made governor of Multan, to which Sind was added in 1649. Two attempts were made, in 1649 and 1652, to recover Samarkand from the Persians, but both failed, and Aurangzeb was appointed viceroy of the Deccan in 1652.

The serious illness of Shah Jahan in 1657 was the signal for a civil war of succession of brother against brother. Two of the brothers, Shuja, governor of Bengal, and Murad, governor of Gujarat, proclaimed themselves emperors. Aurangzeb allied himself with Murad, and the two of them combined to defeat the imperial armies at Dharmat and Samugarh in April and May of 1658. Prince Dara, who was the eldest son and Shah Jahan's first choice for successor, was chased all the way to Agra where he surrendered the fort and its treasures to Aurangzeb 8 June 1658.

Aurangzeb soon disposed of his three brothers. Shuja was pursued to Arakan and perished there with his family. Murad was charged with the murder of the Diwan of Gujarat and executed. Dara was convicted on a charge of apostasy, publicly humiliated and executed 30 August 1659.

Aurangzeb had himself informally crowned 21 July 1658 and was formally enthroned in June of the following year, assuming the title *Alamgir*, which means "Conqueror of the World".

Like other rulers of Hindustan before him, Aurangzeb spent many years consolidating and extending his realm.

In 1661, Palamau was conquered and annexed. The following year his general, Mir Jumlah, conquered the Ahom king of Assam and acquired Darrang. Sandwip Island in the Bay of Bengal and Chittagong were conquered in 1666. The Afghans revolted in 1667, but were not subdued until

1675. The Rajput states were brought into the empire in 1681, and Bijapur and Golkunda annexed in 1686 and 1687, and in 1691 Aurangzeb was able to extract tribute from the Rajas of Tanjore and Trichinopoly.

Aurangzeb's empire, however, had over-extended himself. As Sir Jadunath Sarkar said:

Like the boa constrictor it had swallowed more than it could digest.

There is no doubt that Aurangzeb was an able administrator and a highly qualified general; however, his many wars had depleted the treasury and foredoomed the great Mughul empire. Had he adopted his great grand-father Akbar's policy of conciliation with the Hindu population, his mighty empire might have survived him.

He was never able to conquer the Marathas who were then on the ascendancy, and his preoccupation with the conquest of the Deccan cost him dearly.

He razed Hindu temples, often building mosques on their foundations. He destroyed Hindu idols, forbade Hindu fairs and discouraged the hiring of Hindus in government jobs. To.make matters worse for his subject popu-lation, he reinstated the *jizya*, a toll tax on non-Muslims, which had been abolished by Akbar.

His treatment of Şikhs was no less harsh. He confronted the Sikh leader, Teg Bahadur, with a choice between decapitation and conversion to Islam. Teg Bahadur chose the former.

Aurangzeb died 3 March 1707 in Ahmadnagar to be succeeded by his son Bahadur Shah I and a series of ineffectual "emperors," concluding with Bahadur Shah II in 1858.

After his death Aurangzeb was given the title *Hazrat Khuld- Makán* ("He Whose Place Is in Paradise").

Suggested Further Reading

Sarkar, Jadunath, Sir, 1870-1958.
  History of Aurangzeb. — Calcutta : M.C. Sarkar, 1912-30.
  5 v. in 4 ; 19 cm.

CHAPTER 4

THE SIXTEENTH AND SEVENTEENTH CENTURIES

Albuquerque
João de Castro
Vasco da Gama
Krishnadevaraya
François Martin

Jacob Blanquet de La Haye
Rana Pratap Singh
Sir Thomas Roe
Shivaji

*T*he sixteenth and seventeenth centuries in India belong by right of conquest to the Mughuls. They are dealt with in the chapter devoted just to them.

However, events were occurring in parts of India far from their seat of power in Delhi which would wreak havoc with the Mughul Empire and produce a century of confusion and conflict (the eighteenth) in which the fate of modern India would be decided.

On the West Coast the Portuguese arrived when Vasco da Gama anchored the "São Gabriel" in the harbour of Calicut in 1498. Later Albuquerque and João de Castro established the Portuguese presence with brutal force. The Dutch dislodged them from Malabar, but in the meantime the French, with Martin in Pondichéry and La Haye all over the place, and the English, with their ambassador, Sir Thomas Roe, at the court of Jahangir, were setting up trading companies on Indian soil.

While this was happening, Krishnadevaraya, the great warrior king, was extending the boundaries of the Vijayanagar Empire as far north as Vizagapatam in the east and the Konkan coast in the west.

And in the seventeenth century another great warrior king, Shivaji, the Maratha marauder, established his power on the West Coast which would challenge all comers in the several decades that followed his death in 1680.

These are two fascinating centuries in the panorama of India as told in the stories of the men who left their marks.

AFFONSO DE ALBUQUERQUE
(1453-1515)

A prominent figure in Portuguese imperial history, Affonso de Albuquerque descended from a well-connected lineage. His family seems to have derived its origin from an illegitimate son of King Denis of Portugal in the late thirteenth century. Affonso de Albuquerque was the second son of Gonçalo de Albuquerque and Leonor de Menezes. He had at least three other brothers and two sisters. He was born at Alhandra in the neighbourhood of Lisbon between 1445 and 1462.

He was educated in the royal court of Afonso V, the African (1432-1481), and served in the royal guard of King João II, who succeeded his father on the throne in 1481. While the previous monarch kept up the warlike spirit of the Portuguese through wars against the Spaniards and the Moors, the new monarch turned his attention to further the scientific pursuits oriented towards the expansion of Portugal overseas. Albuquerque was a blend of both the spirits, and was one of that breed of *conquistadores* with their overweening self-confidence and tradition of reaching for the moon. He represented supremely the national tradition of the poor and bellicose Portuguese, who had grown to identify their raids for food, loot and prisoners with a mission from above. Albuquerque carried this zeal and fanaticism from Africa to the Far East, and has rightly been considered the real founder of the Portuguese empire in the East.

In 1503, after an early stint in Morocco, where Albuquerque lost his younger brother and developed a personal hatred for the Moors, the new king Manuel I sent him to the East with a small squadron of three vessels along with two other squadrons of similar strength to threaten Calicut, to help build a fort at Cochin and to establish commercial relations with Quilon. This was his first contact with India and also his first experience with the conflict of sharing responsibility. He had clashes with his cousin Francisco de Albuquerque. His uncompromising and domineering character made such conflicts more painful for himself and for others in the future course of his brief and eventful career.

Apparently, the brilliant performance of the few Portuguese under the command of Duarte Pacheco against the forces of Calicut on sea and land in 1503 had suggested to the king of Portugal that the Portuguese commercial interests in the East would never be sufficiently safeguarded only with fleets and with total dependence upon some local allies on land. The victories of Pacheco had confirmed the viability of a land-based presence of the Portuguese.

On return from India in 1504, Albuquerque seems to have reinforced this thinking of his king with a more grandiose plan of an empire with fort-bases controlling the main entrance-exits of the Indian Ocean. It was decided consequently to enhance the presence of the Portuguese in Asia.

A high ranking nobleman, D. Francisco de Almeida, was appointed the first viceroy, though ironically he did not believe in building forts or attempting to establish direct government in the East. This led to many heartburns and to a stormy relationship between him and Albuquerque, who had also to suffer the initial humiliation of being sent in 1506 to execute the imperial plans only as a subordinate commander under Admiral Tristão de Cunha. However, he had personal command over some vessels, and was given also a secret letter of appointment that entitled him to take over the governance from Almeida on completion of his term in 1508.

On his arrival in the Asian waters, Albuquerque went about terrorizing the ports of Oman and perpetrating deeds of cruelty and vandalism which culminated in the conquest and sack of the key trading port-city of Hormuz. The appalling cruelties — the slicing off of noses and ears — inflicted on enemies real and imaginary had disturbed even his own men, who already had enough grievances against his manner of command. It was the dissension in his ranks and the opposition of the viceroy that blocked for a while the continuation of his imperial mission.

He had to abandon his plans for a fort in Hormuz and return to India where the viceroy refused to hand over to him the charge of his office, and on the contrary detained him in Cannanore. It was only the arrival of the marshal, D. Fernando Coutinho, with a new fleet and with orders to enforce the induction of the new governor that Albuquerque could assume the governorship late in 1509 and pursue his plans. But even this was delayed somewhat as a result of the stubborn attitude adopted by the marshal who demanded total obedience to his decision to storm and sack Calicut. The campaign ended disastrously for the Portuguese as a result of the poor command, and it was only the presence of Albuquerque that saved the situation somewhat. On this occasion he almost lost his life, and definitely the normal use of his left arm.

Albuquerque was incapable of resting idle and as he was on his way back to the Arabian coast, he was met at Mirjan on the Canara coast by a native pirate named Timoja who explained to Albuquerque the discontent of the Hindu population of Goa with the Muslim rulers and induced him to capture Goa. There are indications that this was not the first time that Timoja had been in contact with the Portuguese with such suggestions. Following consultation with his captains, Albuquerque came to the conclusion that the capture of Goa would be strategically very advantageous for the execution of his imperial plans of keeping the Muslims out of the Indian Ocean. The very central position of Goa on the western coast of India and its many natural resources would make Goa a strong base and headquarters of his projected Portuguese empire in the East.

His first attempt at the conquest of Goa in February 1510 was successful, but the counter-attack forced him out soon after, and he had to wait till the end of the monsoon to recapture Goa for good, and that was done 27 November of the same year.

Albuquerque did not want to antagonise the local Hindu population; so he guaranteed their safe existence. He got the cooperation of the native Hindus as a result of the ousting of the Muslims. He proved to be more than a sanguine military man. This was further manifest in his decision to colonise the new conquest by encouraging marriage of his soldiers with local women. This was meant not only to cater to the urgent sexual needs of his men in the heat of the tropics, but also to meet the problem of future supply of personnel to defend the place. It would not be easy for them to acclimatise to the East. He encouraged such marriages with dowries in the form of plots of land, houses, heads of cattle, implements and cash grants.

As he wrote to his king in November 1514: "These Indians will know that we have come to stay, because they see our men planting trees, building houses of stone and lime, and breeding sons and daughters." It is not easy to say that the Portuguese were entirely devoid of racial feelings as this plan was being implemented. We do read again in Albuquerque's letters that he chose women who were "alvas e castas" (fair and chaste). These women belonged to the Muslims who were in control of Goa at the time of its conquest. There are references to batches of women brought from Malabar and replaced from time to time, but they only served the sexual needs of Albuquerque's men.

Following the conquest of Goa, Albuquerque's next major step was the conquest of Malacca, which would give the Portuguese control over the spice islands and over the trade of China and Japan. This was done in 1511 and a fort was established. During his return journey in a vessel laden with incalculable loot, he suffered a shipwreck and escaped only with his life. This incident has been presented as symbolic of the empire established by Albuquerque by one of his most vitriolic critics, António Sérgio, who defines much of the Portuguese imperial tragedies as "albuquerquismo" and calls Albuquerque the most disastrous character in the whole of Portuguese history.

On the return from Malacca, Albuquerque was kept busy defending Goa against attempts by its former rulers to reconquer it. He did succeed in countering these attempts and in February 1513 left for the Gulf area. In spite of heavenly visions, he failed to storm Aden and had to return to Goa where he spent time in organising his "children" (as he called those who accepted his plan of mixed marriages). They were organised into a municipality with special privileges and had a Holy House of Mercy (Santa Casa de Misericórdia) to look after their welfare. Both these institutions contributed immensely to the stability of the Portuguese colonial presence in the East over centuries.

In February 1515, Albuquerque was sent to Hormuz, which he brought under his control without having to repeat his past cruelties. He resumed the construction of the fort which had to be abandoned in 1508. However, this time his strength was giving way, and he decided to return to Goa. In the meantime he had been much maligned by his personal rivals in the royal circles, and it was while he was still on his way to Goa that he learned about the new governor who had been sent to replace him. His enemies had triumphed and this broke his resistance and made him give up his will to live. He did not live to enter Goa again and died within its sight

16 December 1515. But before dying, he had drafted a final letter to the king recommending to his generosity and protection his only illegitimate son, the author of *Commentarios*, the first detailed account of Albuquerque's life and achievements to appear in print.

— **Teotonio R. de Souza**

Suggested Further Readings

Albuquerque, Afonso de, 1500? – 1580.
  The commentaries of the great Affonso Da Albuquerque, second Viceroy of India / tr. from the Portuguese edition of 1774, with notes and an introduction by Walter de Gray Birch ... — London : Printed for the Hakluyt Society, 1875-84.
  4 v. : ill., 4 plates (1 fold.), 6 port. (incl. fronts.), 3 maps, 3 fold. plans ; 22 cm. — (Half-title : Works issued by the Hakluyt Society ; no. LIII, LV, LXII, LXIX)

Sérgio, António, 1883-1969.
  Ensaios. — Lisboa : Livraria Sá da Costa, [1971-74]
  8 v. ; 21 cm.
  (Material on Albuquerque is found in v. 8, pp. 148-160)

Stephens, Henry Morse, 1857-1919.
  ... Albuquerque ... — Oxford : Clarendon Press, 1892.
  222 p. incl. front. (port.) : fold. map ; 20 cm. — (Rulers of India ; v. 2)

An additional bibliographic source for Portuguese persons involved in Indian history is Henry Scholberg's *Bibliography of Goa and the Portuguese in India.*

JOÃO DE CASTRO
(1500-1548)

Introduction

After Vasco da Gama, João de Castro is perhaps the second most important Portuguese admiral to have set sail for India. While Vasco da Gama is justly celebrated in Europe for discovering the sea route to India via the Cape of Good Hope, the story of Castro, the governor of Goa and fourth Viceroy of India is less known to most people. However, his contacts with India, both before and after being made governor, have a value that is of greater depth and breadth than that of Vasco da Gama.

João de Castro's famous *Roteiros* are a precious resource for political records of sixteenth century western India, coastal maps of the seaboard of western India and the Red Sea, descriptions of Indian vegetation; and, most importantly, for historians of science, the *Roteiros* proved a valuable record of the use of navigational instruments of the time, astrolabes, sundials and the magnetic compass. As such, Castro may well be regarded as being of the same tradition as al-Biruni and the forerunner of some British civil servants who have left behind valuable historical records of India for our use today.

Early Years

Born in the year 1500 as the second son of Alvaro de Castro, the civil governor of Lisbon, João was educated at home in the trivium (grammar, arithmetic and humanities) at his father's insistence. He took an early interest in navigation, astronomy and geography, which flourished in Portugal during his early adulthood. He pursued his studies in the company of his contemporaries Pedro Nuñes, the cosmographer, and Infante Dom Luís, an amateur scientist, who was also the younger brother of the reigning monarch, Dom João III. Though Castro left behind work on astronomy and geography, they are not the theoretical works of a scholar but practical compendia for use by sailors.

At the age of 24, he married Leonor Coutinho. They had four sons and three daughters. One son, Fernando, died during the lifting of the second siege of Diu in 1546. Castro himself led the troops that defeated the Turks mounted that siege.

Career and Contributions

João de Castro, an unostentatious knight, found his metier only when he accompanied his brother-in-law, Garcia de Noronha, a Governor of India, to Goa in 1538. The king's brother, and João's friend, Infante Dom Luís, had given Castro a sundial, well-constructed by the cosmographer friend, Pedro Nuñes. First built in Nurenburg, Germany, sundials were considered rather special because with a small magnetic compass incorporated in the base, it was possible to determine the magnetic north and its deviation from the north, the declination. This angle is very important to know, both for navigation and, in modern science, for the discovery that the source of the geomagnetic field lies in its fluid mobile iron core. Castro has left behind a valuable set of declination readings for wherever he had sailed.

The three extant *Roteiros*, or routers, provide "road maps" of the sea from Lisbon to Goa, from Goa to Diu and from Goa to Suez. Castro drew precise maps of the coast, drew buildings and trees and, of course, recorded the magnetic declinations at many points on the route. He also left behind the record of his discovery of an island between Chaul and Bombay where basaltic rocks can possess a permanent magnetization which can even make compass needles point south rather than north.

João de Castro also left behind records of his various military and political exchanges with his contemporaries such as Adil Khan, the Sultan of Bijapur, but these are not as important or informative as his sketches of Indian coastlines, descriptions of trees and other vegetation and of the carvings at Elephanta Caves and the Buddhist stupas at Salcette. As a good Catholic, he was somewhat taken aback by these carvings and their subject matter, but as a good scientist, he described them objectively, including their precise measurements.

He died in Goa on 6 June 1548 in the arms of St. Francis Xavier shortly after having been appointed fourth Viceroy of India without the benefit of returning to Portugal and putting down his mature reflections on India. Much remains to be done to incorporate Castro's contributions into the history of western India of the sixteenth century.

— **Subir K. Banerjee**

Suggested Further Readings

Castro, João de, 1500-1548.
Obras completas de D. João de Castro. — Coimbra : Academia Internacional de Cultura Portuguesã, 1968-76.
3 v. : ill., maps ; 31 cm.

Freire de Andrade, Jacinto, 1597-1657.
The life of Dom John de Castro, the fourth Viceroy of India / translated into English by Sir Peter Wyche. — London : Herringman, 1693.
272 p. ; 30 cm.
There are several Portuguese and English editions of this work.

Sanceau, Elaine.
Knight of the Renaissance : D. João de Castro, soldier, sailor, scientist, and Viceroy of India, 1500-1548. — London, New York : Hutchinson, [1949?]
235 p. : plates, ports., map (on lining papers) ; 24 cm.

DOM VASCO DA GAMA
(c. 1460-1524)

Vasco da Gama was the Portuguese navigator who led the expedition which in 1497-98 opened the sea route between Europe and India by way of the Cape of Good Hope.

The second son of the nobleman and soldier, Estevão da Gama, Vasco was born around 1460-68 at Sines, in southwest Portugal. The king, João II, who entrusted him with important missions, was planning to send a fleet to open the sea route to Asia and so to outflank the Muslims and break their monopoly of trade with India. Estevão da Gama had been chosen to lead this expedition, but after his death the task was entrusted to Vasco, under the new king, Manuel I.

The Portuguese fleet of four vessels — the *naus** São Gabriel (commanded by Vasco da Gama) and São Rafael (under his brother Paulo), the caravel Berrio (under Nicolau Coelho) and a 200-tonne store-shop — left Lisbon 8 July 1497. The fleet was accompanied till the Cape Verde Islands by another ship commanded by Bartolomeu Dias, who had earlier doubled the Cape of Good Hope.

Leaving Cape Verde behind 3 August, da Gama daringly put out to sea, taking a circular course through the South Atlantic, out of sight of land for more than three months, until his ships reached St. Helena Bay (in modern South Africa) 8 November. Ten days later the fleet doubled the Cape and gradually worked its way up the east African coast, reaching Mozambique 2 March 1498, by which time scurvy was taking its toll of the crews.

---

* Sailing ships of 120 tonnes.

After an initial welcome, based on the supposition that the newcomers were also Muslims, the Sultan of Mozambique broke with the Portuguese, who moved off to Mombasa (now in Kenya) and thence to Malindi (also in Kenya), which they reached 14 April. Helped here by a benevolent Sultan, they secured the services of an Arab pilot (long supposed to have been the famous Ahmad ibn-Madjid), who took them to Calicut, which was sighted 18 May.

The Zamorin, Hindu ruler of Calicut, was happy to receive da Gama and the letter he brought from Manuel I, but the Portuguese failed to make an impression on him with their paltry presents and cheap trade goods, and they also had to face the hostility of the powerful Muslim merchants.

After suffering detention and threats, da Gama and his men left without concluding a treaty, but with cargo. They repaired their ships at Anjediva Island (off Goa) and started their return journey 5 October 1498.

After a difficult voyage, in the course of which the São Rafael had to be burned, the Berrio reached Lisbon 10 July. The São Gabriel followed, da Gama having had to stop at Angra (Azores) on account of his dying brother Paulo. Early in September he made a triumphal entry into Lisbon.

The overjoyed Manuel I heaped honours and gifts on the successful navigator, who was granted the title of "Dom" (Sir), given a substantial annual pension, and soon named Admiral of the Indian Ocean.

About this time Vasco da Gama married Catarina de Ataide, who bore him seven sons.

In 1502 da Gama was sent out again to India with a powerful fleet to avenge the deaths and destruction inflicted on the Portuguese at the trading post in Calicut. Off Cannanore, da Gama captured an Arab ship, and, after seizing its cargo, set it afire, killing all on board, including women and children.

He then made an alliance with the ruler of Cannanore, which he bombarded, and where he massacred some defenceless fishermen. In this expedition da Gama displayed a cruelty which is quite indefensible and scarcely explicable. After securing the friendship of the ruler of Cochin, da Gama returned to Lisbon in 1504. He seems to have retired to Evora, continuing to advise Manuel I on Indian matters, and was made by him Count of Vidigueira in 1519.

In 1524 João II appointed Vasco da Gama Viceroy of [Portuguese] India. He was given ample powers to tackle the administrative abuses and corruption which had already made their appearance in Goa. Arriving in Goa in September, da Gama set to work with a will, probably overtaxed his health, and died in Cochin 24 December 1524.

The Portuguese chronicler João de Barros, a contemporary of da Gama, describes him as "of middle stature, a little fleshy, noble in bearing, daring in attempting any deed, harsh in commanding and much to be feared when in a passion, able to bear much labour and a great executor in punishing any fault for the sake of justice."

Vasco da Gama's fame rests upon his discovery of the sea route from western Europe to India, which was the realization of a 200-year-old dream and 75 years of sustained Portuguese effort, and which ushered a new age in world history.

According to K.M. Panikkar, "Without doubt his arrival marks a turning-point in the history of India and Europe." He helped to launch the Portuguese seaborne empire and to make Portugal a world power.

— John Correia-Afonso, S.J.

Suggested Further Readings

Gama, Vasco da, c.1460-1524.

A journal of the first voyage of Vasco da Gama, 1497-1499 / tr. and ed. with notes, an introduction and appendices by E.G. Ravenstein... — London : Printed for the Hakluyt Society, 1898.
xxxvi, 250 p. incl. ill., plates, ports., facsims., front., maps (part fold.) ; 23 cm. — (Half-title : Works issued by the Hakluyt Society ; no. XCIX)

Hart, Henry Hersch.

Sea road to the Indies : an account of the voyages and exploits of the Portuguese navigators, together with the life and times of Dom Vasco da Gama, Capitão-Mór, Viceroy of India and Count of Vidigueira. — London : Hodge, [1952]
296 p. ; 22 cm.

KRISHNADEVARAYA OF VIJAYANAGAR
(1487-1529)

Krishnadevaraya of Vijayanagar occupies a high place among the great monarchs of Indian history. At his accession the kingdom was weak, owing to the misrule of his predecessor and frequent internal and external warfare. He was confronted by hostile rulers like Adil Khan of Bijapur and some feudatory chiefs like the Palagars of Ummatur who rebelled against him.

He had to wage a series of wars (1513-1518) against Prataparudra Gajapati, king of Orissa, in order to recover the lands lost to the kingdom during the previous reign, and he had to fight the Qutb Shah of Golkunda also.

In the process he added much area to the kingdom he inherited. At the end of his campaigns, it embraced the whole region to the south of a line drawn from Ankola on the west coast to Raichur, a few kilometres south of the Krishna River and continued along the river to its mouth on the east coast. He administered and defended the vast kingdom with distinct ability.

Krishnadevaraya was born on Friday, 16 February 1487. He was crowned on the birthday of Lord Krishna, 8 August 1509. Domingo Paes, a Portuguese who had seen him, describes his personality in these words:

This king is of medium height, and of fair complexion and good figure, rather fat than thin; he has on his face signs of small pox. He is the most feared and perfect king that could possibly be, cheerful of disposition and very merry.... He is a great ruler and a man of much justice.

He had several wives of whom Chinnadevi and Tirumaladevi were his favourites. Their copper images along with his own adorn the precincts of the temple of Sri Venkateshwara at Tirupati. Jagamohini, daughter of the defeated king of Orissa, was a third wife. He had two sons and two daughters. The elder son, Tirumala was anointed crown prince at the age of six, but was killed by poisoning the next year. The younger son was a child of 18 months at the death of the king. The daughters were Terumalamba and Vengulamba. The former was married to Ramaraya who later on became king of Vijayanagar (1543-1565). Vengulamba was married to Ramaraya's brother, Tirumalaraya.

Though a Hindu and devotee of Tirupati Venkateshwara, Krishnadevaraya was tolerant towards other religions. He allowed Luis de Salvador, a Franciscan friar from Portugal, to move about freely in the kingdom, with permission to convert peacefully and to build churches and chapels. And he was tolerant towards Islam in spite of his political hostility towards Adil Shahis and other Sultans of the Deccan.

He was not only a patron of literature, but a man of letters himself. Remarkable works were produced in Sanskrit, Telugu, Kannada and Tamil. In fact, his reign is regarded as the Augustan Age of Telugu literature. *Amuktamalayada*, the Telugu work, is ascribed to his authorship. It mentions five works in Sanskrit as composed by him: *Madalasa Charita*, *Rasamanjari*, *Satyavadhupreranam*, *Suktinaipunijnana*, and *Sakalakathasara Sangraham*. None of these survives. *Jambavati Kalyanam* is the seventh work ascribed to him. A copy of this Sanskrit drama is in the Oriental Manuscripts Library, Madras.

Among the Sanskrit literary figures in his court were Lolla Lakshmidhara and Diwakara, poets; Timmarasu and his nephew Nadindla Gopa, scholars and commentators; Yusa Decha, Bandam Lakshminarayana, musicologist ; Ishwara Dikshita, the commentator of Valmiki's *Ramayana*, and Tukka Devi, poetess and one of the wives of Krishnadevaraya.

Numerous Telugu classics were produced by Allasani Peddanna, the greatest of the Telugu poets during Krishnadevaraya's reign; Purandaradasa, Kanakadasa, Timmanna and Kumara Valmiki (Narahari) were among the great Kannada writers of the times. Jnanaprakasar, Hariharadasa and Kumara Sarasvati were some of the Tamil writers.

Krishnadevaraya patronised art and architecture, including sculpture, painting, music, dancing and theatre. He built a number of towns, temples, dams, tanks and canals. Nagalapura, located in the suburb of the capital and known today as Hospet, was a new town named after his mother. Tirumaladeviyara Pattana was another town built and named after one of his wives. He constructed a tower and an assembly hall at the Virupaksha Temple on the occasion of his coronation. The Krishnasvami Temple was built in 1513 to mark his conquest of Udayagiri. The temples of Hazara Ramasvami and Viththalasvami are also attributed to his reign and patronage.

Many of the hundred-pillared and thousand-pillared *mandapas* belong to his reign. In 1521 the dam and canal at Koragal and the Basavana Canal were constructed. Another great work by Krishnadevaraya was a huge tank, or dammed-up lake, at the capital. A Portuguese engineer helped in its construction. The work in progress was seen in 1520 by two Portuguese men, Domingo Paes and Fernão Nunes, who were at the capital. The enormous statue of Narasimha at the capital was made in 1528 under Krishnadevaraya's patronage.

The economic prosperity of his reign was mainly responsible for the progress in literature, art and architecture. The population of the kingdom in 1520 was calculated to have been around 18,000,000.

Krishnadevaraya promoted agriculture by providing irrigation facilities in the form of numerous tanks and canals and by giving lands on a favourable rate of assessment to poor farmers for cultivation. Trade and commerce, crafts and industries, mining and metallurgy were also advanced, leading to a higher standard of living for the people of the kingdom of Vijayanagar.

Krishnadevaraya, the great king of Vijayanagar, died in November 1529 at the age of 42.

— B.S. Shastry

Suggested Further Reading

Oruganti, Ramachandraiya.
    Studies on Krsnadevaraya of Vijayanagara. — Waltair : Andhra University, 1953.
    2 v. : 23 cm.

FRANÇOIS MARTIN
(1634-1706)

The French merchant who played a seminal role in the establishment of French trading activities in India during the late seventeenth century was François Martin. Born in 1634, he was the illegitimate son of a rich Persian grocer. Upon his father's death in 1650 he was expelled from the family house.

Later he married Marie Cuperly, the daughter of a fish wife.

In 1664, Martin arranged a position as *sous-marchand* (under-merchant) in Colbert's newly formed *Compagnie Royale des Indes Orientales* and sailed with the fleet to Madagascar. By October 1668 he had risen to the rank of "merchant" and was in Surat, then the Company's main factory. After a trading voyage to Combroon (Bandar Abbas) in Persia, Martin returned to Surat in 1669 to find internal quarrels in the Company hierarchy centering around the enigmatic director-general, François Caron.

In October 1671, Colbert's great *Escadron Perse* (Persian Squadron), commanded by La Haye, reached Surat. La Haye's instructions called for the establishment of strategic fortresses in Ceylon and Indonesia to ensure French power in the region at the expense of the Dutch. Martin, a potential rival to Caron, had earlier been "exiled" to the Company factory at Masulipatam in Golconda where he did much to augment French trade there.

La Haye and Caron, after a disastrous voyage down the Malabar coast and Ceylon reached the Coromandel Coast in June 1672. The French fleet captured San Thomé in July, thus beginning a war with Abdul Hasan of Golkunda (and the Dutch) that lasted until September 1674.

Martin joined La Haye's force in January 1673, performing valued diplomatic missions, despite La Haye's overbearing personality, during this crucial period for French pretensions in the Asian trade.

Following La Haye's surrender, Martin travelled to Pondichéry and strove to continue the Company's activities in the face of the daunting defeat of Colbert's grand strategy.

Martin remained in Pondichéry, which had been granted to one of La Haye's officers by Sher Khan Lodi in late 1672, from 1674-1681.* His enlightened trading practises in Pondichéry, and those of François Caron in Surat, did much to establish a solid basis for the French Company.

In 1681, Martin was called to Surat to take over the Company's operations there. For the next five years he sought to reduce the factory's debt, to develop a "country" trade with Persia, Bantam, Siam and the Coromandel, and to increase the number of sailings to Europe. These efforts were only partly successful due in part to the legislation of 1686 that undermined the trade in calicoes with the home market.

Martin returned to Pondichéry in May 1686. During his absence direct trading relations had begun with France, and efforts had been made to develop the country trade with Bengal and Golkunda.

For the next 20 years Martin did his utmost to continue these practises in the face of the dislocation caused by Louis XIV's wars. Martin's son-in-law, André Boureau-Deslandes, was responsible for entrenching French activities in Bengal and the foundation of Chandernagore between 1677 and 1701.

During the War of the League of Augsburg (1689-97) Martin, recognising the fragile nature of European power in Asia and the definitive role of sea power, urged the Crown, without success, to despatch another large squadron to Asia to destroy Dutch pretensions. Instead, Pondichéry was besieged by a Dutch fleet in the summer of 1693 and Martin, after directing a gallant defense, was forced to surrender in September.

He and his family were permitted to join Deslandes in Bengal, and they remained there until the Dutch evacuated Pondichéry in October 1699.

In the years before the War of Spanish Succession broke out in India (1703), Martin did much to recreate Pondichéry's prosperity: plans were made for a stronger fortress and to erect a wall around the town, the trade

---

* Martin is credited by many historians as being the founder of Pondichéry.

association of local merchants was established, and trade began anew with Achin, China and the Philippines.

Once the war began, the French held their own on the Coromandel and in early 1705, Martin was able to obtain a suspension of hostilities on that coast with the Dutch East India Company.

On 25 August 1706, Martin dedicated the new fort at Pondichéry, his last public act. He died 31 December 1706 after four decades of loyal service to the French cause in Asia, having done much to ensure the survival of the French Company during the tumultuous years in Europe and the East.

— Glenn Ames

Suggested Further Readings

Kaeppelin, Paul.
  La Compagnie des Indes Orientales et François Martin. — Paris : Challamel, 1908.
  673 p. : maps, plan ; 23 cm.

Martin, François, 1634-1706.
  Mémoires de François Martin, fondateur de Pondichéry. — Paris : Societe d'editions geographiques maritimes et coloniales, 1931-34.
  3 v. : ill., map ; 23 cm. — (Bibliothéque d'histoire coloniale)
  (This work was recently translated by Lotika Varadarajan as *India in the Seventeenth Century : Social, Economic, and Political*.)

An additional bibliographic source for Martin and other Frenchmen involved in Indian history is Henry Scholberg's *Bibliographie des Français dans l'Inde*.

JACOB BLANQUET DE LA HAYE
(1615?-1676)

Jacob Blanquet de La Haye, the scion of an old aristocratic family, was the French viceroy of "the Indies" from 1671 to 1674.

After receiving a traditional education in the arts of war and statecraft, La Haye began a distinguished military service to the Crown that included serving as a second colonel in the *Regiment de la Fère*, commanding the French fortress at Aimeries, and as a full colonel in that regiment.

By all accounts La Haye possessed the overbearing and arrogant personality common to his class. Above all, however, he was a fearless and skilled soldier determined to serve Louis XIV in his quest for *gloire*. The French king's love of war afforded him every opportunity to do so.

La Haye distinguished himself during the first of Louis XIV's wars, the War of Devolution (1667-68).

A year later Colbert was in the midst of forming his famed *Escadron Perse* (Persian Squadron), consisting of five men-of-war, a frigate, three store ships, 238 guns, 2,100 men that would, it was hoped, finally entrench the struggling *Compagnie des Indes Orientales*, while challenging Dutch pretensions in the Asian trade.

In late 1669, La Haye was chosen to command this expedition, perhaps the most important French fleet sent to Asian waters during the *Ancient Régime*. Louis XIV's powers to La Haye of January 1670 gave him the rank of "Lieutenant-general of the king on the islands of Dauphine and Bourbon, and other islands and lands that are obedient to us in the East Indies" and the power to appoint governors in the lands he occupied in Africa and Asia.

Colbert's instructions made it clear that the main objective of the fleet was to establish fortified settlements in Ceylon and Indonesia (according to the advice of the Director-General François Caron) that would ensure French power in the region.

The *Escadron Perse* departed from Rochefort in March 1670. After a slow and costly voyage that included long stopovers at the Bay of Saldanha and Madagascar (where La Haye became involved in a needless war with Malagasy tribes that refused to pay him homage), the grand French fleet reached Surat in October 1671.

The enigmatic Caron, however, was off in Bantam, attempting to establish a French factory on that island, and did not return until November. Thereafter, in discussions between the Caron and La Haye (who had taken the title of Viceroy upon his arrival in India) it was decided that the expedition would make for Goa and then Ceylon.

In Goa abortive talks were held with the Portuguese Viceroy, Luís de Mendonça Furtado, about the possibility of arranging a joint campaign against the Dutch. After re-taking the Malabar coast town of Alicot from a small Dutch garrison in February 1672, the French fleet encountered a Dutch fleet under Rikjloff Van Goens off Cape Comorin. Despite enjoying every advantage, Caron (who had previously toiled for over 20 years in the Dutch East India Company) prevented La Haye from engaging the Dutch fleet, thus beginning a debate over his true loyalties that has continued to the present day.

After missing this crucial opportunity, La Haye and his force succeeded in occupying and fortifying the strategic bay of Trincomalee in Ceylon, but an eventual blockade by Van Goens and Caron's continued refusal to sanction La Haye's rebellious plans forced the French to abandon Ceylon and make for supplies on the Coromandel coast in July 1672.

On the Coromandel, La Haye finally received delayed dispatches from the Crown which informed him of the outbreak of hostilities against the Dutch in Europe, thus freeing him from the constraints of Caron's policy.

In July 1672, frustrated by the refusal of a Qutb Shahi garrison in San Thomé to reinforce his fleet, La Haye attacked and captured the town. This act began a two-year war with Golkunda which included two bloody sieges of San Thomé by Abdul Hasan's armies (the last in conjunction with Van Goens' fleet) and an abortive attack by La Haye on Golkunda's most important port, Masulipatam.

During this war La Haye displayed the true extent of his military prowess: organising the defence of the town, leading sorties, overrunning the

Qutb Shahi camp (March 1672) to lift the first siege, sending out envoys like Bellanger de Lespinay to arrange support from indigenous rulers along the coast (resulting in the granting of Pondichéry to the French by Sher Khan Lodi in December 1672) and withstanding a force five times that of his own in a harsh, foreign climate.

In the end, however, not even La Haye's skill could overcome the combined Qutb Shahi-Dutch siege, lack of support from his nominal English allies in nearby Madras, and, above all, a crippling dearth of reinforcements from home.

In September 1674 La Haye was forced to surrender San Thomé.

Abdul Hasan, recognising the bravery he had shown in the campaign, offered him a lucrative position in his own army. La Haye, however, refused this offer, having arranged, in the articles of capitulation, passage back to France aboard Dutch ships for the surviving members of his garrison. Thus ended Colbert's grand thrust into the Asian trade.

La Haye reached Port Louis in May 1675. After detailing his experiences to Colbert in Paris, he went to Flanders where Louis XIV was campaigning against the Dutch. La Haye was honorably received by Louis and given command of a cavalry regiment.

He was killed, perhaps fittingly, in an attack against a Dutch convoy in 1676.

— **Glenn Ames**

Suggested Further Readings

Carré de Chambon, Barthelémy.
    The travels of the Abbé Carré in India and the Near East 1672-1674. — London :
    Cambridge University Press, 1947-48.
    3 v. ; 23 cm. — (Half-title: Works issued by the Hakluyt Society ; Series 2 ; Nos. 95-97)

La Haye, Jacob Blanquet de, 1615?-1676.
    Journal du voyage des grandes Indes. — Orléans : 1697.
    2 v. ; 23 cm.

RANA PRATAP SINGH OF MEWAR

The sixteenth century in India is replete with men who failed several times, but finally succeeded. One thinks of Babar, Humayun, Sher Shah Suri as rulers who triumphed and came to rule after set-backs that would have disheartened lesser men.

Rana Pratap Singh of the Sisodia clan never conquered his foe, but he himself was never conquered; so today he stands tall as a hero, a tribute to tenacity and to the fighting spirit of the Rajputs. Tod, the historian of Rajputana, said of him:

Had Mewar possessed her Thucidides or her Xenophon, neither the wars of the Peloponnesus nor the retreat of the Ten Thousand would have yielded more diversified incidents for the historic muse than the deeds of this brilliant reign among the many vicissitudes of Mewar. Undaunted heroism, inflexible fortitude, that sincerity which keeps honour bright, perseverance — with fidelity such as no nation can boast of, were the materials opposed to a soaring ambition, commanding talents, unlimited means, and the fervour of religious zeal; all, however, insufficient to contend with one unconquerable mind.

Pratap Singh was the son of Rana Udai Singh of Mewar. The date of his birth is not known with any certainty, but he succeeded to the throne on the death of his father.

In 1567, Akbar, intent on bringing Rajputana into the Mughul Empire, had sent his armies against Mewar. Udai Singh retreated to the hills for safety and left the defence of his capital at Chitor in the care of Jaimall and Patta and 8,000 Rajput soldiers. The siege, perhaps the most famous in Indian history, lasted from 20 October 1567 until 23 February 1568. Jaimall was killed by a bullet fired by Akbar, and Patta died later. When they saw their leaders were dead, the remaining soldiers charged the enemy and were annihilated. Young women in the fort committed *jauhar* (self-immolation) rather than succumb to the enemy. Akbar entered the fort and ordered the massacre of all survivors.

After Akbar departed, Udai Singh came down from the hills and continued the work in which he had been engaged before the battle, that of building his palaces.

The fall of Chitor was followed by the submission in succession of other Rajput kingdoms to the rule of Akbar: Ranthambhor, then Kalinjar, followed by Bikaner and Jaisalmer — an early display of the Domino Theory.

However, Rana Pratap Singh, who came to the throne on the death of his father in 1572, did not surrender. Nor did he do what other Rajput chiefs had done, concur in a marriage alliance with the Mughuls.

Pratap Singh's first act was to strengthen his small kingdom by reorganising the government and putting his fort garrisons under capable officers. Then he told his people to flee to the mountains whenever they were attacked by Mughul forces.

Akbar sent his general, Man Singh, to Mewar to reason with Pratap Singh, but Pratap Singh, who received him politely, would not accede to his overtures. On his departure, Man Singh was insulted by Pratap Singh who told him to bring his *phupha* (father's sister's husband, Akbar) with him the next time he came to Mewar.

On his return to the court, Man Singh persuaded Akbar that he should humiliate the upstart Pratap Singh. Akbar then gave Man Singh the exalted title of *Farzand* (son) and put him in command of the campaign against Pratap Singh.

Leading an army of 5,000 horses and commanded by both Rajput and Mughul officers, Man Singh marched on Mewar in April 1576. They met Pratap Singh in a fierce battle at Haldighat (after which both sides claimed victory), and Pratap Singh was forced to escape into the hills. He carried on guerrilla warfare against the Mughuls for the rest of his life.

On one occasion he found he had captured the harem of one of his enemies; however, to prove that chivalry was not dead in India, he treated the ladies like his own daughters and returned them to his enemy, who happened to be the crown prince.

Pratap Singh endured great hardship during these years of battle. A tribute was paid to them by the poet, Mirza Khan:

> All is perishable in this world; powers and riches will disappear, but the virtue of a great name will live forever.

Rana Pratap Singh died in 1597. He was succeeded by his son Amar who tried to carry on the fight his father had so gallantly fought. He was defeated in 1599 by a Mughul army commanded by Man Singh. Finally, during the reign of Jahangir, he succumbed, and Mewar came under the suzerainty of the Mughul Empire.

Suggested Further Readings

Sharma, Sri Ram.
  Maharana Pratap. — Hoshiarpur : V.V.R. Institute, 1954.
  xi, 156 p. : ill., map ; 19 cm.

Tod, James, 1782-1835.
  Annals and antiquities of Rājasthān; or, The central and western Rajput states of India. — London : Smith, Elder, 1829-32.
  2 v. : map ; 32 cm.

SIR THOMAS ROE
(1580 or 1581-1644)

Sir Thomas Roe, the son of Robert Rowe, was born at Low Leyton, near Wanstead in Essex in 1580 or 1581. His grandfather, Sir Thomas Rowe (or Roe), was a merchant tailor, alderman, sheriff (in 1560) and lord mayor of London in 1568. Robert Rowe died when his son was quite young; so the boy was brought up by his mother, Elinor, the daughter of Robert Jermy of Worstead, Norfolk. She then married someone named Berkeley of Redcomb, Gloucestershire.

Young Thomas matriculated as a commoner of Magdalen College, Oxford, 6 July 1593 at the age of 12. Through family influence, either from his father's side or his mother's, he obtained appointment as esquire to the body of Queen Elizabeth I, and in 1605 he was knighted by King James I.

He was popular in the royal court, particularly with the prince of Wales, who sent him on a journey in 1609 "upon a discovery to the West Indies." He reached the Amazon River and sailed 300 kilometres up it. After coming down the river, he spent several months exploring the coast, but failed to find what he was looking for: the gold that was supposed to be there. He returned to the Isle of Wight in July 1611, and made two more voyages to South America before his historic trip to India.

In 1614, he was elected M.P. for Tamworth, after which he was assigned by King James to be ambassador at the court of the Mughul emperor, Jahangir, in 1615. He was sent out at the behest of the East India Company to negotiate a treaty and to secure the right to build factories in India.

The East India Company had been formed 31 December 1600, and its first attempt to establish a factory at Surat in 1608 met with stiff resistance on the part of the Portuguese who at this time were strong on the West Coast of India and in the Indian Ocean. However, with the help of the Dutch, the perennial enemies of the Portuguese during this period, the English were able to begin trading at Surat in 1613.

Sir Thomas arrived in India and presented himself at the court of Jahangir in 1615. He was unable to negotiate the treaty he wanted, but he succeeded it getting *firmans* (permits) to build factories in various parts of India which were under Mughul control. The English thus established factories at Masulipatam, Armagoan and in the Bay of Bengal at Balasore, Hugli, Dacca and Cassimbazar.

Roe remained in India until 1618, and although no one may have realised it at that time, he had laid the groundwork for the future British Empire in India. He disapproved of the military activities of both the Portuguese and the Dutch and recommended that England indulge only in trade and commerce.

On his return it was rumoured that he returned rich, but it seems more likely that the silk goods he brought back were presents for his king.

He never set foot in India again. However, he was not finished with the Orient. He was ambassador to the Ottoman Empire from 1621 to 1628. He obtained increased trading privileges for the English in the Levant, and in 1624 he negotiated a treaty with Algiers by which several hundred English prisoners who had been captured by Barbary pirates were set free. (At that time Tangiers was under Ottoman control.) He also mediated a peace treaty between Poland and the Ottomans.

Roe continued his diplomatic activities in Europe, and retired in 1631. From 1631 to 1642, he participated in conferences in Hamburg, Ratisbon and Vienna aimed at ending the Thirty Years War.

In 1640, he was made privy councilor and was elected a member of the Long Parliament for the University of Oxford. His health failed after his return from the Vienna conference of 1642, and the following year he retired to Bath where he died in November 1644.

Suggested Further Readings

One of the most important contributions of Sir Thomas Roe to the study of India in the early part of the seventeenth century is his journal. It was published in two volumes by the Hakluyt Society in 1899 with the title *Embassy of Sir T. Roe to the Court of the Great Mogul.*
See also:
Roe, Thomas, Sir, 1580 or 1581-1644.
Travels in India in the seventeenth century. — London : Trübner, 1873.
474 p. ; 23 cm.

SHIVAJI
(1627-1680)

In Maharashtra, the name Shivaji calls to mind the exploits of the greatest Maratha hero. Surrounded by several Muslim powers (preeminently
the Adil Shahi of Bijapur to the south and the Mughuls to the north), Shivaji
used a combination of warfare and diplomacy to win a measure of Hindu
independence that was to survive until the British era.

Shivaji's father, Shahji Bhosle, was a soldier of fortune who gained
prominence in the service of rival sultans in Ahmadnagar and Bijapur.
Shivaji's mother, Jijabai, was in effect abandoned by Shahji when he took a
younger wife in Bijapur. Shivaji was born at the hill fort of Shivneri, near
Pune, and moved to Pune in his youth. His father provided for him and
Jijabai by granting him the Pune district, whose tax revenues he controlled
as a servant of Bijapur.

As a minor, Shivaji was placed under the care of a Brahman counsellor,
Dadaji Khonddev. Jijabai, daughter of the noble and legendary Jadav clan,
may have filled her son's head with ideas of heroism from Hindu epics,
perhaps even notions of Hindu independence from Muslim rule.

While still a young man Shivaji embarked on his military career (contrary to the wishes of his counsellor). In 1646, he took several hill forts near
Pune; but after his father was imprisoned in Bijapur, he remained quiet for
several years. In 1655, however, he resumed his conquests, moving to Javli,
near modern Mahabaleshwar in the mountains of Satara district. He was
ruthless in his military pursuits, not above having rival Hindu chieftans
assassinated when they blocked his advances.

In these years Shivaji maintained peace with the Mughuls who no doubt
saw him as a useful ally against rival Muslim powers. The sultan of Bijapur
was threatened by this rebel Hindu prince and sent a large force to Javli to
suppress his activities.

There Shivaji agreed to a diplomatic meeting with the Bijapuri general,
Afzal Khan. According to Hindu legend, Shivaji was warned by his patron
goddess Bhavani to expect trouble. He wore concealed weapons to the meeting; and when Afzal attempted to stab him, be responded quickly and killed
him. His hidden troops were signalled, and they routed the Adil Shahi army.
This victory quickly became the stuff for legends, and Shivaji's greatness
was sung in ballads throughout the land.

From 1660 to 1664 Shivaji continued in a cat-and-mouse warfare after
the Mughuls had turned against him. Aurangzeb first sent Shaistah Khan
to Pune to claim it as Viceroy. He was attacked in the night in a secret assault
and he fled. After several years of fighting, Aurangzeb sent the able Rajput
general Jai Singh against Shivaji in 1664. In a long campaign Jai Singh forced
Shivaji to give up some 23 forts and retain 12 as a *mansabdar* (vassal) of the
Emperor. He encouraged Shivaji to go to Aurangzeb's court in Agra and
guaranteed him safety.

There Shivaji felt insulted at court and stormed out. He was then placed under house arrest, but skipped away in a characteristically clever and daring escape, assuming the disguise of a holy man and taking a circuitous route home.

While Jai Singh was continuing his military efforts against Bijapur, Shivaji was able to recoup many of his losses, and the Mughul emperor was reluctant to oppose him. By 1670, however, Shivaji was again at war with the Mughuls. After several years of successful campaigning he announced his coronation by both Vedic and Tantric rites in 1674. There was much debate over Shivaji's claim to Kshatriya status, but ultimately he was invested with the sacred thread and crowned *Chatrapati* ("Lord of the Umbrella") in Raigarh. His beloved mother died soon after that.

In the final years of his life Shivaji turned his attention to the south. He asked for his half-brother Vyankoji's support in extending his Hindu dominion, but Vyankoji remained in allegiance to the Bijapuri sultan. Nonetheless, Shivaji captured much new territory in Karnataka and the far south and returned from these campaigns with an enriched treasury.

In 1678, Shivaji's alliance with the Golkundas in Hyderabad broke down, and his son Sambhaji defected to the Mughuls for a brief time.

Shivaji died in 1680 after a period of illness, his life of adventure and conquest and heroism thus coming to a troubled and anticlimatic end. Although he was (and is) often compared with the heroes of the Hindu epic tradition, Shivaji died with the tragic disappointment that he had never united with his half-brother, nor could he confidently trust in his son's succession. Sambhaji was tortured and executed in 1684 by Aurangzeb.

Nonetheless, the spark of Maratha independence smoldered and flared up again in the eighteenth century when Hindu Peshwas ruled Maharashtra from Pune and gave only nominal allegiance to Delhi. Morover, when the later day *swaraj* movement leader Lokamanya Tilak sought to cast off British rule in the 1890s, he revived Maharashtrian memories of Shivaji which persist to this day.

— James W. Laine

Suggested Further Readings

Sardesai, S.G.
> Shivaji : contours of a historical evaluation. — New Delhi : Perspective Publications, 1974.
> 36 p. ; 18 cm. (Presentation of the thesis that the struggle for power of Raja Shivaji was not for religious, but for economic and political reasons. cf. Library of Congress)

Sarkar, Jadunath, Sir, 1870-1958.
> Shivaji and his times. — 3rd ed. — Calcutta : M.C. Sarkar, 1929.
> 431 p. : ports. ; 22 cm.

Sen, Surendra Nath, ed. & tr.
> Foreign biographies of Shivaji. — London : Kegan Paul, Trench, Trübner & Co., Ltd., [1930]
> lvii, 492 p. : ports. ; 23 cm. — (Extracts and documents relating to Maratha history ; v. II).

CHAPTER 5

THE EIGHTEENTH CENTURY

Haidar Ali	Dupleix
Tipu Sultan	La Bourdonnais
Clive	Bussy-Castelnau
	Lally-Tolendal

$\mathcal{T}$he eighteenth century in India was one of the most fascinating, complex and important centuries in the history of the subcontinent. A vacuum had been created with the death of Aurangzeb and the decline of the Mughul Empire in 1707, and the scramble to fill that vacuum came from several quarters. Some quarters were content to get a piece of the pie, but one wanted it all.

By mid-1800, the Mughul Empire had shrunk to an area about the size of Kansas City. The once great Vijayanagar Empire was no more. But the Marathas, based in Poona, had conquered a large chunk of western and central India. Hyderabad was an on-again, off-again ally of the British, was located where Andhra Pradesh is today. And then there was Mysore, constantly struggling for the right to dominate south India.

The Portuguese were content to carry on, as they had in the previous centuries, with small enclaves on the West Coast, but the French under Dupleix had dreams of a French Empire in India.

It was the British, however, who won the day, and the year, at Plassey when in 1757 they established themselves in the Ganges Delta with the conquest of Bengal. This, plus their mastery of the Coromandel Coast at Madras, gave them a leg up on other powers seeking to control the destiny of India.

In 1799, Mysore was eliminated after the fourth of its wars with the British. The French were in decline after 1754 when their great leader was sent home in disgrace and finished after they lost the Battle of Wandiwash in 1760. In 1818, the last of the Maratha Peshwas was beaten and exiled.

Some strong men, some courageous men and some unlucky men played their roles in full view of history's stage. In this chapter are the stories of some of them: Haidar Ali and Tipu Sultan, who faced a whirlwind of circumstances they could not control; Dupleix, who almost won it all for France, and a supporting cast of La Bourdonnais, Bussy-Castelnau and Lally-Tolendal.

But Robert Clive, to continue the metaphor, was the main character in the drama. He maintained that only one European power should rule India, and that European power, he said, should be England. His skill, his luck, his leadership and his courage brought India into the British Empire in the eighteenth century, and there it stayed until another important century: the twentieth.

HAIDAR ALI
(1722?-1782)

Haidar Ali Khan was the son of Fatah Ali Muhammad, military commander and Jagirdar of Budikota, who had distinguished himself in the service of Aurangzeb. Haidar was born in 1722 (some authorities say 1717), the second son of his father's second wife.

The father was killed while fighting Saadat Ullah Khan, the Nawab of Arcot, after which his family was tortured and plundered by the son of the the Nawab. They became refugees and found a home in Bangalore where the elder brother, Shahbaz Khan, became an officer in the Mysore army. Haidar, having learned about military tactics from the French under Dupleix, persuaded his brother to purchase artillery from the English at Bombay and hire Europeans as gunners. He thus became "the first Indian who formed a corps of sepoys armed with firelocks and bayonets, and who had a train of artillery served by Europeans."

He joined his brother at the siege of Devanhalli in 1749 and, as a result of his performance, was given an independent command in Mysore.

By 1763 he made himself master of Mysore. In 1755, he was appointed *Faujdar* (military governor) of Dindigul, and it was here that he established a base from which he could conduct future campaigns. With the aid of French soldier mechanics from Pondichéry, he built up a formidable arsenal.

India in the mid-eighteenth century was at the mercy of several forces: the English with their base in Bengal, the French at Pondichéry, the Nizam of Hyderabad in the Deccan and the Marathas at Poona. The Vijayanagar Empire was in a state of advanced decay, and in the north the Mughul "emperor" was feasting on past glory.

The English and Marathas were watching with some anxiety the growing strength of Haidar Ali in Mysore. In March 1757, the Marathas under Peshwa Balaji Baji Rao invaded Mysore, demanding heavy reparations. Haidar counselled the Raja to renege on the payments, which brought the Marathas back in 1759 for a second invasion. This time Haidar Ali's forces were strong enough to drive the Marathas away, in recognition of which he received the title Fatah Haidar Bahadur. (He had previously gone simply by Haidar Nayak.)

Haidar came very near to losing it all when he was deceived by his general, Khande Rao. It seems the youthful Raja of Mysore was chafing under the thumb of the mayor of the palace, Nanjraj. The dowager queen called upon Haidar to rescue the boy, and he did so with the help of Khande

Rao. However, Khande Rao took advantage of his position, and defeated Haidar in a surprise attack at Seringapatam.

Haidar battled Khande Rao at Nanjangud, about 50 kilometres south of Seringapatam but was defeated. In desperation he threw himself at the feet of Nanjraj, professing object loyalty. Nanjraj gave him the title *Dalwai* (commander-in-chief) and a good-sized army. With this Haidar ultimately defeated his enemy and demanded that Khande Rao be surrendered to him for punishment.

The story is told that the ladies of the court interceded for Khande Rao; whereupon, Haidar assured them that he would cherish him like a parrot. He kept his word, putting Khande Rao in a cage and feeding him rice and milk for the rest of his life.

In 1763, Haidar conquered the stronghold of Bednur and its treasure, estimated to have been in the region of 12,000,000 sterling. With this treasure Haidar found himself in a stronger position than anything he had known thus far.

He continued his conquests by conquering the Nayars of Malabar, capturing Calicut in 1765 and in the same year, invaded the Carnatic. He fought against the combined forces of the English and the Nizam, but at a critical moment the Nizam deserted the English and went over to Haidar. However, Haidar was soon deserted by his erstwhile ally who went back to the English side. Haidar fought on alone, defeating the Bombay troops on the west coast and capturing Mangalore. At Mangalore there is a small circular fort which is called Haidar's Redoubt.

On 4 April 1769, he was within eight kilometres of Madras and in a position to dictate terms of peace. In the treaty that was signed with the English a mutual restitution of all conquests and exchange of prisoners was agreed upon as well as a defensive alliance by which the English agreed to help Mysore if it should by attacked by another power.

The English did not fulfill their side of the agreement. When the Marathas invaded Mysore in 1771, the English sat on their hands. Then, in 1778 when the French and English were again at war with each other, the English grabbed Mahe' on the Malabar Coast, an action Haidar considered a violation of neutrality.

He formed a confederacy against the English together with the Nizam and the Marathas, the latter of whom were at war with the English, anyway. In July 1780 the Second Mysore War began. Haidar with 80,000 and 100 guns descended on the Carnatic "like an avalanche carrying destruction with him."

Governor-General Warren Hastings sent General Sir Eyre Coote, the commander-in-chief, south to "stand forth and vindicate in his own person the rights and honour of British arms." Haidar had defeated Colonel Baillie in October 1780 at Polilore and taken him prisoner and had captured Arcot. In the words of Sir Alfred Lyall:

The fortunes of the English in India had fallen to their lowest watermark.

The English managed to disengage the Nizam from his alliance with Mysore. Then Coote defeated Haidar's troops in a decisive battle at Porto Novo, and the English captured Negapatam in 1781.

In the following year the French entered the war when Admiral Suffren appeared in Indian waters on the side of Mysore.

Haidar, however, did not live to see how the war ended. That would be left to his son Tipu Sultan. Fatah Haidar Bahadur died of cancer 7 December 1782 at Chitor. He had restored the finances of his country and left his successor a full treasury and a well-trained army.

An illiterate, brave and cruel man, Haidar Ali had made a brilliant fight against unbeatable foes in unwinable wars, but had beaten some of his foes and had won some of his wars.

TIPU SULTAN
(1753-1799)

Fatah Ali Tipu, known in history as Tipu Sultan the Tiger of Mysore, inherited from his famous father, Haidar Ali, an efficient army and a large treasury. He was also left with perennial foes and a legacy of war.

He was born in 1753 at a time when his father was building a power base in Mysore. His birth occurred in Devanhalli, the place where his father first distinguished himself. His mother was Fakhr-un-Nissa, the daughter of Mir Moin-ud-Din, an erstwhile governor of Kadapa. It is said that as the time of her delivery drew near, she visited a holy man, got a blessing from him and decided on Tipu as a name for the child she would bear.

Unlike his father, who was illiterate, Tipu was well read and fluent in Persian and could speak Urdu and Kannada.

He adopted the tiger as his emblem, and is quoted as having said once that he would rather live two days as a tiger than 200 years as a sheep. In fact, a mechanical toy from this period is a tiger which, when wound up, devours an English soldier.

In addition to inheriting a well-trained army, Tipu was educated in the art of warfare by French officers who had been hired by his father. During the wars with the Marathas, he commanded a cavalry corps in 1767 and fought against them in 1775 and 1779. In 1782, in the Second Mysore War, he defeated Colonel John Braithwaite at the Colrun River.

On the death of Haidar Ali 7 December 1782, Tipu took over the army and continued the war. Bednur had been captured by a force led by General Richard Mathews, but Tipu retook the place and sent Mathews and his men to Seringapatam as prisoners. Mathews died there, either from eating poisoned food or by being beaten by the butt ends of his guards' matchlocks.

In 1784, the English, anxious for an end to the war, sued for peace, and negotiations with Tipu were begun at Mangalore. In the Treaty of Mangalore which ended the Second Mysore War, mutual restitution of conquests and the liberation of prisoners were agreed to. Governor-General Warren Hastings was not pleased with the Treaty. He said of Lord Macartney, governor of Madras who had wanted peace with Tipu:

> What a man is this Lord Macartney! I believe that in spite of the peace, he will effect the loss of the Carnatic.

In the years that followed the Treaty of Mangalore, Tipu conducted a series of campaigns against the Marathas and in 1786 declared himself Sultan of Mysore, something his father had never done. (Haidar Ali was content to be commander-in-chief and the real power behind the throne.)

Tipu believed that another war with the British was inevitable; so to secure his base he needed Travancore on the Malabar coast. It happened that Travancore was allied with the English; therefore, when he invaded the state in 1789, he was inviting British intervention.

He attacked the fort at Cranganore in December but was repulsed. The fort had been built by the Portuguese in the sixteenth century, but had been taken over by the Dutch as the Portuguese were being expelled from Malabar. The Dutch, in turn, had sold the fort (called Kottapuram) to the Raja of Travancore.

A second assault led by the French general, Lally, captured and destroyed the fort. (Today Kottapuram lies in overgrown ruins.)

Tipu's invitation to the British to go to war again was accepted, and the Third Mysore War broke out when Governor-General Cornwallis in 1790 sent General William Medows to Mysore to carry on the campaign. Previously Cornwallis had made alliances with the Nizam of Hyderabad and the Marathas for the purpose of conducting a war which he knew would come against Tipu. This was in direct contradiction of Pitt's India Act which forbade the East India Company from conducting warfare against Indian rulers unless for defensive purposes. Mark Wilks, a historian of south India commented:

> It is highly instructive to observe a statesman, justly extolled for moderate and pacific disposition, thus indirectly violating a law, enacted for the enforcement of these virtues, by entering into a very intelligible offensive alliance.

Under Medows the war dragged on until Cornwallis complained that "we have lost time and our adversary has gained reputation, which are the two most valuable things in war."

In December 1790, he himself went south to lead the troops. He captured Bangalore 21 March 1791 and was within about 15 kilometres of Seringapatam when the rains set in, and he had to retreat to Mangalore. When fighting resumed, Tipu captured Coimbatore, but Cornwallis advanced on Seringapatam and forced Tipu to sue for peace.

In the treaty that followed Tipu had to surrender half of his territory. Much of it went to the Marathas and the Nizam, and the English got Malabar, Dindigul, the Baramahal district and sovereignty over the Raja of Coorg.

Tipu now sought aid from many countries, but mainly from the French, and sent an embassy to Paris. Frenchmen in his service hailed him as "Citoyen Tipou," but no help from France was forthcoming. He also sent a mission to Mauritius, and the governor there issued a proclamation urging Frenchmen to join Tipu in driving the English out of India.

In 1798, the new governor-general, Lord Wellesley, learned of this proclamation, and invited Tipu to enter into an alliance, but when Tipu dallied, Wellesley sent troops south to force Tipu either to negotiate or fight.

They advanced on Seringapatam and captured it 4 May 1799. Tipu was killed during the fighting, and the war was over.

Sir Thomas Munro said of him that "a restless spirit of innovation, and a wish to have everything to originate from himself, was the predominant feature of his character."

Suggtested Further Reading

Bowring, Lewin B.
  Haidar Ali' and Tipu' Sultán and the struggle with Musalmán powers of the south. — Oxford : Clarendon, 1899.
  233 p. : fold. map ; 20 cm. — (Rulers of India ; v. 10)

ROBERT LORD CLIVE, BARON OF PLASSEY
(1725-1774)

Robert Clive emerged into history during the mid-eighteenth century Anglo-French war in South India. A "writer" became a soldier by accident. The lucky general and man of business became an administrator and diplomatist. The Baron of Plassey became the grandee of the Mughul Empire. He was not a planner or founder of empire; he was a "forerunner of the British-Indian Empire."

Robert Clive was born 29 September 1725 at Styche, England, as the eldest child of Richard and Rebecca Clive of a small landed family. On 1 June 1744, he arrived in Madras as a clerk ("writer") in the East India Company's service on an annual salary of five pounds. The melancholic youth was rescued from the monotony of a clerical job by the First Carnatic War (1746-48), an offshoot of the War of Austrian Succession. Clive became a prisoner of war when the French fleet under La Bourdonnais occupied Madras in September 1746 but escaped to Fort St. David and soon obtained an ensign's commission (March 1747).

The young civilian's military talents, displayed during the sieges of Fort St. David and Pondichéry and in the Tanjore expedition, impressed the authorities. In 1749, Clive won promotion to steward, lieutenant and commissary for supply of provisions to European troops, and then reverted to civil employment.

The Siege of Arcot

The Second Carnatic War (1749-54) raised his life to a new dimension. He returned to the army with a captaincy in July 1751 and at the siege of Arcot won his great reputation. It was a glorious feat of arms. The Arcot-Trichinopoly episode (1751-52) turned the balance of success against the French and largely contributed to the frustration of Dupleix's design to dominate south India. But without Dupleix "there would have been no Clive." On 18 February 1753, Clive married Margaret Maskelyne at St. Mary's Church, Madras. Next month he left for England with his charming wife and a fortune of 40,000 pounds sterling. Clive was 27, famous and wealthy. The ugly duckling had returned a pretty swan.

Clive returned to India in October 1755 and captured Gheria, Tulaji Angria's stronghold (February 1756). On 22 June he took over the governorship of Fort St. David. The news of the capture of Calcutta 20 June by the Nawab of Bengal and the "Black Hole Tragedy" reached Madras in August. In October a full scale expedition was despatched to Bengal under the command of Lt. Col. Clive. He recovered Calcutta 2 January 1757, and Siraj-ud-Daulah agreed to a generous restoration of the Company's privileges by the Treaty of Alinagar 9 February. The Seven Years War (1756-63) had broken out in Europe, and England and France were on opposite sides. Clive attacked the French settlement at Chandernagore, and it surrendered 23 March after a brave resistance. The French being removed, Siraj and the English confronted each other.

In the spring of 1757, Siraj was faced with a crisis. Clive and the Calcutta Council became involved in a conspiracy against him. Some influential persons at Murshidabad (the capital of Bengal) planned to overthrow Siraj and had selected Mir Jafar, a prominent general, as their alternative Nawab. The English decided to support Mir Jafar and concluded a secret treaty with him 5 June. Clive's role in this intrigue was not creditable. Omichand, who acted as a go-between between the English and Mir Jafar, was tricked by Clive.

The Battle of Plassey

Clive marched against Siraj and defeated him at Plassey 23 June. The Battle of Plassey was hardly a battle at all. It added nothing to Clive's military reputation. The casualties were minimal. Intrigue had done its work. Siraj had been betrayed. He fled, was taken captive and then put to death by Miran, Mir Jafar's son. On 29 June, Clive installed Mir Jafar as the Nawab of Bengal, and the era of puppet Nawabs commenced with the East India Company as king-maker.

Clive had learned his lessons from Dupleix. Clive was a "British de Bussy." Plassey was a breakthrough in his career. In theory Plassey only restored the situation in Bengal that had existed in 1756. The agreement concluded by the new Nawab with the English was a cooperative one. Legally the English did not become political masters of Bengal in 1757, but

Plassey gave them certain immediate advantages — commercial, military and political. It undermined the foundations of the Nawab's government and created a field for the establishment of British political influence in Bengal. Plassey was decisive for the East India Company.

Governor of Bengal

Mir Jafar started with a financial handicap. The value of his gifts and donations to the English in 1757 has been estimated at 1,250,000 pounds; Clive's share amounted to 234,000 pounds. He was the largest beneficiary. On 8 March 1758, he was appointed governor of Bengal. He repulsed external invasions and gave Mir Jafar security, but the weak and irresolute Nawab became more and more dependent on English support. In 1759, Clive helped him in expelling the Mughul prince, Ali Gauhar, from Bihar which he had invaded. The grateful Nawab rewarded Clive with a *jagir*. Its value amounted to 30,000 pounds per annum. Clive had already become a Mughul *mansabdar* of six thousand.

On 25 November 1759, a Dutch force was defeated by the English at Bidera. Thus, both the French and the Dutch were eliminated from Bengal as political and commercial competitors.

During his first government, Clive started the organisation of the Bengal Army and created the first Bengal artillery unit. He also selected the village of Govindapur for the new Fort William. It is the sole material survivor of Clive's work in Bengal today. Clive left for England 21 February 1760. On his return home he was lionised by his countrymen. The University of Oxford conferred a doctorate on him 21 September 1760, and he was raised to an Irish peerage in 1762. He renamed his estate Plassey and was created a Knight of the Bath in 1764.

When Clive returned to Bengal 3 May 1763 as governor for the second time, he found the military situation improved, but his problems were two-fold: political and administrative. He had to deal with the political problems created by the English victory at Buxar in 1764. The Mughul emperor, Shah Alam II, had found shelter with the English, and the territories of Nawab Shuja-ud-Daulah of Oudh were under English occupation. It was Clive's task to settle British relations with the Mughul emperor, the Nawab of Oudh, and the puppet Nawab of Bengal.

First, he took up the Bengal problem and by 9 July 1763, reorganised Mir Jafar's government. On 2 August, Clive met Shuja at Benares and settled the conditions of restoring his dominions. He then hastened to Allahabad and secured a *firman* from the emperor which granted the Company the *diwani* of Bengal, Bihar and Orissa. It legalised the Company's position in Bengal; the Company had entered the Mughul imperial system.

On 16 August Shuja signed the Treaty of Allahabad and got back his territories. He entered into a defensive alliance with the Company, and Oudh became a dependent buffer state. The Company's agreement with the Nawab of Bengal on 30 September completed the Nawab's military and financial dependence on the Company. He sank into a position of mere pensioner of the English, and the English became the *de facto* rulers of Bengal.

"Sucking the Orange Dry"

Clive, however, was not prepared to assume direct responsibility for administration. Shah Alam's *firman* authorised the Company to collect revenues and administer civil justice, but Clive set up a "masked system" — a double government in Bengal in which power was separated from responsibility. It enabled the English to "suck the orange dry." Its impact on Bengal was deplorable.

The administrative problems that required solution were no less important. The Company's servants were intoxicated by the dazzling prospects of wealth in a unique situation. It was stated in a Select Committee letter to the Court 30 September 1765: "Public spirit was lost and extinguished in the unbounded lust of unmerited wealth."

Clive took some steps to remove corruption and to restore discipline in the Company's civil and military services, but he himself had been the leading present-taker among the Company's servants. He also prohibited Company servants from participation in inland trade and tried to set up a Society of Trade for the benefit of "superior servants" of the Company, but it was disallowed by the Court of Directors.

His attempt to reduce the double *batta* (or field allowance of Bengal officials) led to the "White Mutiny" which he suppressed with characteristic vigour. He also used Mir Jafar's legacy of five lakhs to set up a fund for the relief of military widows and invalid officers. On 29 January 1767, Clive quitted Bengal forever.

Clive's military and financial success had aroused jealousy in many quarters. Many influential persons in England turned against the "Nabobs" of whom Clive was a conspicuous example. He was charged with corruption and had to face a parliamentary enquiry. He was acquitted in May 1773 but did not long survive the ordeal. On 22 November 1774, Clive died by his own hand.

The "heaven-born general" never succeeded in becoming a "major Anglo-Indian statesman." He lacked the integrity, the sense of balance, the imagination and the patience which mark "the higher statesmanship."

— **Niharkana Majumdar**

Suggested Further Readings

Forrest, George William, Sir, 1846-1926.
    Life of Lord Clive. — London, etc. : Cassell, 1918.
    2 v. : front., plates, ports., fold. map ; 24 cm.

Malleson, George Bruce, 1825-1898.
    Lord Clive and the establishment of the English in India. — Oxford : Clarendon, 1900.
    229 p. : fold. map ; 20 cm. — (Rulers of India ; v. 6)

MARQUIS JOSEPH FRANÇOIS DUPLEIX
(1697-1763)

Dupleix had more influence on Indian history than any other French-man. During the eighteenth century, he dreamed of building a French empire in India and came close to realizing it.

He was born in December 1697 in Landrecies, France, and died in obscurity in Paris 10 November 1763.

In 1720 his father, who was "Fermier Général et Directeur Général de la Compagnie des Indes," had him appointed to a responsible post with the Company in Pondichéry.

Colbert in 1664 founded the *Compagnie des Indes Orientales*, and sent François Caron to India to establish factories. Later, settlements were founded in Mahé, Masulipatam, Karikal, Chandernagore, etc. Pondichéry was founded in 1674 by François Martin and was the capital of the French holdings in India.

Since he was an enterprising young man, Dupleix soon made a fortune in Pondichéry in private trade, a practice that was sanctioned by the Company at that time. However, he eventually came into conflict with the administration in Pondichéry and in 1726 was dismissed and ordered home.

He refused to return to France, appealed against the decision of the Directors, and was vindicated after waiting four years. His next assignment was to serve as governor of Chandernagore in Bengal.

Chandernagore, which had been founded in 1676, had the most important of the French factories in Bengal. The settlement he found there was in a deplorable condition, but he changed all that. In the words of K.C. Kormocar, "In 1731 Dupleix did not find a ship in Chandernagore, and in 1742 one saw there from 12 to 15 vessels being used daily in commerce."

Dupleix often used his own money to finance the commercial ventures of others in the settlement and succeeded in setting up for Chandernagore trade relations with countries as far north as Tibet, as far west as Persia and as far east as China.

By the time he left Chandernagore to take over his duties as Governor General of the French possessions in Pondichéry in 1741, he had, according to George Toynbee, "rendered it (Chandernagore) at once a place of the greatest commercial importance and the centre of great political renown."

It was in Pondichéry that Dupleix developed his scheme for extending French political influence in India.

In 1744, the War of the Austrian Succession broke out, and England and France found themselves on opposite sides both in Europe and India. The French, under Mahé de la Bourdonnais, captured Madras from the English and later they tried to take Fort St. David as well. However, the treaty of Aix-la-Chapelle in 1748 restored the status quo ante bellum, and the French had to return Madras to the English.

Dupleix was now free to pursue his grand design, which was to enter into alliances with Indian rulers and extend French influence and power throughout south India.

The first opportunity came when Muzaffar Jang laid claim to the throne of the Nizam of Hyderabad and Chanda Sahib to the Nawabship of the Carnatic. Both of these positions were being contested, and this was an excellent chance for the French to display their political and military prowess in India.

At Ambur in 1750 a decisive battle was fought. The French, with Chanda Sahib and Muzaffar Jang, were on one side, and Anwar-ud-Din, the incumbent Nawab of Carnatic, his eldest son, Maphuz Khan, and Muhammad Ali, who would later contest for the Nawabship of the Carnatic, were on the other side.

The French and their allies won the battle. Anwar-ud-Din and his son were killed, and Muhammad Ali fled to Trichinopoly which was still in the hands of France's enemies.

The English championed the cause of Muhammad Ali in the Carnatic and that of Nadir Jang, a son of the late Nizam, who had himself declared Nizam of Hyderabad in contradiction of his father's will and a *firman* from the Mughul emperor in Delhi.

Had Chanda Sahib marched immediately on Trichinopoly as urged by Dupleix, he might have captured it. However, he delayed and attacked Tanjore instead. With the help of the French he defeated the Raja of Tanjore and by the terms of surrender demanded money. The Raja stalled, during which time he sent urgent messages to Nadir Jang for help.

The stall worked. Nadir Jang and his forces arrived in the Carnitic, and the English with their troops sided with Muhammad Ali. In the face of overwhelming numbers, the French and their allies were forced to retreat to Pondichéry.

All was lost when Robert Clive, then a mere captain, marched on Arcot, the capital of the Carnatic which at that time was held by the French and the forces of Chanda Sahib. He captured it and held it against a siege that lasted 55 days.

The fall of Arcot can be considered the turning point of the French struggle for India. Dupleix had spent much of his own money to wage the several campaigns which had been lost.

In 1754, he was replaced by Robert Charles Godeheu and sent home in disgrace. He spent his last years trying to regain his honour and the fortune he had lost in India.

Had Dupleix had the support of competent military and naval officers and the backing of the home government, the world might have had a French India, rather than a British India. This writer has seen two statues of Dupleix. One is in Landrecies, the other in Pondichéry. The latter was located outside as late as 1964, but, because its outdoor presence was offensive to a few super Indians, it was moved inside some place.

Suggested Further Readings

Malleson, George Bruce, 1825-1898.
History of the French in India : from the founding of Pondichéry in 1674 to the capture of that place in 1761. — Edinburgh : Grant, 1893.
614 p. : map ; 23 cm.

Martineau, Alfred Albert.
Dupleix et l'Inde Française ... — Paris : E. Champion, 1920-28.
4 v. : plates, maps ; 23 cm.

BERTRAND-FRANÇOIS,
COMTE DE MAHÉ DE LA BOURDONNAIS
(1699-1753)

Comte Bertrand François Mahé de La Bourdonnais, French naval commander, adventurer, and victor over the British at Madras (1746), was born in Saint-Malo 11 February 1699.

After several voyages to the Indies, La Bourdonnais formally began a long career with the *Compagnie des Indes* in 1718 as a lieutenant. He was promoted to captain in 1724 and first came to prominence the following year when he led the French forces that captured the town of Mahé on the Malabar Coast, taking his title from that victory. His considerable military skills brought him to the attention of France's rivals in the Asian trade, and he was persuaded by the viceroy at Goa to serve the Portuguese cause for two years during a time of mounting difficulties for the *Estado da India*.

In 1733, he returned to France where he was lured back to the service of the French Company. By 1735, La Bourdonnais was back in Indian Ocean waters, with the title of governor of the Île de France (Mauritius) and Île de Bourbon (Réunion).

La Bourdonnais played a notable role during the War of Austrian Succession (1740-48), the initial stage of the "great war of the mid-eighteenth century" that in India witnessed a struggle for dominance between England and France. The outbreak of hostilities found La Bourdonnais in France. He returned to Mauritius in 1740-41 with a sizable fleet, but to his chagrin was ordered to send these ships back to Europe to assist in the campaign there in 1742. Nevertheless, he demonstrated great skill and energy in combining French Company Indiamen and country ships into a respectable squadron of eight ships.

This naval force sailed for India, the focus of hostilities, in 1746. La Bourdonnais' squadron succeeded in saving Mahé and holding its own against an English fleet of four ships of the line under the less than inspired leadership of Lord Peyton.

Peyton thereupon sought refuge in Ceylon and Bengal, while La Bourdonnais sailed up the Coromandel Coast to Pondichéry, relieving Dupleix's forces and taking on badly needed supplies. Reinforced, his fleet and land forces under Dupleix began a siege of the English stronghold of Madras, capturing the place in September 1746.

The French, however, did not exploit this stunning success, as the two men quarrelled over the disposition of the town and the subsequent conduct of the campaign. La Bourdonnais offered to ransom back the town at a sum that, according to the English governor's correspondence, far exceeded the amount he publicly demanded. Dupleix strongly opposed this course of action, and a destructive stalemate developed that was broken only in October 1746 when a severe storm badly damaged La Bourdonnais' fleet and forced him to return to Mauritius. Madras was subsequently plundered, before being returned to the English in 1748.

Upon his arrival in Mauritius, La Bourdonnais found that he had been replaced by a supporter of his rival and that charges of corruption had been levelled against him by Dupleix. He embarked for Europe aboard a Dutch ship, determined to present his case to the Crown.

However, he was captured by the British, and did not reach France until 1748, whereupon he was promptly arrested on charges of "peculation and maladministration."

La Bourdonnais was held in the Bastille for two years, before being acquitted of the charges in 1751. He died in Paris 10 November 1753.

— **Glenn Ames**

Suggested Further Readings

Anandaranga Pillai.
Les François dans l'Inde : Dupleix et La Bourdonnais, extraits du journal d'Anandarangapoullé / tr. du tamoul par Julien Vinson. — Paris : 1894.
339 p. : maps, plan ; 23 cm. — (Publications de l'Ecole des Langues Orientales Vivantes; III sér., vol. XV)

La Bourdonnais, Bertrand François Mahé de, Comte, 1699-1753.
Me'moires historiques de B.-F. Mahé de La Bourdonnais, gouverneur des Îles de France et de Bourbon / recueillis et publiés par son petit-fils. — Paris : 1827.
368 p. ; 23 cm.

CHARLES-JOSEPH PATISSIER, MARQUIS DE BUSSY-CASTELNAU (1720-1785)

Charles-Joseph Patissier was born 8 February 1720 in Ancienville, a small town located between the Oureg River and the Villers-Cotterêts Forest.

His father, who later took the name Bussy, was a petty lord, having, according to his son's biographer, "scarcely any fortune other than his sword." He was a lieutenant-colonel of infantry who had won the Croix de Saint-Louis. His wife, Sophie-Ernestine Passavat, was *d'origine plus modeste encore.*"

Charles-Joseph's godfather was Joseph-Clément, his brother, eight years his senior, and his godmother was Charlotte, daughter of Patissier de Chateauneuf.

At the age of 13 he was provided with a lieutenancy by his father, but since one had to be 15, his birth records were altered to have him born in 1718 in Bucy-de-Long, near Soissons.* At 15, he was named captain under orders of his father who died in 1735 in Wissenbourg.

The controller-general of French, Philibert Orry, took the family under his care and in 1736 proposed to send Bussy to the Iles of France and of Bourbon (Réunion and Mauritius). He arrived there between October 1736 and October 1737 and remained there until he went to India probably in 1742.

The exact date of his arrival in India is a matter of conjecture, but he is known to have been in Pondichéry in 1742. He was present at the siege of Madras in 1746 and of Pondichéry in 1748. (Details of these events may be found in the sketches of La Bourdonnais, Dupleix and Clive.)

Bussy remained in India until he returned to France in 1761 at which time he married Arthémise de Choiseul, daughter of Antoine-Nicolas, Seigneur de Sommeville and Marquis de Choiseul. The happy event occurred 14 May 1761.

Bussy proved himself to be an able commander, often utilizing a minimum of troops for a maximum of results. He commanded the victorious troops at Amber in the campaign against Chanda Sahib in the Carnatic in 1750, and in 1751 he commanded 250 European and 1,200 sepoys (called "sipahis" by the French) in the capture of Jinji Fort, defended by 10,000 to 12,000 troops.

He then was attached to Muzaffar Jang, *Subedar* of the Deccan and an ally of the French, and was in command when Muzaffar was slain in hand-to-hand combat with the *Nawab* of Cuddapah. He immediately appointed Muzaffar's second son, Salabat Jang, as the new *Subedar* (and puppet) and had him installed with great pomp and ceremony in Aurangabad.

As was the custom in India in those days, the first son of Muzaffar Jang, Ghazi-ud-Din, coveted the seat of power. To achieve this he entered into an alliance with Balaji Baji Rao, Peshwa of the Marathas, a Hindu power on the west coast.

Once again Bussy was faced with an army that greatly outnumbered his forces, this time about ten to one. As the Maratha hosts approached Aurangabad, Bussy advanced to meet the challenge and defeated them at Rajapur during a moon eclipse. Bussy's forces then threatened Poona and were within about 30 km. of the Maratha capital when an armistice was agreed upon between Salabat and Balaji.

Shortly after this Bussy became ill and was forced to leave for Machlipatam to recuperate. Before leaving, however, he appointed Syed

---

* This has caused G.B. Malleson and a number of his biographers to give his date and place of birth incorrectly.

Laskar Khan, *Diwan* (Prime Minister) of the Deccan. He thought Laskar was on the side of the French, but instead he was conspiring against them.

When Bussy learned of this treachery, he rose from his sick bed and marched 800 km. to Aurangabad with 500 troops, rounded up at Hyderabad. There he confronted a frightened Syed Laskar and signed a treaty with him whereby France gained almost 800 km. of sea coast and the districts of Ganjam, Vizagapatam, Godavari, Yanaon and Krishna. These later came to be known as the Northern Sirkars.

At this point French influence in India was at its zenith, and from here French influence in India began to wane. Dupleix was replaced by Charles Robert Godeheu.

Godeheu arrived in Pondichéry 1 August 1754, and before the month was out had surrendered much of France's territory and influence to the English (called "les Goddamns" by the French).

Bussy remained in Hyderabad as "advisor" to Salabat Jang and administrator of the Northern Sirkars which France retained. In 1756, he led a successful campaign against Savanur, and in June 1758, he was summoned to Arcot by Comte Lally-Tolendal who had arrived in Pondichéry as governor-general and commander-in-chief of French forces in India.

Lally-Tolendal and Bussy, who disliked and distrusted each other, took part in the capture of Arcot 4 October and the following month led an abortive assault on Madras, the British capital in south India. Following the siege of Madras, Bussy remained in Pondichéry, suffering from one malady after another. Finally, in late 1759 he was summoned to Wandiwash where Lally-Tolendal planned to dislodge the British.

The Battle of Wandiwash was a disaster for the French. Bussy was taken prisoner and Lally-Tolendal forced to retreat to Pondichéry which he surrendered to the British. French dominion in India was at an end.

Bussy returned to France in 1761 and joined in the legal proceedings against Lally-Tolendal which resulted in the latter's execution in 1763.

The remaining years of Bussy are sad to relate. He had amassed an enormous fortune while in India, and this enabled him to live for 20 years, a life, in the words of Malleson, "of sloth and luxury." He was now Marquis de Bussy-Castelnau.

In 1781, he was summoned to India for the second and last time. The Second Mysore War was being fought, and Bussy was to aid Haidar Ali in his struggle with the English. He did not arrive in India until March 1783, four months after the death of Haidar Ali. Instead of acting with the vigour he had shown during his first tour in India, he remained in his tent at Porto Novo and did nothing.

After the war he retired to Pondichéry where he died 7 January 1785 at 10 P.M. following a whist party at the home of M. Monneron.

Bussy was a brilliant soldier with statesmanlike qualities. When he returned to India in 1783, he was in his sixties and suffering from the gout. Had he then been in his prime, he might have turned the tide of battle in the Second Mysore War and possibly restored, for a time at least, French influence in India.

Suggested Further Readings

Malleson, George Bruce, 1825-1898.
French struggles in India ... . Delhi : Inter-India Publications, 1977.
xvi, 286 p. ; 19 cm.
First published in 1884. [Rpt. of 1878 ed.]
Martineau, Alfred Albert.
Bussy et l'Inde Française, 1720-1785. — Paris : Société de l'Histoire des Colonies Françaises, 1935.
459 p. : plates, map ; 25 cm.

THOMAS-ARTHUR, COMTE DE LALLY, BARON DE TOLENDAL (1702-1766)

Thomas-Arthur Lally was born at Romans in Dauphiné 13 January 1702. He was baptized two days later at Saint-Nicolas Church. His father, Sir Gerard O'Lally, was an Irish exile who entered the service of France after the Battle of Limerick in 1690. He married Anne-Marie de Bressac de Faventine, widow of Philippe du Vivier, in 1701. From his Jacobite and Catholic father, Thomas-Arthur inherited an intense hatred of the English. As a youth, he served under his father at Gerona and Barcelona, and before he was 19, he obtained the command of a regiment of the Irish Brigade.

During the Franco-Austrian War of 1734, he distinguished himself at Kehl and Philipsburg, and after the peace, he was sent on a diplomatic mission to Russia to negotiate a secret alliance between Russia and France.

He served in the War of the Polish Succession and later in the War of the Austrian Succession, during the latter of which he saw action at Dettingen (1743) and served with particular excellence at Fontenoy (1745) after which, Louis XV made him a brigadier in the field.

In July 1745, he went to Scotland with the pretender Charles Edward to carry out a Jacobite plot which failed. Following the Battle of Falkirk (January 1746) he returned to France and served in the Low Countries. He was present at Laffeldt and at Bergen-op-Zoom where he was taken prisoner. He was soon released and before the conclusion of the war had achieved the rank of maréchal de camp.

When the Seven Years War broke out in 1756, Lally was put in command of a French expedition to India. He arrived in Pondichéry in April 1758 and celebrated the occasion by capturing Cuddalore, Fort St. David and Devikota.

However, he failed in an attack on the Raja of Tanjore, attempting to force the Raja to pay a debt he owed to the French. This failure lowered French prestige in India, but it was lowered even further when he besieged Madras and when he recalled Bussy-Castelnau from Hyderabad. The Madras siege was lifted when a British fleet under Admiral Sir George Pocock showed up off shore. The recall of Bussy-Castelnau from Hyderabad enabled the British to capture the Northern Sirkars which Bussy-Castelnau had won for the French.

The last campaign of Lally was at Wandiwash where the fate of the Carnatic was to be decided between the British and the French. The British were firmly entrenched in the fort of Wandiwash, but the town of Wandiwash was for the taking. Lally took it, but the assault on the fort failed. Bussy-Castelnau was made prisoner, and Lally returned to Pondichéry which was attacked by forces under the command of Colonel Sir Eyre Coote.

Lally was forced to surrender Pondichéry 1 January 1761, and the French were no longer a serious threat to the English in India.

Lally was taken to London where he learned that the French were accusing him of treachery. He insisted on returning on parole and was imprisoned. He remained in prison for two years, awaiting trial. When the trial was finally held, he was found guilty as charged and beheaded three days later, 9 May 1766.

Lally was a brilliant general, but he had a ferocious temper and no understanding of how one must conduct oneself in an Eastern country. He antagonized those who might have been helpful to him. Bussy-Castelnau, for example, was one of those who testified against him when he stood trial. The trial was a sham. Voltaire may have summed it up best when he wrote:

*La mort de Lalli ne rendit pas la vie de la Compagnie des Indes: elle ne fut qu'une crauté inutile.**

Suggested Further Readings

Chassaigne, Marc.
  Le Comte de Lally. — Paris : Société de l'Histoire des Colonies Françaises, 1938.
  334 p. : front. ; 24 cm.

Voltaire, François Marie Arouet de, 1694-1778.
  Fragments sur l'Inde, sur le général Lalli, sur le procès de comte de Morangies et sur
  plusieurs autres sujets. — Londres : 1774.
  400 p. : 23 cm.

An additional bibliographic source for Frenchmen involved in Indian history is Henry
  Scholberg's *Bibliographie des Français dans l'Inde*.

---

* Voltaire. *Fragments sur l'Inde et le général Lalli,* 1773 ed., p 158. Translation: "The death of Lally did not revive the *Compagnie des Indes.* It was only a useless act of cruelty."

CHAPTER 6

THE NINETEENTH CENTURY

Mountstuart Elphinstone   Mahadev Govind Ranade
Allan Octavian Hume   Ranjit Singh
T.B. Macaulay, 1st Baron   James Skinner
Sir John Malcolm   William Henry Sleeman
Sir Thomas Munro   Dwarkanath Tagore
Sir Charles James Napier   Jamsetji Nusserwanji Tata

$\mathcal{T}$he nineteenth century in India was a time of consolidation. The old foes of the eighteenth century had been, for the most part, vanquished. The Mughuls had faded with the death of Aurangzeb in 1707. The French were eliminated as a power in mid-eighteenth century. Mysore, with the death and defeat of Tipu Sultan at Seringapatam in 1799, was no longer a threat. Hyderabad was brought into the British sphere by diplomacy. The Marathas and their Peshwas were still troublesome, but they would succumb at the Battle of Seoni in 1818.

It then remained for the British to consolidate their empire. There was the Mutiny of 1857 that turned into the Great Rebellion, but it was put down and the East India Company abolished in 1858. Then, in 1877, Queen Victoria was named empress of India, and India became the jewel in her crown.

Some fascinating people left their signatures. This chapter is the story of some of them. The governors-general and viceroys who served during these 100 years are treated in Chapter 8. Those who fought against each other in the Revolt of 1857 are in Chapter 7. The century produced writers, educators and religious reformers of distinction, and they are sketched in their appropriate chapters.

What the nineteenth century produced was a group of civil servants, men like: Elphinstone, Malcolm, Munro, Hume, Napier, Sleeman and Macaulay who brought to India some of the best administrative talent Britain had to offer.

India has never lacked in men of military acumen, and these are found in James Skinner, the Eurasian who raised himself above the prejudices of the time, and Ranjit Singh, a Sikh leader who gave his enemies all they could handle.

At the start of the century we find in Dwarkanath Tagore the beginnings of Indian banking and the founder of a great family, and at the close of the century in Jamshed Nusserwanji Tata, we find the building of India as an industrial power.

The scene changed and attitudes changed as the years of the century rolled by. At first there was subservience to a foreign nation with great might and power. This changed to resentment which flared up in a conflagration in 1857. Then, 15 years before the century ended, a brave and noble states-man, Allan Octavian Hume, set wheels in motion by founding a society called the Indian National Congress which would, in the century to follow, at last bring freedom to India.

MOUNTSTUART ELPHINSTONE
(1778-1859)

Mountstuart Elphinstone was born to comfortable circumstances, the fourth son of John, 11th Baron Elphinstone, sometime governor of Edinborough Castle, 6 October 1779 in Dumbartonshire, Scotland.

Young Elphinstone was educated in Scotland and through the patron-age of an uncle obtained, at age 16, an appointment in the Bengal Civil Service as a writer, arriving in Calcutta in 1796. He was posted to Benares where he began what would be a lifelong study of the classical literature of both Greece and India.

In the May 1798 attack upon Benares by the deposed ex-Nawab of Oudh, Vizir Ali, Elphinstone escaped barely with his life. After a brief stay at the College of Fort William, he took up appointment as an assistant to the Gov-ernor-General's agent to the Peshwa at Poona in 1802. The following year during hostilities between the Company and Daulat Rao Sindhia, Elphinstone was attached to the staff of Arthur Wellesley, the future Duke of Wellington, and was an active participant in the Battle of Assaye (23 September 1803) and other engagements. Wellesley praised Elphinstone's services to him as a military officer, and on the general's recommendation, his young colleague was appointed resident at the Bhonsle Court at Nagpur (1803-08). There Elphinstone continued his education, both through exten-sive reading of European classics and by observing the working of a Maratha administrative system. His next posting came in 1808 when he was de-puted to be ambassador to the court at Kabul of Shah Shuja in quest of a treaty with the ruler of Afghanistan against a potential French and Persian military invasion. In fact, Elphinstone never reached Kabul, meeting the erstwhile Afghan ruler at Peshawar where a pact of friendship was finally agreed upon, little more than one month before a rebellion had pushed Shuja from the throne.

During 1810, Elphinstone resided at Calcutta before his next appoint-ment — the difficult and sensitive post as resident at the court of the Peshwa at Poona. There between 1811 and 1816, he soon found himself engaged in political confrontations with the Peshwa Baji Rao II. In the aftermath of the murder of Gangadhar Shastri Patwardhan, representative of the Baroda ruler, the British determined to bring the Peshwa under greater control, and Elphinstone was British signatory to a revised treaty with the Peshwa (June 1817). Baji Rao moved in October 1817 to throw off his British over-lords, leading the following month to an open conflict which by 1818 had resulted in the annexation of the Peshwa's territories by the East India Company.

Elphinstone himself was opposed to this policy of annexation; but once that policy became a settled fact, he undertook to establish British rule in the Deccan and along the Konkan Coast in a manner which would provide the least disruptive impact upon the existing social and economic order. Appointed commissioner of the Deccan, he organized the new Deccan ad-ministration with an eye to avoiding innovations and retaining Indian forms and agency wherever possible. He sought openly to reconcile the newly conquered population through policies which would assure respect for the traditions of the region. He stated that his goal was "to learn which system is in force and to preserve it unimpaired."

His period as resident at Nagpur and Poona had given him insight into the Maratha administration, and he thought it more suitable than a trans-plantation of the so-called Cornwallis system of Bengal with its elaborate and complicated regulations and separation of powers. In this view he was much influenced by his friend Thomas Munro, later governor of Madras.

Elphinstone gave particular encouragement to landed Maratha inter-ests, attempting to create a loyal, stable gentry as a foundation of the new regime. In addition, Elphinstone adopted politics of reconciliation with Brahmans, particularly those who had been influential in the previous Peshwa regime.

His policies may be said to have created the basis for the accommoda-tion to British rule by the Brahman castes of western Maharashtra, thus providing a foundation for the prominence of the Chitpavan or Konkanastha community awakening in that region in the nineteenth century.

In 1819, Elphinstone was appointed successor to Sir Evan Nepean as governor of Bombay. He held this office until his retirement in 1827. As governor, Elphinstone pursued similar policies of trying to settle the East India Company's government of the Bombay Presidency in such a way as to cause the smallest impact upon its people and ultimately to engage those people in its active acceptance and support.

Elphinstone was a strong believer in the value of education and his tenure witnessed some of the instances of government support for education at all levels in western India. He was especially concerned with elite edu-cation as a key to social and cultural regeneration. At the time of his retire-ment in 1827, the leading people of Bombay, irrespective of religion, caste or race, paid him a high tribute and resolved to found a college bearing his name. The Elphinstone Institution (later Elphinstone College) became ulti-mately a premier institution under what came to be the University of Bombay.

Elphinstone's reign as governor of Bombay was marked by the same sensitivity to Indian circumstances as had prevailed during his period as commissioner in the Deccan. While he accepted the expansion of British power in India as perhaps inevitable, his appreciation of Indian institutions suggested that he did not see conquest as unalloyed progress.

While still at Poona he wrote to Sir James Mackintosh that he did not expect the new British Indian empire would be long-lived, observing, "The most desirable death for us to die should be, the improvement of the natives reaching such a pitch as would render it impossible for a foreign nation to retain the government; but," he added cautiously, "this seems at an immeasurable distance."

Elphinstone's return to England and retirement offered him an opportunity to enter public affairs, including an offer of the governor-generalship of India which he declined, preferring to engage in research and writing his *History of India* of which the first sections, *History of Hindu and Muhammadan India,* enjoyed critical success.

Elphinstone did not find writing to be an easy task and brought out the volume to publication only after great encouragement from friends who hoped, for the most part in vain, that his judicious and sympathetic account of India's past would offer a counterweight to the widely read and strongly biased historical work of James Mill. A companion volume, *The Rise of British Power in the East,* was completed by others and published posthumously.

Elphinstone's only political activity appears to have been restricted to giving evidence before the House of Lords' Select Committee in connetion with the renewal of the East India Company's charter. He was a notable critic in later life of the annexation policies of Lord Dalhousie. At the time of the annexation of Sind, Elphinstone characterized Lord Ellenborough's action as being done in the style of "a bully who has been kicked in the streets and goes home to beat his wife in revenge."

Mountstuart Elphinstone's Indian career was characteristic of that generation of remarkable leaders whose energy and imagination framed many active policies of the East India Company's expanding rule in the subcontinent at the opening of the nineteenth century. His unusual combination of vigourous activity and military prowess with a brilliant and sensitive mind and skill as a diplomat and administrator marked him for a distinguished career.

His role as governor of Bombay might be compared to that of Munro in Madras. Not only did Elphinstone's term see the basic establishment of the geographical outlines of the modern Bombay Presidency, it also witnessed the formation of the basic administrative, judicial and educational policies which gave shape and substance to public life in western India for the next century and a quarter.

As a man of enlightenment, Elphinstone was a student of history who grasped the extraordinary complexities of Indian life and tradition and sought to impose foreign rule on the subcontinent in such a way as to do the slightest damage to India's on-going life.

That his policies and those of his successors did not fail to disrupt or dislodge the existing Indian society and economy was a reflection of the nature and dynamics of colonial rule itself and of the revolutionary character of new forces introduced by British domination into the subcontinent.

Mountstuart Elphinstone died in Hookwood, Surrey, England 20 November 1859.

— Frank F. Conlon

Suggested Further Readings

Ballhatchet, Kenneth A.
Social policy and social change in western India, 1817-1830. — London : Oxford University Press, 1957.
335 p. : port., maps ; 23 cm. — (London oriental series ; 5)

Choksey, Rustom Dinshaw.
Mountstuart Elphinstone : the Indian years, 1796-1827. — Bombay : Popular Prakashan, 1971.
viii, 465 p. : ill. ; 23 cm.

Colebrooke, Thomas Edward.
Life of the Honourable Mountstuart Elphinstone. — London : J. Murray, 1884.
2 v. : ill., ports. ; 23 cm.

Elphinstone, Mountstuart, 1778-1859.
An account of the kingdom of Caubul and its dependencies in Persia, Tartary and India. — London : Bentley, 1842.
2 v. : fronts., plates, map ; 23 cm. — [1st pub. 1815]

Forrest, George William, Sir. 1846-1926.
Selections from the minutes and other official writings of the Honourable Mountstuart Elphinstone, governor of Bombay. — London : R. Bentley, 1884.
x, 578 p. ; 23 cm.

ALLAN OCTAVIAN HUME
(1829-1912)

The founder of the Indian National Congress, which led the struggle for Indian independence, was an English ornithologist.

Allan Octavian Hume, the son of Joseph Hume, was born 6 June 1829. He came by his non-conformist views honestly. His father, Joseph Hume (1777-1855), was a Scottish reformer and radical who went to India in 1797 and returned home with a fortune with which he bought a seat in the House of Commons. Later, when Hume was serving in India, he could recall the days when his father had fought against the corn laws in 1834.

Allan Octavian interrupted his studies at the age of 13 and joined the Royal Navy as a midshipman. Later he resumed his studies by enrolling at Haileybury College where future Indian Civil Servants were being trained.

In 1849, he was sent to India and he joined the Bengal Civil Service, being posted as a clerk in a police station. This was as lowly a job as one could get in the I.C.S. Two months later he was made sub-inspector in another larger police station and still later was made inspector in a smaller station.

After having "paid his dues" with small jobs of this sort, Hume was promoted to assistant magistrate and later joint magistrate and deputy collector of Etawah district in what is today Uttar Pradesh.

Hume was magistrate in Etawah when the Revolt of 1857 broke out, and his measures of restraint in maintaining law and order in his district won the praise of government.

Hume was deeply moved by the Revolt and felt the need for social reform and friendlier relations between the ruler and the ruled. "History, alas!" he said, "presents us with too many examples of the long obstructed stream hurling aside at last roughly, its opposing barriers and sweeping onwards an ungovernable flood, heaping up desolation where it should have scattered flowers. Let it be ours to smooth and not impede its path, ours not by cold explanations of policy but by enlisting the sympathies and affections of the people in the cause, to watch and direct its progress and turn it, under God's blessing, to good and good alone."

To this end, from 1859 until his retirement in 1882, Hume carried out a policy of befriending the people. He published a vernacular daily, *The People's Friend*, he opened 181 primary schools in Etawah district (where as many as 5,000 children were educated), he effected prison reform by establishing a juvenile reformatory so that young offenders would not be locked up with hardened criminals and he tried, unsuccessfully, to stop the curse of alcoholism in his district.

He noted that the *akbari* revenue was one cause of the problem of alcoholism. He stated this in a note of 14 September 1860 to government:

> Financially speaking, bearing in mind the almost unexplained distress in the face of which this settlement was concluded, it may be regarded as eminently successful. To me, however, the constant growth of the *akbari* revenue is a source of great regret. Year after year, but alas in vain, I protest against the present iniquitous system which first produced and now supports a large class whose sole interest is to reduce their fellows into drunkenness and its necessary concomitants, debauchery and crime. Unfortunately, these tempters are too successful, and year by year the number of drunkards and the demands for drugs and spiritous liquors increases.

He went on to point out that the monies received from *akbari* do not represent any profit to government because "for every rupee additional that the *akbari* yields, two at least are lost to the government by crime, and spent by the government in suppressing it."

Hume worked hard for the abolition of the customs barrier after he was promoted to commissioner of customs in 1867. He was made secretary of the home department of the Government of India in 1870, but he was keenly aware of the agricultural problems of the country and had himself transferred to the post of secretary of the department of revenue, agriculture and commerce.

In 1879, he brought out a pamphlet entitled *Agricultural Reforms in India.* In it he pointed out that government should hire specialists to deal with the problems of agriculture and that judges should go from village to village to settle debt cases involving poor peasants who were being exploited by greedy money-lenders.

Hume's reforms and attempted reforms did not gain favour with the senior bureaucrats of the I.C.S. and in 1879, the year his pamphlet was published, he was transferred to an insignificant post in the revenue board in Allahabad. The private secretary of Lord Lytton explained that "the decision (to transfer Hume to Allahabad) was based entirely on the consideration of what was most desirable in the interest of public service."

Several Indian newspapers were outraged at this treatment of Hume, but *The Englishman* expressed it best:

> The plea advanced in justification of this arbitrary act was that Mr. Hume habitually, in his minutes on measures coming up for discussion in his department, expressed his views with great freedom, without regard to what might be the wishes or intentions of his superiors. If he believed a particular policy to be wrong, he opposed it without hesitation, using plain language for the expression of his view. We cannot find that any other charge has been brought against him. He is notoriously a hard worker, and Government will not easily find his equal in knowledge or the special subjects dealt with in his department.

After three years, in 1882, Hume retired from government service. Now, free from government restraint, he devoted his time and energy in urging Indians to speak up and demand their rights. He addressed a circular letter 1 March 1883 to the graduates of the University of Calcutta, and ended it with these strong words:

> You are the salt of the land. And if amongst you, the elite, fifty men cannot be found with sufficient power of self-sacrifice, sufficient love for and pride in their country, sufficient genuine and unselfish heartfelt patriotism to take the initiative, and if needs be, devote the rest of their lives to the cause — then there is no hope for India.

This appeal resulted in the formation of the Indian National Union whose aim it was to seek justice for the people through constitutional means, while "insisting that unswerving loyalty to the British Crown shall be the key-note of the institution."

The first meeting of the Union was scheduled for Poona, but since cholera had broken out there, it was held in Bombay instead. Convened 27 December 1885, it was presided over by W.C. Banerjee, and its secretary was none other than Allan Octavian Hume.

At about the same time that the Indian National Congress, as it was now called, was holding its first meeting in Bombay, the Indian National Conference was holding its second meeting in Calcutta. Since the aims of the two organizations were similar, they merged and continued under the name of the Indian National Congress.

At first the I.N.C. was looked upon with favour by the viceroy and other high government officials, and its leaders were invited to garden parties. However, in time, it came to be regarded, in the words of Lord Dufferin, as a "microscopic minority." The Congress objectives did not often win the hearts of the administration, which prompted Hume to remark:

> The National Congress had endeavoured to instruct the Government, but the Government had refused to be instructed.

While in India, Hume made a study of the birds of India and Asia. He published till 1899 a journal entitled *Stray Feathers.* Among his books on birds are *Nests and Eggs of Indian Birds* and *Birds of India, Burmah and Ceylon.*

He returned to England in 1894 and settled in Norwood where he died 31 July 1912.

It is not possible to over-estimate the impact that Hume had on the history of modern India. The Indian National Congress which he founded was the leading force which eventually brought about independence in 1947. Only an Englishman — an Englishman of the stature of Hume — could have founded the Indian National Congress. Gopal Krishna Gokhale stated:

> No Indian could have started the Indian National Congress. If the founder of the Congress had not been a great Englishman and a distinguished ex-official, such was the disgust of political agitation in those days that the authorities would have at once found some way or the other to suppress the movement.

Suggested Further Readings

Hume, Allan Octavian, 1829-1912.
   A speech on the Indian National Congress : its origin, aims and objects, delivered at a
   great public meeting in Allahabad 30th April 1888. — [Calcutta : 1888?]
   18 p. ; 21 cm.

Wedderburn, William, Sir.
   Allan Octavian Hume, C.B. : father of the Indian National Congress. — London : T.
   Fisher Unwin, [1913]
   vi, 182 p. : port. ; 21 cm.

THOMAS BABINGTON MACAULAY,
FIRST BARON OF ROTHLEY
(1800-1859)

How does one do justice to Thomas Babington Macaulay, historian, essayist, poet and law-giver, in a few words or a few paragraphs? Here was a man of enormous energy and tremendous output whose career touched two countries: England and India. He spent less than four years (June 1834-January 1838) in India, but his influence there was greater than that of many who devoted life time careers to the country. It is the India side which will be examined in the paragraphs that follow.

He was the eldest child of Zachary Macaulay, born 25 October 1800 at Rothley Temple, Leicestershire. There were several children, and Macaulay was particularly devoted to his sisters, Hannah and Margaret. A third sister, Jane, had died in 1830.

Zachary Macaulay had been governor of Sierra Leone and was a friend of the abolitionist William Wilberforce and a pious Christian. Mrs. Macaulay, was a quaker and the daughter of a Bristol bookseller.

Before he was eight years old, Thomas wrote a *Compendium of Universal History* and a poem entitled *The Ballad of Cheviot*.

He went to a good private school and when he turned 18, he enrolled at Trinity College, Cambridge. He won a number of prizes and scholarships there, but failed to appear in the Tripos because he was weak in mathematics.

He was called to the bar in 1826 and joined the northern circuit. He was made commissioner of bankruptcy in 1828, and in February 1831, he became an M.P. for the "pocket borough" of Calne. However, his initiation to fame came not from the law courts, but from an essay on Milton which he wrote for the *Edinburgh Review* in 1831.

Macaulay was a good speaker as well as a good writer. When the Reform Bill was being debated in 1831, Sir Robert Peel said of the first of his speeches that, "portions of it were as beautiful as anything I have ever heard or read." Following the passing of the Reform Bill in 1832, Macaulay became one of the commissioners, and later secretary, of the board of control of the East India Company, and in 1833, helped carry the bill which renewed the charter of the Company. He was appointed law minister in the governor-general's executive council in 1834 and arrived in India 10 June of that year. Margaret was married; so he took his sister Hannah with him to India.

He was at first stationed in Madras where he met Lord William Bentinck at Ootacamund. Later he moved to Calcutta. When his sister married Charles Trevelyan in 1835, he lived with them in their house on Chowringee (now Nehru Sarani).

In his capacity on the council, Macaulay supported freedom of the press and equality of Europeans and Indians before the law. He wrote a minute on education which inaugurated a system of liberal Western learning through the medium of English, and he wrote, almost single-handedly, the penal code, the code of civil procedure and the code of criminal procedure. The penal code was revised and drafted into law in 1860, and the civil and criminal codes were promulgated in 1859 and 1861 respectively.

He resigned his post 15 January 1838 and returned to England, but he did not lose his interest in India.

He wrote essays on Clive and Hastings and in 1855, argued in parliament in favour of the introduction of competitive examinations for admission to the Indian Civil Service.

He continued to be active the remainder of his life, devoting much of his time to writing. Among his publications are: *Armada* (1832), *Lays of Ancient Rome* (1842), and his most important work, *History of England* (1849-55), in four volumes. In addition to these books, plus his minute on education in India and the law codes he wrote, he produced numerous articles for the *Edinburgh Review, Knight's Quarterly Magazine* and *Encyclopaedia Britannica* (eighth edition).

His work in education, law and civil service during a period of three-and-a-half years was his great contribution to India, although his educational policy was, and perhaps still is, controversial among orientalists.

He died 28 December 1859 in his library at Holly Lodge, Campden Hill, and was buried in Westminster Abbey in a grave in the Poets' Corner, at the foot of a statue of Addison.

His versatility and wide knowledge prompted Lord Melbourne to say of him:

I wish I were as cocksure of one thing as Macaulay is of everything.

Suggested Further Readings

Macaulay, Thomas Babington, 1st Baron, 1800-1859.
    The works of Lord Macaulay complete / edited by his sister, Lady Trevelyan. —
    London : Longmans, Green, 1879.
    8 v. : front. (port.) ; 23 cm.
Trevelyan, George Otto, Sir, 1838-1928.
    The life and letters of Lord Macaulay. — Oxford ; New York : Oxford University Press,
    1978.
    2 v. in 1 ; 19 cm.

SIR JOHN MALCOLM
(1769-1833)

Sir John Malcolm, the son of George Malcolm, was born in Burnfoot in the parish of Westerkirk, Dumfriesshire, Scotland, 2 May 1769. His mother was Margaret, the daughter of James Pasley of Craig, Dumfriesshire.

John left school at the age of 12 at a time when his father had fallen on hard times due to unfortunate speculation. The boy's maternal uncle, John Pasley, took John to London with him, hoping to get him a job with the East India Company.

When John, not yet 13, appeared before the directors, they were all for rejecting his application. One of them asked him, "Why, my little man, what would you do if you met Haider Ali?" John replied:

"I'd cut his head off."

His commission was dated October 1781, and he sailed for India in the autumn of 1782, arriving at Madras in April 1783. His first duty was as an ensign assigned to two companies of sepoys whose duty it was to protect the safety of English prisoners who had been surrendered by Tipu Sultan following the treaty of 11 May 1784 which ended the Second Mysore War. "Boy Malcolm," as he was called, spent the next six years soldiering, getting into scrapes at times and into debt at times. In 1790, at 19, he was made adjutant to the wing of his regiment, the 29th Battalion of Native Infantry.

His career took off that year when his regiment was ordered to cooperate with the Nizam's army and took part in the siege of Copoulee during the Third Mysore War.

It was when his regiment was stationed with the Nizam's main army in Hyderabad that Malcolm became acquainted with some members of the Company's diplomatic corps, and it was here that he determined he would like to go into the diplomatic service. To this end he began a study of Persian and was described as "a careless, good-humoured fellow, illiterate, but with pregnant ability."

He failed to get into the diplomatic service, and that fall he became ill and was sent to the coast for rehabilitation. In 1792, Malcolm, now a lieutenant, joined Lord Cornwallis's camp at Seringapatam and was appointed Persian interpreter for the Nizam's troops.

Then in 1794, still in bad health, he went home on furlough. The sea voyage must have been good for him because by the time he landed, he was in good health and good spirits. He wrote a paper on the grievances of the East India Company's officers and got acquainted with Henry Dundas, president of the board of control, and Sir Alfred Clarke who was about to leave for Madras as commander-in-chief. He spent some time with his parents in Burnfoot and sailed for India in May 1795. He never saw his parents again.

On his return to India, Malcolm served as secretary to Clarke and to Clarke's successor, General George Harris, until 1798. When the new governor-general, Lord Mornington (later Wellesley), arrived in India that year, Malcolm presented him with a paper he had prepared on the Indian states, and when a vacancy occurred for the post of assistant resident in the court of the Nizam of Hyderabad, Malcolm applied for it and got it.

His first duty almost cost him his life. The Nizam had been forced by the British to disband his "French corps" which had been trained and officered by Frenchmen. The corps mutinied, seizing their officers and attacking Malcolm. He was saved by some deserters from his old regiment, the 29th. He returned to the residency, rounded up some loyal troops and so overawed the mutineers that they surrendered.

In 1799, Malcolm sailed with the governor-general to south India where he joined the Nizam's contingent and was present at the siege of Seringapatam, the last battle of the Fourth (and last) Mysore War.

He was next appointed joint secretary (with Thomas Munro) of the commission to arrange for the future disposal of Mysore and other territories and for the settlement of questions arising out of the recent war.

The governor-general was then in diplomatic negotiations with Persia, and he selected Malcolm as his envoy to Teheran. Malcolm concluded two protocols with the Shah: one a commercial treaty providing for unrestricted trade with the East India Company and the cession of some islands to the British, and the other, a political treaty which would exclude French troops from Persia, in exchange for which the English would come to the aid of Persia in the event of a French invasion of the country.

The treaties were never ratified by either government, but Malcolm had established his ability and reputation as a diplomat. On his return from Persia in 1801, he was appointed private secretary to Lord Wellesley, and it was said that his influence with the governor-general was so great that he was called "the factotum of Lord Wellesley and the greatest man in Calcutta."

In December 1803, he drew up the Treaty of Surji-Arjungaon by which Sindhia of Gwalior agreed to give up all his territories between the Ganges and the Jumna and his forts and territories north of Jodhpur, Jaipur and Gohud. He also surrendered to the British, Ahmadnagar, Broach and all his lands west of the Ajanta Hills, and he renounced all claims on the Mughul emperor, the Peshwa, the Nizam and the East India Company's territories.

Malcolm was appointed resident in his court and in February 1804, concluded another treaty whereby Sindhia agreed to allow a defence force of 6,000 Company troops near his frontier.

The following year he was resident at Mysore, and in the war against Holkar he served under Lord Lake. He concluded a treaty with Sindhia in 1805 which restored Gwalior and Gohud to Daulat Rao and in 1806, a treaty with Holkar whereby Jaswant Rao I had to give up all claims to Tonk, Rampura, Bundi, Kuch, Bundelkhand and all places north of the Chambal River, but got back most of his lost territories.

In 1808, Malcolm was sent on a diplomatic mission to Persia, but he was foiled in his efforts by French influence there. He returned to India and in 1809 put down a mutiny of Madras troops at Masulipatam, but was called back into diplomatic service again the following year when he was deputed to serve in a mission in Persia with Sir Harford Jones, the king's ambassador to Persia.

Malcolm was home on furlough from 1812 to 1817 and returned to become a political agent to the governor-general and brigadier-general with the army of the Deccan during the Pindari-Maratha War. He won the Battle of Mahidpur 21 December 1817 and obliged Peshwa Baji Rao II to abdicate in 1818.

Malcolm was disappointed in not being appointed governor of Bombay and was assigned to administrative duties in Central India instead. He also hoped for the governorship of Madras, but that was denied as well. He took another furlough (1822-1827) and returned as governor of Bombay. He served three years, resigning after a series of judiciary disputes in 1830.

On his return to England he was elected M.P. for Launceston (1831-32) and continued writing his *Life of Lord Clive*.

He died 30 July 1833 at his lodgings on Prince's Street, Hanover Square, London.

Malcolm, in addition to being an active soldier, diplomat and administrator, was a prolific writer. From his pen, besides his biography of Clive, came: *Political History of India* (1811), *Observations on the Disturbances in the Madras Army 1809* (1812), *History of Persia* (1815), *Central India* and *Sketch of the Sikhs*.

Sir John Malcolm was one of a parade of British officers who dominated the Indian scene in the nineteenth century. His courage and diplomacy won the respect of both friend and foe, but he was not always treated well by those in high positions who could have advanced his career.

Suggested Further Readings

Chakravorty, U.N.
  Anglo-Maratha relations and Malcolm, 1798-1830. — New Delhi : Associated, c1979. x, 200 p. ; 22 cm.

Kaye, John William, Sir, 1814-1876.
  Life and correspondence of Sir John Malcolm, ... — London : Smith, Elder, 1856. 2 v. : front. (port.) ; 22 cm.

SIR THOMAS MUNRO
(1761-1827)

Sir Thomas Munro was born 27 May 1761, the son of Alexander Munro, a Glascow merchant who traded principally with Virginia. Thomas was the second of five children. His mother was a sister of Dr. Stark, a prominent anatomist. In his childhood, Thomas suffered a severe attack of measles, and this caused slight deafness, a condition that worsened in his latter years.

He finished grammar school at the age of 13 and went from there into the University of Glasgow where he remained for almost three years. He excelled in chemistry and mathematics, and he read widely in literature and history.

He arrived in India 15 January 1780 as a cadet in the mercantile marine of the East India Company. He saw military action almost immediately, serving in the Second Mysore War under Sir Hector Munro and Sir Eyre Coote from 1780 to 1783.

During the course of the campaign Munro kept a journal of his activities, and these provide an excellent eye-witness account of the Second and
Third Mysore Wars, and of the final war with the Marathas. Following are
excerpts from "Memorandum of the Services of Sir T. Munro, written by
himself:"

> I was present at the retreat of Sir Hector Munro from Conjeveram to
> Madras, after the defeat of Colonel Bailie by Haider Ali on the 10th of
> September, 1780.
>
> I was with the army under Sir Eyre Coote, at the relief of
> Wandiwash, on the 24th of January, 1781. At the cannonade by Haider
> Ali, on the march from Pondichérry to Cuddalore. At the assault of
> Chidambaram, 18th of June, 1781. At the battle of Porto Novo, 1st July,
> 1781....
>
> I was with the advanced division of the army, under Colonel Owen,
> when that officer was attacked and defeated by Haider Ali, near
> Chittor....
>
> I was present at the taking of Chittor on the 11th of November,
> 1781.... At the attack of the French lines and battle of Cuddalore, on the
> 13th of June, 1783; on which occasion I acted as aide-de-camp to Major
> Cotgrave, field officer of the day, who commanded the centre attack.
>
> In April, 1792, I marched with the force ordered to occupy the
> Baramahal, ceded by Tipoo to the British Government.
>
> From April, 1792, until March, 1799, I was employed in the civil
> administration of that country.
>
> On the breaking out of the war with Tipoo Sultan, I joined the army
> under Lieutenant-General Harris, intended for the siege of
> Seringapatam ... on the 5th of March, 1799.

Except for his involvement in the war with the Marathas in 1817 and
1818, Munro was engaged after 1799 (and the fall of Tipu Sultan) in civil
administration. The last paragraph of his memorandum reads:

> On the 8th of August, 1818, having received the surrender of Paurghur,
> the last fort held for the Peishwah, resigned my command, after hav-
> ing, in the course of the campaign, reduced all the Peishwah's territo-
> ries between Toombudra and Kistna, and from Kistna northward to
> Akloos, on the Neemah, and eastward to the Nizam's frontier.

After the Fourth (and last) Mysore War, Munro and Captain (later
Major-General Sir) John Malcolm were appointed joint secretaries to the
commissioner to arrange for the future disposal of Mysore and other
territories and for the settlement of questions arising out of the recent war.
From July 1799 until October 1800 Munro (now Major Munro) was in
charge of the Kanara district on the West Coast, south of Goa. He was not
happy with the assignment because he had to leave his friends and his
work in Baramahal. However, he performed his duties well, putting down
disturbances and establishing an efficient government throughout the
district.

As a reward for this excellent service, he was appointed collector of the so-called Ceded Districts south of the Tungabhadra which included Cuddapah and Bellary. Three months after assuming his new duties, Munro described the situation:

> The ten years of Mughal government in Cuddapah have been almost as destructive as so many years of war, and this last year, a mutinous unpaid army was turned loose during the sowing season to collect their pay from the villages. They drove off and sold the cattle, extorted money by torture from every man who fell in their hands, and plundered the houses and shops of those who fled; by which means the usual cultivation has been greatly diminished.

The first thing Munro did to settle the districts was to pension off or expel the *poligars* (petty chieftans) and force them to disband their armies. He then established a *ryotwari* system for collecting revenue whereby the village head-man was held responsible to defaulting or absconding *ryots* (peasants). The system was so successful that Gribble in the *Manual of the District of Cuddapah* commented:

> It is astonishing how Munro was able, with rapidity, to organize an establishment, and carry through a work which was not only new, but detrimental to the village head-men, whose false accounts and concealments of cultivation were thus brought to light.

Munro was in England on furlough from 1807 until 1813, during which time he testified before the House of Commons regarding the renewal of the East India Company charter.

On his return in 1814, with his wife, Jane, the daughter of Richard Campbell of Craigie House, Ayrshire, Colonel Munro was appointed president of a commission to inquire into and reform the judicial systems of the Madras and Bengal presidencies.

He returned to military service as a brigadier-general in 1817 and fought in the Maratha and Pindari Wars. After the wars, General and Mrs. Munro returned to England. While at sea, "in the latitude of the Azores," their son, Thomas, was born, 30 May 1819.

The following year, Major-General Sir Thomas Munro and Lady Munro returned to India. Munro had been named governor of Madras, and it would be in this position that he would end his career and his life.

As governor, he instituted a number of reforms, establishing a "Native Board of Revenue" to give Indian Civil Servants more responsibility in the collection of revenue, improving education and installing the *ryotwari* system for revenue collection. His administration was conducted with such efficiency and fairness that when he died, his passing was greatly deplored by subjects.

A couple of generations later Rev. W. Robinson of Salem said of him:

> Munro's name is held in the greatest reverence in this district, and the highest compliment they can pay a native is to compare him to Munro.

Parents would name their children after him, "Munrolappa", and in one district he was designated *Mundava Rishi,* meaning "Munro Deified".

While on a tour of Puttaconda in the Ceded Districts, Sir Thomas Munro, governor of Madras, died 6 July 1827. He was survived by Lady Munro and two sons: Campbell and Sir Thomas.

Suggested Further Readings

Bradshaw, John.
  Sir Thomas Munro and the British settlement of the Madras Presidency. — Oxford :
  Clarendon, 1906.
  231 p. ; 20 cm. — (Rulers of India ; v. 13)

Gleig, George Robert, 1796-1888.
  The life of Major-General Sir Thomas Munro. — London : Colburn and Bentley, 1830.
  2 v. : front. port., fold map ; 23 cm.

Krishnaswami, P.R.
  Tom Munro Saheb : governor of Madras. — [Madras : Higginbothams, 1947]
  xiii, 237 p. : port. ; 19 cm.

SIR CHARLES JAMES NAPIER
(1782-1853)

Charles James Napier, the eldest son of Colonel the Hon. George Napier and Lady Bunbury (née Lennox), was born 10 August 1782 in London. His brother was the soldier-historian Sir William Francis Patrick Napier.

He was commissioned in the 53rd regiment at the tender age of 12 and, thanks to the efforts of his cousin Charles James Fox, was promoted to major by 1806. He led the 50th Regiment in the ill-fated La Coruña campaign under Lieutenant-General Sir John Moore during the Peninsular War of 1808-09.

Following his battle against Napoleon he returned to England in 1811 and was sent to do battle against the United States in the War of 1812.

He served in Greece from 1819 to 1830 and was a friend of Lord Byron. He also took a Greek mistress by whom he had two daughters. He was unemployed from 1830 until 1839, at which time he was given command of the northern forces during the Chartist agitation. Promoted to general, he succeeded in keeping the situation under control in north England.

By 1841 he was in financial straits, with two illegitimate daughters to support; so he was happy to have a good-paying job in India. He arrived in India in August 1841 and took command of the army in Sind in August of the following year.

His military career in Sind (1842-1847) can be described by the word "aggressive." When Napier assumed command, replacing Major James Outram, he recognized it was his duty to carry out the wishes of the new governor-general, Lord Ellenborough, who was anxious to annex Sind.

By a treaty proposed by Lord Ellenborough it was stipulated that if the Amirs were not loyal, their territories could be transferred to loyal Bahawalpur. Napier was convinced they were not loyal; so he bullied them until one by one they fell under British control. He is credited with saying that "the barbaric chiefs must be bullied or they think you are afraid: they do not understand benevolence or magnanimity." A diary entry of his is also revealing of his character:

> We have no right to seize Sind, yet we shall do so, and a very useful, humane piece of rascality it will be.

In January 1843, without a formal declaration of war, he attacked the desert fortress of Imamgarh. This greatly disturbed the neighbouring Baluchis; so they attacked the British residency. In the Battle of Miani 17 February 1843, Napier defeated a force of 22,000 with a force of 2,800 troops. In March he won a battle at Hyderabad (Sind), subduing the Amir Sher Muhammad, "the Lion of Mirpur."

Following the battle, he sent a message in Latin to Ellenborough: "*Peccavi*". Translation: "I have sinned."

Prize money for the conquest to the amount of 50,000 pounds sterling went into Napier's pocket. Outram, who was resident in Sind at the time, received only 3,000, which he gave to charity. Outram, who was not an admirer of Napier, wrote a letter to him, stating:

> I am sick of policy; I will not say yours is the best, but undoubtedly it is the shortest — that of the sword. Oh, how I wish you had drawn it in a better cause.

The Amirs of Sind, who had sided with the British during the First Afghan War (1839-42), were dealt with cruelly and deceitfully by the British. Referring to Lord Ellenborough's administration, Innes wrote:

> If the Afghan episode is the most disastrous in our annals, that of Sind is morally even less excusable.

Following the annexation of Sind, Napier was made G.C.B. and governor, and remained in the position until he went home on leave in 1847. His administration of the province of Sind was efficient but autocratic. He established a competent police force, started building canals and encouraged trade. He also checked marauding hill tribes.

He was recalled to India in 1849 by Lord Wellington during the Second Anglo-Sikh War (1848-49) to take over as commander-in-chief. However, by the time he arrived, the war was over; so he occupied himself in reorganising the army. He soon came into conflict with Governor-General Dalhousie over the issue of compensation for Indian troops, and resigned, returning to England in May 1850. In his book, *Defects, Civil and Military, of the Indian Government*, he showed he had a premonition of the Revolt of 1857. He died 29 August 1853 at Portsmouth. His statue in St. Paul's Cathedral, London, reads:

A prescient general, a beneficent governor, a just man.

Some people would have disagreed with that last part.

Suggested Further Readings

Lawrence, Rosamond (Napier), Lady.
    Charles Napier : friend and fighter. — London : Murray, 1952.
    236 p. ; 23 cm.

Napier, William Francis Patrick, Sir, 1785-1860.
    The conquest of Scinde. — London : Boone, 1845.
    2 v. : maps, plans ; 22 cm.

Napier, William Francis Patrick, Sir, 1785-1860.
    The life and opinions of General Sir Charles James Napier, G.C.B. — London :
    Murray, 1857.
    4 v. : fronts., (ports.), map ; 20 cm.

MAHADEV GOVIND RANADE
(1842-1901)

Though perhaps best known for his unstinting efforts for social reform, Mahadev Govind Ranade was also a tireless worker encouraging public consciousness of political affairs and activity. He also made distinguished contributions during his career as a journalist, economist and historian.

He was born 18 January 1842 in Niphad, District Nasik, into a family of landowners and government servants belonging to the elite Chitpavan Brahman caste. His education commenced in Kolhapur state where his father had taken up an appointment. Mahadev (or Madhav, which was his true given name) entered Kolhapur English School and after three years of study, he was sent to Bombay's Elphinstone Institution prior to admission to Elphinstone College. He was among the first students to appear for and pass the new University of Bombay matriculation examination in 1859 and, in 1862, was among the first graduates of that University. He completed his degree with first class honours in economics and history, then received the M.A. degree with honours in the same subjects. In 1866, he passed the LL.D. examination also with honours.

His style of study involved intense reading of all available material which left him a master of his subjects, but at the cost of a severely strained eyesight which troubled him throughout his career. His academic accomplishments were recognized during his university studies in his appointment as a Junior Fellow. Ranade was an active member of the Students' Literary and Scientific Society and there became interested in issues of social reform.

This led him in 1862 to journalism when he became the English editor of the Anglo-Marathi *Indu Prakash* which had been begun by Gopal Hari Deshmukh (*"Lokahitavadi"*). He soon had to resign the editorship under pressure of studies, but continued to contribute articles to the paper.

Ranade's interest in reform was not limited to secular reflections of his university education. He was also drawn to the indigenous theistic religious reform of Hinduism which led to the founding in 1867 of the Prarthana Samaj in Bombay. Throughout his life he was a deeply committed theist who drew special inspiration and comfort from the *bhakti* hymns of the saint-poets of western India such as Eknath and Tukaram.

Following completion of his studies in 1866, Ranade held the post of *Karbhari* under the princely states of Akalkot and Kolhapur successively. In 1868, he returned to Bombay as assistant professor of English and History at Elphinstone College, a post which he held until 1871 when he passed the Bombay advocate's examination. He then opted for the judicial branch of government service and was made judge of the Small Causes Court at Bombay.

In November 1871, Ranade was appointed judge of Small Causes Court at Poona where he became an active supporter of the Poona Sarvajanik Sabha. He was soon a prominent figure in Poona's political society, emphasizing constructive work and a moderate ideology which could incorporate the widest possible membership.

This activity, coupled with a general suspicion of "Poona Brahmans," made Ranade's superiors to doubt him, leading ultimately to punitive transfers, first in 1878 to Nasik and, in the aftermath of the uprising of Wasudeo Balvant Phadke, the following year to Dhulia in Khandesh.

In 1880, he was passed over for appointment to the Bombay High Court due to official suspicions of his "strong patriotic, national feelings."

The following year, however, he was promoted to be Additional Presidency Magistrate, Bombay, and then Sadr Amin at Poona where he was also placed in charge of inspection in Poona and Satara districts under the Deccan Agriculturalists' Relief Act.

It was in this context that Ranade began writing his studies of economic subjects. In 1885, he was made Law Member in the Bombay Legislative Council and named a member of the Indian Finance Commission.

In appreciation of this work he was awarded the C.I.E. in 1887 at the same time that he was appointed a Special Judge for the Deccan Agriculturalists' Relief Act. In 1893, he was at last appointed a Justice in the Bombay High Court, which position he held until his death in 1901.

During the period after 1878 Ranade was a frequent contributor to the *Poona Sarvajanik Sabha Quarterly Journal*, addressing issues of land tenures and settlement, agrarian development and other economic subjects. He was a strong advocate of industrialization as a key to India's economic improvement. Ranade also continued his promotion of social reform, taking a lead in the establishment of the National Social Conference which met yearly in conjunction with the new Indian National Congress.

Ranade had attended the inaugural meeting of the Congress, but was barred by his official appointment from direct participation in a political association.

In the context of promoting social reform, he came increasingly into conflict with conservative, orthodox Hindus and faced a direct confrontation with Bal Gangadhar Tilak over the relationship of the Social Conference with the Congress. In these affairs Ranade attempted to avoid further trouble, recognizing the unconstructive nature of confrontation.

He became a guru to the young Gopal Krishna Gokhale and other young men of reform, although Ranade himself understood that each individual had somehow to evolve a personal equation and posture *vis-a-vis* these difficult issues.

When Ranade's first wife died in 1873, he resolved not to marry again. His father, fearing that he would marry a widow, arranged a marriage with a young girl. Although he was opposed to every aspect of the situation, Ranade ultimately acceded to his father's will, recognizing the limits of acting entirely without ties to family and community. Unlike some social reformers, Ranade felt strongly that reform would not be advanced by merely taking a radical position which offended the orthodox majority.

When queried about what reforms he favoured, he observed in 1898 that the issue was not that of concrete details of a particular reform, "but the general spirit of purity, justice, equality, equity, temperance and mercy which should be infused into our minds and which should illumine our hearts." He believed that, without regeneration of Indian society through reform, political independence would be meaningless for the Indian people. Thus his views came into direct conflict with those of his younger contemporary Tilak.

In 1893, Ranade was appointed a justice of the Bombay High Court, the highest position available to an Indian in government service. Thenceforth he resided principally at Bombay and, given the nature of his position, took little active role in Indian politics, although he maintained close ties with Gokhale and other so-called "moderates."

It was in this period that Ranade began work on Maratha history. At a time when Tilak had already appropriated Shivaji to the demand for *swaraj*, Ranade sensed that historical myth-making alone would be insufficient to serve the long term interests of Maharashtra. Recognizing his interests in social reform and his recognition of the potential mischief of caste intolerance, Ranade's interpretation sought to find a common ground of Maratha identity rooted not just in the martial exploits of the hero Shivaji.

In his *Rise of the Maratha Power* (1900) Ranade emphasized the emergence of the Marathas as an expression of genuine nationality, based on organic evolution of social-cultural tolerance, rooted in the "Maharashtra dharma" of the region's medieval poet-saints — a legacy which he glimpsed in the faith of the reformist, theistic Prarthana Samaj of which he continued to be a member.

Nevertheless, such solace as Ranade might find in the history of his people could scarcely overcome the wounds of public criticism from the so-called extremists and the growing recognition that social and religious reform were at best options followed by the few, not the many.

Ranade's health failed late in 1900 and 16 January 1901 he died in Bombay.

His life encompassed many of the difficulties and contradictions of the educated elite of colonial India, but it symbolized all that was best in rational and sensitive quest for reform and regeneration of Indian society.

Ranade was sometimes criticized as being too sympathetic to British colonial rule and by extension, too Anglicized; yet in fact he remained a devout Hindu who viewed reform only as the path by which Hinduism would regain lost lustre. Ranade was also a champion of the history and culture of the Marathi-speaking people.

Near the beginning of his career he wrote essays on Maratha history and a report evaluating the range and content of published Marathi books. He opposed the dropping of Marathi as a required subject in the Bombay examinations in 1867. When, after 1893, he became a member of the University Senate, he worked tirelessly for the restoration of Marathi, arguing that the University curriculum was too Western in orientation, and that the result was a diminishing of what he called a Marathi language renaissance.

Although in his life he failed to obtain the restoration of Marathi, after his death the policy was reconsidered and altered in posthumous recognition of his commitment. During the final years of his life he also pursued his interest in Maratha history, desiring to free the subject from the interpretive framework given to it by English historians of an earlier generation.

He published a series of lectures in his interpretive volume, *Rise of the Maratha Power*, which emphasized the view that the Marathas' emergence was an expression of a genuine nationalism whose vital spark derived from the inspiring reformist ideals of the medieval *bhakti* poet-saints. He also found the keys to Maratha decline in the influence of caste and a failure to recognize the egalitarian import of the poet-saints' teachings.

Ranade was not a professional historian; yet his writings were among the most influential published because they offered an intellectually challenging and politically inspiring reinterpretation of Maharashtra's history.

Ranade's is the legacy of a remarkable individual talent harnessed to important social and political issues of the day, who evolved his own formula of enlightened reform and personal living, but who held back from offering his own career as a model to be followed thoughtlessly by others.

— **Frank F. Conlon**

Suggested Further Readings

Chintamani, Chirravoori Yagneswar, 1880-1941, ed.
 Indian social reform. — Madras : Minerva Press, 1901.
 2 v. : 369, 390 p. : port. ; 21 cm.

Heimsath, Charles H.
 Indian nationalism and Hindu social reform. — Princeton : Princeton University Press, 1964.
 xiii, 379 p. ; 25 cm.

Jagirdar, P. J.
    Studies in the social thought of M. G. Ranade. — Bombay : Asia Publishing House,
    1963.
    vi, 148 p. ; 22 cm.

Kellock, James.
    Mahadeo Govind Ranade. — Calcutta ; Association Press, 1926.
    ix, 204 p. : front., plates, ports. ; 19 cm.

Parvate, T.V.
    Mahadev Govind Ranade : a biography. — Bombay : Asia Publishing House, 1963.
    x, 326 p. : port. ; 23 cm.

MAHARAJA RANJIT SINGH
(1780-1839)

The Lion of the Punjab was born 13 November (or 2 November) 1780
in Budrakhan. He was the son of Sardar Maha Singh whom he succeeded
in 1792 as head of the Sukerchakia *misl* (branch) of the Sikh confederacy.

Early in life he lost an eye from small pox. Little is know of his childhood education, but it is evident from the manner in which he conducted
his court in later years that he had a deep appreciation of religion and of
the outside world, for he surrounded himself with people of all faiths and
nationalities.

He allied himself with the Afghan ruler Zaman Shah when the latter
invaded the Punjab, and was given Lahore in 1799.

In 1801, he defeated the most powerful of the Sikh *misls*, the Bhangis,
capturing Amritsar the following year.

On 1 January 1806 he took Ludhiana which put him in conflict with the
British who claimed the land up to the Sutlej River. He respected British
military prowess because he knew of their victory over Tipu Sultan in
Mysore and of their successes against the Marathas.

(It is said that he was so impressed with the relentlessness with which
England was acquiring territory that he once said, while looking at a map
of India, "*Sab lal hojayega.*"*)

He therefore welcomed the arrival of Charles Metcalfe, the rising young
political officer who had been sent by Lord Minto to negotiate with him at
Amritsar. The result was the Treaty of Amritsar of 25 April 1809 by which
Ranjit Singh was left in possession of his territories south of the Sutlej River,
but was to leave the cis-Sutlej chiefs alone, while the East India Company
agreed not to interfere north of the Sutlej.

During the negotiations, an escort of two companies which had
accompanied Metcalfe was attacked by a band of Akali fanatics brandishing
steel quoits and two-handed swords. They were beaten off with ease, and
this convinced Ranjit Singh of the need to employ European officers to train
his army. Among these were Generals Court, Ventura and Allard who had

---

*   "It will all be red."

fought under Napoleon, Colonel Alexander Haughton Gardner, an Irish artillery officer, and Paolo de Bartolomeo Avitabile, a Neapolitan general.

Officers such as these built up Ranjit Singh's army to a force of 29,000 men and 192 guns. It came to be known as the Army of the Khalsa.

In 1810, he subdued the Nakkai and Kanheya confederacies and in 1812 declared himself Raja of the Punjab.

Not wanting to be in conflict with the British, he then expanded his kingdom to the north and west.

In 1818, he captured Multan. The stronghold was held by an aged Afghan Nawab, Muzaffar Khan, and his eight sons. The siege began in January 1818 and lasted over six months. Ranjit Singh brought up his powerful Zam Zam gun to batter down the walls with huge stone missiles. But as soon as the walls were breached, they were filled up and the attackers driven back in hand-to-hand fighting.

Finally, on 2 June, a party of Akalis seized an important bastion, but still the defenders held out, crying, "Come on! Let us perish like men!"

The Nawab and five of his sons were picked off by matchlocks, but the remaining three surrendered, bringing to Ranjit Singh spoils estimated at two million pounds.

By 1820 he had consolidated all of the Punjab between the Sutlej and Indus Rivers and had proclaimed himself Maharaja.

His conquest of the Punjab was completed by his capture of Peshawar which was held by the Afghan general, Yar Muhammad Khan. One of Ranjit Singh's reasons for attacking Peshawar was to get possession of Lailli, an Arab mare renowned for her beauty throughout Afghanistan and the Punjab. She was not surrendered until Yar Muhammad Khan was arrested and told he would have to remain in prison until she was given up.

Afterwards, Ranjit Singh boasted that Lailli had cost him sixty lakhs of rupees and 12,000 good men.

In 1823, he made the city and province of Peshawar tributary to him, received Shah Shuja, then a fugitive from Afghanistan, and obtained the Koh-i-Nur diamond from him.

(Ultimately this gem ended up in the crown of Queen Victoria.)

In 1835, Dost Muhammad of Afghanistan attacked the Sikhs at Peshawar but was repulsed. In 1838, he agreed to the tripartite treaty with Lord Auckland and Shah Shuja for the restoration of the latter to the Afghan throne.

Ranjit Singh died at Lahore 27 June 1839, but the kingdom he had built with military genius, a strong will and capacity for hard work, did not last.

He was succeeded by a series of rival chieftans who quarrelled with each other and, in violation of Ranjit Singh's policy, fought the British. They were finally defeated by the British at Gujarat in 1849. As they were surrendering their swords and matchlocks, an old Sikh warrior cried:

*Aj Ranjit Singh mar gya!**

---

* "Today Ranjit Singh is dead."

Suggested Further Readings

Gardner, Alexander Haughton Campbell. 1785-1877.
    Soldier and traveller : memoirs of Alexander Gardner, colonel of Artillery in the service
    of Maharaja Ranjit Singh. — Edinborough : Blackwood, 1898.
    xxxiv, 399 p. : 3 port. (incl. front.), 2 maps ; 23 cm.

Griffin, Lepel Henry, Sir, 1840-1908.
    Ranjit Singh. — Oxford : Clarendon Press, 1892.
    223 p. : fold. map ; 20 cm. — (Rulers of India ; v. 19)

Singh, Khushwant.
    Ranjit Singh, Maharaja of the Punjab. — London : Allen G. & Unwin, [1962]
    237 p. : ill., ports., geneal. tables ; 23 cm.

JAMES SKINNER
(1778-1841)

James Skinner was born in Bengal in 1778 and died in Hansi 4 December 1841. His father, Hercules Skinner, was a Scotsman and a captain in the East India Company army, and his mother was a Rajput, the daughter of a zamindar. She died by suicide in 1790 because her daughters had been taken out of purdah.

When sixteen James was apprenticed to a printer in Calcutta but hated it so much he ran away after three days with only four annas in his pocket. Shortly after that his brother-in-law gave him a job copying legal papers, but his real ambition was to be a soldier.

At that time it was not possible for half-castes or country-borns as they were called then, to hold officer rank in the army of the East India Company. (The term Eurasian was little used then, if at all, and Anglo-Indian was used to denote Englishmen who were domiciled in India.)

Armed with a letter of introduction, James Skinner, then seventeen, met Benoît de Boigne, a Frenchman in the service of Madhaji Sindhia, and received a commission in Sindhia's Maratha army.

He distinguished himself in a number of battles including the capture of Delhi in 1798 and the storming of Hansi, the stronghold of the Irish adventurer, George Thomas, in 1799. In 1803, he was dismissed from the Maratha service by General Perron who had succeeded de Boigne as commander of Sindhia's army and was asked by Lord Lake to organise a body of horsemen who had deserted from the Maratha army. He agreed to do so on the condition he would not be required to fight against Sindhia. His men agreed to serve the British only on the condition that they be allowed to chose their own leader, "*the Bara Sikander.*"

This unit was originally known as Captain Skinner's Corps of Irregular Horse. This was abbreviated to Skinner's Horse, and its leader was called Sikander Sahib, an allusion to Alexander the Great, Sikander being the Urdu rendition of Alexander. The men of Skinner's Horse were called "Yellow Boys," because of the colour of their uniforms. Their motto was "*Himmat-i-*

marda'na va madad-i-Khudá" which in translation is "By the courage of men and the help of God."

Skinner and his men then distinguished themselves in campaigns against Jeswant Rao Holkar in 1805 and the Pindaris in 1817-19. In 1815, he had received the honorary title of lieutenant-colonel, and as a reward for services against the Pindaris, he was given *jagirs*, or grants of land in Aligarh district.

As a landlord, Skinner spent considerable sums on irrigation works and was highly regarded by his tenants. They are reported to have said of him, *"Vu'h tha' ba'dsha'h tha'!"* meaning "Ah! He was a king!"

He was also highly respected by the British. Men like Sir John Malcolm, Marquis Wellesley, Sir David Ochterlony, the Earl of Auckland and Bishop Reginald Heber all spoke glowingly of him. In 1818, he was awarded the C.B. (Companionship of the Bath).

A lasting monument of his is St. James Church which he built near Kashmiri Gate in Delhi. It was consecrated 21 November 1836. He died at Hansi 4 December 1841 and was buried there. A month and a half later his body was exhumed, taken to Delhi by escort of his regiment and was buried 19 January 1842 in St. James Church.

Lt.-Col. Skinner's importance in Indian military history according to his biographer, Dennis Holman, was his bringing "to perfection a multipurpose light cavalry that could be used in a remarkable variety of roles: long-range reconnaissance and pursuit, internal security, escort duties ... indeed anything requiring for its success the elements of speed, ingenuity, surprise, or just sheer hard work."

Author's Note: Some of the data in this sketch were contributed by Skinner's great-great-grandchildren, Mrs. Lillian Skinner Singh and Lt.-Col. M. A.R. Skinner, and do not appear in any published accounts of their forebear's life.

— Henry Scholberg

Suggested Further Readings

Holman, Dennis.
    Sikander Sahib : the life of Colonel James Skinner, 1778-1841. — London, etc. : Heinemann, [1961]
    x, 275 p. : ill., front. port., map ; 22 cm.

Skinner, James, 1778-1841.
    Military memoirs of Lieut-Col. James Skinner ... [edited by J. Baillie Fraser] — London : Smith, Elder, 1951.
    2 v. : front. ; 20 cm.

Brief sketches of Skinner may be found in Dictionary of National Biography and Buckland's *Dictionary of Indian Biography.* Also of interest would be Philip Mason's *Skinner of Skinner's Horse,* a fictional account.

SIR WILLIAM HENRY SLEEMAN
(1788-1856)

The conqueror of the thugs was an Englishman who began his career as a soldier and concluded it as a civilian.

He was William Henry Sleeman, born 18 August 1788 in Stratton, Cornwall, the son of Philip Sleeman of Pool Park, St. Judy, Cornwall, and his wife Mary Spry. Philip Sleeman was a yeoman and supervisor of excise. He died when William was ten. William was nominated to an infantry cadetship in the Bengal army in 1809. He went to India that year, and in the following year, 24 September, he was gazetted ensign. Then 16 December 1814 he was promoted to the rank of lieutenant.

He fought in the Nepal War (1814-1816) and suffered from jungle fever. In 1820, he was appointed junior assistant A.G.G.* for the Sagar and Nerbudda districts.

After this he never resumed military duties, though he continued to rise in rank. He was gazetted captain 23 September 1823, major 1 February 1837, lieutenant-colonel 26 May 1843, colonel 5 December 1853 and major-general 28 November 1854.

In 1829, Sleeman married Amélie Josephine, daughter of Count Blondin de Fontanne. A son, Henry Arthur, was born in 1833.

For ten years beginning in 1825, Sleeman was a magistrate and district officer in parts of India which later came to be known as the Central Provinces and still later came to be known as Madhya Pradesh. It was during this period, beginning in 1829, that Sleeman performed the work for which he is best remembered, the abolition of thugee.

The words *"thug"* and *"thugee"* have been adopted into the English language. The Hindi word is *thag*. In Marathi it is *thak* and in Sanskrit *sthaga*, meaning "a cheat, swindler." According to Yule and Burnell in their *Dictionary of Indian English*, "the proper designation of these criminals was *phansigar*, from *phansi*, a noose," which was usually the means by which the victims were murdered.

In 1829, Sleeman was named assistant to the officer whose duty it was to suppress *thugee*, and in January 1835 he was made general superintendent of the operation.

A word about *thugee* is in order here. Thugs would prey on travellers, joining them in their journeys and posing as innocent fellow-travellers. Then, during the night, they would strangle them, take their valuables and vanish into the dark. Although some of them were Muslims, they claimed to be worshippers of the goddess Kali and that they were carrying out her will for them. From 1826 to 1835 over 1,400 thugs were hanged or transported for life. One confessed to having murdered over 700 victims.

While posted in the Jubbulpore district in 1828 , Sleeman issued a proclamation forbidding anyone from aiding or abetting in a *sati*. However, on one occasion he was actually forced to witness a *sati*. He had been persuaded that if the woman did not commit herself to the flames of her husband's funeral pyre, she would starve herself to death.

---

*   Agent of the governor-general.

In 1841, Sleeman turned down the lucrative job of resident at Lucknow, capital of Oudh, so that a colleague who had been impoverished by the failure of a bank could have it. Then in 1842 he was assigned to Bundelkhand to investigate troubles there, and in 1843 was named resident at Gwalior and served in that capacity until 1849.

In 1848, the job of resident at Lucknow became vacant, and Sleeman was offered it by Lord Dalhousie. This time Sleeman accepted.

He served there from 1849 until 1856. During a three-month tour of Oudh, Sleeman issued reports of bad government on the part of the Nawab and noted the urgent need for reforms. The court of directors used these reports to bolster their excuse for annexing Oudh in 1856, even though both Sleeman, who believed reform could be instituted, and Dalhousie both opposed annexation.

Sleeman became ill in 1854 and was sent to a hill station to recover, but he never fully recovered. He was ordered home and died 10 February 1856 off the coast of Ceylon.

Four days before he died, Dalhousie conferred on him the Civil Cross of the Bath.

Sir William's greatest achievement was the elimination of *thugee*. Had his advice on Oudh been accepted by the court of directors, it is possible he would have been credited with an even greater contribution: the prevention, or at least the delay, the the Great Rebellion of 1857.

Suggested Further Readings

For the student who wishes to know more about *thugee*, the following books are recommended:

Sleeman, William Henry, Sir, 1788-1856.
    Ramaseeana; or, A vocabulary of the peculiar language used by the thugs. — Calcutta : Military Orphan Press, 1836.
    270, 115 p. ; 23 cm.

Taylor, Meadows, 1808-1876.
    Confessions of a thug. — London : Bentley, 1839.
    3 v. ; 21 cm.

Autobiographical sources on Sleeman may be found in:

Sleeman, William Henry, Sir, 1788-1856.
    Rambles and recollections of an Indian official. — Karachi : Oxford University Press, [1973]
    xxxvii, 667 p. : map ; 19 cm.
    Reprint of 1844 ed.

Sleeman, William Henry, Sir, 1788-1856.
    A journey through the kingdom of Oude, 1849-50. — London : Bentley, 1858.
    2 v.: map ; 20 cm.

DWARKANATH TAGORE
(1794-1846)

Dwarkanath Tagore of Calcutta is known primarily as the grandfather of the poet Rabindranath Tagore, a protegé of Rammohun Roy, a merchant prince and a philanthropist. Aside from that, he is notable as the first modern Indian business entrepreneur. He was the father of the age of steam in India — the first businessman in India to apply steam power to commercial undertakings on a large scale. Directly or through his business partners he founded India's first coal company, tea company and steam tug and river steamer lines. He also pioneered in the introduction of such business institutions as the managing agency system, the joint stock company and commercial banking.

Dwarkanath Tagore was born in Calcutta in 1794 into a wealthy family of Pirali Brahmans, a Brahman subcaste considered impure by the dominant castes of Bengal. Even in the eighteenth century, the Tagores were the most westernized of the great families of Calcutta..Dwarkanath was adopted by his childless uncle Ramlochan and in 1812, at the age of 18, assumed personal supervision of Ramlochan's estates and began his own business career. He became a legal agent for some of the wealthiest zamindars of Bengal and simultaneously added to his own landholdings which he developed commercially. He also served as *Dewan* to the Board of Salt, Customs and Opium, acted as a moneylender to both Indian and British, and became associated with the agency house of Mackintosh and Company. Mackintosh, along with all the other major houses, banks and insurance companies, crashed in the commercial crisis of 1830-33.

Because of his zamindari estates, Dwarkanath emerged from this crisis as the dominant figure in the Calcutta business world. In 1834, he took on British partners and established his own agency house, Carr, Tagore and Company. His house promoted a series of joint-stock companies, some successful — the Calcutta Steam Tug Association, Bengal Coal Company, Bengal Tea Company, and India General Steam Navigation Company; and some abortive — the Bengal Salt Company and the Ferry Bridge Company. He and his partners also became the leading directors of the Union Bank, the city's joint stock commercial bank. On his own account Tagore invested in a fleet of opium clippers and in the major English-language newspapers of the city. His last important entrepreneurial undertaking was to become one of the leading promoters of the Great Western of India Railway Company.

As the civic leader of Calcutta, Tagore tried to promote an interracial partnership in every aspect of civic life. He led his countrymen in the support of Western-style charities, including funds for modern medical facilities and medical education, and the improvement of roads, sanitation and communications. He forged an interracial alliance with the non-official European community to support freedom of the press, an improved judicial system, local control of steam shipping between India and Europe, the abolition of the East India Company, the rights of landlords and the development of India's resources. He patronized the Western theatre and opera and took pleasure in the company of European actors and artists.

At his suburban mansion, Belgatchia, he lavishly entertained everyone of importance in Calcutta, including the governor-general and foreign visitors together with the Bengali elite. He did all this alone since the women of his family, including his wife Digambari had ostracised him from his ancestral home, Jorasanko, for his friendship with impure Europeans, wine-drinking and allegedly libertine behaviour. His four sons, including the eldest, Debendranath (1817-1905), were raised by the women with little input from their father.

In 1842, he undertook his first voyage to Europe, visiting Egypt, Malta and Italy en route. During his four months in Britain he was entertained by royalty, including Queen Victoria and Prince Albert, the directors of the East India Company, and leading figures in the arts and theatre world. He visited the industrial midlands and Scotland and travelled to France where he was received by King Louis-Philippe. Because he thought of himself as the "loyal opposition," he brought to Calcutta with him George Thompson, a leading British radical, who inspired the college-educated "Young Bengal" to form a liberal-radical political organization, the British India Society, in 1843. This was the link between Dwarkanath and the younger generation.

During the next few years Dwarkanath's health began to fail. In addition, he was disappointed in his eldest son, Debendranath, who was not interested in business, and his enemies united to attack the monopoly of his house and its poor management of the various joint stock companies under its control. Dwarkanath left for his second, and final, voyage to Europe in 1845 and died in England 1 August 1846. He is buried at Kensal Green Cemetery in London.

Soon after his death the commercial crisis hit Calcutta. Carr, Tagore and Company folded as did the Union Bank and many of the other commercial institutions of the city. His family, however, was left with the landed estates, and under the careful management of Debendranath their value increased over the years.

Dwarkanath's legacy to his talented family, including his grandson Rabindranath, was his breadth of vision, his universalism and his liberal spirit.

But Dwarkanath's dream of an interracial partnership and the rapid development of India as an economic power in the British Empire died with him.

— Blair B. Kling

Suggested Further Readings

Kling, Blair B.
    Partner in empire : Dwarkanath Tagore and the age of enterprise in eastern India. —
    Berkeley : University of California Press, 1976.
    xii, 276 p. : port. ; 25 cm.

Kripalani, Krishna.
    Dwarkanath Tagore. — New Delhi : National Book Trust, 1980.
    viii, 305 p. : plates, ill., facsims., ports. ; 21 cm.

JAMSETJI NUSSERWANJI TATA
(1839-1904)

Jamsetji Nusserwanji Tata was the leading entrepreneur of modern times and founder of the largest corporate group in the private sector. His work, which laid the foundation for the diversified industrial development of India in the twentieth century, was distinguished by its grand scale and its focus on the technologically advanced nation-building industries.

J.N. Tata was born 3 March 1839 into a Parsi family in Navsari. His father, Nusserwanji (1822-1886), migrated to Bombay and started his own trading firm. He was a shrewd businessman and, until his death, provided Jamsetji with sound business advice and capital resources.

He gave his son a liberal education at Elphinstone College and arranged for his marriage to Heerabai (1844–1904). They had two sons, Dorabji (1859–1932) and Ratanji (1871–1918), and a daughter who died at the age of 10 in 1871.

In 1859, Jamsetji entered his father's trading firm and was sent to open branches in Hong Kong and Shanghai. He followed this with four years in England (1864–1868) where, in addition to his work as the firm's agent, he studied the latest developments in science, technology and manufacturing.

Nusserwanji's trading firm barely survived the commercial crisis of 1865 but recouped its losses by supplying the goods and transportation for a short-term British military expedition to Abyssinia in 1867-68. In the next few years Jamsetji, wealthier, better educated and more travelled than his peers, became a leading figure among the younger, progressive Parsis of Bombay and a close friend of Pherozeshah Mehta.

Though Jamsetji had strong feelings about economic imperialism and Indian poverty, he avoided political activity and gave only token support to the Indian National Congress.

In 1869, with his share of profits from the Abyssinian adventure, Jamsetji joined a few other merchants and purchased an old oil mill at Chinchpoogly which they converted into a cotton mill. A few years later the group sold the mill at a profit, and, after a visit to England to study the latest developments in cotton-mill technology, Jamsetji formed a joint stock company to raise money for a new mill. The Empress Mill, which opened in 1877, was unique among Indian mills and eventually became the most successful one in India. Jamsetji located the mill in Nagpur, an economically backward region, far from other cotton mills, but near raw materials and an untapped labour market. Through trial and error he learned the advantage of scientific management, a liberal labour policy and utilizing the most advanced technology available. The Empress Mill became the model for all subsequent Tata enterprises.

In 1886, he founded the Svadeshi Mills Company Ltd. to make yarn of high-count to compete with British imports. He bought an old, dilapidated mill at Kurla near Bombay and after years of struggle with antiquated machinery and labour problems, finally made it pay by 1890, an effort which took its toll on his health. Although cotton mills represented Jamsetji's major industrial investment during his own lifetime, he worked on many other projects simultaneously. He was committed to the development of Bombay, and after 1890 began to purchase property and buildings until he became the city's largest landlord. His most famous real estate venture was the Taj Mahal Hotel, opened in 1903, and is regarded as the finest hotel east of Suez.

Other ventures included a shipping line which failed to survive the freight-rate war with P. and O. and other experiments with new agricultural commodities such as Egyptian cotton and sericulture. His manifold enterprises were coordinated and managed by Tata and Sons, established in 1887, consisting of himself, his son, Dorabji, and his nephew, R.D. Tata.

Jamsetji is best remembered for three schemes which he inaugurated, but did not live to complete. The first of these, the Indian Institute of Science, was designed to be India's first modern post-graduate teacher-research university. It was opened at Bangalore in 1911 after years of controversy between the Tatas and an over-cautious government.

The hydro-electric project, suggested to Jamsetji by a British engineer in 1897, harnessed the water from the Ghats above Bombay to provide clean and economic power for the burgeoning needs of the city. It was completed in 1915.

The third scheme, the manufacture of iron and steel, was the most important both for India and his house. In 1882, Jamsetji began a long process of thorough investigation of India's coal and iron resources and negotiations with the government for mining concessions. In 1902, he toured steel plants in the United States and hired a consulting engineer, Charles Perin, to help him select a site and design for the first modern integrated steel mill in India. The Tata Iron and Steel Company Ltd was founded in 1907, three years after Jamsetji's death. Manufacturing began in 1911, and in 1919 the steel town of Sanchi was renamed Jamsetpur after the founder. The founding of the steel mill represented the apex of Jamsetji's entrepreneurial genius and reflected his finest qualities — his boldness in taking on a project of enormous vision and scope, his willingness to take great risks, the careful, scientific and deliberate pace of his investigations, his talent for finding the best advice and assistance, his faith in the future of India and his insistence on a decent environment for those who would eventually make the steel.

Jamsetji died 19 May 1904 at Bad Nauheim in Germany where he had gone for medical treatment. He was buried in London at Brookwood Cemetery.

— **Blair B. Kling**

Suggested Further Readings

Harris, Frank Reginald.
Jamsetji Nusserwanji Tata : a chronicle of his life. — London : Humphrey Milford, Oxford University Press, 1925.
xix, 348 p. : front., plates ; 23 cm.

Saklatvala, Beram & Khosla, K.
Jamsetji Tata. — New Delhi : Publications Division, Ministry of Information and Broadcasting, 1970.
ix, 141 p. ; 19 cm. — (Builders of modern India)

CHAPTER 7

THE GREAT REBELLION

The Indian Side	The English Side
Bahadur Shah II	Gen. Havelock
Lakshmibai	Gen. Lawrence
Nana Sahib	Gen. Neill
Tatya Tope	Gen. Nicholson

$\mathcal{T}$he Indian Revolt of 1857 has also been called the Sepoy Mutiny, the Great Mutiny, the Indian Mutiny, the Great Rebellion, a Revolution and the First War of National Independence. For purposes of dramatic effect we are entitling this section "The Great Rebellion"; for purposes of brevity here we are calling it the "Revolt." It began as a mutiny when the sepoys in Meerut rebelled 10 May 1857; it ended as a full-scale revolt.

The Doctrine of Lapse was one casus belli. Under this doctrine, promulgated by Lord Dalhousie, whenever the ruler of a "Native State," as they were called then, would die without leaving a natural male heir, his state would revert to the Paramount Power, the East India Company. Problems arose when the only existing male was adoptive. According to Hindu custom, an adoptive son had the same status as a natural son. According to British law, or the law that prevailed in India at the time, this was not the case. This caused two of the persons being discussed in this Chapter to rebel: Rani Lakshmibai of Jhansi whose son, Damodar, had been adopted by her late husband on his deathbed, and Nana Sahib, the adoptive son of ex-Peshwa Baji Rao II, who was made to go without his late father's handsome pension.

Another, and more immediate cause of the revolt was the issue of the greased cartridges. In order for the new Enfield rifles to fire properly, they first had to be greased. The rumour spread among Hindu sepoys that cow fat was used, and among Muslim sepoys that pig fat was being used. Naturally, there was grumbling in the ranks!

In this chapter we treat eight persons who played their parts with varying degrees of honour and distinction: four Indians (Bahadur Shah II, Rani Lakshmibai, Nana Sahib and Tatya Tope) and four Britishers (Sir Henry Havelock, Sir Henry Lawrence, General James George Smith Neill and Sir John Nicholson).

Much of the fighting occurred in north central India; so it is inappropriate to use the adjective "national," as in "the First War of National Independence," to describe the Revolt. In 1857 few Indians had a genuine sense of nationhood. They were fighting to right wrongs which had been done to their persons or to their realms, and there was no single national leader behind whom all the rebels could, would or did assemble.

When one compares the military and administrative training and leadership of men like Havelock, Neill, Nicholson and Lawrence with that of Bahadur Shah, Lakshmibai, Nana Sahib and Tatya Tope, it is not surprising the rebellion failed.

The rebels may not have achieved their objectives, but in 1858 the East India Company was abolished that was something.

BAHADUR SHAH II
(1775-1862)

Bahadur Shah II was 22nd in the line of succession from Babar, the founder of the Mughul Dynasty. He was the titular King of Delhi and his official designation was Emperor of Hindustan. His "empire" existed only within the city walls of Delhi. He received a pension from the British government of Rs.100,000 per month, and he wrote lovely poems in Persian.

His name was Abul Muzaffar Siraj-ud-Din Muhammad Bahadur Shah. Born 24 October 1775, he was the son of Akbar Shah II. On 28 September 1837 he succeeded to the throne on the death of his father, and 20 years later, much to his consternation, he found himself up to his eye balls among mutinous rebels.

His house came tumbling down with the outbreak of the Revolt of 1857, and ultimately he was sent into exile in Rangoon where he ended his days. However, even before the occurrence of the Revolt, the British had determined that his royal titles and prerogatives would be withdrawn after his death.

Following the mutiny in Meerut 10 May 1857, the rebels headed for the sanctuary of Delhi and proclaimed Bahadur Shah their Emperor of Hindustan. They arrived 11 May, demanding an audience with their leader. When they were informed that they had been receiving their pay from the English and Bahadur Shah had no money in his treasury with which to pay them, they said they would "bring the revenue of the whole empire to your treasury."

The next day all the shops in Delhi were closed, and the soldiers demanded that their king should go through the city with his army and demand that the shop owners open up. He did so on the back of an elephant. Some shops were opened, but many shop owners ignored Bahadur Shah's orders. In the evening some officers approached him saying, *"Are, Badshah! Are, buddhe!"** Some even touched his beard.

Such was the treatment he received from his "followers." Chaos reigned in the city, and no one commanded enough respect to keep order

---

* "Hey, Emperor! Hey, Old Man!"

among the rebels. To steady the situation, Bahadur Shah appointed Prince Mirza, Mughul commander-in-chief of the rebel army, and he gave high military ranks to other princes.

They were unable to keep the rebels in check, partly because of their incompetence, and partly because they themselves were engaged in looting and robbing.

Bahadur Shah was helpless and tried to shut himself up and hide from the mutineers. He developed superstitions and at one point expressed the idea of becoming a faqir and leaving the troubles of the world to others. Sir Syed Ahmad Khan wrote:

> The ex-King had a fixed idea that he could transform himself into a fly or gnat, and that he could in this guise convey himself to other countries, and learn what was going on there. Seriously, he believed that he had the power of transformation.

In September 1857 the British captured Delhi and took Bahadur Shah prisoner. His sons were brutally murdered by Captain William Hodson at Humayan's tomb.

He was put on trial from 29 January until 9 March. Four charges were levelled against him:

1. Aiding and abetting the mutineers.
2. Encouraging and assisting divers persons in waging war against the British Government.
3. Assuming the sovereignty of Hindustan.
4. Causing and being accessory to the murder of Christians.

He was sentenced to spend his last days in exile in Burma and died there in 1862.

His favourite wife, Zinat Mahal, accompanied him there and died in 1882.

Bahadur Shah's *Diwan,* or "Book of Odes," was written in Persian and published in Delhi. In addition to being a poet, Bahadur Shah was an excellent scholar. He wrote his poetry under the pen name "Zafar."

During the revolt he had a coin minted with the following inscription:

> Siraj-ud-Din, that hero bold,
> Adorned his triumph with this gold.

Suggested Further Readings

There are a number of works in Urdu on the life and times of Bahadur Shah. Among them:

Amir Ahmad Alavi.
    Bahadur Shah Zafar. — Lucknow : Nami Press, 1935.
    152 p. ; 24 cm.
    This is a character study of the subject.

Faruqi, Abdullah.
    Bahadur Shah Zafar ka afsana'i-gham aur hangamah-i-Dehli. — [N.p.] : Daftar Risalah Khatun-i-Mash-Riq, 1940.
    56 p. ; 20 cm.
    Bahadur Shah and his trial.

In English, sketches may be found of him in Beale's *Oriental Biographical Dictionary* and Buckland's *Dictionary of Indian Biography*.

LAKSHMIBAI, RANI OF JHANSI
(1827 or 35-1858)

Lakshmibai, Rani of Jhansi, was born in Benares. Her birth date is uncertain, but was probably 19 November of either 1835 or 1827. The augurs of her birth were propitious, for not only was she born in the holiest of cities, but astrologers foretold that she would combine the qualities of the Hindu deities: Durga (valour), Sarasvati (learning), and Lakshmi (prosperity). Her father, Moropant Tambe, was a Karhada Brahman employee of the brother of the last Maratha Peshwa.

When his employer died, Moropant moved with his wife and small daughter, called Manu, to the court of the Peshwa at Bithur, not far from Cawnpore. Manu's mother died early, and Manu grew up not as a conventional Brahman girl but as a tomboy playing with the boys at the Peshwa's court, among them were Nana Sahib of the later Cawnpore notoriety, Rao Sahib, and reputedly also Tatya Tope, guerrilla hero of the Indian Revolt of 1857. Manu at an early age consequently became an accomplished equestrienne and sword fighter, and also learned to read and write.

She was married at the usual age, just following puberty, to an older widower, the Maharaja of the small state of Jhansi. There she was given the name Lakshmibai, but felt restricted in the *zenana** under the strict supervision of her conventional husband and the palace women. However, since her father had accompanied her to Jhansi, an unusual departure from custom, she gained more freedom than she otherwise would have been allowed. She raised a women's military unit of her friends from Bithur and younger palace women and drilled them in her horsemanship and swordsmanship skills.

Lakshmibai gave birth to a son and heir who died in infancy. Her husband died not long after, in 1853, but on his deathbed he adopted a boy as heir, in accordance with the Hindu custom. Governor-General Dalhousie refused to recognize the heir and proclaimed Jhansi to have lapsed to the British paramount power. The young widow vigourously protested this action in several closely argued memorials chronicling the record of the Newalkar family's loyalty to and treaties with the British. Her protests elicited only the most perfunctory refusals by British officials.

British resumption of the state was followed by other British actions repugnant to Hindu sensibilities: lifting the ban on cow slaughter, refusing Lakshmibai the use of funds from her son Damodar's trust for his sacred thread initiation ceremony, and resuming the revenues from the two

---

*   Women's quarters.

villages that had supported temples in Jhansi. The Rani continued her spirited protests during 1854 and 1855, but to no avail.

When the Indian Revolt erupted in May 1857, all English men, women and children took refuge in the fort of Jhansi, but were enticed out and massacred by the rebels. The British, convinced that the Rani was "nursing grievances and resentments" and had ordered the killings, hoped to capture and "try" her. The British sent a two-pronged Central India Field Force from Madras and Bombay under General Sir Hugh Rose of Crimean War fame, and several other generals. This army spent several months marching towards Jhansi, and the part of central India where rebels still held out under Tatya Tope and Rao Sahib.

Meanwhile, following the outbreak at Jhansi, Lakshmibai wrote the English official in closest communication with her, W. C. Erskine, asserting that she had been helpless in preventing the rebel actions at Jhansi and that she had been forced to supply them with money, guns, and elephants. Erskine replied that she should try to restore order in Jhansi until the British could resume control there. She did take effective control of the Jhansi administration between the sepoy uprising and the arrival of General Rose's army at Jhansi in late March 1858.

As late as February and early March of 1858, Lakshmibai was still in two minds — whether to fight or make peace — as she sent letters to Robert Hamilton seeking to resume communication with the English. Her letters went unanswered.

The Central India Field Force began its siege of the Jhansi fort in late March. The Rani's army was commanded by nine generals from neighbouring Dinara and Karera and included a force of loyal *valayati** palace guards. During the siege Tatya Tope brought an army of 20,000 to rescue the Rani and Jhansi. But Rose's force turned to face Tatya Tope while not letting up its assault on the fort, and the rescuing army, composed mostly of raw recruits, turned and fled in disarray. The British enfiladed the city wall, fought in the streets of the city, and prepared to force a breach in the fort wall on the morning of 4 April. During the night, much to Rose's dismay, the Rani escaped from the fort, probably let down over the wall by rope, and rode north eastwards with a force of *valayati* and women guards.

(*Editor's note*: If you go to Jhansi, you will hear a tale that Lakshmibai on horseback, with Damodar on her back, took off from the parapet of the fort. Guides at the fort will even show you where it happened!)

Joined now by Tatya Tope, Rao Sahib and other rebels, she fought a battle against Rose at the town of Koonch, then retreated to the Kalpi fort overlooking the Jumna River, where the rebels had their ammunition cache. Again the rebel army fled after several of the Rani's guards were killed, including two women.

When the British learnt that the rebels had ridden for Gwalior, the state ruled by the staunchly loyal Scindia Maharaja, they were amazed by the

---

* Pathans.

bold rebel plan of winning over Scindia's army and ensconcing themselves in the Gwalior fort, one of the most formidable in north India.

When Rao Sahib celebrated the taking of the fort and the uniting of the rebel and Gwalior forces, Lakshmibai took him to task for wasting time "celebrating before victory" while the British advanced on Gwalior. Instead of joining in the celebrations, Lakshmibai marched to the Morar sector east of the city with several followers. There at Kota-di-serai, the access to Gwalior most difficult to defend, she fought and was killed in action by the 8th Hussars.

She thus became a martyr to the cause of independence, praised by her opponent General Rose as "the best and the bravest of the rebels." Today her legend lives on in song and ballad, in poetry, painting and sculpture her valourous deeds celebrated as though they happened yesterday.

— Joyce C. Lebra

Suggested Further Readings

Lebra-Chapman, Joyce.
   The Rani of Jhansi : a study of female heroism in India. — Honolulu : University of Hawaii Press, 1986.
   xii, 224 p. [3 p. of plates] : ill., maps ; 22 cm.

Smyth, John, Sir.
   The rebellious Rani. — London : Frederick Muller, 1966.
   223 p. : front., 8 plates, maps ; 23 cm.

Tamhankar, Dattatraya Vishvanath.
   The Rani of Jhansi. — Bombay : Jaico, 1961.
   166 p. : ill. ; 23 cm. — (Jaico books ; J-160)

NANA SAHIB
(1820?-1859?)

Nana Sahib, alias Dhundu Pant Nana, alias the Maharaja of Bithur, etc., etc., was born around 1820. The date of his birth is uncertain, but the date of his adoption by ex-Peshwa Baji Rao II was 1827.

The erstwhile Peshwa was defeated by Sir John Malcolm at the battle of Seoni 2 June 1818. In the terms of the treaty that followed, he was guaranteed an annual pension of Rs.800,000. He wanted to spend his retirement in Benares, Mathura or some other holy city, but he was given a plot of land and a palace in Bithur, a few kilometres northwest of Cawnpore.

When he died in 1851, he was survived by four adoptive children, two sons and two daughters, and Nana Sahib was the eldest of those who survived him. In the years, then, between the death of his adoptive father and the outbreak of the Revolt, Nana Sahib spent much of his time and energy attempting to persuade the English that as the legitimate heir of Baji Rao he was entitled to the pension which ceased with Baji Rao's death.

(In Hindu law, the adoptive son has the same status as the natural son. The East India Company did not see it that way.)

Nana Sahib had no luck in the courts in India; so he sent an agent, Azimullah Khan, to London to plead his case there. He did have a reasonably strong case inasmuch as the East India Company was drawing revenue from the late Peshwa's lands, using part of the revenue to pay his pension; therefore, the argument ran, the pension should be continued to his heirs as long as the Company was receiving revenue from the late Peshwa's lands. Azimullah's efforts in London failed to bear fruit.

Another source of annoyance for Nana Sahib was that he was not getting the 11-gun salute to which Baji Rao had been entitled. In fact he did not get any salute at all.

So even before the Revolt began, he and his friend Azimullah were travelling about northern India, spreading intrigue. One of his *gurus* predicted Nana Sahib "would become as powerful as the Peshwa had once been," and claimed to have had a dream in which Nana Sahib was victorious in battle.

The Revolt broke out in Meerut 10 May 1857 when 90 sepoys attacked the English as they were coming out of church* and then fled 60 kilometres south to take refuge behind the skirts of the Mughul king, Bahadur Shah II, and his court.

Cawnpore, some 300 kilometres to the southeast of Delhi, was an important military station for the English. Reports circulated that Nana Sahib appeared before the authorities there, feigning friendship and warning them of an impending mutiny on the part of the sepoys. Most authorities discount these reports today, but the feeling among a number of Englishmen at the time was that Nana Sahib was on their side.

When the mutiny reached Cawnpore, the rebels broke into the jail, released the prisoners, torched government offices and captured the magazine. They also plundered the treasury.

It is not known at which point Nana Sahib joined the rebels. That he had meetings with them prior to the outbreak in Cawnpore is a fact. However, two years later while hiding out in Nepal, he wrote to the British authorities to say that "he joined the rebels from helplessness." According to Tatya Tope's pre-execution testimony, Nana Sahib's complicity in the Cawnpore mutiny was forced on him by the mutineers.

Whatever the truth, after the initial burst of activity, the Cawnpore rebels headed for Delhi. At some point they joined Nana Sahib (or he joined them) and on 5 June, returned to Cawnpore to attack the English forces there. Before the battle started, the rabble was turned loose to plunder and kill in the city. Not only were Europeans and Indian Christians at the mercy of the mob, but wealthy Indian citizens as well.

The bombardment of the English entrenchment began 6 June. Three days later with a drum roll it was announced that the rule of the Peshwa

---

* The "Mutiny Church" still stands. In the interior one finds gun racks behind the pews — reminds, perhaps, of that fateful Sunday in 1857.

had begun. It began with a vengeance. According to Nanakchand, one of Nana Sahib's lieutenants, "the rebels murdered Goredhun, agent of the Baees ... and slew the people of his house and blew up his house with guns. The other agent Appaji ran away, and the attendants of Chimnaji Appa ... were all put to death; their hands and noses being cut off first."

On 23 June Nana Sahib decided to celebrate the centenary of the Battle of Plassey by making a general assault on the Cawnpore entrenchment. It failed. It was tried again the following day. Again it failed.

Finally, 25 June a letter from Azimullah Khan arrived which assured the British that if they would surrender, they would be granted safe passage to Allahabad. The English by this time were in no condition to continue the fight; so General Wheeler accepted the terms, which included immediate evacuation of the entrenchment.

At Sati Chaura Ghat where the British were to board boats which would take them to Allahabad, the rebels opened fire on them, and only four escaped alive to tell about it. Those who had not boarded the boats were taken back to the city.

The extent of Nana Sahib's complicity in the massacre at Sati Chaura Ghat is a mystery which may never be solved. No witness ever came forward to claim having seen him give the order to fire on the English. Later he claimed innocence. If he did give the order, he may have been forced to do so by the sepoys, whom he was supposedly at this point, leading. In his biography, *Nana Sahib and the Rising at Cawnpore*, Pratul Chandra Gupta sums it up:

> Undoubtedly Nana Sahib was very much dominated by his advisers and had hardly the power to go against the wishes of his troops, but it is difficult to see how he can be absolved of responsibility.

Havelock did not arrive in Cawnpore until 17 July, but before he got there, a group of refugees from Fatehgarh, unaware of what had been happening in Cawnpore, showed up, asking for shelter. Nana Sahib put most of the men in the group to death and the 40 or so women he confined to *bibighar** where those who had been brought from Sati Chaura Ghat were being held.

On 15 July the few men who were being confined in *bibighar* were taken out and shot. Then some men with swords entered the chamber and slaughtered the women and children confined there. Their bodies were thrown into a nearby well. Nana Sahib may not have given the order for this atrocity, but that evening he ordered a *nautch*** in his hotel headquarters and passed the evening in song and dance.

When Havelock entered Cawnpore 17 July, he discovered that Nana Sahib and his troops had courageously fled towards Bithur. Nana Sahib disappeared from view for some time and news about him came to the English only in the form of rumours.

---

*   House of the women.
**   Dance performed usually by women.

A bizarre twist occurred in the autumn of 1857 when Nana Sahib tried to elicit help from the French. He sent two emissaries to Chandernagore in an attempt to reach Napoleon III through the governor there, M. Moras. Apparently the message got through to Napoleon, but it was never answered. (The English did not learn about all this until 1859.)

Where Nana Sahib was between July 1857 and March 1858 was a mystery to the English then, and is a mystery to us today. In March he was reported in Shahjahanpur and Bareilly. Then in April he was said to be near Bithur, and later in Rohilkhand. In June the Rani of Jhansi's troops proclaimed him Peshwa, but this was meaningless because she died shortly after this, and her armies were soon defeated.

In December Nana Sahib was seen in Bahraich, and after that he crossed over into Nepal, where he was reported to have died in 1859. His life and death in Nepal has remained a mystery to this day. His last "appearance" occurred in 1895 when a crazed beggar was found in Rajkot who claimed to be Nana Sahib.

Nana Sahib was a prominent figure in the Revolt of 1857. Yet, when one studies his life, one searches in vain for accomplishments that can be attributed to him. He is not seen gallantly leading his troops in battle or carrying on guerrilla warfare with his enemy. His prominence must then be found in the symbol of revolt that he became, both in his life time and in the years following his mysterious death.

Suggested Further Readings

Gupta, Pratul Chandra.
    Nana Sahib and the rising at Cawnpore. — Oxford : Oxford University Press, 1963.
    xviii, 227 p. : ill., ports., map ; 23 cm.

Majumdar, Ramesh Chandra, 1888-1980.
    The Sepoy Mutiny and the Revolt of 1857. — Calcutta : Mukhopadhyay, 1957.
    xxiv, 289 p. : fold. map ; 22 cm.

TATYA TOPE
(1813?-1859)

Tatya Tope, whose name is sometimes spelled "Tantia Topi," was born around 1813 into an orthodox *Deshastha* Brahman family in Poona. He was given the name Ram Chandra Pandurang by his father, Pandurang Rao Tope, a noble at the court of Peshwa Baji Rao II.

After the Third Maratha War (1817-1818) when Baji Rao was pensioned off in Bithur, Pandurang Rao Tope and his family moved there to be with the ex-Peshwa. It was here that, as a child, Tatya Tope made the acquaintance of Nana Dhundu Pant, better known as Nana Sahib. He is also said to have been a childhood friend of Rao Sahib, the nephew of Nana Sahib, and a girl named Manu, who would be better known later as Rani Lakshmibai of Jhansi.

As the day of the Revolt was about to dawn, Tatya Tope, in collaboration with Nana Sahib, was busy stirring up intrigue against the English among the troops in Cawnpore. Once the sepoys mutinied at Meerut 10 May 1857, and the revolt was on in earnest, Tatya Tope established Nana Sahib's authority and became commander-in-chief of his forces.

Following the defeat of these forces by Henry Havelock at Cawnpore 16 July, Tatya Tope gathered some 4,000 troops at Bithur. There he was met by Havelock who had left Cawnpore to go to the relief of Lucknow. When Havelock heard of Tatya Tope's activity at Bithur, he turned back, met him in battle, and once again Tatya Tope was defeated.

Following this Tatya Tope was ordered by Nana Sahib to proceed to Gwalior to win over the sepoys of the Gwalior contingent. He succeeded, and with his mutinous troops captured Kalpi, a few kilometres east of Gwalior. Tatya Tope now seemed to be getting his orders from Rao Sahib who told him to capture Cawnpore. He returned north with a force 20,000 strong, defeated General Charles Ash Windham and captured the city of Cawnpore, but not the entrenchment there, in late November.

This time it was Sir Colin Campbell who was on his way to the relief of Lucknow and who turned back and utterly defeated Tatya Tope 6 December. Cawnpore was never fought over again.

On returning to Kalpi, Tatya Tope received orders from Nana Sahib to attack the Raja of Charkhari. He did so, acquiring 23 guns and Rs.300,000 from the Raja. At this point several nearby rulers joined him, and he had at his command 20,000 to 25,000 men (which he called "The Peshwa's Army").

He received an urgent appeal for help from the Rani of Jhansi who was being besieged by General Sir Hugh Rose. With 22,000 men he arrived at Jhansi 31 March, but with a force of only 1,500 men a contingent of Rose's army defeated Tatya Tope and sent him back to Kalpi. A few days later Lakshmibai escaped from the fort and met Tatya Tope at Kalpi.

Rose marched towards Kalpi and was met by the combined forces of Tatya Tope and the Rani at Koonch. He defeated them, and Tatya Tope went to the home of his parents in Chirki. Lakshmibai and the Nawab of Banda made a stand at Kalpi, but were defeated there by Rose 22 May.

Lakshmibai and Rao Sahib, whom the Rani had encountered at Kalpi, were joined in Gopalpur, about 70 kilometres southwest of Gwalior, by Tatya Tope. Here one of them, probably Lakshmibai, hatched a plot to capture Gwalior and win over the troops of Sindhia, who was loyal to the English.

They met the army of Sindhia 1 June and defeated it. They entered the fort, declared Nana Sahib Peshwa, and Rao Sahib, in an elaborate ceremony, was declared his viceroy. They virtually ignored Lakshmibai who thought they should have been preparing to battle the British rather than celebrating a victory not yet won.

Sir Hugh, who had thought the campaign in Central India was over, returned to Gwalior in mid-June, and in the battle that followed, Rani Lakshmibai fell and Tatya Tope escaped.

From then until his betrayal by his friend, Man Singh, and capture on 7 April 1859, Tatya Tope led the British on a merry chase. He engaged in guerrilla tactics, and it was at this activity that he displayed his genuine skill as a soldier and fighter.

After his capture he was tried and court-martialled 15 April on a charge of "having been in rebellion against the British Government between January 1857 and December 1858 especially at Jhansi and Gwalior."

He was hanged 15 April. On the first try the rope broke. He was strung up again, and this time he was hanged properly.

Aside from the Rani of Jhansi, Tatya Tope may have been the only rebel leader during the Revolt who had any skill as a military leader. Also, he may have been the only one besides Lakshmibai who attained anything approaching heroic stature.

Suggested Further Readings

Considering the important part that Tatya Tope played in the events in north and central India from 1857 to 1859, it is unfortunate that a really good biography of him in English does not, to the best knowledge of this writer, exist.
In Hindi there is:
Hardikar, Srinivas Balaji.
    Tatya Tope. — Delhi : National Publishing House, 1965?
    14, 258 p. : ill., pl., maps ; 19 cm.

Otherwise, one can find an excellent analysis of Tatya Tope in R.C. Majumdar's
    Sepoy Mutiny and the Revolt of 1857 and sketches of him in Buckland's *Dictionary of Indian Biography* and S.P. Sen's *Dictionary of National Biography*.
Unfortunately these outlines are rather sketchy, and not fairly accurate.

SIR HENRY HAVELOCK
(1795-1857)

Sir Henry Havelock was the son of William Havelock, shipbuilder. The family lived at Ford Hall, Monk Wearmouth, and Henry was born there 5 April 1795.

The family had moved from Monk Wearmouth around the turn of the century and settled in Ingress Hall, near Dartford, Kent. Here Henry received his early schooling at a seminary there run by a Rev. Bradley. When he was 10, he went to school at Charterhouse, and here he learned the meaning of discipline. His mother, a devout woman who brought her sons up with religious training and Bible-reading, died in 1809.

After completing his education at Charterhouse, Henry studied at the Middle Temple but left after one year. His elder brother, William, had gone off to war to fight Napoleon and was wounded at Waterloo. When he came home on sick leave, he used his influence with his general and obtained for Henry in the fall of 1815 a commission as second lieutenant in the 95th regiment, and the next year Second Lieutenant Havelock reported for duty at Shorncliffe. In 1821, he was promoted to lieutenant. Two years later he sailed for India to join the 13th Foot, arriving in Calcutta in May 1823.

The very next year war broke out between Britain and the Kingdom of Ava, and Lieutenant Havelock was sent to Rangoon. Being of a religious turn, Havelock had organised a group of men into a Bible-studying prayer group. Being men of sobriety, as opposed to many of the English soldiers who were intoxicated much of the time, "Havelock's Saints," as they were called, could always be depended upon in emergencies.

Havelock became very ill during the Burma campaign and was sent to India on sick leave for about six months. On his return to Burma in June 1825 he fought in several engagements and the next year was chosen to go to Ava to receive the ratification of the treaty which ended the First Burmese War.

The campaign over, Havelock rejoined his regiment at Dinapore and wrote his *Campaigns in Burma*. It was published in 1828 and was not a best seller.

During his service as adjutant of the depot of the king's troops in Chinsura in 1827 he made the acquaintance of two Baptist missionaries in Serampore: Dr. William Carey and Rev. Joshua Marshman. He fell in love with Rev. Marshman's daughter, Hannah, married her 9 February 1829 and joined the Baptist congregation. Hannah's brother, John Clark Marshman, would later be a biographer of Havelock.

In 1838, after years of yearning for it, Havelock received his captaincy and was appointed aide-de camp to Sir Willoughby Cotton at the outbreak of the First Afghan War. Captain Havelock was in the march to Kandahar and later to Ghazni and was present at the blowing up of the Kabul Gate.

After the occupation of Kabul, Sir Willoughby was put in command of the army of occupation and wanted Havelock to remain as his aide-de-camp. Havelock had other ideas. He had been taking careful notes during the campaign and was anxious to get into print with another book; so he declined the offer and returned to Serampore where he wrote his *Narrative of the War in Afghanistan.*

By 1841 Captain Havelock was back in Afghanistan, serving under General William Elphinstone. He served with distinction, and when he retired from Afghanistan in 1842, he received three medals and a promotion to brevet-major.

Major Havelock spent a few years in Cawnpore as Persian interpreter to the commander-in-chief, Sir Hugh Gough. He served with Sir Hugh in the First Anglo-Sikh War (1845-46) and in the year that followed, was made adjutant-general of queen's troops in Bombay by the Duke of Wellington.

In 1849, his health was failing, and he was given home leave which he spent in Plymouth. On his return in 1851, he took up his old post in Bombay, and in 1854 he was appointed quarter-master-general of the queen's troops in India. Later in the year he obtained his lieutenant-colonelcy and brevet-colonelcy, and when a vacancy occurred for the post of adjutant-general of the queen's troops in India, he was awarded that appointment.

When war broke out between England and Persia 1 November 1856, Colonel Havelock served under General Sir James Outram in the Persian Gulf. He directed the attack on Mohumra. It succeeded 5 April 1857, after which the English learned that a treaty between England and Persia was signed 4 March.

By the time Havelock reached Bombay 15 May, word was received of mutinies in Meerut, Ferozepore and Delhi. The only way Havelock could reach the scene of fighting from Bombay was via Ceylon and Calcutta. He reached Calcutta 17 June and was immediately despatched to Cawnpore to relieve General Sir Hugh Wheeler there. He met resistance along the way at Futtehpore and Aong, reaching the outskirts of Cawnpore 16 July. He had to fight his way in and arrived a day late. Over 200 English, mostly women and children had been slaughtered either by Nana Sahib or his sepoys and their bodies thrown into a well.

He left a small garrison at Cawnpore and advanced towards Lucknow to relieve the Residency there. Once again his efforts to relieve a beleaguered stronghold were thwarted by a series of skirmishes. On 16 August he fought an important battle at Bithur against Tatya Tope and utterly defeated him.

He relieved Lucknow in September, in the culmination of a brilliant career. It might be said of him that he saved the Indian people from their rebels.

He became ill shortly after the relief of Lucknow and died at Dilkusha 24 November 1857 with his son and aide-de-camp, Henry at his side. General Sir Henry Havelock's last words were:

See how a Christian dies.

Suggested Further Readings

Cooper, Leonard.
Havelock. — London : The Bodley Head, [1957]
192 p. : front. port., maps ; 22 cm.

Marshman, John Clark.
Memoirs of Major-General Sir Henry Havelock. — 2d ed. — London : Longman, Green, Longman, Roberts, 1861.
x, 462 p. : front. port., 2 fold maps, plan ; 23 cm.

SIR HENRY MONTGOMERY LAWRENCE
(1806-1857)

Henry Montgomery Lawrence was the fourth son of Colonel Alexander William Lawrence who had emigrated from Northern Ireland and served in the British Navy in the American Revolutionary War. When it was over, he was discharged and sailed as a 16-year-old volunteer in the 36th Hereforshire Regiment for Madras, arriving there in 1783. He saw most of his service in south India and Ceylon. He was at Seringapatam when Tipu Sultan fought his last battle. In 1798, he married Letitia Catherine Knox, and they had 12 children. Henry was born in Matura, Ceylon, 18 June 1806.

The Lawrence family was a distinguished one. In addition to Henry, who would later be remembered as *Lawrence of Lucknow*, there were Sir George St. Patrick Lawrence who served in north India and Afghanistan and wrote *Forty-Three Years in India*, Richard Lawrence who became the British resident in Nepal and Lord Lawrence, governor-general and vice-roy of India (1864-1869).

The family moved to Ulster when Henry was two years old, and in 1815 he and his brothers enrolled at Foyle College. After Foyle, Henry spent a year at College Green School in Bristol, and in 1820 enrolled in the East India Company's military college at Addiscombe. While there he did well at fortification, military drawing, mathematics and Hindustani.

He graduated in 1822, and the next year he found himself in India in the Bengal Artillery, stationed at a camp at Dum-Dum near Calcutta. His first military action was as a subaltern at Arakan in the First Burmese War (1824-26). During the campaign he contracted "Arakan Fever" (malaria), which would stay with him all his life. A first lieutenant now, he was "invalided home" and while there joined the Trigonometrical Survey of Ireland.

He returned to India in 1830 and the following year was transferred to the Horse Artillery. In 1833, having qualified himself in Hindi, Urdu and Persian, he was appointed assistant revenue surveyor in the Survey Department of the North-Western Provinces (later United Provinces, still later, Uttar Pradesh).

He worked in this capacity five and a half years, and during this time he married Honoria Marshall, a distant cousin of his and the daughter of a Rev. George Marshall 21 August 1837.

In 1839, he was appointed assistant to the political agent at Ludhiana, and from 1840 to 1842 served, after being promoted to the rank of captain, as assistant to the A.G.G.* for the North-West Frontier, first at Ferozepore and later at Peshawar and in Afghanistan. It was during this period that Henry and Honoria Lawrence collaborated on their novel *Adventures of an Officer in the Service of Runjeet Singh*. They wrote it in serial chapters for the Delhi Gazette.

Captain Lawrence led a Sikh regiment to Kabul in 1842 as part of General Sir George Pollock's Army of Retribution, and after the Afghan War he was appointed Resident in Nepal. He served there two years (1843-45), and when the First Anglo-Sikh War (1845-46) broke out, he was appointed A.G.G. for the Punjab, and in 1846 Agent and later Resident in Lahore.

---

*   Agent of the governor-general.

After the treaty which ended the First Anglo-Sikh War 16 December 1846 was signed, Lawrence reorganised district administration, made judicial appointments and prepared a code which forbade infanticide, *sati,* and forced labour.

In 1848, he went home on leave, was knighted and returned in time for the Second Anglo-Sikh War. He took part in it and was present at the siege of Multan in January 1849. Lord Dalhousie had become governor-general in 1848, and following the war, he annexed the Punjab. Sir Henry was appointed A.G.G. for the Punjab and president of the board of administration, a position he held until 1852 when he resigned over differences with his brother, John, and Lord Dalhousie, and the board broke up. Years later, Sir Henry wrote regarding his leaving the Punjab:

> But ever since I was so cavalierly elbowed out of the Punjab, I have fretted over my health.

In January 1853 he took up his duties as A.G.G. in Rajputana and served there until 1857 when he was called upon by Lord Canning to be Chief Commissioner and A.G.G. in Oudh.

He arrived in Lucknow and assumed his duties 20 March. He proved in letters to Canning that he was aware of weaknesses in the British military system in India. There were not enough European officers, and the senior officers that were there were senile. Also, no incentives were offered to sepoys who might have the ambition and ability to rise in the ranks.

He was also aware of dissatisfaction among the sepoys over the business of greasing the cartridges.

Once the trouble started in Meerut 10 May, he prepared the Residency in Lucknow for the fate that he knew lay in store for it. The siege began in June, and it would last six months.

Sir Henry did not live to see it end. He was wounded 2 July, and died 4 July. Before dying, he wrote his own epitaph:

> Here lies Henry Lawrence, who tried to do his duty.

After his death high tribute was paid to him. Sir Robert Montgomery wrote that it was "Henry Lawrence's foresight, humanly speaking, that saved *every one of the garrison.* But for him I do not believe that one would have escaped."

His biographer had even higher praise:

> It is just possible that, with Sir Henry Lawrence as Chief Commissioner when Oudh was annexed, the risings of 1857, might have been, if not avoided, at least reduced to manageable proportions.

Suggested Further Readings

Morison, John L.
Lawrence of Lucknow 1806-1857; being the life of Sir Henry Lawrence retold from his
private and public papers. — London : G. Bell, 1934.
viii, 348 p. : ports., maps ; 23 cm.

Innes, James John McLeod.
Sir Henry Lawrence : the pacification. — Oxford : Clarendon, 1898.
208 p. : front. port., fold. map ; 20 cm.

JAMES GEORGE SCOTT NEILL
(1810-1857)

"He died young," they said afterwards, "but not too young for his
fame." But others might have said, "Nor too young for his infamy."

James George Scott Neill, the eldest son of Colonel Neill of Burnweill
and Swendridge Muir, Ayrshire, was born 27 May 1810 in the vicinity of
Ayr. He received his education in Ayr and at the University of Glasgow.

He arrived in India at the age of 17 with an army cadetship in the service of the East India Company and was posted to the Madras First European Regiment stationed at Machlipatnam. He rose steadily in the ranks,
and in 1837 Lieutenant Neill went home on furlough.

Anxious to get into the First Afghan War, he broke his furlough early,
returning to Madras 15 July 1839. He failed to make it, but in 1841 he was
appointed to the general staff as assistant adjutant general in the ceded
districts and in 1843 published his one and only book, *Historical Records of
the Madras European Regiment.*

By the time the Second Burmese War broke out in 1852, Lieutenant
Neill had become Captain and, later, Major Neill. He was ordered to the
seat of the war. He did well there, and after it was over, he stayed on and
put down several insurrections. This activity was injurious to his health; so
in 1854 he was sent home to recover.

At the outbreak of the Crimean War, Colonel Neill was put in charge of
an unruly Turkish regiment which he soon brought under control with strict
and severe discipline. When the war was over, he returned home, but in
February 1857 he left for India and arrived in March in good time for the
Revolt which was about to occur — and about to make his reputation.

News of the mutinies in north India reached Madras 16 May, and by
the 23rd Neill and his Madras regiment were in Calcutta. Their first objective was Benares where the sepoys were restless. The day after he got there
they mutinied. He brought order out of chaos quickly. He took over in place
of Brigadier-General Ponsonby who was suffering from sunstroke. Because
of the speed with which he restored order in Benares, Neill was promoted
to brigadier-general and ordered to Allahabad where the 6th Native Infantry Regiment had mutinied on 5 June.

The methods which Neill had used in Benares received this assessment from T.R. Holmes:

> Old men who had done us no harm, helpless women with infants at their breasts, felt the weight of our vengeance.

Sir John William Kaye, another historian of the Revolt, added horror stories of his own:

> Already our military officers were hunting down criminals of all kinds and hanging them up with as little compunction as though they had been pariah dogs or jackals or vermin of a baser kind. Volunteer hanging parties went out into the districts, and amateur executioners were not wanting to the occasion. One gentleman boasted of the numbers he had finished off quite in an artistic manner, with mango-trees for gibbets and elephants for drops, the victims of this wild justice being strung up as though for pastime, in the form of the figure eight.

Word of Neill's atrocities reached the rebels at Cawnpore and may have inflamed the passions which led them to commit equally savage atrocities on innocent people there.

Brigadier-General Neill despatched 50 men to Allahabad immediately and soon followed with more troops, and with the help of both Europeans and Sikhs he had the situation under control and was prepared to march to the relief of Cawnpore.

Neill arrived in Cawnpore too late to save the men, women and children who perished at Sati Chaura Ghat and *Bibighar**.

Let Neill tell it in his own words:

> Whenever a rebel is caught he is immediately tried; and, unless he can prove a defence, he is sentenced to be hanged at once: but the chief rebels, or ring leaders, I make first clean up a certain portion of the pool of blood still two inches thick, in the shed [*Bibighar*] where the fearful murder and mutilation of women and children took place. To touch blood is most abhorrent to the high-caste natives; they think, by doing so, they doom their souls to perdition. Let them think so. My object is to inflict a fearful punishment for a revolting, cowardly, barbarous deed, and to strike terror into these rebels.

It is not necessary here to reveal additional examples of Neill's justice. Suffice it to say that Neill did not believe that punishment in this world was adequate. If a Hindu was hanged, he was buried; if a Muslim was hanged, he was cremated.

After civilizing Cawnpore, Neill hastened to the relief of Lucknow. As he and his troops were approaching the Residency 25 September, Neill was shot and killed.

---

* House of the women. Sati Chaura Ghat and *Bibighar* are discussed in grizzly detail in the Nana Sahib sketch.

A bronze statue of him stood on Mount Road in Madras until recently when some patriots persuaded the city to remove it. It was removed to the Conamara Museum. Another statue stands tall in Wellington Square in Ayr, Scotland.

In the basement of the Aryshire Historical Society is a Burmese bell gathering dust. It was sent by Neill to the Society after the Second Burma War. No one knows what to do with it.

Neill has not always gotten good press, even from English writers. The Rev. Fitchett in his *Tale of the Great Mutiny* thought his conduct "un-English."

He was a church-going, God-and-queen-loving soldier. He was a violent man living in a violent time.

Suggested Further Readings

A full-fledged biography of Neill may be hard to come by. However, you can find out more than you ever wanted to know about him by looking him up in S.N. Sen's *Eighteen Fifty-Seven* or R.C. Majumdar's *The Sepoy Mutiny and the Revolt of 1857*. Biographical sketches of him appear in the *Dictionary of National Biography* and Buckland's *Dictionary of Indian Biography*.

JOHN NICHOLSON
(1821-1857)

John Nicholson was the eldest son of Dr. Alexander Nicholson, a physician of Dublin. He was born in Dublin 11 December 1821.* Dr. Nicholson died in 1830, and the widow, with her two daughters and five sons, moved to Lisburn, County Wicklow, to stay with her mother.

John attended college at Dungannon, after which his uncle, Sir James Weir Hogg, obtained for him a cadetship in the Bengal Infantry. He was commissioned as ensign 24 February 1839, sailed for India and arrived the following July. He was stationed in Benares with the 41st Native Infantry, but in December of that year was transferred to the 27th Native Infantry in Ferozepore on the Sutlej River.

The First Afghan War had begun, and Nicholson in October 1840 went with the 27th to Jalalabad, Kabul and Ghazni. In Ghazni the garrison was besieged by Afghan troops and, greatly outnumbered, forced to surrender. The British troops were promised safe conduct to the Punjab border and were put in quarters in the city of Ghazni near the citadel, but the Afghans attacked the *kafir feringhis.*** Nicholson, and a fellow-lieutenant managed to escape by digging a tunnel with bayonets, but were soon captured again

---

* Some authorities give his birth date as 1822. There appears to be no disagreement, however, about 11 December.
** Infidel foreigners.

and in August 1842 taken to Kabul. They were finally rescued by a force sent by General George Pollock.

On his return to India in May 1843 Lieutenant Nicholson was made adjutant of his regiment, and in 1845 he passed the interpreters' examination. In this capacity he saw action in the First Anglo-Sikh War in the campaign of the Sutlej and at the battle of Feroze Shah.

After the war, he and a companion, Captain Broome of the artillery, were sent by Sir Henry Lawrence, to instruct the troops of the Maharaja of Kashmir.

In 1846, he was appointed assistant resident at Lahore, and in that post he put down rebellions in Multan and Attock. By the time the Second Anglo-Sikh War started, Nicholson had been promoted to captain. He distinguished himself at Chilianwala and Gujrat. He was promoted to brevet-major in 1849, and in December 1849 took a two-year furlough during which he studied the military systems of the countries of Europe.

When he returned to the Punjab, Sir Henry Lawrence, now president of the administrative board for the Punjab, appointed Major Nicholson assistant commissioner. He was promoted to brevet-colonel and served five years at Bannu with such distinction that Lord Dalhousie called him a "Tower of Strength." He so impressed the people under his charge that they came to regard him as a demi-god. In fact, a number of *faqirs* called him "Nikkul Seyn" and themselves Nikkul Seynis and would fall at his feet and worship him whenever they saw him. Nicholson tried unsuccessfully to put an end to this form of adoration.

On the outbreak of the Revolt of 1857, Nicholson was deputy-commissioner of the Punjab at Peshawar. Mutinies were breaking out in Nawshahra and Mardan, and he put them down. When General Neville Chamberlain was appointed adjutant-general of the army at Delhi, Nicholson succeeded him 22 June at the rank of brigadier-general and commander of the Punjab movable column.

He learned that troops were in mutiny in Jhelum and Sialkot, and he put these down, also. Then, 21 July he received orders to march on Delhi. On the way to Delhi he fought a brilliant battle at Najafgarh which won the praise of Lord Lawrence. He arrived at the walls of the city in August, and before the next month was over, Delhi had been recaptured. The area between the Ridge where the British were positioned and Kashmiri Gate where the breach in the walled city was made, is called *Tees Hazari* (meaning 30,000) because 30,000 men died there during the siege of Delhi. Once inside Delhi, Nicholson was shot in the chest.

He lingered for nine days and died 23 September. He was buried in a cemetery not far from the Kashmiri Gate. His mortal remains are still there, and the cemetery, now rather badly kept up, is named after him.

Nicholson exemplified the kind of administrative ability and military skill the British were able to tap during the Revolt of 1857. He was one of the several outstanding men who won the day for the East India Company.

If the other side could have had leaders with comparable training and leadership, the result might have been different.

During the Revolt, many folk songs were song, praising the rebel side and cursing the *feringhi* side. The Rani of Jhansi was the subject of many of these.

This is a translation of a portion of a Punjabi song in which Nikkul Seyn is the subject:

> Oh, Brother! See the English charge, the Chandni Chauk is won,
> In the Red Fort of the kings their bloody work is done.
> The quaking Natives hear the tale and curse their losing fate.
>
> Now magic peace the conquerors bring where carnage reigned so late,
> While merchants vend again their goods 'neath British arms secure,
> The warriors lay aside their hate to feed the needy poor.
> Oh, Lion-hearted Nikkul Seyn! Couldst thou but live once more,
> We'd slay, and leave each Native dog to welter in his gore!

Suggested Further Readings

Pearson, Hesketh.
> The hero of Delhi : a life of John Nicholson, savior of India and a history of his times.
> — London : Collins, 1948.
> 293 p. : front., ill., port., map ; 23 cm.

Trotter, Lionel J.
> The life of John Nicholson, soldier and administrator, based on private and hitherto
> unpublished documents. — London : John Murray, 1908.
> x, 333 p. : ports., fold. maps ; 22 cm.

CHAPTER 8

THE VICEROYS &
GOVERNORS-GENERAL

The Governors-General	The Viceroys
Hastings (1772-1785)	Canning (1856-1862)
Wellesley (1798-1805)	Lawrence (1863-1869)
Bentinck (1828-1835)	Curzon (1899-1905)
Dalhousie (1848-1856)	Mountbatten (1947)

$\mathcal{D}$uring almost 200 years that England was the "Paramount Power" in India, there were 14 governors-general and 20 viceroys. Technically, Clive was neither a governor-general nor a viceroy. He served two terms as governor of Bengal (1758-1760 and 1765-1767), and he is often included in the ranks of those who served as governors-general or viceroys between 1757 and 1947.

However, we have a Chapter which deals with the eighteenth century, and when one considers Clive's place in the events and personalities of eighteenth century India, that is where he belongs.

Warren Hastings, on the other hand, was governor of Bengal from 1772 to 1774 and stayed on to be the first governor-general of Bengal (1774-1785). Cornwallis was governor-general twice (1786-1793 and 1805), and Bentinck, with the renewal of the East India Charter in 1833, became the first governor-general of India. Canning was a governor-general for two years (1856-1858) and, after the abolition of the East India Company, viceroy for four (1858-1862). Mountbatten, after being viceroy from March to August in 1947, stayed on as governor-general of the Dominion of India until June 1948.

Only three viceroys could be said to have been knowledgeable about India in a personal way prior to their appointments: Lord Lawrence, who had first served as chief commissioner of the Punjab, and Lord Curzon who had travelled to India and made a serious study of the country, and Lord Mountbatten who served from time to time in New Delhi during World War II.

Suggested Further Readings

Bence-Jones, Mark.
  The viceroys of India. — London : Constable, 1982.
  xviii, 343 p. : ill. ; 25 cm.

Mersey, Clive Bigham, 2d vscount, 1872-1956.
  The viceroys and governors-general of India, 1757-1947. — London : Murray, 1949.
  179 p. : front., ports., map (on lining paper) ; 22 cm.

Morris, Henry.
  The governors-general of British India. — Delhi : Discovery Publishing House, 1984.
  2 v. ; 23 cm.
  Reprint. First published in 1907.

WARREN HASTINGS
(1732-1818)

Warren Hastings was the first governor-general of Bengal. He was governor from 1772 to 1774 and then governor-general from 1774 to 1785, at which time he went home to face the longest impeachment trial in history.

He was born in Churchill, Oxfordshire, 6 December or 18 December (depending on whether one is using the Julian or the Gregorian calendar) 1732. In later years Edmund Burke will refer to him as being of "low, obscure and vulgar origin," but Hastings could trace his ancestry back to a Lord Hastings who performed loyal services for Richard III. Lord Hastings' successor was granted the Earldom of Huntington by Henry VII.

However, the family was visited with bad times, and by 1715 the family estate was gone. Warren's great-grandfather, Samuel Hastings, was a Bristol merchant. His son, Pynaston, was rector of a small parish. He had a son, also named Pynaston, who in 1730 at the age of 15 married a farmer's daughter from Gloucestershire named Hester Warren. Hester died shortly after the birth of little Warren, her second child. The young widower soon disappeared, and the care of Warren and his brother was left to his paternal grandfather, who took a curacy in Churchill.

Warren's early education took place in a village school in Churchill, and when he was eight, his uncle, Howard Hastings, transferred him to a school at Newington-Butts near London. After a time he was transferred again, this time to Westminster where his school chums included Elijah Impey, William Petty Fitzmaurice (later Lord Shelburne), William Cowper and Edward Gibbon.

In 1749, his Uncle Howard died, and Warren was taken out of school by a distant relative, Joseph Creswicke, and nominated for a writership with the East India Company. He sailed for India in January and arrived in Calcutta 9 October 1750.

After three years, in October 1753, Hastings was transferred to Kasimbazar where there was an English factory, and two years later he was made a member of the local council.

When war broke out between Siraj-ud-Daulah, the Nawab of Bengal, and the English in 1756, Hastings was taken prisoner after the fall of Calcutta in June, but was soon released. He joined the other English refugees at Fulta, and when the war was over, following the battle of Plassey, Clive appointed Hastings resident at the court of the new Nawab, Mir Jafar, at Murshidabad. Hastings had just married the widow of a Captain Buchanan, a daughter of C.F. Scott. There were two children by this marriage, but both children and Mrs. Hastings died a few years later.

Hastings was appointed to the council in Calcutta in 1761, and was given the task of arranging terms with the new Nawab for the English factory at Patna. He was not successful, but he drafted some proposals for regulating trade with the new Nawab Mir Kasim, which Mir Kasim accepted, but the council did not accept. Finally, in 1764, Hastings resigned in disgust and went home. Unlike many of his colleagues, he did not take enough money home with him.

While in England Hastings continued his interest in India. He was keen to set up a training school for future East India Company employees and to establish a Persian scholarship at Oxford. He succeeded at neither, but 40 years later Haileybury was founded.

By 1768 Hastings was out of money and out looking for work. He was appointed second-in-council in Madras and took up his post there in 1769. In order to get there, he had to borrow passage money. On board ship he met a German portrait painter, Baron von Imhoff, who was travelling with his wife. Hastings became ill during the voyage, and the Baroness nursed him back to health, during the process of which the two fell in love.

When, in 1772, Hastings was appointed governor of Bengal, the Baroness followed him. Then, in 1777, the Baron obtained a divorce from his wife, and Hastings and the Baroness were married. The situation was stated with typical British understatement by one of Hastings' biographers, Viscount Mersey:

His social position did not suffer in any way from this marriage.

The Calcutta that greeted Hastings in 1772 was at peace, but the financial structure of the East India Company was in a sorry state. Corruption was rampant and spreading. In order to put an end to this, Hastings instituted a system whereby Indian officials would collect revenue under the supervision of English officers. This caused disaffection among those who had profited by the old system, and it brought in less revenue to the Company.

In 1773, Lord North's Regulating Act was passed by which the British possessions in India would be administered by a governor-general with a small council, and in 1774 Hastings was appointed the first governor-general of India.

Hastings' old school chum, Elijah Impey, was appointed chief justice of the new supreme court, but most of the council opposed Hastings, particularly Sir Philip Francis, and often thwarted his efforts at administration. Sir Philip was later described as "a man prone to the error of mistaking his malevolence for public virtue."

Once in control of the council following the death of one of his chief opponents, Hastings pursued a vigorous foreign policy of eliminating French influence in India, and reducing the power of the Indian states.

His generals defeated the Maratha princes, Sindhia and Holkar, and occupied Gwalior and Gujarat. Through diplomacy Hastings was able to neutralise the Nizam of Hyderabad.

Due to incompetent management on the part of the government of Madras, Mysore had risen in power under the leadership of Haidar Ali and his son Tipu Sultan. Hastings suspended the governor of Madras and sent Sir Eyre Coote south to lead the fight against Mysore. Peace was finally restored in 1784 by the Treaty of Mangalore.

Meanwhile, back in Calcutta. Hastings' arch enemy, Nanda Kumar, a wealthy Calcutta merchant, brought false charges of bribery against him. Eventually, Nanda Kumar was himself put on trial, convicted and executed.

Hastings founded the Asiatic Society of Bengal in 1784, and laid the foundation for the Indian Civil Service.

In 1785, Hastings returned to England and in 1787 impeachment proceedings were started against him by the House of Commons. He had been preceded by Sir Philip who stirred up Parliament against him. His trial lasted from 1788 until 1795. He was acquitted on all charges, including his severe treatment of Raja Chait Singh of Benares and his conduct of the Rohilla War.

In 1806, Hastings was offered a peerage by the prince regent, but he refused to accept it unless his impeachment was revoked. The government would not revoke it.

Warren Hastings died 22 August 1818 at Daylesford, the old family estate which he had bought back. To some extent he saw himself vindicated for the work he had done in India.

In 1813, when he appeared in the House of Commons to speak on the renewal of the Company charter, the entire House gave him a standing ovation. In the words of Viscount Mersey:

> He it was who really founded the British system of administration and finance in the Indian Empire.

Suggested Further Readings

Glieg, George Robert, 1796-1885.
	Memoirs of the life of the Right Hon. Warren Hastings. — London : Bentley, 1841.
	3 v. ; 22 cm.

Trotter, Lionel James, 1827-1912.
	Warren Hastings. — Delhi, etc. : S. Chand, [1962]
	179p. ; 19 cm. — (Rulers of India ; v. 7)
	First Indian reprint.

RICHARD COLLEY WELLESLEY,
MARQUESS & 2nd EARL OF MORNINGTON
(1760-1842)

Richard Colley Wellesley was the eldest son of Garrett Wesley, 1st Earl of Mornington. In 1789, he changed his surname to Wellesley. He was born at Dangan Castle, County Meath, Ireland 20 June 1760. His mother was Anne Hill-Trevor, the daughter of Viscount Dungannon. In later life when her sons, Richard Colley and Arthur (later Duke of Wellington), became famous, she used to say she was the mother of the Gracchi.

Richard came from a talented family. The father was a musician, and four of the six brothers became peers. The family was related to Samuel and John Wesley, the founders of Methodism.

Richard went to school at Trim and later at Harrow, where he got in trouble for helping to bar out the headmaster. He then went to Eton where he showed great proficiency in the classics and poetry. It is said that when he recited Stratford's speech at the Speeches in 1777, he gave it with such feeling that he made King George III weep. The speech even got plaudits from David Garrick, the famous actor.

At Christ Church, Oxford, he won the Chancellor's prize for Latin verse. His father died before he could complete his studies at Christ Church; so he dropped out and went to Ireland to settle the family estate.

Now, as Lord Mornington, he took a seat in the Irish House of Peers, and in 1784 he was elected to the House of Commons, representing in turn Bere Alston, Saltash, Windsor and Old Sarum until 1796. In the House of Commons he became acquainted with William Grenville and Grenville's cousin, the younger Pitt. He was made lord of the treasury in 1786 and appointed to the board of control in 1793.

In 1794, he married his mistress, Mlle. Hyacynthe Gabrielle, the daughter of Pierre Roland whom he had met at the salon of Madame de Genlis in Paris.

Lord Cornwallis, who had served as governor-general in India from 1786 to 1793, had come home, and the talk was that he would be returning for another term on the retirement of Lord Tiegnmouth. Wellesley, as he was now called, was appointed governor of Madras in 1797 with the proviso that he would take the governor-generalship if Cornwallis did not return.

Cornwallis took over as lord-lieutenant of Ireland; so Wellesley became governor-general, arriving in Calcutta early in 1798. While at the Cape of Good Hope he had the good fortune to meet Lord Macartney, who had been governor of Madras, and several other Englishmen who had just been in India and could acquaint him with the situation he would encounter on his arrival there.

The situation he encountered was that Tipu Sultan was causing trouble in Mysore, the Nizam of Hyderabad harboured a number of French advisers, and the Marathas were known to be in league with the French.

Wellesley saw it as his duty to rid India of French influence inasmuch as the English on the continent were having enough trouble with Napoleon. The first thing Wellesley did was to neutralize the Nizam by signing a treaty with him which compelled him to dismiss his French advisers and use only English advisers.

With Hyderabad neutralised, Wellesley was free to address the crisis in Mysore. He knew that Tipu Sultan was courting the French because of known correspondence between him and Governor Malartie of Mauritius. A proclamation, dated January 1798, was published in a Calcutta newspaper the following June. It called for French volunteers to fight along side of Tipu Sultan to drive *"les goddamns,"* as the English were called, out of India.

Wellesley entered into correspondence with Tipu in the hope of reaching an accommodation short of war, but at the same time preparing for war. Finally, he despatched armies from both Bombay (under General Stewart) and Madras (under General Harris). They converged on Mysore. Tipu Sultan was defeated and killed at his stronghold of Seringapatam 4 May 1799.

After Tipu's defeat, a Hindu Raja was put on the throne of Mysore, and Tipu's territories were divided up among Hyderabad, the Marathas and the English, the English getting Malabar. He could now turn his attention to three powerful Maratha chiefs: Scindia of Gwalior, Holkar of Indore and the Peshwa of Poona.

He first signed a treaty with the Nawab of Oudh, after which he made war on the Maratha chiefs, defeating them at Assaye, Argaum, Delhi and Laswari; however, the cost of the war was more than the court of directors could appreciate, and he was recalled in 1805. He was even threatened with impeachment.

The remaining years of his life were not happy ones. He was separated from his wife, who had not accompanied him to India, and his friend William Pitt was dying.

He had been made a marquess after the fall of Seringapatam, and following his India service he took several posts. He was ambassador to Spain in 1809 and later became foreign secretary. However, he did not get on with the cabinet. In 1821, he accepted the lord-lieutenancy of Ireland, but did not fare well in that post, though he kept it until 1827.

His wife, from whom he had been separated, died in 1816, and in 1825 he married Mrs. Marianne Patterson, the wealthy daughter of Richard Caton of Baltimore.

In his last years Wellesley suffered from hallucinations and mental distress. He wanted to be made Duke of Hindustan, a title that would equal that of his illustrious brother, the Duke of Wellington. He died at Knightsbridge 26 September 1842.

His biographer, Sir William Wilson Hunter, said of him:

It is ill comparing the trophies of heroes; but if it was Clive who won and Hastings who preserved the English foothold in the great peninsula, it was Wellesley incontestably who founded the British Empire in the East. He found the East India Company a trading body: he left it, almost in spite of itself, the mightiest power in the land.

Suggested Further Reading

Hunter, William Wilson, Sir, 1840-1900.
  The Marquess Wellesley, K.G. — Oxford : Clarendon, 1894.
  219 p. : ill., front. port., fold. map ; 20 cm. — (Rulers of India ; v. 11)

LORD WILLIAM CAVENDISH BENTINCK
(1774-1839)

Lord William Cavendish Bentinck's governor-generalship of India (1828-1835) was a period of peace, but he himself had a checkered career. The second son of William Henry, 3rd Duke of Portland, and Lady Dorothy Cavendish, daughter of the 4th Duke of Devonshire, he was born 14 September 1774. Both his father and his maternal grandfather were ministers of England.

In 1791, at the age of 17, William was gazetted an ensign in the Coldstream Guards, and the following year became a captain in the 2nd Light Dragoons. Two years later he was promoted to lieutenant-colonel in the 24th Light Dragoons and served as aide-de-camp to the Duke of York in Flanders in the not too memorable campaign of 1794.

In 1796, he was elected M.P. for Camelford, but he later exchanged it for Nottinghamshire. In 1799, he was back in the field, seeing action in Switzerland, northern Italy and Egypt. He was present at the battle of Marengo where Napoleon won a decisive victory.

Shortly after the Treaty of Amiens which brought a brief period of peace to Europe, Bentinck returned to England and 19 February 1803 married Lady Mary Acheson, the daughter of the 1st Earl of Gosford.

Three months later he was nominated by the East India Company to the governorship of Madras. At this time it was feared that Napoleon might have designs on India; so the British needed a man of military experience on the Coromandel Coast. (Goa had been occupied by the British in 1799 to protect the Malabar Coast.)

By the time of Lord Bentinck's arrival at Fort St. George in Madras, the British power was concentrated in Calcutta in the Ganges Delta. Lord Wellesley was governor-general then, and military operations were concentrated mainly in the Deccan and central India against the Marathas. Thus, the problems of Madras were local ones requiring peaceful solutions, that is, until the Vellore mutiny in 1806.

Bentinck opposed the *zamindari* system which prevailed in Bengal and preferred the system of *ryot*, or peasant cultivators, which his subordinates recommended.

His administration of Madras came to an abrupt close when sepoys at Vellore mutinied because their British officers forbade them to wear beards, turbans and caste marks when in uniform. It was believed that members of Tipu Sultan's family who were interned in Vellore were responsible for instigating the mutiny.

Whatever the cause, Bentinck was held responsible for it, and called home in 1807, an action he understandably resented.

On his return to England, as a major-general, Bentinck was sent to fight in the Peninsular War, serving in both Portugal and Spain, and ultimately as a lieutenant-general over a division under Sir Arthur Wellesley (later Duke of Wellington).

Bentinck continued to serve in the battles against Napoleon, even though Wellington was not impressed with his military prowess, despite the G.C.B. and other decorations he had won.

His fighting days over, Bentinck retired to Rome where he was unemployed for over a decade. His name kept coming up as a possibility for service in India, but the feeling at the India Office was that he was too young and impetuous. Finally, in 1827, Prime Minister George Canning appointed him governor-general of Bengal to succeed Lord Amherst.

When Lord Bentinck took up his duties in Calcutta 4 July 1828, his concerns were economic rather than military. The First Burmese War (1824) had drained the treasury, and the expenditures exceeded the revenue by over a crore (10,000,000) of rupees or 1,000,000 sterling. The instructions from the court of directors was quite vague, except in the matter of *bhatha*, or extra pay for the Company's Indian servants. Originally, this was sort of an incentive payment which the servant received on the basis of exceptional performance or hard duty. However, over the years it came to be expected as part of the income, and many servants claimed they could not subsist without it.

Bentinck was forced to cut it to half, which resulted in a great deal of wailing and gnashing of teeth on the part of Company servants who felt their very livelihood was being taken away.

Another action of Bentinck which did not gain favour with the populace was his edict forbidding *sati*, the practise whereby the grieving widow throws her body on the funeral pyre of her dear departed husband. This was looked upon as evidence that the East India Company was planning to Christianise India.

In finance Bentinck reduced expenditure while increasing revenue from unassessed lands and slapping a tax on opium. As for the civil service, Bentinck admitted many "natives" (as they were called then) to government posts, and in civil liberties he initiated freedom of the press. He concluded treaties with the Amirs of the Punjab and of Sind, and he took over the administration of Mysore and Coorg. His educational reforms included making English the official language of India, thereby making it possible for educated people to talk to each other. The influence of this act is fully evident to this day.

By 1834 his health was failing; so he returned to England the following year in March. He was elected an M.P. from Glasgow, but was not politically active. He refused a peerage, and died in Paris 17 June 1839.

In 1892, his biographer, D.C. Boulder, summed up his career:

> The part of his life-work which will endure was performed in India, and although to him fell less of the pomp and circumstance of war which has formed so prominent a feature of our history in that country, and more of the unattractive internal reform, he can never be excluded from the list of eminent rulers who made India a British possession, and who have kept it so, as much by the tacit assent of the subject population as by superior force.

Suggested Further Reading

Boulger, Demetrius C.
  Lord William Bentinck. — Oxford : Clarendon, 1892.
  214 p. : fold. map; 20 cm. — (Rulers of India ; v. 16)

JAMES ANDREW BROUN-RAMSAY, FIRST MARQUESS & TENTH EARL OF DALHOUSIE (1812-1860)

Let us dispel a popular misconception at the outset. Dalhousie did not invent the Doctrine of Lapse, a policy which is often blamed, along with its supposed inventor, for being the main cause of the Indian Revolt of 1857. Under the Doctrine of Lapse an Indian state could be annexed by England on the failure of a natural heir to the throne.

The Doctrine was applied to Mandavi in 1839, to Kolaba and Jalaun in 1840 and to Surat in 1842. According to Innes, "there was fully adequate precedent for every one of his (Dalhousie's) annexations. But his predecessors had acted on the general principle of avoiding annexation if it could be avoided; Dalhousie acted on the general principle of annexing if he could do so legitimately."

James Andrew Broun-Ramsay Dalhousie was born at Dalhousie Castle, Midlothian, Scotland, 22 April 1812, was the third son of George Ramsay, the 9th earl, who was a lieutenant-general of Wellington and commanded a regiment at Waterloo. He was governor-general of Canada (1819-1828) and commander-in-chief in India (1829-1832).

James went with his parents to Canada when his father became governor-general there. At the age of 10 James returned to England in a small sailing brig. He spent the next seven years at Harrow, and when his father in 1829 went to India to take the post of commander-in-chief, James continued his education at Christ Church, Oxford. Here he made friends with two gentlemen who would follow him to India: Charles Canning and James Bruce (later, Lord Elgin). He also made the accquaintance of William Gladstone.

In 1839, Dalhousie was elected M.P. from Haddingtonshire, first as a Conservative and then as a Peelite. The following year he succeeded his father and took a seat in the House of Lords. When Sir Robert Peel became prime minister in 1843, Dalhousie was appointed vice-president of the board of trade under Gladstone, and two years later succeeded him as president.

Before leaving office, Peel made Dalhousie Lord Clerk Register in Scotland. Lord John Russell, the new prime minister offered him a cabinet post, but Dalhousie refused it; whereupon he was made Knight of the Thistle.

Then, in 1847 Russell offered him the office of governor-general of India, and Dalhousie accepted it. He was 35.

He took up his duties in Calcutta 12 January 1848, and during the eight years of his rule as governor-general the Punjab and Burma were conquered, seven Indian states were consolidated, railway lines were established in many parts of India, telegraph stations were set up all over the country and a half-anna letter post system was installed.

The Second Anglo-Sikh War broke out shortly after Dalhousie's arrival in India, and he took it upon himself to go to the Punjab-Sutlej frontier and direct the campaign. On the successful conclusion of the war, he was made a Marquess.

In 1852, he declared war on Burma, and he himself went to Rangoon and directed operations much as he had done at the Sutlej in the war with the Punjab. The war won, he annexed Pegu.

Nor was he inactive on his northern frontier. He made treaties with the king of Kelat and the Amir of Afghanistan.

But his greatest contribution to the building of the Indian Empire was in the area of internal administration. Not only did he lay a railroad, post and telegraph system throughout the country, but he established a public works department and started steam communication between India and England. He also developed canals and agriculture, lowered taxes and expanded education. Oudh provided a major problem for Dalhousie. Here was a state which had been, since a treaty of 1801, a "protected feudatory state" in which the Nawab of Oudh was given responsibility without power. It was so badly mismanaged that it appeared that the only solution was annexation by the East India Company. Dalhousie opposed annexation, but he was voted down by his court of directors.

The last years of Dalhousie in India were not happy ones. His health was failing. His wife, Lady Susan Hay, the daughter of the Marquess of Tweeddale, whom he married in 1836, had died in 1853. When he returned to England, he was a broken man.

He was — and still is — blamed for the Revolt which followed his tenure of office in India, and he lived to witness it from afar. He died 19 December 1860 in Dalhousie. He had two daughters but no sons; so his marquessate died with him.

Writing in 1890, Sir W.W. Wilson said this of Dalhousie:

Lord Dalhousie did three things in India. He extended its frontiers, so as to bring them into inevitable though indirect contact with a great European nation on the one side, and with an ancient Asiatic power on the other. He at the same time consolidated the East India Company's internal possessions and the intervening Feudatory States, into the true beginnings of a united Indian Empire. But perhaps his most permanent claim on the gratitude of his country is that by his far-reaching schemes on railways, roads, canals, and public works, he inaugurated the great revolution which has converted the agricultural India of antiquity into the manufacturing and mercantile India of our own day. Expansion of territory, unification of territory, and the drawing forth of material resources, these were the three labours given to Lord Dalhousie to accomplish in India; and in the three words, conquest, consolidation, and development, his work may be summed up.

Suggested Further Readings

Ghosh, Suresh Chandra, 1937-
    Dalhousie in India, 1848-56 : a study of his social policy as governor-general. — New Delhi : Munshiram Manoharlal, 1975.
    166 p. ; 22 cm.

Hunter, William Wilson, Sir, 1840-1900.
    The Marquess of Dalhousie and the final development of the Company's rule. — Delhi : S. Chand, 1961.
    160 p. ; 20 cm. — (Rulers of India ; v. 20)
    First published in 1895.

CHARLES JOHN CANNING, EARL
(1812-1862)

"Clemency Canning," as he came to be known in later life, belonged to an illustrious family. William Canynges was a wealthy cloth-worker and ship-owner and bailiff of Bristol in 1361. He was six times its mayor, his son was also mayor, and one of his grandsons became Lord Mayor of London. In 1718, a branch of the family settled in Londonderry and one of its members was killed by a Papist during O'Neill's rebellion.

Charles John Canning was born 14 December 1812 at Gloucester Lodge in Brompton. He was the third son of George Canning who was foreign secretary (1822-1827) and prime minister of England for four months (1827). Charles was educated at Eton and later at Christ Church, Oxford, where he made first class in classics and second class in mathematics. His mother had been created a viscountess shortly after the death of her husband, and Charles became heir to the peerage on the death of his two elder brothers.

He married Charlotte Stuart, the eldest daughter of Lord Stuart de Rothsay, in 1833.

In 1836, he was elected M.P. for Warwick and the following year succeeded his mother in the House of Lords. He became under-secretary for foreign affairs, a job he held from 1841 to 1846. He was also chief commissioner for woods and forests. On the resignation of Lord John Russell in 1851 he was offered the post of foreign secretary, but he turned it down because he could not agree with the policies of the prime minister, Lord Derby. In the coalition cabinet of Lord Aberdeen in 1852 Canning accepted the position of postmaster-general. He remained in that post until 1855 when he was appointed governor-general of India, arriving at his new post in Calcutta 29 February 1856.

In his acceptance speech 1 August 1855 before the court of directors of the East India Company in London, he said:

> I know not what course events may take. I hope and pray that we may not reach the extremity of war. I wish for a peaceful time in office, but I cannot forget that, in our Indian Empire, that greatest of all blessings depends upon a greater variety of chances and a more precarious tenure than in any other quarter of the globe. We must not forget that in the sky of India, serene as it is, a small cloud may arise, at first no bigger than a man's hand, but which, growing bigger and bigger, may at last threaten to overwhelm us with ruin.

The India that greeted Lord Canning was nearing the brink of rebellion, but his first crisis involved Persia which was on the march against Herat, in western Afghanistan. England was pledged to the independence of Herat; so war was declared on Persia, and Canning sent General Outram to command the British forces. The war, successful for the British, lasted only a few months.

Canning inherited from his predecessor, Lord Dalhousie, the problems incurred by the Doctrine of Lapse by which an Indian state which was left without a natural heir to its throne would be annexed by the Paramount Power, which, of course, was the East India Company. Oudh was the largest of several states which had been taken over by the Company, and many of the former rajas and nawabs were, as might be expected, seething with discontent.

There were other reasons for unrest in India. England's poor showing in the Crimean War had damaged her reputation of invincibility; the activity of Christian missionaries had convinced many Indians that England planned to Christianise all India; a prophecy was current that England's domination of India would end on the 100th anniversary of the Battle of Plassey (23 June 1757), but the most immediate cause is generally believed to have been the matter of the greased cartridges.

The new Enfield rifle had been introduced, and before bullets could be fired from it properly, they had to be greased. Word spread among Hindu sepoys that cow fat was being used, and among Muslim sepoys that pig fat was being used.

Finally, Sunday, 10 May 1857 some sepoys in Meerut rebelled against their officers. Before British reinforcements could arrive, the sepoys had fled to Delhi and hailed poor old Bahadur Shah II, the last of the Mughul rulers, "Emperor of India." The mutiny spread throughout the Doab of the Ganges and Jumna Rivers and soon it took on the proportions of a full scale rebellion.

Fortunately for England, she had at her disposal a number of soldiers who could claim military experience: James George Smith Neill had fought in Burma and the Crimea, John Nicholson in Afghanistan and the Anglo-Sikh Wars, James Outram in Afghanistan and Persia and Sir Henry Lawrence in Burma, Afghanistan and the Punjab. Against leaders with all this experience were arrayed Tatya Tope, Nana Sahib, the Rani of Jhansi and other rebel leaders who, until the Revolt, had little or no wartime experience.

Canning responded to the crisis with haste. He detained English troops which were about to sail for China, and he sent troops to the affected areas of north India. He made Lawrence chief commissioner of Oudh with the responsibility for preparing the defence of the Lucknow Residency. Sir Henry's brother, John Lawrence, brought a column from the Punjab to besiege Delhi.

Because of his policy of insisting that rebels were entitled to fair trails and that ringleaders should be distinguished from those who may have been innocently caught up in the Revolt, Canning received the derisive nickname "Clemency Canning."

However, clemency was the expedient course for the English to adopt at the end of 1857 by which time the British armies had for the most part put the rebellion down. It was a time for reconciliation in India. Canning's last years in India were spent restoring order and gaining enemies at home. However, in 1859 he was made an earl, and shortly after his return to London, in ill health and grieving for his wife whom he had lost the previous year, he died 17 June 1862.

Suggested Further Readings

Cunningham, H.S., Sir.
    Earl Canning. — Oxford : Oxford University Press, 1892.
    220 p. : fold.map ; 20 cm. — (Rulers of India ; v. 25)

Maclagen, Michael.
    "Clemency Canning : Charles John, 1st Earl Canning, Governor-General and Viceroy of India". — London, etc. : Macmillan, 1962.
    xvi, 419 p. : ill., ports., maps ; 23 cm.

JOHN LAIRD MAIR LAWRENCE, FIRST BARON
(1811-1879)

John Laird Mair Lawrence, the sixth son of Lieutenant Colonel Alexander William Lawrence, was born at Richmond, Yorkshire, 4 March 1811. He was the most famous brother of several famous brothers: Sir George St. Patrick, a major-general during the Revolt of 1857, Sir Henry Montgomery, the Hero of Lucknow, and General Richard Lawrence, who served as British resident in Nepal. His father also distinguished himself in India, serving mainly in Ceylon and south India, seeing action at Seringapatam.

One biographer, Viscount Mersey, said of John's childhood that he "was educated at a number of schools as his father's regiment moved from garrison to garrison, but he did not particularly distinguish himself at any of them."

He was fascinated by history and wanted to be a soldier. When he had a chance to go to India as a writer with the East India Company, he took it and (after two years of study at Haileybury) sailed for India in 1829.

He arrived in Calcutta in February 1830 and was posted as an assistant to the resident at Delhi. Later he was a magistrate and collector in Panipat and Gurgaon.

He worked hard at learning about the agriculture and customs of the people and became fluent in their language. After eight years he was promoted to the post of settlement officer and transferred to Etawah, which he described as a "hole." His health failed him, and he was sent home in 1840. While in Ireland, he married Harriet Catherine, the daughter of the Rev. Richard Hamilton, rector of Culdaff and Donegal, 26 August 1841.

He was back in India again in November of the following year. This time he started in Delhi as civil and sessions judge, but later was appointed magistrate and collector.

In 1846, he was appointed by Governor-General Lord Hardinge to be the commissioner for the district acquired from the Sikhs in the Jullundur Doab. Hardinge had met him the previous year and had been impressed by "this vehement, swift-riding man."

The country assigned to Lawrence was called the Trans-Sutlej Territory and was not an easy one to administer. It was peopled in the plains by Jats and other agricultural Hindu tribes, in the north by Mongolian elements who spoke Tibetan, and in the lower ranges, the Rajputs of Kangra.

In 1848, the Rajas of Kangra, Jaswan and Datarpur, with the the Vizir of Burpur and some Sikh leaders, revolted against the English, but they were put down in a bloodless campaign by Lawrence with a small force. Robert Cust, a subordinate, reported it thus:

> By the orders of John Lawrence, I issued a Proclamation to the headmen of the villages to meet us at difference points in our hasty march to grapple with the insurgents. At each halting-place they were assembled in scores, and when a sword and a pen were placed before them to

select the instrument by which they wished to be ruled, the pen was grasped with enthusiasm. With the genius of a general, Lawrence planned and carried into execution this bloodless campaign ...

The leaders were sent into exile and their palaces and fortresses razed to the ground. This marked the end of the Kangra Rebellion of 1848.

After the annexation of the Punjab in 1849 Lawrence became a member of the board of administration with his brother Sir Henry and Charles Grenville Mansell, and the three of them ran the Punjab. Sir Charles Napier had little respect for this arrangement. "Boards rarely have any talent," he stated, "and that of the Punjab offers no exception to the rule."

(In support of this statement, John Lawrence once disparagingly referred to the board as a "Triumvirate.")

In 1853, John Lawrence was made chief commissioner of the Punjab, after the break-up of the board of administration — partly due to differences with his brother.

Two years later he negotiated the Treaty of Peshawar with Amir Dost Muhammad by which the independence of Afghanistan was recognized by the East India Company, and in 1857 he negotiated a second treaty by which the Amir would get a subsidy from the British.

Chief Commissioner Lawrence was knighted in 1856, and during the Revolt of 1857 he was of invaluable aid to the Company's army in his civilian capacity. He supplied the British with guns, ammunition and transport and raised both regular and irregular troops. Perhaps most important of all he kept the Punjab out of the conflict and was a constant adviser to Governor-General Canning. Following the Revolt, Canning said of "Jan Larin," as he was called by the Indians:

Through him Delhi fell and the Punjab became a source of strength. It is difficult to exaggerate the value of such ability, silence and energy at such a time.

Sir John returned home a hero in 1859 and remained there until 1863 when he was called upon to be viceroy of India.

He took over his duties 12 January 1863 and relinquished them 12 January 1869. His tenure was a peaceful one, broken by the annexation of Bhutan in 1864 and the Orissa famine of 1866. His concerns were primarily peaceful and domestic: finance, sanitation, railways, forestry, canals and the *ryotwari* system of revenue collecting.

He never considered himself properly suited for the job of viceroy. He was a commoner who was not familiar with the niceties of protocol. He was impatient and uncompromising. However, his service to England in her hour of need and his service to India in its moment of peace won him a place among the most distinguished civil servants to serve in India.

After his retirement, he was made Baron of the Punjab and of Grately. He died in London 26 July 1879 and was buried in Westminster Abbey.

They remembered him as "The Saviour of the Punjab."

Suggested Further Reading

Aitchison, Charles Umpherston, Sir, 1832-1896.
    Lord Lawrence and the reconstruction of India under the crown. — Oxford : Oxford
    University Press, 1894.
    vi, 216 p. : fold. map ; 20 cm. — (Rulers of India ; v. 26)

CURZON OF KEDLESTON, GEORGE NATHANIEL CURZON, FIRST MARQUESS
(1859-1925)

George Nathaniel Curzon was born 11 January 1859 at Kedleston Hall, Derbyshire, the eldest son of the Rev. Alfred Curzon, 4th Baron Scarsdale and rector of Kedleston. His mother was Blanche, the daughter of Joseph Senhouse of Netherhall, Cumberland.

The Curzons, not surprisingly, could trace their ancestry back to the Crusades. Though he was "born with a silver spoon in his mouth," he had a difficult childhood under a tyrannical governess. However, when he went to Eton, things changed for him, and he met with nothing but success. He also met with success later at Balliol College, Oxford.

He became president of the Union Society in 1880 and was elected in 1883 a fellow of the All Soul's College. Early on he had acquired a knowledge of India; so that by the time he became viceroy, he was quite well informed. In fact, he was the only viceroy, except Lawrence and Mountbatten, who had a personal knowledge of the India before his appointment.

At Oxford he developed curvature of the spine and was forced to wear a back brace all his life. This gave him a haughty appearance which seemed to reflect his personality.

After Oxford, Curzon made a trip to the Middle East with Edward Lyttleton, and to supplement his income he wrote articles for the newspapers and became private secretary to Lord Salisbury. He stood for Parliament, but was defeated in his first try for South Derbyshire, but later made it as a Conservative M.P. for Southport (in 1886).

During the next two years he travelled extensively in Persia, Central Asia, India, the Far East, Canada and the United States. The story is told that when he was in Calcutta in 1887, he lunched one day with Lord Dufferin at Government House. After lunch as he was walking back to the Great Eastern Hotel across the street, he remarked: "The next time I enter those gates it shall be as viceroy." This was prophetic. He had always told his friends he would be appointed viceroy before the age of 40. He assumed the office 6 January 1899, five days before his 40th birthday.

In 1891, he was appointed under-secretary for India, and in 1895 for foreign affairs. He married Mary, the daughter of Levi Leiter, an American millionaire, in April 1895. This permitted him to live in a style to which he soon became accustomed.

By the time of his appointment as viceroy in 1898, Curzon had published: *Russia in Central Asia* (1889), *Persia and the Persian Question* (1892) and *Problems of the Far East* (1894).

As viceroy, Curzon created the North-West Frontier Province in 1901, reorganised Indian finance, established the imperial cadet corps, made a treaty with Tibet, reduced the status of the Bombay and Madras Presidencies, settled with the Nizam of Hyderabad the question of the districts of Berar, created a chief commissionership of the Trans-Indus districts, enforced the blockade of Waziristan and partitioned Bengal (an act which caused consternation among Indian nationalists) in 1905.

One of Lord Curzon's most lasting achievements, and one for which both Indians and non-Indians, scholars and non-scholars, should be eternally grateful, was the passage of the Ancient Monuments Preservation Act which served to protect many of India's great monuments, such as the Taj Mahal, which had fallen into disintegration and decay. Today they are objects of tourist attraction as well as historic sites of value to scholarship.

Curzon left the viceroyalty under a cloud of disappointment. He had been reappointed to a seven-year term in 1904, but a quarrel developed between him and Lord Kitchener, commander-in-chief, over the issue of civilian control of the army in India. In 1904, Curzon went home on leave, and on his return at the end of that year, he resumed the struggle for control of the army with Kitchener. A compromise was reached without Curzon's consent, and he resigned in protest. To his surprise his resignation was accepted, and he returned to England disappointed and understandably bitter.

However, his public career was not over. After his wife died in 1906, he was elected a representative peer for Ireland which gave him a seat in the House of Lords and he became president of the Royal Geographical Society and later chancellor of Oxford University. In 1911, he was promoted to an earldom.

After the outbreak of war in 1914 Curzon became lord privy seal in the coalition ministry of Lord Asquith. When Lloyd George became prime minister in 1916, Curzon was appointed to the inner wartime cabinet.

After the war he took temporary charge of the foreign office in Lord Balfour's absence at the Paris Peace Conference. On the resignation of Lord Balfour in October 1919, Curzon became foreign secretary, but he did not get along well with Prime Minister Lloyd George because the latter preferred to conduct foreign affairs himself. In 1921, he was created a marquess even though many of his suggestions and policies had either been unsuccessful or rejected. Curzon remained as foreign secretary when Bonar Law became prime minister in 1922. He represented Britain at the Lausanne Conference.

The following year, Law resigned due to ill health, and Curzon fully expected to be appointed prime minister. Once again, he was disappointed. Stanley Baldwin was named instead.

However, he continued to support the Conservative government, and after the election of 1924, he resumed the post of lord privy seal.

He became ill in Cambridge early in 1925 and died in London 20 March of that year.

His tenure as viceroy had been marked by rising feelings of nationalism in India, feelings which were exacerbated by his stern measures. He was a brilliant statesman at a difficult time. Perhaps his greatest tribute came from Clemenceno:

Orgveil immense – justifié! ("Immense pride - justified.")

Suggested Further Reading

Fraser, Lovat.
India under Curzon and after. — New Delhi : Lakshmi, 1969.
x, 496 p. : ill., front. port., fold. map ; 25 cm.

MOUNTBATTEN OF BURMA,
LOUIS MOUNTBATTEN, FIRST EARL
(1900-1979)

Louis Mountbatten was the last viceroy of British India. He also had the distinction of being the only viceroy born in the 1900s and the only naval person to become viceroy.

He was the second son of Admiral of the Fleet, Prince Louis of Battenberg, afterwards first marquess of Milford Haven, and Princess Victoria, daughter of Louis IV, grand duke of Hesse, and Princess Alice of Great Britain. He was born 25 June 1900 at Frogmore House, Windsor. He had plenty of blue blood flowing in his veins, being also a great-grandson of Queen Victoria.

He was educated at Osborne, Dartmouth and Christ's College, Cambridge, after which he served in H.M.S. "Lion" and "Queen Elizabeth," Lord Beatty's flagships. He also did submarine duty during World War I, and in 1919 he became lieutenant R.N.

Three years later he married Edwina Ashley, elder daughter of Wilfred, Lord Mount Temple, and grand daughter of Sir Ernest Cassel, a financer and friend of Edward VII.

Because he was mechanically inclined, Mountbatten became a senior instructor in the Royal Navy Signal School in 1929 and fleet wireless officer in the Mediterranean. In 1930 he was promoted to commander R.N.

He commanded H.M.S. "Daring" and later served in the Admiralty Naval Air Division, being promoted to captain. He saw action early in World War II, commanding the 5th Destroyer Fleet and then the H.M.S. "Kelly" which was sunk off Crete. In 1941, he was posted to the H.M.S "Illustrious," an aircraft carrier, after which he was given a desk job.

In 1942, he was made chief of combined operations and became a member of the chiefs of staff committee, being given the rank of acting vice-admiral. He was also made an honorary lieutenant-general and air vice-marshal.

Following the Quebec Conference of 1943, he was made supreme commander of the Southeast Asia Command with headquarters first in New Delhi, India, then in Kandy, Ceylon, and finally in Singapore. His forces were both British and American, consisting of all three services, and his area of command included Burma, Malaya and the Indian Ocean. He worked with Generals Mac Arthur and Stillwell as well as Chinese generals.

He remained in control of Southeast Asia at the end of the war, and was raised to the peerage as Viscount Mountbatten of Burma. He was later dubbed a Knight of the Garter.

As the day of India's independence was drawing near, he was summoned by Prime Minister Attlee (18 December 1946) and asked to serve as the last viceroy of India.

Hesitant at first, he agreed after persuading Attlee that a time limit on British rule must be set. Attlee suggested that the summer of 1948 was the earliest date at which the transfer of power could occur. Ultimately, Mountbatten set the date at 15 August 1947.

The India that greeted Mountbatten was a divided one, perhaps even more so than the India that greeted other governors-general and viceroys. Jinnah and the Muslim League wanted to partition India and create Pakistan because they did not believe Indian Muslims would be treated fairly in Hindu India. Gandhi, Nehru and the Indian Congress party wanted an undivided India. The Indian states, each of which had treaties with Britain, did not want the British to leave.

It was to Mountbatten's credit that he worked with the factions and personalities he encountered in an atmosphere of mutual respect. He himself was opposed to the idea of partition, but his hand was forced by the adamant behaviour of Jinnah, and he finally relented and agreed to divide the subcontinent on the basis of religion.

It was decided Indian states which would be surrounded by India would go to India, and those which were surrounded by Pakistan would go to Pakistan. This arrangement was viable for all the states except Kashmir whose borders were surrounded by neither country. When independence occurred, Kashmir simply sat there, but not for long. It became a cause of war and a bone of contention between the two countries from the start, and, at this writing, is a scene of renewed communal violence.

In mid-August of 1947 India got her independence and is today the world's largest democracy. Pakistan got Jinnah, but he died 11 September 1948, and, except for occasional moments of respite, has suffered through one dictatorship after another.

In the aftermath of independence millions died in the slaughter as Hindus in Pakistan migrated to India and Muslims in India hastened to Pakistan. It was the most violent period of South Asia's violent history.

Mountbatten stayed on as governor-general of the Dominion of India until June 1948. He was fourth sea lord (1950-52), commander-in-chief of the Mediterranean fleet (1952-54) and first sea lord (1955-59).

He became an admiral of the fleet in 1956 and was killed when Irish terrorists blew up his yacht off the coast of Britain 27 August 1979.

There is no question that Mountbatten was a great and good man, and it is sad to think that he was forced to accede to the iron will of Jinnah and permit the creation of Pakistan.

Suggested Further Readings

Collins, Larry.
> Freedom at midnight / Larry Collins and Dominique Lapierre. — New Delhi, etc. : Vikas, [1976]
> 500 p. : ill., maps ; 22 cm.

Collins, Larry.
> Mountbatten and the partition of India / Larry Collins & Dominique Lapierre. — [New Delhi] : Vikas, 1984.
> viii, 191 p. ; 25 cm.
> (A series of interviews with Lord Mountbatten regarding events between 22 March and 15 August 1947)

CHAPTER 9

THE TWENTIETH CENTURY

Charles Freer Andrews	Gopal Krishna Gokhale
Annie Besant	Motilal Nehru
Subhas Chandra Bose	Sir Tej Bahadur Sapru
Ramananda Chatterjee	Lokamanya Tilak
Chittaranjan Das	Mahatma Gandhi
Aurobindo Ghosh	

*I*t is not surprising that the chapter dealing with India in the twentieth century should be filled with heroes of the struggle for independence.

(It should be pointed out that this chapter is devoted only to those political leaders who made their mark prior to 26 January 1950, the date of birth of the Republic of India. The leaders who followed, Nehru, Shastri, Mrs. Gandhi, etc. are sketched in the next chapter.)

The outstanding figure in India in the first half of the twentieth century was, of course, Mahatma Gandhi. It was he who led the way, right up to and through the day of independence, 15 August 1947, and until his tragic death in January 1948.

The twentieth century dawned with several bright stars shining in the heliacal rising. One was Ramananda Chatterjee with his *Prabasi* and *Modern Review*, the latter of which became India's major national monthly during those early days.

Another was Aurobindo Ghosh, a barn-burning, flag-waving Bengali radical who was not above the use of terrorism to achieve noble ends. As the government closed in on him, he fled to Pondichéry, the French settlement, for refuge and to devote the balance of his life to peaceful contemplation and integral philosophy.

On the other side of the country was G.K. Gokhale who, like Chatterjee, was a journalist and a political leader.

Another Maharashtrian, Tilak, was a militant nationalist, a *Lokamanya*, revered leader of the people.

Sapru, on the other hand, was noted for his keen legal mind and strove to achieve by constitutional means what others were trying to achieve by popular movements.

Two Europeans got into the act: Charles Freer Andrews and Annie Besant. Freer was a constant companion, friend and supporter of Mahatma Gandhi. Mrs. Besant, who appeared earlier on the scene, was a theosophist, a supporter of Benares Hindu University and one of the early presidents of the Indian National Congress.

A puzzling figure is Subhas Chandra Bose. He is honoured and streets and parks are named after this man who was prepared to sell out his country to Japanese imperialism.

But Motilal Nehru wás an aristocrat, a Kashmiri Brahman, who gave the struggle a real glimmer of patriotism, maturity and steadiness. He also gave it his son.

CHARLES FREER ANDREWS (DEENBANDHU)
(1871-1940)

Charles Freer Andrews was born 12 February 1871 in Newcastle-on-Tyne, the son of a minister of the Catholic Apostolic Church.

He studied at King Edward VI College with a scholarship, and, being a superior student, in 1890 he won an open scholarship at Pembroke College at Cambridge University. In 1893, he got a first class with distinction in the classics, and in 1895 he cleared Theological tripos, also with distinction.

His first job on graduation was at Pembroke College Mission in South London. His next job was as vice-principal Westcott House, a theological seminary for training high church clergy at Cambridge.

Andrews was inspired to go into mission work in India by the life and words of Basil Westcott who had died in Delhi. Westcott had spoken highly of Indian culture, maintaining that as Greece had been the leader in Europe, India would some day be the leader in Asia. Andrews arrived in India 20 March 1904.

He joined the Cambridge mission and was employed as a teacher in St. Stephen's College in Delhi. Sushil Rudra initiated Andrews into life in India, and years later Andrews would say of him:

> I owe to Sushil Rudra what I owe to no one else in the world, a friendship which has made India from the first not a strange land, but a familiar country.

When the principalship became vacant in 1907, the position was offered to Andrews, but he turned it down, arguing that it should go to Rudra instead. The authorities hesitated because no "native" had ever held that position before. However, Andrews prevailed, and Rudra did well as principal of St. Stephen's College.

While teaching at St. Stephen's, Andrews moved his residence to *Chamar Basti* in *Sabzi Mandi** and worked among the cobblers. He had his students come and organise health and temperance campaigns in the slums there,

---

*　　*Chamar Basti* was where the cobblers lived, and *Sabzi Mandi* was a place where there were numerous vegetable markets.

thus showing them the evils of drink and drugs, and teaching them to work for the betterment of the poor.

At about this time Andrews became aware of the nationalist movement that was gaining strength and momentum in India, and he sided with India. In 1906, he said in Lahore:

> My one great wish is to express to you whole-heartedly, as a Christian missionary and as a loyal Englishman, I sympathize with the higher aspirations of Indian nationalism today.

Then, in an article entitled "The Indian Point of View" in 1908 he said:

> The pulse of a new life is beating in Indian hearts.... They feel subjection and inequality as they never did in the past. What will be the Church's answer to this new spirit? The Anglo-Saxon Church, even in the early missionary days, led the English people into freedom, unity and self-dependence. Can the Indian Church, tied as she is to a foreign State Establishment, do the same in India?"

And he supplied his own answer:

> The awakening in the East in its effect upon politics, art, literature and thought may well be called a Renaissance. With very much of this Renaissance — with the longing for freedom and enlightenment, the love of country, the desire for a true and healthy national existence, the wish to elevate over the countless myriads of the common people — no thoughtful Christian can fail to sympathise. As an Englishman, he may feel at times that the day of his power is on the wane, but as a Christian he cannot but rejoice and welcome into the brotherhood of man the new nations that are now being born.

In the course of his activities Andrews met leaders of the freedom movement like Gokhale, Tilak, Srinivasa Shastri, Malaviya, Tagore and Lajpat Rai, and in 1913 Gokhale urged him to go to South Africa to help the Indian community there. He accepted the challenge.

Arriving in South Africa in 1914, he was met by Gandhi, and the two of them struck up a life-long friendship. They worked together for the Indian community of South Africa, the fruition of which was the passing of the Indian Relief Act of 1914.

On his return to India after the work in South Africa was done, Andrews lived at Shantiniketan, Tagore's foundation in Bengal. He was furious when the House of Lords acclaimed General Dyer, the man who perpetrated the Jalianwalla Bagh massacre, as a conquering hero, and he wrote many books to express his views: *How Can India Be Free?*, *Indian Independence: the Immediate Need*, *The Indian Problem and the Claim for Independence* and *Within or Without the British Empire*.

He worked closely with Gandhi during the freedom movement, and because of his compassion for the depressed classes, he earned the epithet,

Deenbandhu (Friend of the Poor). Even so, Andrews and Gandhi did not always agree, as when Gandhi openly attacked Christian missionaries for their work in India.

However, Gandhi was at his side when Deenbandhu died 5 April 1940. Among his last words were these spoken to Gandhi:

"*Swaraj* will come, Mohan." Seven years later it came.

Andrews was buried, at his own wish, near St. Paul's Cathedral in Calcutta.

Suggested Further Readings

Roy Chaudhuri, Pranab Chandra.
  Charles Freer Andrews : his life and times. — Bombay : Somaiya, [1971]
  vi, 200 p. : port. ; 22 cm.

Tinker, Hugh.
  The ordeal of love : Charles Freer Andrews and India. — Delhi : Oxford University Press, 1979.
  xxi, 334 p., [5] leaves of plates : ill. ; 23 cm.

ANNIE BESANT
(1847-1933)

Annie (Wood) Besant was born in London 1 October 1847, the daughter of William Persse Wood, an Irish businessman and Emily Mary Roche who was also Irish. She was educated privately and married in 1867 to Rev. Frank Besant, an Anglican clergyman.

They had two children and were divorced in 1873.

The following year she became an associate of Charles Bradlaugh, a prominent atheist, and soon was made co-editor with him of the *National Reformer*. She was the first prominent woman in England to support birth control and, with Bradlaugh, was prosecuted by the government on a charge of obscenity for having published in England the American pamphlet *The Fruits of Philosophy; or, The Private Companion of Young Married People.* Her children were taken from her, and she and Bradlaugh were sentenced to heavy fines and imprisonment, the punishment being later set aside on technicalities.

She parted company with Bradlaugh in 1885 when she turned her interests to socialist and labour politics. Her close friendship with George Bernard Shaw had led her to reject radical politics in favour of Fabian socialism. She edited a journal called *Our Corner* and eventually joined the Social Democratic Federation, a more Marxist organization.

She soon became a leading labour organiser, strike leader and reformer, but her political wheel took another turn in 1889 when she read Madame Blavatsky's *The Secret Doctrine* and became an ardent theosophist. By the time of Madame Blavatsky's death in 1891, Mrs. Besant was theosophy's most famous and prominent member, and in 1907 she was elected president of the Theosophical Society, a position she held for the remainder of her life.

On 16 November 1893 she arrived in Tuticorin for her first visit to India. She turned her back on the first two religions of her life, Christianity and atheism, and adopted Hinduism as her new faith. She believed in reincarnation and decided that in a previous life she had been an Indian.

She got involved in political and educational activities and set up a number of schools and colleges, the most important of which was Central Hindu College High School at Banaras which she started in 1913. It was the base from which Banaras Hindu University grew under the leadership of Madan Mohan Malaviya.

Her interest in politics and her views on India's struggle for independence predated her arrival in India. As early as 1879 she wrote in *England, India and Afghanistan*:

> Few records of conquest show stains so foul as the story of the subjugation of Hindustan by this originally merchant association (the East India Company). What is our duty to this great land, and how may we best remedy our crimes of the past? The answer comes in one word: Liberty. The work cannot be done in a day, but it must be begun by slow stages. Let a system of representative government gradually replace the centralized despotism of our present sway.

She believed that one way to gain freedom for India would be to put political pressure on parliament; so she started a journal called *New India* and founded the Home Rule League in 1916.

Because of her inflammatory writings, in 1917 she was imprisoned in Ootacamund, but released only after Subramania Iyer, vice president of the Theosophical Society, smuggled a letter to President Wilson of the United States, asking him to intercede with the British government to release her, which he did. Shortly after she was freed, she was elected president of the Indian National Congress.

As the campaign for independence heated up after 1919 with Gandhi's programme of non-violent non-cooperation, Mrs. Besant found herself in disagreement with Gandhi. She did not see *satyagraha* as the most effective means for achieving the objectives they both desired. She hoped to bring about a transformation in British heart by educating public opinion as to the plight of the Indian people. For this purpose, she toured Britain and used her considerable oratorical powers extensively.

With the help of a political science professor, Bhagat Ram Kumar, a Constitution of India Bill was framed and presented to the House of Commons by George Lansbury, but it was rejected.

The campaign of Mahatma Gandhi developed momentum in the early 1930s, and Annie Besant was left behind.

Her career as a leading theosophist was marred by her association with Jiddu Krishnamurti. She had undertaken his education in 1909 and soon was hailing him as some sort of messiah. However, he objected to the eso-teric section of the Theosophical Society and broke away from it and Mrs. Besant and formed his own society.

She suffered from ill health in 1931 and retired to Adyar in Madras and died there 20 September 1933, confident that she would be reincarnated and continue the mission which her occult hierarchy would assign to her.

Among her many publications are her *Autobiography, Religious Problem in India* and *How India Wrought for Freedom*. However, that is only a small fraction of her publishing efforts. The actual number (of books and pam-phlets) is 506: pre-theosophical 105, biographical 6, theosophical 219, on religion 32, London Queen's Hall lectures (published) 17, Indian culture, education, social reform, etc. 48, Indian politics 79.

She received many tributes during her life time. Perhaps the most beau-tiful one came from Sarojini Naidu:

> Mrs. Annie Besant was a great woman, a warrior, a patriot and a priest-ess... Many creeds were reconciled in her. Her essential qualities were her unquenchable thirst for freedom, her warmth of love and the radi-ant spirit with which she inspired her followers. Whenever I think of Mrs. Besant, I think of the following line of Keats:

> "Eternal beauty wandering on her way."

Suggested Further Reading

Nethercott, Arthur Hobart.
    The last four lives of Annie Besant. — [Chicago] : University of Chicago Press, [1963]
    483 p. : ill. ; 23 cm.

SUBHAS CHANDRA BOSE
(1897-1945)

Subhas Chandra Bose was born in 1897 in Cuttack, Orissa, ninth child of Janakinath and Prabhavati. His father was a lawyer of the Kayastha caste who, in the reformist atmosphere of nineteenth century Bengal, resigned posts in the bureaucracy to protest against British policies.

Subhas and his brothers were educated first in a Baptist Mission School where they learned English and Latin and studied the Bible. When Subhas entered Ravenshaw Collegiate School in Cuttack, other students laughed at him because he knew so little Bengali. At age 15, he read the works of Vivekananda and Ramakrishna and began to practice yoga.

At 16, Bose was sent to Presidency College in Calcutta. There he en-countered student activists and also was influenced by the religious nationalism of Aurobindo Ghosh and Surendranath Banerjee. World War I and the treatment of Indians by the English in Calcutta combined to raise

Bose's political consciousness. An Englishman teaching at Presidency College was especially offensive to students, and Bose was expelled in the aftermath of a skirmish between the teacher and students. Bose then matriculated in Scottish Church College before being sent to Cambridge to prepare for the civil service examinations in England. There he continued to encounter discriminatory treatment of Indians.

Bose passed the ICS examination and was given a posting, but he spent several months in introspection, then decided to resign the posting out of the conviction that the best way to end a government was to withdraw from it. Bose had taken his first step as a revolutionary.

Bose returned to Calcutta, where he wrote for the newspaper *Swaraj* and took charge of publicity for the Bengal Provincial Congress Committee. He took as his mentor C.R. Das, a lawyer who moved from membership in the Extremist Party in the Indian National Congress and president of the All-India Swaraj Party, to mayor of Calcutta and president of the Congress successively. Bose and his elder brother Sarat worked under Das's leadership to organise political demonstrations.

By 1924 Bose became chief executive officer of the Calcutta Corporation and in the same year he was arrested and held without specific charge. He worked within the Congress and in the late 1920's cooperated with Gandhi. He also worked actively in the trade union movement and became president of the All-India Trade Union Congress.

Subhas spent most of the period from 1932 to 1938 either in prison or in Europe, where he assumed the role of spokesman for Indian nationalism and culture. He visited several countries, attended conferences and made international friendships, most importantly in Vienna with his secretary, Emilie Schenkl, whom he married secretly. The couple had one daughter. While in Europe Bose wrote two books, *The Indian Struggle*, and his autobiography, *An Indian Pilgrim*.

Bose's attitude toward Gandhi was ambivalent, as *The Indian Struggle* reveals. He saw Gandhi not only as being supported both by the masses and by wealthy capitalists, but also as a restraint on the militant nationalists with whom Bose identified. He also viewed himself as differing from Gandhi over the force of science and modernity. Despite their differences, Gandhi supported Bose when he was unanimously chosen Congress president at Haripura in 1938. The following year, however, Gandhi and his followers, including Nehru, objected to Bose's insistence that a six-month ultimatum be issued to the British. Despite this opposition, however, Bose won the presidency in a close election and met with Gandhi to seek agreement on the composition of the Congress Working Committee.

When the Congress met in its annual session at Tripuri, Bose was ill and arrived on a stretcher, following incarceration in Rangoon. Frustrated by the split between the political left and right wing followers of Gandhi, Bose in late 1939 formed the Forward Bloc to consolidate factions on the left.

In July 1940, Bose was arrested again for leading a demonstration demanding removal of a memorial to Black Hole of Calcutta victims and was also held for sedition. The government released him from prison but kept him under house arrest.

In January 1941, he escaped from the family home at night and made his way by car, then by train to Afghanistan disguised as a deaf mute Muslim. This began the saga of his journey to Italy and Germany. In Germany, he organised the Indian Legion of POWs in Germany and also launched a broadcast offensive of political appeals to Indians in Britain and Southeast Asia, calling on Indians overseas to rise and fight for liberation from Britain. While in Berlin, he met Hitler and Von Ribbentrop; but Berlin proved a disappointment to him; so he turned to the Japanese.

He met the Japanese military attache' and the Japanese ambassador, General Oshima, and urged them to send him to Asia. The resulting German-Japanese agreement to send Bose to Singapore first by German, then by Japanese submarine, was one of the few Axis military agreements reached during the war. Bose arrived in Singapore in the summer of 1943 and was given a tumultuous welcome by the waiting Indians.

Indian POWs of the Japanese had in December 1941 cooperated in the Malayan jungles with Major Iwaichi Fujiwara, an idealistic young intelligence officer, in organising the Indian National Army to fight for independence with Japanese cooperation.

In early 1942, however, the leader of the INA, Captain Mohan Singh, ran afoul of Fujiwara's successor and superior, Colonel Hideo Iwakura. Mohan Singh was put under house arrest for the duration of the war and the INA languished until the arrival of Bose who, hailed as *"Netaji"* (Leader), galvanized the Indian population of Singapore — POWs, civilians and young women alike — behind the struggle for independence. The rallying of young girls to Bose's Rani of Jhansi Regiment was one of the more romantic phases of the INA struggle. Bose organised a Free India Provisional Government as a government in exile and the civil arm of the movement.

Bose went to Tokyo where he met Prime Minister Tojo and Army Chief of Staff General Sugiyama, both of whom were impressed with his passion for independence. But they had more pressing problems than Indian policy demanding their attention, and their responses left him disappointed as he returned to Southeast Asia.

In November 1943, Bose made a second trip to Tokyo to attend the Greater East Asia Conference, the result of a political strategy by Tokyo leadership to enlist Southeast Asian civilian support for Japan's cause. Bose in his speech at the conference said that the fate of all Asia was linked. While at this conference Bose was promised a request he made to Tojo: the formal transfer of the Andaman and Nicobar Islands to the jurisdiction of the Free India Provisional Government. The transfer, however, was to remain more nominal than real. The announcement, however, served both Japanese and FIPG purposes.

The INA remained from the Japanese perspective part of a political campaign to encourage overseas Indian disaffection from Britain, although Bose saw it as a real weapon to use in the struggle for freedom from British rule. The INA did see action in Burma in the ill-fated Imphal campaign which crossed the Indo-Burma border into the state of Manipur. By the time the joint Japanese-INA operation got under way in March 1944, it had no air cover, long supply lines were without logistic support, and the prospect of success was virtually nil, as events proved.

Bose moved the INA and FIPG headquarters to Bangkok in May 1945. There he met Japanese officials and requested that he be sent to the Soviet Union, in the belief that Japan's cause was lost but that Russian help might still save the fight for Indian independence. This was Bose's intent as he left Bangkok for Saigon aboard a Japanese military plane on 16 August 1945, the day after the surrender by Japan. An Indian secretary, Habibur Rehman, accompanied him on the secret flight. The plane stopped in Taihoku, Taiwan, to refuel on the 18th. Immediately after take-off one engine fell off and the plane plunged to the ground. Bose was burned fatally. He was cremated and his ashes taken to Tokyo by a Japanese officer. To this day the remains are kept in the Renkoji Temple.

Millions of Indians refused to believe that Netaji was dead, and the myth that he lives on in the hills of Assam or in Mongolia or Russia awaiting an opportune moment to return to India survives till today, especially in Calcutta. The British after the war tried several INA officers for treason in the Delhi Red Fort, but such a popular outcry arose in support of the freedom fighters of the INA that they were released and their sentences commuted. This popular support was one factor that convinced the British that their hold on India was no longer tenable. In this sense, then, Bose's struggle for independence succeeded.

— Joyce C. Lebra

Suggested Further Readings

Bose, Subhas Chandra, 1895-1945.
    An Indian pilgrim. — New York : Asia Publishing House, [1965]
    viii, 199 p. : facsims., geneal tables, port. ; 23 cm.

Das Gupta, Hemendra Nath.
    Subhas Chandra. — Calcutta : Jyoti Prokasalaya, [1946]
    viii, 254 p. : ports. ; 21 cm.

RAMANANDA CHATTERJEE
(1865-1943)

Ramananda Chatterjee was born in Bankura, Bengal, 29 May 1865. He was educated at Presidency and City College in Calcutta, and received his B.A. in 1887 and M.A. in 1890. Before the completion of his studies, he began his association with the three interest areas — teaching, social reform and the press —which would remain priorities in his life's work and inform his role as a nationalist. In 1888, he began teaching at City College, joined the Sadharan Brahmo Samaj in the following year and began writing editorial notes for the *Indian Mirror* in 1890. He was appointed principal of Allahabad Kayastha Pathsala College in 1895 and retained that post until 1906, when he committed himself to a full time career as a journalist.

Throughout this period Chatterjee had undertaken writing and editorial responsibilities in a range of newspapers and journals: the *Indian Mirror, Dharmabandhu, Sanjivani,* the *Indian Messenger* (the Brahmo weekly), *Dasi, Makul* (a children's magazine), *Pradip,* and *Kayastha Samachar.*

In 1901, he became the founder-editor of *Prabasi* and in 1907, he established the *Modern Review.* He would engage in a number of literary, political, academic, and general public activities throughout his long life and career; but it was these two journals which would engage most of his attention and be the source of his influence on the public life of Bengal and India generally. The *Modern Review,* in particular, became India's major national monthly — attracting a readership throughout the sub-continent and a group of writers from India's political, literary and academic elite — and successfully reaching out as well to a larger gallery in Britain, Europe and North America.

Chatterjee's formal participation in the nationalist movement began in 1892 when he attended the Allahabad Congress session as a delegate. Subsequently he attended the annual Congress sessions on a regular basis, eventually committing himself as well to the Hindu Mahasabha. He was president of the Mahasabha's Karachi session in 1931. In 1934, he served as president of the Congress Nationalist Party. In both these contexts Chatterjee combined his commitment to the Congress and the nationalist movement with a politicised Hindu identity and perspective which he defined and reiterated in the pages of his journals.

Chatterjee believed that an appreciation of the profound cultural impact of the Western imperial power in its Indian setting was a prerequisite for independence; and the whole of the *Modern Review* was calculated to stimulate a positive and dynamic view of India and Indian national identity. Indian writers, poets, artists and political leaders filled its pages with samples of their views and creative powers. While emphasising the common humanity which Indians shared with all others, special emphasis was always given to India's distinctive culture and the differences which separated Indians from other people, particularly in the West. Chatterjee was convinced that the particular nature of the Indian genius had to be identified and understood, and it was this cultural perspective which would bring him to a Hindu community viewpoint of nationalist struggle and national goal, often at odds with the secular priorities of Congress leaders at the centre.

In Rabindranath Tagore, Chatterjee found the ultimate symbol of contemporary Indian achievement and excellence, and he worked to make Tagore the symbol of Indian nationality. There was rarely an issue of the *Review* without at least one Tagore contribution, and English translations of many of his works appeared first in its pages. Chatterjee was convinced that Tagore represented the best opportunity to revive and sustain an Indian identity that would be appreciated by the Indian people as a whole, and by the West as well.

Chatterjee's response to the major issues and personalities generated by the nationalist movement reflected his commitment to rational debate, constitutional process, and cultural renewal as prerequisites to the achievement of independence. While he warned the British that it was possible to pay a very high price for peace and order, Chatterjee remained ambivalent about the non-cooperation programme of M.K. Gandhi. He applauded Gandhi's successful challenge to India's dependent mentality which had been a major goal of Chatterjee's own writing, but the apparent rejection of all Western experience as applicable to India made him an opponent.

In his analysis of the sources of India's malaise, Chatterjee had identified Hindu isolation and rejection of change as a principal element in Britain's success. Before the British could be effectively challenged, he insisted, the old dynamism would have to be revived.

Bengali history and culture were far too significant in his life to give place to an All-India perspective completely shorn of its provincial loyalty. A substantial proportion of the contributors to the *Modern Review* were Bengalis, and he often drew upon Bengali events to illustrate a point of significance for the national future.

Frequently the "nation" is Bengal, and it is clear that Bengal's cultural Renaissance, social reform commitment and early leadership of the nationalist movement were fundamental to Chatterjee's ideal for all India.

More significantly, Hinduism was inseparable from his concept of India, and he was convinced that a strong, reformed and united Hinduism was essential to the achievement of national political health and unity. As a young convert to Brahmo Samaj, he committed himself to a view of India's problems, centered on the need for a revitalized Hindu India to be accepted and appreciated by Christian Europe on terms of equality. This ideal was intrinsic to his identity as a nationalist.

For 35 years as editor of the *Modern Review*, Chatterjee was a principal patron and publicist of a modern and vital Indian culture, essential, in his view, to the achievement of national freedom. While he was attacked as a communalist by those who feared any challenge to the secular ideal, the self-awareness he offered those who read his monthly lesson reflected the complexity of Indian society, and the reality of competing loyalties.

Chatterjee died in Calcutta 30 September 1943.

— **Milton Israel**

Suggested Further Readings

Bose, Nemai Sudhan.
  Ramananda Chatterjee. — New Delhi : Publications Division, Ministry of Information and Broadcasting, 1974.
  165 p., plates : ill. ; 21 cm. — (Builders of modern India)

Israel, Milton.
  "Ramananda Chatterjee and the Modern Review" in *National Unity : the South Asian Experience* / edited by Milton Israel. — New Delhi : Promilla, 1983.

CHITTARANJAN DAS
(1870-1925)

Chittaranjan Das, better known as *Deshbandhu* (Friend of the Country), was born in Calcutta 5 November 1870. His father, an ardent Brahmo, poet and social reformer, was Bhuban Mohan Das, and his mother was Nistarini Devi, a woman of less than high educational attainments but gifted with courage and common sense. Chittaranjan's grandfather, Kashishwar Das, was a government pleader of Barisal, and two of Chittaranjan's uncles, as well as his father, were *vakils* (lawyers).

Chittaranjan started school at the age of nine at the London Missionary Society's Institution at Bhawanipore, Calcutta, and in 1886 passed the entrance examination for Calcutta University. Later he entered Presidency College.

In 1890, after graduating from Presidency, he went to London to qualify for the Indian Civil Service. Two years later he sat for the Civil Service examination, but did not take all the papers because he feared he would not pass. Then in 1893 he took it again, feeling sure he would make it. The top 42 candidates made it. Chittaranjan came in 43rd.

It was believed at the time that Chittaranjan had failed because of his political activities. This belief was supported by a letter from Sir Richard Garth, ex-Chief Justice of the Calcutta High Court, to Bhuban Mohan which contained this paragraph:

I tried my best, but the fiery speeches of your son at Oldham have spoiled everything. I could not persuade the India Office.

At the urging of his father, Chittaranjan studied for the Bar, joined the Inner Temple and was called to the Bar in 1893. In December of that year Chittaranjan was sworn in as an advocate of the Calcutta High Court, and his career as a lawyer began. The first years were difficult. His father, who was not a good money manager, had become insolvent, and this placed a heavy burden on the entire family.

In 1897, Chittaranjan married Basanti Devi, the daughter of Barada Nath Haldar, *Dewan* of Bijni Estate in Assam.

In 1907, his reputation was engendered when he defended Brahmo Bandhoy Upadhyaya and Bipin Chandra Pal who were accused of sedition, and it was further enhanced in 1908 when he successfully defended Sri Aurobindo Ghosh in the famous Alipore Bomb Case.

The succeeding years were years of success and prosperity for Chittaranjan, and during this time he became more and more involved in the independence struggle. In 1917, he presided over the Bengal Provincial Conference and in that same year supported Annie Besant in her election as president of the Indian National Congress.

The following year he opposed the Montagu-Chelmsford Reforms as inadequate, and in 1919, he was a member of the non-official Jallianwala Bagh Enquiry Committee.

It was not until 1920, however, that he fully supported Gandhi's non-cooperation campaign. He gave up his luxurious house in Calcutta and devoted himself entirely to the cause of Indian independence. He was elected president of the Indian National Congress at its 1922 session at Gaya.

He tried to bring together Hindu and Muslim elements of the country by effecting in 1923 the Bengal Pact between Hindus and Muslims of Bengal.

He joined Motilal Nehru in forming the Swaraj Party which captured the seats of the Corporation of Calcutta in 1924 and was elected mayor of Calcutta that year, being reelected in the following year. He died 16 June 1925 in Darjeeling.

In his presidential address at the Gaya session of the Indian National Congress, Chittaranjan stated the case for independence and non-violence:

> I am one of those who hold to non-violence on principle ... It is for India to show light to the world — *Swaraj* by non-violence and *Swaraj* by the people.

Rabindranath Tagore said of him in eulogy:

> You brought with you the gift of deathless life,
> In your death you have left it as a gift to your countrymen.

Suggested Further Readings

Das Gupta, Hemendranath.
  Deshbandhu Chittaranjan Das.— [New Delhi] : Ministry of Information and Broadcasting, Publications Division, [1969]
  x, 234 p. : front. ; 19 cm. — (Builders of modern India)

Deshbandhu Chittaranjan Das memorial volume. — Calcutta : Deshbandhu Chittaranjan Das Memorial Committee, 1976.
  ca. 150 p. : ill. ; 26 cm.
  In English or Bengali.

SRI AUROBINDO GHOSH
(1872-1950)

He began his career as an ardent nationalist and extremist and ended it as a revered saint.

Aurobindo Ghosh, known popularly as Sri Aurobindo (or sometimes "Aravinda") was born in Calcutta 15 August 1872. He was the son of Krishna Dhone Ghosh of the Ghosh family of Konnagar, district Hugli, Bengal, and Svarnalata, the eldest daughter of Raj Narayan Bose, a pioneer in Indian nationalism.

Aurobindo began his education at Loretto Convent School in Darjeeling and in 1879 was taken to England by his father who wanted to give him "an entirely European upbringing." The boy was enrolled in St. Paul's School in London where he did well in Latin. He continued his education in the classics at Cambridge and excelled in Greek and Latin as well as in several modern European languages: French, German, Spanish and Italian. It is said he could read Goethe, Calderon and Dante in the original with facility.

Although he effortlessly passed the Indian Civil Service examination, he failed because he was unable to get high marks (some said on purpose) in riding.

He returned to India in 1893 and joined the Baroda State Service, first in the revenue department, then at Baroda College as a teacher of French and English, and finally as vice principal. While at Baroda he learned Sanskrit, Marathi, Gujarati and Bengali.

He also became politically active, writing articles for *Indu Prakash*, calling for Indian National Congress to take a radical stand and he started organizing secret societies in Bombay Presidency and Bengal. Later he became a leader, with Bal Gangadhar Tilak, of a newly formed National Party and published three short-lived journals: *Bandemataram, Karmayogin* and *Dharma*.

In 1901, Aurobindo married Mrnalini, the daughter of Bhupal Chandra Bose, and shortly after that he went to Bengal to serve as principal of National College. He later (in 1910) deserted his wife to live out his life in French India; so she spent her last days in religious pursuits, thinking well about her saintly husband. She died in 1918.

Aurobindo was deeply affected by the partition of Bengal in 1905. His journal's articles inflamed young radicals and are thought to have resulted in a number of terrorist acts, the most celebrated of which was the Alipore Bomb Case.

Two young terrorists, Khudiram Bose and Profulla Chaki, threw a bomb at the district judge of Muzaffarpur, Mr. Kingsford. They missed him, but when the bomb exploded, it killed two Englishwomen. Chaki shot and killed himself as he was being captured, but Bose was put on trial, sentenced and hanged.

Not satisfied that justice had been done, the British put Aurobindo and a number of "co-conspirators" on trial 19 October 1908. Although it was a trial of several, the British were anxious to put Aurobindo away because he was the most prominent of the defendants and was thought to be the real instigator of the terrorism. Unlike many nationalists at this time, Aurobindo was calling for total independence for India.

Defending him was Chittaranjan Das, a.k.a. *Deshbandhu*. The aim of the court was to prove beyond a shadow of doubt that Aurobindo had incited the men to commit the terrorist act and was therefore guilty of sedition and conspiracy. The chief piece of evidence was a letter which Aurobindo had written to his loving wife:

> At present I have no work of my own. I am always busy with His work. My mind has undergone a radical change. I do whatever I am commanded by Him to do. I have no will of my own. God will also be kind to you and He will show you the true path. You are my wife (*Sahaḍharmini*): won't you help me in my mission?
>
> Divine energy (*Brahmatej*) is necessary for the salvation of the country.

The prosecution held that this proved conspiracy. Das held, on the other hand, that this was evidence of deep spiritual commitment on the part of Aurobindo.

Other evidence was advanced, and Das countered it with great skill. Ultimately, Aurobindo was released, but the British kept a close watch on him, fearing that he might be the instigator of further acts of terror.

In 1910, he left the maelstrom of politics in British India and fled to the sanctuary of French India were he founded an ashram which bears his name and exists to this day.

In Pondichéry he gave up politics and devoted his energies to more peaceful pursuits. He started a monthly philosophical journal, *Arya*, and wrote a number of books: *Essays on the Gita* (1928), *The Life Divine* (1940), *The Synthesis of Yoga*, (1948) and *Savitri* (1950), being among the better known ones.

In 1914, Aurobindo met Madame Richard, a Frenchwoman, whose spiritual qualities were similar to his own. They collaborated in founding *Arya*, but the outbreak of war in August of that year forced her to return to France to settle personal affairs there. However, she was back in Pondichéry in 1920, and in 1926 Aurobindo turned over the running of the ashram to Madame Richard, by now known as *"La Mére"* in French and "The Mother" in English.

Aurobindo retired to a life of concentration. His biographer, Sri Rishabhchand, said of him:

> Sri Aurobindo saw that unless earthly life undergoes a radical transmutation, and the whole being and nature of men are converted into the divine being and nature by the Light-Force of the Supramental Truth-Consciousness, the manifestation of God on earth cannot be perfect. So, he strove for long years of unrelaxed concentration, in collabora-

tion with the Mother, to bring down the Supramental Truth-Consciousness into Matter.

When India gained her independence on his 75th birthday, Aurobindo took this coincidence "not as a fortuitous accident, but as the sanction and seal of the Divine Force that guides my steps on the work with which I began life, the beginning of its full fruition."

He died three years later, 5 December 1950, but he issued during his lifetime a warning to his biographers:

No one can write about my life because it has not been on the surface for men to see.

This, however, did not stop his contemporaries from praising him. Rabindranath Tagore exclaimed:

Arabinda Rabindrer laha namaskar!" (Rabindranath, O Aurobindo, bows to thee!)

In a more sedate statement Romain Rolland said:

He is the most noble representative of a great Neo-Vedantic spirit.

Suggested Further Readings

Purani, Ambalal Balkrishna.
    Life of Sri Aurobindo. — 4th ed. — Pondicherry : Sri Aurobindo Ashram, 1960.
    vi, 372 : plates, ill. ; 23 cm.

Srinivasa Iyengar, K.R.
    Sri Aurobindo. — Calcutta : Arya, 1945.
    viii, 425 p. : plates, ports. ; 22 cm.

GOPAL KRISHNA GOKHALE
(1866-1915)

G.K. Gokhale, born in 1866 in tiny Kotlak village south of Bombay to a poor Brahman family, became the chief representative of moderate nationalism in the first 15 years of the twentieth century. A Chitpavan, the dominant intellectual caste of the Maharashtra area, his life was devoted to education and politics.

The nature of his legacy to India is two-fold: the forwarding of the aims and the work of the Indian National Congress and the exposition of a rational and scholarly approach to India's social and economic problems. Gokhale's second legacy can be seen in the renowned Gokhale Institute of Politics and Economics in Poona, a fitting tribute to his broad interests and scholarly nationalism. Gandhi called him his political guru.

After graduating from Elphinstone College in Bombay, Gokhale became a life member of the Deccan Education Society in Poona, a group whose members pledged their lives to higher education for Indian youth. He taught English literature, mathematics and history at Fergusson College in Poona for 18 years, and from his students' reports was a committed and excellent teacher. A mathematics text he wrote sold some 300,000 copies. While he was teaching, Gokhale also served in politics, bringing to the nationalist scene the clear expository vision that marked his educational work.

Gokhale became a member of the Indian National Congress when he was 23, and within a few years held the important offices of secretary of the Bombay Provincial Conference (1893) and joint secretary (1895). He was president of the Congress at its Benares session in 1905.

A product of the moderate nationalist school exemplified by Dadabhai Naoroji, Pherozeshah Mehta, G.V. Joshi and, above all, Mahadev Govind Ranade, Gokhale carried on and extended their tradition. His pragmatic, rational, secular approach, however, brought him into conflict with the extremist leader, Bal Gangadhar Tilak, also of Poona, also a member of the Deccan Education Society, also a Chitpavan Brahman. From 1895 until his death, Gokhale attempted to guide the Congress into moderate demands in a sympathetic way, battling the extremists' bold and emotional approach as well as British conservative intransigence.

Gokhale's first opportunity to press for reform came in 1897, when, as the Deccan representative to the Welby Commission on Expenditure in London, he outlined the financial and economic grievances of India. Although Gokhale continued to be a severe critic of British economic policy in India all his life, that first trip to London involved a failure that made him even more moderate in all his public presentations. Acting on reports from Poona, Gokhale accused the British plague officers of the violation of women, and when this charge could not be proved, Gokhale had to apologise. The British reaction negated the triumph of his first public speech on finance, and the extremists accused him of cowardice. From 1897 on, Gokhale was the model of accurate and moderate criticism of the British.

In addition to the Indian National Congress, Gokhale's public platforms were the Bombay Legislative Council, to which he was elevated in 1899, and the Imperial Legislative Council, which he became a member of in 1909. His budget speeches were legendary. The subjects indicate the concern of the nationalists of his day: reduction of the salt tax, abolition of excise duty on cotton goods, Indianisation of the bureaucracy, compulsory elementary education, relief to agriculturists and the promotion of industrial and technical education. He was seen by liberal Englishmen as the proof of Indian ability, but by the conservatives as a dangerous man whose belief in eventual self-government and whose criticism of British errors made him the object of mistrust. Nevertheless, Gokhale was offered a knighthood in 1914, which he refused.

Journalism was another of Gokhale's abilities, and he served as editor of *Sudharak* ("The Reformer") and the *Quarterly Journal of the Poona Sarvajanik Sabha*. To develop leadership for all his nationalist concerns, Gokhale founded the Servants of India Society in 1903. Members lived in voluntary poverty and devoted all their energies to social reform and nationalism. The Society did organisational work for Congress, founded the newspaper *Dnyanprakash* ("Light of Knowledge") and two others, developed a library, ran the influential Aryabushan Press and mobilized support for such efforts as the Free and Compulsory Education Bill.

Gokhale elicited respect from the educated nationalist elite all over India and was probably the first truly all-India leader. However, he discouraged any personal following, and he disapproved of the kind of mass activity exemplified by Tilak's development of the Ganapati Festival, a religio-nationalist community effort very effective in the Marathi-speaking area.

Gokhale gave his life to a humane, liberal, secular nationalism, creating a respect among some Englishmen that led to the Labour Party's reforms and furthering the belief among both English and Indians that self-government was India's right and possible future. He died 19 February 1915, and his last words were: "This side of life has been good to me. It is time I should go and see the other side."

— **Eleanor Zelliot**

Suggested Further Readings

Gokhale, B.R.
    Speeches and writings of Gopal Krishna Gokhale. — Bombay : Asia Publishing
    House, 1962-67.
    3 v. : ill. ; 26 cm.

Nanda, B.R.
    Gokhale : the Indian moderates and the British raj. — Princeton : Princeton University
    Press, 1977.
    x, 520 p. [5 leaves of plates] : ill. ; 23 cm.

Wolpert, Stanley A.
    Tilak and Gokhale ... . — Berkeley : University of California Press, 1962.
    370 p. ; 23 cm.

PANDIT MOTILAL NEHRU
(1861-1931)

Motilal Nehru, the father, grandfather and great-grandfather of three Indian prime ministers, was born 6 May 1861 in Delhi. Hailing from a distinguished Kashmiri Brahman family, his grandfather, Lakshmi Narayan, was the first *vakil* (lawyer, or authorized representative) of the East India Company at the Mughul court. His father, Gangadhar, was a police officer in Delhi at the time of the Revolt of 1857. During the siege of Delhi, Gangadhar and his wife, Jeorani, moved to Agra. Gangadhar died there, three months before Motilal was born.

Motilal's childhood was spent in Khetri, Rajputana, where his elder brother, Nandalal, was a *Dewan* (high government official). In 1870, Nandalal went to Agra to practise law, and when the high court moved to Allahabad, he joined him there.

Motilal passed the matriculation examination from Cawnpore and then entered Muir Central College, Allahabad. He began his law practice in Cawnpore, but three years later shifted to Allahabad where Nandalal had a going practice. Nandalal died in April 1887 and was survived by seven children. These became the responsibility of Motilal, and he bore it well.

Motilal was very successful as a lawyer, and in 1896 he was admitted to the roll of advocate of the Allahabad high court.

In 1889 his wife, Swarup Rani, had given birth to a boy whom they named Jawaharlal. Then in 1900 and 1907 two girls were born, Sarup (later Vijayalakshmi Pandit) and Krishna (later Krishna Hutheesingh).

Motilal visited England in 1899 and 1900. By now the Nehrus were quite Westernized, using silverware at the table and hiring European nannies for the children. In 1905, Mr. Nehru took his family to England, putting Jawaharlal in school at Harrow.

Motilal's entrance into politics was tentative at first. He was listed among the delegates to the 1888 Congress in Allahabad as: "Pandit Motilal, Hindu, Brahman, Vakil, High Court, N.W.P." He was more a spectator than participant in subsequent Congress meetings, but was drawn deeper into politics in 1907 over the issue of the partition of Bengal, at which time he stood on the side of the moderates.

However, he became more active after 1912 with the return of his son from England. He was incensed at the internment of Annie Besant in 1917 and later was elected president of the Allahabad chapter of the Home Rule League. In 1918, he attended the Bombay Congress which demanded social changes in the Montagu-Chelmsford reforms, and in 1919 he founded the newspaper, the *Independent*, to oppose the local *Leader*, which was the voice of the moderates.

After the passing of the Rowlatt Acts of 1919, which severely restricted individual freedom, and the massacre at Jallianwala Bagh, Motilal became even more active. He defended in court many persons accused of crimes under the provisions of Rowlatt, and in 1921 both Motilal, who had given up his Western style of living and was wearing homespun, and Jawaharlal were sent to prison for six months. In the meantime he had given his house, which he called Ananda Bhavan, to the Congress Party.

In 1923, Motilal and C.R. Das formed the Swarajya Party, which was a party within the Congress Party. It contested the central legislative assembly election of that year and was the largest party to be seated. It also won a number of seats in several provincial assemblies.

However, a rift over the issue developed between Motilal and Gandhi, the latter holding that non-cooperation was a more effective weapon in the struggle for independence than participating in the legislative councils.

In 1928, Motilal drew up a report, known as the Nehru Report, which demanded immediate dominion status for India. The report was opposed by the Aga Khan and Muhammad Ali Jinnah, representing the Muslim League, and by Subhas Chandra Bose and Jawaharlal Nehru, both of whom believed it was a regression from the stand of total elimination of British rule from India.

Gandhi stepped in with a compromise solution in which Congress would initiate a civil disobedience campaign if dominion status was not granted within a year. It was not, and this left the way clear for Gandhi to resume active leadership of the civil disobedience movement, which he did with a vengeance with the celebrated Salt March of 1930.

Motilal was imprisoned in the aftermath of this campaign and suffered physically from the incarceration. He was released, but he died in Lucknow a short while later, with both Jawaharlal and Gandhi at his side, 6 February 1931.

A touching epitaph for him was delivered by Dr. Patabhi Sitaramaiah, Congress historian:

> Though he was an aristocrat of wealth, yet he recognized, under the inspiration of Gandhiji, the need to chasten life and character by passing through the discipline of poverty and self-abnegation. His gift to the Congress of the Ananda Bhavan is not his greatest legacy; his greatest gift is the gift of his son.

Suggested Further Readings

Nanda, B.R.
    The Nehrus : Motilal and Jawaharlal. — London : G. Allen & Unwin, 1967.
    357 p. : ill. ; 23 cm.

Chablani, S.P., ed.
    Motilal Nehru : essays and reflections on his life and times. — Delhi : S. Chand, [1961]
    xvi, 292, 27 p. : ill., ports. ; 23 cm.

SIR TEJ BAHADUR SAPRU
(1875-1949)

Sir Tej Bahadur Sapru was the greatest constitutional lawyer of his time. He was born in December 1875 at Aligarh of Kashmiri Brahman parents. His early education was in Mathura, after which he attended Agra College. Here he received both his B.A. and M.A. degrees, English literature being his speciality for the latter, winning top place in the first division.

He qualified for the Bar and practised for two years before getting his L.L.B. degree at the district court in Moradabad. He moved to Allahabad to practise in the high court, but met severe competition from Pandit Motilal

Nehru and Pandit Sundarlal, both of them being prominent lawyers. Undismayed, he went on to earn his L.L.M. and L.L.D. degrees.

In 1907, he joined the moderate wing of the Indian National Congress and contributed to the *Leader*, a moderate newspaper. In 1910 he was made secretary of the Congress. He served in the United Provinces legislative council from 1913 to 1916 and in the imperial legislative council from 1916 to 1920. In 1917, he was among the first to join Annie Besant's Home Rule League which was protesting her imprisonment.

He served on Viceroy Lord Reading's executive council (1920-23) and was appointed law member of the group. When Gandhi proposed a boycott at the time of the arrival of the Prince of Wales in 1921, Sapru advised Gandhi that such a move was unwise. His advice was not taken. Then, after Gandhi's trial and imprisonment following the Chauri Chaura incident, Sapru resigned from the council and went back into private practice.

While in government service Sapru had taken the lead in abolishing the Criminal Law Amendment Act of 1908 and in removing restrictions on freedom of the press from the Press Act of 1910.

On his resignation from the viceroy's council, Sir Tej Bahadur (who had been knighted) was free to work for the cause of Indian independence as a private citizen and one who had a thorough knowledge of the working of the government under the British. He was elected president of a national convention to draft a bill for dominion status for India. The convention had the support of many parties, but not that of Congress. He believed that the time had come for full provincial autonomy and responsibility at the centre.

The national convention drafted the Commonwealth of India Bill which was introduced in the House of Commons by George Lansbury, a Labour Party M.P.

In 1928, Sapru was an important member of the all-parties committee which drafted the Nehru Report (named Motilal Nehru), calling for dominion status for India.

He was an influential member of the Indian delegation that attended the Round Table Conference of 1930-31 and was chiefly responsible for the Gandhi-Irwin Pact by which Gandhi, as the only representative of Congress, would be permitted to take part in the second session of the Conference.

Sapru played an important role in bringing about the Poona Pact of 1932 which granted depressed classes almost twice as many seats in the provincial legislatures as had been allowed by Ramsay MacDonald's so-called Communal Award.

In 1934, Sapru was elected to the privy council, and he supported, somewhat reluctantly, the Government of India Act of 1935, holding that it was important because it could ultimately lead to full self-government.

Due to ill health Sir Tej Bahadur stayed in the background of the freedom struggle, stepping forward only when it seemed urgent or when he was summoned to do so. He was disappointed with the failure of the Cripps mission of 1942, and, although he thought the Quit India movement was a tactical blunder, he was critical of the reaction of government for its whole-sale arrests of Congress leaders.

In December 1942, he appealed to Prime Minister Winston Churchill to grant India equal status with the dominions and a thorough overhauling of the central government.

After Gandhi's release, Sapru was summoned to Sevagram to work out a compromise solution with Jinnah, the leader of the Muslim League, who was demanding partition and the creation of Pakistan. Sapru strongly opposed partition and favoured a constitution for a united India which would include safeguards for Muslims and other minorities.

He was strongly supported by Gandhi as a candidate for the constitu-ent assembly in 1946, but his poor health forced him to decline. Though not a member of the assembly, Sapru was often consulted by it, particularly on questions relating to the judiciary. He died in Allahabad 20 January 1949.

C.F. Andrews said of him:

He was by far the clearest thinker whom I had ever met so far in India, and my mind went along with his all the way as I recognised his rugged honesty of purpose.

Suggested Further Readings

Bose, Sunil Kumar.
Tej Bahadur Sapru. — New Delhi : Publications Division, Ministry of Information and Broadcasting, 1978.
232 p. : plates, port. ; 22 cm. — (Builders of modern India)

Mohan Kumar.
Sir Tej Bahadur Sapru : a political biography. — Gwalior : Vipul Prakashan, 1981.
2, 2, 160 p. : plates, port. ; 23 cm.

LOKAMANYA BAL GANGADHAR TILAK
(1856-1920)

Bal Gangadhar Tilak was born into a modestly situated orthodox Chitpavan Brahman family, the son of a school master. Though he was given the name Keshav, his family called him Bal, and this name was used through-out his life. Tilak's early education was begun with his father and was con-tinued in schools at Ratnagiri and Poona. He was a precocious and rather high-spirited lad who often showed personal independence.

In 1872, he passed the University of Bombay matriculation examina-tion. As a youth Tilak had been rather sick and weakly, but during his first year at Deccan College he sought to remedy this with physical training, wrestling and body building. Perhaps for this reason he failed his first year examination, but he never regretted this as he was thereafter a man of robust constitution and an advocate of physical fitness.

In college Tilak became highly proficient in mathematics, but his wide reading covered Sanskrit, English literature and politics. In 1876, he obtained a first class B.A. degree of Bombay University. During the following two years he prepared for the L.L.B. examination with an eye to a career in law. With his friend Gopal Ganesh Agarkar he planned opening an independent school of high educational standards. Instead, as Agarkar tried to finish his M.A., Tilak became an instructor in the New English School which had been founded at Poona in 1880 by Vishnushastri Chiplunkar. The school immediately established a reputation for high standards of academic excellence coupled with an inculcation of independent thought and patriotic spirit.

In 1881, Chiplunkar, Tilak and Agarkar launched two weekly papers which would become the influential standard-bearers of Indian nationalist ideals in Maharashtra, the Marathi language *Kesari* and the English language *Mahratta*. Chiplunkar's sudden death the following year left Tilak and Agarkar in charge of the papers, but their plans were interrupted when they were jailed on charges of defaming the *Dewan* of Kolhapur state. This imprisonment served in fact to strengthen the reputation of *Kesari* and *Mahratta*, and, along with growing recognition of their school's excellence, made Tilak and Agarkar celebrities.

In 1884, they created the Deccan Education Society under the patronage of the Governor, Sir James Fergusson, and on 2 January 1885 Fergusson College was formally inaugurated at Poona.

From 1885 a growing strain developed between Tilak and Agarkar arising from differences in personality and issues of school management leading in December 1890 to Tilak's resignation from the Deccan Education Society. Personal enmities coincided with philosophical differences over public issues of social reform.

Subsequently Tilak employed the columns of *Kesari* to attack the Age of Consent bill pending in the Legislative Council as well as its backers, including Agarkar. He argued that reform by legislation forced changes upon a society not yet ready for them. He was also suspicious of reform arguments which placed social issues ahead of political advance. Any government action to raise the age of consent seemed to him to be British interference in Indian religious customs. His campaign did not halt the legislation, but it did reveal the depth of orthodox Hindu concern and suggested its potential for future mobilisations.

In the 1885 Poona session of the Indian National Congress Tilak took a lead in forcing the reformers' Indian Social Conference to forego the use of the Congress *pandal** as had been previously customary practice.

Communal tensions and violence of a nature unusual to Maharashtra occurred in 1893. In the aftermath Tilak joined with traditional leaders of Poona to find an alternative to Hindu participation in the Muslim Muharram festival. By enlarging the scope of the annual Ganapati festival to unite

* From the Tamil: A shed or arbour constructed for temporary use.

Hindu society, Tilak saw further an opportunity to promote the growth of nationalist consciousness. He introduced a number of innovations such as popularising the use of public (*sarvajanik*) Ganesh images and singing parties (*melas*) of marchers whose songs included political and social commentary.

Publicised by Tilak's papers, the movement spread throughout Maharashtra with the effect of broadening the appeal of nationalism, albeit with a distinctly Hindu flavour.

Tilak next took up the tradition of the Maratha hero Shivaji as a symbol of nationalist regeneration. In so doing he appealed directly to the emergent non-Brahman movement and particularly to the Maratha princes. Nevertheless, as the non-Brahman sentiment spread in Maharashtra, Tilak's clear identification with Brahmanical status, traditions and power contributed to a cleavage within the public life of the region which was never fully overcome in his lifetime.

Although he would later be dubbed "the Father of Indian Unrest," Tilak was prepared to work within the colonial system to some degree. He served a term from 1895 to 1897 as member of the Bombay Legislative Council and would have continued had it not been for his sedition conviction. While a member of the council, he did not refrain from criticism of the government. When failure of the monsoon produced a famine, *Kesari* opened a drive for remission of land revenue demands.

The outbreak of bubonic plague in 1896 led to a fresh crisis as government sanitation measures intruded upon the orthodox homes of Poona. Tilak attacked the British plague campaign's insensitivity to Indian circumstances. Subsequently in 1897 the officer-in-charge was killed by two young men of Poona who, the British charged, were inspired by Tilak and other extremists who had interpreted Maratha history to emphasize the lesson that the end justifies the means, appealing to the higher principle of patriotism. Tilak was charged with committing sedition, convicted and sentenced to 18 months imprisonment. This judicial martyrdom did nothing to dampen Tilak's, patriotic ardour nor diminish his reputation.

Tilak entered the twentieth century as a committed nationalist, linking his essentially practical view of politics and public affairs to an idealistic imperative to free India of foreign rule. He continued to argue that attaining political independence should take precedence over social reforms. He forged links with politically active men throughout Maharashtra and beyond such as Dadasaheb Khaparde in Berar, Dr. B.S.Moonje of Nagpur and Gangadharrao Deshpande in Mysore. In provincial conferences he repeatedly offered trenchant criticism of the flaws of colonial rule and criticised those "moderates" who would practice what Tilak regarded as political mendicancy.

In the testing time of the Indian National Congress following Curzon's partition of Bengal in 1905, Tilak was a strong proponent of militancy and *swadeshi* leading to *swaraj*. Freedom was not something to be given; it was by nature a birthright. Moving beyond politics, Tilak took a lead in organising *swadeshi* industries and the Paisa Fund to promote them as practical measures to advance Indian economic independence.

The following year Tilak pushed Congress to accept the legitimacy of boycott, but at the cost of a bruising contest with older, more moderate leadership. Tilak now spoke of a "New Party" whose fundamental view was that power lay in the hands of the Indian people if they would but take it, using the weapons of boycott and passive resistance.

During 1907 Tilak lost an advantage to his opponents when the Congress venue was transferred from Nagpur, a stronghold of his supporters, to Surat, dominated by moderate interests. However, it was not Tilak, but Indian nationalism which was the ultimate loser at Surat when there occurred the tragic split in the Congress, in which Tilak and other "nationalists" challenged the "moderates" and were expelled for not adhering to "peaceful and constitutional methods."

By 1908 growing instances of anti-British political terrorism had occurred in India. While Tilak deplored violence, he was prepared to explain it in terms of repressive acts of the British government. Allegations of connections with terrorism led in July 1908 to his second sedition trial. He was convicted and sentenced to six year's transportation to Mandalay, Burma. Tilak survived imprisonment with great discomfort and poor health, but maintained his composure through intellectual work, the writing of his *Gita Rahasya*, a cogent commentary on the *Bhagavad Gita*. He was released in 1914 and returned to Poona.

It was ironic that Tilak's first public campaigns after imprisonment were on behalf of the British war effort. Still he sought to find all realistic paths toward realisation of self-rule for India. However, Tilak found his "New Party" virtually disintegrated. Congress was dominated by the old moderate leaders, aside from the new presence of Annie Besant. Tilak sought to re-enter the Congress along with others who had been excluded. In 1916, he founded the Home Rule League which accepted the Congress creed and served as a focal point of political mobilisation. He rejoined the Congress and attended the 1916 Lucknow session, promoting the ideal of home rule.

As the British moved in the contradictory directions of developing what would be known as the Montagu-Chelmsford Reforms while at the same time passing the repressive Rowlatt Acts, Tilak's energies were divided somewhat by an expensive and unsuccessful libel prosecution of an English journalist, Valentine Chirol, in London, but while there he made active appeals to the British public on behalf of the Indian people.

Tilak returned home in 1919 again to enter the political arena. He was active in the Congress and proposed a strategy of taking the opportunity of the new Montagu-Chelmsford Reforms and turning them to India's advantage. Thus he and his protégés were not enthusiastic about the Gandhian strategy of full non-cooperation. It was an ironic twist that on the very day that the Congress was meeting to embrace Gandhi's plans, Bal Gangadhar Tilak died in Bombay. In death he was embraced by the now dominant Gandhian influence as a symbol of nationalism, yet his practical political insights were brushed aside. His close followers in Maharashtra remained on the periphery of the Congress movement during the following years.

In many respects Tilak was in his time India's most influential and important proponent of militant nationalism. His mobilisations broadened political consciousness and participation, although in some respects their nature necessarily had limited appeal to certain communities and regions. His political legacy was a clear-eyed pragmatism which reflected the circumstances of the late nineteenth century Poona affairs.

His surviving lieutenants were among the few consistent and coherent critics of Gandhian strategies, although their regional focus and emerging anti-Brahman mobilisation of the times effectively limited their influence. Tilak's major work as a political leader earned him the sobriquet "Father of Indian Unrest." His political endeavours should not be comprehended without recognition of his other contributions to modern India. His educational efforts were part of the core of a tradition of academic excellence that characterised the intellectual life of Poona and Maharashtra. His own research on religious history provided interpretations which became important components of the developing modern Hindu self-image. His journalism gave a fresh and provocative stimulus to the growth of public affairs in Maharashtra. In all of these activities, Tilak did not labour alone — he inspired and encouraged others to pursue the development of Indian strength and pride in order that all might recognise *swaraj* as a birthright to be demanded.

He was truly a *lokamanya*, revered leader of the people.

— **Frank F. Conlon**

Suggested Further Readings

Cashman, Richard I.
    The myth of Lokamanya : Tilak and mass politics in Maharashtra. — Berkeley : University of California Press, 1975.
    viii, 246 p. : maps ; 24 cm.

Keer, Dhananjay.
    Lokamanya Tilak : father of the Indian freedom struggle. — Bombay : Popular Prakashan, 1969.
    x, 463 p. : ill., ports. ; 23 cm.

MAHATMA GANDHI
(1869-1948)

Mohandas Karamchand Gandhi was the last son of Karamchand Gandhi (1822-1885), the Dewan (Prime Minister) of Porbandar in Gujarat. He was born 2 October 1869 into the Modh Bania caste. He was married at the age of 13 to Kasturba, the daughter of Gokaldas Makanji, a merchant of Porbandar. They had four surviving sons: Harilal (1888-1948), Manilal (1892-1956), Ramdas (1897-1969) and Devdas (1900-1957).

After high school in Rajkot, Gandhi went to England to study law, arriving in London in September 1888. He enrolled in the Middle Temple. After a slow start, he passed his law exams and the University of London matriculation exam. Association with the London Vegetarian Society and the Theosophical Society brought him into contact with Englishmen who shared certain Indian values, and gave him experience in organisational work.

Upon qualifying as a barrister-at-law, he promptly returned to India, where he encouraged his family to adopt European ways. His effort to establish a law practice was ineffectual, and in 1893 he agreed to perform elementary legal work in a lawsuit between Indian firms in South Africa.

On 31 May 1893, soon after arriving in Natal, he was ejected from a train at Pietermaritzburg. His decision that night to finish the work he had undertaken was a formative event in his career. For the first year he was occupied with the lawsuit, which was settled by compromise. When Christian missionaries sought his conversion, he chose (following the advice of the Jain philosopher, Rajchandra Mehta) to remain a Hindu, although he was stimulated by the unorthodox Christianity of Tolstoy.

In May 1894, he was invited to remain in Durban as an attorney for the Indian merchants. As the first Indian barrister in the country he did very well financially. He helped form the Natal Indian Congress through which he defended the rights of the community through representations and publications. In 1896, he returned to India to get his family and to publicise the South African situation. At this time he met Gopal Krishna Gokhale with whom he increasingly allied himself. On his return to Durban he was assaulted and nearly killed.

During the South African War (1899-1902) he organised a corps of Indian stretcher-bearers which served on the Natal battlefields, believing that Indians should demonstrate their acceptance of community responsibilities. In 1901, believing that the impending British victory would improve the position of the Indians, he returned to India to practise law and enter politics.

Called back in late 1902, he settled in Johannesburg to struggle against increasing restrictions on Indian residence and trade in the Transvaal. In June 1903 he began publication of *Indian Opinion*, a quadrilingual weekly. At the end of 1904 he bought land near Durban to establish the Phoenix settlement, at which the interracial press staff could live in a cooperative colony and reduce expenses of the newspaper. He acknowledged the influence of Ruskin and Tolstoy in this experiment.

He had some success in overturning discriminatory ordinances through appeals to the higher courts, but events in the summer of 1906 set him in a new direction. Service in a stretcher-bearer corps in the Zulu Rebellion led him to a deeper personal commitment to public service sealed by a vow of *brahmacharya**. An unexpectedly oppressive new Transvaal registration law

---

* Lifelong chastity.

led 11 September to a vow of non-compliance by the Indian community. Over the next two years Gandhi redefined the concept of *satyagraha**. He was first jailed in January 1908, struck a compromise with General J.C. Smuts, but on his release was assaulted by disappointed followers. Gandhi was imprisoned twice more under conditions of increasing severity.

After an attempt in 1909 to negotiate a settlement in London, at which time he debated with Indian radicals, he wrote his manifesto, *Hind Swaraj; or, Indian Home Rule*.

In June 1910, he established Tolstoy Farm near Johannesburg where he conducted experiments in education, stressing manual labour, simple food, natural medicines and public service. He gave up law practice and was supported by grants from supporters such as R.J. Tata in India. Active resistance was suspended in 1911, and, when resumed in 1913, it extended into Natal with the first large scale involvement of Indian labourers. Gandhi led over 2,000 strikers in an illegal crossing into the Transvaal.

Soon after this he began wearing the clothing of an Indian labourer. The crisis involved the government of India and resulted in passage of the Indians Relief Act of 1914, after which Gandhi left Africa.

Returning to India, Gandhi, at 45, was a national hero, hailed by Rabindranath Tagore as a *mahatma***. He established an ashram at Ahmedabad, the major industrial city of Gujarat, and continued training a core of disciplined workers. Soon he accepted an untouchable family into membership. Invited to the Champaran district of Bihar in 1917, he trained local lawyers, including Rajendra Prasad, in documenting the exploitation of indigo workers and obtained relief from excessive rents.

In 1918, he took up the cause of peasant cultivators in the Kaira district of Gujarat. He also led a mill-workers strike in Ahmedabad which saw his first political use of fasting. In the summer of 1918 he recruited for the Indian army despite sharp criticism from many followers.

The Rowlatt Acts of 1919, continuing wartime restrictions on civil liberties, finally turned Gandhi against loyalty to the Empire. He called for a nationwide *hartal**** 30 March and 6 April, followed by the sale of prohibited literature. The protests led to the Jallianwala Bagh massacre of nearly 400 civilians 13 April. As violence increased, Gandhi suspended civil disobedience 18 April.

In 1919, he acquired control of two weeklies, *Young India* and *Navajivan*, and increased his influence in the Indian National Congress, so that in 1920 its constitution was revised to transform it into a mass organisation reaching into the villages.

His programme for "*swaraj***** in one year" through non-cooperation was adopted, calling for the boycott of British courts, schools, councils and

---

    * Truth force.
   ** Great soul.
  *** Strike.
**** Home rule.

cloth. Thousands were jailed, including Motilal Nehru, C. Rajagopalachari and many others who accepted Gandhi's leadership at this time. He now reduced his clothing to the *dhoti* and *chaddar**.

He was arrested after he called off the campaign in February 1922 following violence in Chauri Chaura, U.P. His speech at the trial won him many admirers worldwide. The unity of purpose between Muslims and Hindus in this campaign was never equalled again, despite adherence of many Muslims to the Congress, and the achievements of Khan Abdul Ghaffar Khan ("the Frontier Gandhi") among the Pathans.

On his release from prison in 1924, Gandhi devoted himself to his "Constructive Programme," including the *charkha, khadi***, Hindu-Muslim unity and the eradication of Untouchability. He also completed his two autobiographies, *Satyagraha in South Africa* (1925) and *My Experiments with Truth* (1929).

At the end of 1929, with Jawaharlal Nehru as president, the Congress declared independence and Gandhi was asked to renew civil disobedience. He left his ashram 12 March 1930 to walk the 300 or so kilometres to the sea at Dandi, where he broke the salt laws and launched a nationwide wave of protest. The role of women such as Sarojini Naidu in this campaign was notable. Though imprisoned, Gandhi was released in 1931 to negotiate the "Gandhi-Irwin Pact" to end the campaign. In September he was in London as the sole Congress delegate to the Round Table Conference on the Indian constitution. His efforts to explain the Indian case to the English people were more successful than the negotiations.

On returning to Bombay, he was immediately jailed under a new wave of repression. In prison he conducted a "fast unto death" against separating Untouchables from caste Hindus in the electoral rolls, and obtained a settlement with Bhimarao Ramji Ambedkar. Released in 1933, he resigned from the Congress and concentrated on his social and economic programmes. In 1936, he settled in the centre of India at a village renamed *Sevagram****. Here he demonstrated his belief that service to the poor, through education in basic skills and simple technology, offered the most immediate hope for India's millions.

In 1939, he intervened in Congress politics to force the resignation of Subhas Chandra Bose who had a more radical programme. After the outbreak of war Gandhi demanded a promise of freedom for India after the war. Not receiving it, he announced a programme of "individual *satyagraha*" in October 1940, designating Vinoba Bhave as the first to go to jail. By 1942 he was calling the British to "Quit India," and upon the declaration of mass *satyagraha* on 8 August was immediately arrested. During his imprisonment at Poona he saw the deaths of his secretary Mahadev Desai and his wife Kasturba.

---

* Loin cloth and shawl.
** Spinning-wheel, Hand-woven cloth.
*** Service village.

Upon his release in 1944 the question of agreement with the Muslim League became paramount. Gandhi met Muhammad Ali Jinnah and accepted the Muslim claim to cultural and economic autonomy, but resisted the demand for partition. Communal massacres made him go to Calcutta and then into the villages of the Noakhali district of present Bangladesh to restore peace.

The appointment of Lord Mountbatten as the last viceroy in February 1947 made the question of national unity more urgent. When Congress leaders began to recognise the need to choose between partition and anarchy, Gandhi, though still against partition, urged the Congress to follow the advice of their leaders. He returned to the riot-torn villages of Bihar and the Punjab, and on Independence Day, 15 August, he was in Calcutta where he obtained peace through fasting.

Afterwards he moved to Delhi and struggled against communal violence while advising the new leaders of independent India.

He called for fair treatment for Pakistan, and was murdered in the garden of G.D. Birla's house 30 January 1948.

Gandhi was one of the most important persons leading India from colonial status to independence. His philosophy of satyagraha and service to the poor is a significant model for human development worldwide.

— **James D. Hunt**

Suggested Further Readings

Brown, Judith.
  Gandhi: Prisoner of Hope. — New Haven: Yale University Press, [1989]
  440 p.

Green, Martin
  Gandhi: Voice of a New Age Revolution. — New York: Continuum Publishing
  Company, [1993]
  424 p.

Parekh, Bhikhu C.
  Gandhi's Political Philosophy: A Critical Examination. — Basingtoke: Macmillan
  [1989]
  248 p.

CHAPTER 10

THE REPUBLIC OF INDIA

B.R. Ambedkar	V.K. Krishna Menon
Vinoba Bhave	Jawaharlal Nehru
Sardar Patel	Lal Bahadur Shastri
S. Radhakrishnan	Indira Gandhi

*I*ndia became a republic 26 January 1950, commemorating the day in 1930 when the Indian National Congress celebrated its first Independence Day.

India had gained *swaraj* 15 August 1947, and its Constituent Assembly under the chairmanship of B.R. Ambedkar wrote a constitution which incorporated elements of the American and British systems of government. There would be a president with mainly ribbon-cutting authority, and the real executive power would be in the hands of a prime minister. The country would be divided into states, the borders of which would be determined on the basis of language. There are now many more states than there were at the beginning, and bushels of amendments have been added to the constitution.

Rajendra Prasad was the first president and Jawaharlal Nehru was the first prime minister. Even before becoming a republic, the government had to deal with the issue of the Indian states which until 1947 had diplomatic ties with Great Britain as the paramount power in India. Hyderabad, the largest of these states, was abruptly taken over by the government when Sardar Patel, the Iron Man of India, marched the troops in. Kashmir was a different problem, situated as it was (and is) between India and Pakistan. Kashmir, with a Hindu raja and a Muslim population, was a matter of dispute between the two countries, and its status probably will not be changed before this book comes out.

Nehru, who acquired his political philosophy from Fabian socialists when he was getting his education in England early in the twentieth century, made socialism the sacred cow of politics in India, and it has remained that ever since. The country has been inflicted with one five-year plan after another during the brief period of its nationhood and remains one of the poorest countries on earth because corruption has devoured the body politic and bureaucratic red tape has stifled economic growth.

Vinoba Bhave was a brave soul who tried through his Bhoodan Movement to enact land reform, and many noble attempts have been made to abolish untouchability and caste, the worst social system known to mankind.

The Republic of India produced many noble leaders, men of the calibre of Radhakrishnan and Lal Bahadur Shastri, but it also brought to centre stage statesmen of less appealing qualities, embodied in a man of the calibre of V.K. Krishna Menon.

The Indian National Congress, though split into factions, was the dominant political party during most of the past 50 years, but it lost power following the death of its leader, Indira Gandhi, in 1984 and the defeat of her son and successor, Rajiv Gandhi, in 1990.

Jai Hind!

BHIMRAO RAMJI AMBEDKAR
(1891-1956)

Dr. B.R. Ambedkar, author, statesman, leader of the Untouchables, draftsman of the Indian Constitution, was born at Mhow in the Central Provinces (present day Madhya Pradesh). Originally from Ratnagiri, the area south of Bombay, Ambedkar's father was a teacher in a school of the Indian Army, stationed at Mhow at the time of the birth of his 14th child.

A member of the untouchable Mahar caste, traditionally the lowly servants of the village, Ambedkar built on the progress his family had made to become one of the first Mahars to receive a B.A. degree (at the University of Bombay). With the help of reformist non-Brahman princes, he also secured a Ph.D. from Columbia University in New York and a D.Ds. from London University, and passed the Bar from Grey's Inn in London.

Ambedkar came of age at a time when the British reforms allowed greater participation in Indian politics, and he took advantage of the changes to press for the rights of Untouchables and to present his ideas on democracy. Even before he completed his education, he returned to India to testify at great length before the Southborough Commission on franchise, securing few of his demands but beginning the process of allowing representation of Untouchables in all legislative bodies.

Muknayak

Two years later, in 1920, he started his first newspaper in an attempt to prepare Untouchables for greater responsibility. He called it *Muknayak**; it was the first of the three Marathi newspapers that he founded, and even though Untouchables were hardly one percent literate, the news was spread throughout the Marathi-speaking area. Ambedkar continued this dual thrust of attempting to change law and at the same time organising the low castes after his return from London in 1923 until his death.

Thoughts on Pakistan, Ambedkar's first book, appeared in 1940. Up until that time, much of his thinking on political and social matters can be gleaned

---

* "The Leader of the Dumb."

from his testimony to government commissions and his speeches to the conferences of the "Depressed Classes."* Ambedkar testified to the University Commission, the Starte Committee on the Depressed Classes, and the Round Table Conferences of 1930-32 which planned further democratising of the legislatures. These conferences created the Government of India Act of 1935 which was to allow Indian-dominated provincial legislatures, and which put Untouchable castes on a "schedule" to receive special benefits.

A major disagreement with Mahatma Gandhi marked Ambedkar's participation at the Round Table in London. One of the few Untouchable leaders who spoke for independence, Ambedkar began to fear the Untouchables' rights would be diminished in an India run by upper castes. He joined Muslims, Sikhs, Christians and other minorities in pressing for separate electorates. Gandhi opposed recognising the separateness of the Untouchables, and in 1932 began a Fast Unto Death. Ambedkar capitulated, but, in exchange for separate electorates, won the right for special representation which still obtains in all Indian legislative bodies.

In 1937, Ambedkar founded his first political party, the Independent Labour Party, in an attempt to mobilise all the dispossessed to press for rights in the newly organised Provincial Legislative Councils. The first of three parties, it won most of the 15 seats it contested, but had little effect in the Council. The Scheduled Castes Federation followed in 1942, and in 1956 Ambedkar returned to a more inclusive basis for his Republican Party. The parties provided a voice for Untouchables, but Ambedkar was never able to find a way to overcome the dominance of the Indian National Congress.

As independence approached, Ambedkar was still at odds with Gandhi and Congress, and a scathing book, *What Congress and Gandhi Have Done to the Untouchables*, appeared in 1945. However, after Ambedkar won a place in the Constituent Assembly, Congress seemed to value his abilities over his criticism, and Nehru named him chairman of the drafting committee for the Constitution and the first law minister of independent India. Disagreement over the slow progress of Ambedkar's Hindu Code Bill and over the non-aligned position of India's foreign policy brought about Ambedkar's resignation in 1951.

The Last Years

During the last years of his life, Ambedkar continued to speak and write, but he also pursued more seriously his life-long interest in a rational religion that would allow equality to all people. He had declared in 1935, after a series of unsuccessful temple entry efforts, that he "would not die a Hindu." In the years before the announcement of his conversion to Buddhism in 1956, the year of his death, Ambedkar visited Buddhist countries, compiled *The Buddha and His Dharma*, undertook the reprinting of books on Buddhism, and established a celebration of Buddha's birth day. His actual

---

*   The official name for Untouchables until 1935 when "Scheduled Castes" came into use.

conversion with some half a million people, most of them Untouchables, took place in Nagpur in October 1956. Ambedkar died in December, and his massive funeral procession in Bombay resulted in another mass conversion. Over 4,000,000 people, many of them Mahars of Maharashtra, have converted to Buddhism under Ambedkar's inspiration.

The affectionate name *"Babasaheb"* was given to Ambedkar some time around 1930, as Ambedkar was gaining fame both outside and inside his community. It symbolises his caring leadership, and Babasaheb Ambedkar is still an inspiration to India's Untouchables, now ex-Untouchables since the practise of untouchability is forbidden by law. The conversion movement, the three colleges and many educatioṇal institutions he founded, his newspapers, his writings, the political rights he won, and the very fact of his accomplishments, continue to make him the most influential of Untouchable leaders. In the years since his death his political parties have diminished in importance, but the literary movement called *Dalit Sahitya** which grew from his movement, the politicised elite which his colleagues and his winning of special government benefits helped create — all these continue to influence the Indian scene.

— **Eleanor Zelliot**

Suggested Further Readings

Ambedkar, Bhimrao Ramji, 1891-1956.
  Dr. Babasaheb Ambedkar : writings and speeches. — Bombay : Education Department, Government of Maharashtra, 1979 -
  v. : ill. ; 26 cm.

Keer, Dhananjay.
  Dr. Ambedkar : life and mission. — 2nd ed. — Bombay : Popular Prakashan, 1962.
  528 p. : ill. ; 23 cm.

Zelliot, Eleanor.
  "Gandhi and Ambedkar — a study in leaderships" in *The Untouchables in contemporary India*, edited by J. Michael Mahar. — Tuscon : University of Arizona Press, 1972. Reprinted by Triratna Grantha Mala, Pune, 1983.

VINOBA BHAVE
(1895-1982)

Vinayak ("Vinoba") Nasahari Bhave was born 11 September 1895 in Gadoda (near Bombay) in what is now the State of Maharashtra. His was a family of well-educated landowners belonging to the Chitpavan Brahman caste. Vinoba's home life included material security, much encouragement to study, and a religious atmosphere to which the asceticism of his mother contributed greatly. At the age of 12, the reclusive Vinoba had taken a vow

---

*   Literature of the oppressed.

of life-long chastity. He was later encouraged to attend Baroda College where he excelled in mathematics and languages. At the age of 20, however, Vinoba resolved to abandon his studies in order to seek *moksha* (self-realisation) in the holy city of Benares.

It was on 4 February 1916, that Vinoba's path first crossed that of M.K. Gandhi. Not yet known as Mahatma, Gandhi was among the speakers participating in the opening ceremonies of Benares Hindu University. Vinoba was a commoner in the audience that boasted bejewelled maharajas and high government officials, including the viceroy of India. Gandhi confronted his listeners with his national shame at having to speak to them in English and challenged them to renounce their wealth and power in order to serve the poor and develop Indian self-rule. Gandhi's words caused such a commotion that Annie Besant adjourned the meeting even before his speech was finished. Vinoba wanted to hear more.

Acting in opposition to his father's wishes, Vinoba was admitted as a member of Gandhi's Sabarmati Ashram in June 1916. In 1921 Gandhi sent Vinoba to establish a new ashram called Paunar, near Wardha in central India.

An Adopted Son

Gandhi came to declare Vinoba an adopted son, calling him a spiritual *Bhim* — a Hercules.

In 1940, Gandhi selected Vinoba above Jawaharlal Nehru for the honour of initiating an individual resistance campaign against British rule in India. All totalled, Vinoba spent five years in prison during the independence movement.

During the period that followed the granting of independence to India in 1947, and even more so after the assassination of Gandhi in 1948, many people considered Vinoba to be Gandhi's spiritual heir. Vinoba helped to establish the new Sarvodaya (Welfare for All) Association, and assisted refugees suffering as a result of the partition of India and Pakistan.

In 1951, he was approached by 40 landless Harijan (Untouchable) families from the village of Pochempelli in Hyderabad (now Andhra Pradesh) whose poverty was increasing as a result of communist agitation for land reform and violent police repression. As Vinoba sought a solution to this problem, on 18 April 1951 a landowner from Pochempelli presented him a gift of 40 hectares (100 acres) to be distributed to the landless. This began the Bhoodan (Land-Gift) Movement.

Vinoba came to believe that the land problem was the main problem for the whole of Asia and began propagating the saying of Tulsi Das that *"sampati sab raghupati ki hai,"** Interpreting God, in this case, to mean society, Vinoba called upon the rich and poor alike voluntarily to give up land for redistribution to the most desperate of their villages.

---

* "All wealth, including all land, belongs to God." Tulsi Das was Hindi poet of the sixteenth and seventeenth centuries.

For 14 years, between 1951 and 1965, Vinoba carried this message on a great walking tour that would cover over 500,000 kilometres and take him throughout every state of India. Eventually, Vinoba and his co-workers collected over 3,200,000 hectares of land from over 700,000 donors. About one-quarter of the donated land was found to be either unsuitable for cultivation or not legally available, and distribution of the remainder proceeded very slowly.

Beginning in 1956, Vinoba added a new dimension to his programme which encouraged Gramdan (Village-Gift) as well as Bhoodan. After several changes, a village came to be defined as a Gramdan village when at least 75 percent of the people owning at least 50 percent of the land signed a pledge relinquishing their private ownership of one-twentieth of their land. By 1969, one-quarter of India's villages (140,000) had been declared Gramdan, but little development or social reconstruction had yet been undertaken in them. Such practicalities were of little concern to Vinoba since, as a renunciant and believer in *Advaita Vedanta*, he was content that the Bhoodan and Gramdan Movements reflected the ideals of Gandhian Sarvodaya and served to remind India of Gandhi's principles of trusteeship and self-reliance.

The Sarvodaya Movement

In 1969, at the age of 74, Vinoba retired from active leadership roles and returned to his ashram at Paunar. What came to be known as the Sarvodaya Movement (including Bhoodan and Gramdan) evolved to include a call for "Total Revolution" under the leadership of Jayaprakash Narayan ("JP") in Bihar.

Vinoba urged JP to challenge the government of Indira Gandhi and even denounced participation in election campaigns as a means which Mahatma Gandhi might have used to bring about change. Stressing cooperation rather than conflict, conversion rather than coercion, Vinoba encouraged a life of committed service which neither seeks power over others nor relinquishes power to elected representatives.

During the State of Emergency (1975-77) when Indira Gandhi suspended civil liberties and jailed Jayaprakash Narayan, among others, Vinoba ended a year of self-imposed silence and tried to help all parties see the common good he believed they all shared. The Sarvodaya Movement split as a result of Vinoba's continued opposition to JP's methods and Vinoba's reluctance to condemn as autocratic the rule of Indira Gandhi. Although this split was modified somewhat by the victory of the Janata Party in the 1977 elections, the cleavages were reaffirmed with the return of Indira Gandhi to power in 1980.

In the last years of his life, Vinoba championed the causes of cow protection and the prohibition of alcohol.

After ailing for several months, a heart attack prompted Vinoba to decide it was time to be free of bodily existence. A fast to the death 10 days later, brought about his death at Paunar Ashram 15 November 1982.

— **Michael W. Sonnleitner**

Suggested Further Readings

Ostergaard, Geoffrey.
   The gentle anarchists : a study of the leaders ... in India. — Oxford : Clarendon Press, 1971.
   x, 412 p. ; 23 cm.

Ostergaard, Geoffrey.
   Nonviolent revolution in India. — New Delhi : Gandhi Peace Foundation, 1985.
   xxiii, 419 p. ; 23 cm.

Ramabhai, Suresh.
   Vinoba and his mission. — Kashi : Akhil Bharat Sarva Seva Sangh, 1962.
   516 p. : ill. ; 26 cm.

SARDAR VALLABHBHAI JHAVERBHAI PATEL
(1875-1950)

Born on 31 October 1875, Vallabhbhai Jhaverbhai Patel came from a lower middle class peasant family of Nadiad, Gujarat. He was one of six children of Jhaverbhai Patel who, it was said, had fought with the Rani of Jhansi and had been taken prisoner by Malharrao Holkar. Not much else is known of him.

Not being affluent, Vallabhbhai started education late and passed the matriculation examination in his late teens. After that, not being able to pursue further education in the general line, he took up law and after passing the examination, he set up practice as a country lawyer in Nadiad. He moved to Brosad in 1902 and had a brilliant practice there as a criminal lawyer.

It is recorded that while he was conducting a cross-examination, he was informed that his wife had died. Rather than ask for a recess to recover from the shock, he hid his grief and continued the cross-examination as though nothing had happened.

The following year (1910) he went to England where he joined the Middle Temple and topped in Roman law and was called to the bar in two years, instead of the stipulated three years.

On his return to India in 1913 he set up practice at Ahmedabad, usually defending those who were the objects of the wrath of British officials. He was drawn into politics by the leadership of Mahatma Gandhi. In 1917 he was elected municipal councillor at Ahmedabad, and from 1924 to 1928 he was chairman of the municipal committee. This period was marked by social service and reform.

The Kheda *Satyagraha*

His secretaryship in 1917 of the Gujarat Sabha was a great assistance to Gandhi's work, and he and Gandhi became close friends during the Kheda *satyagraha* of 1918, launched to secure exception from land revenue since the crops had failed that year. When it was over, Gandhi said that without

Patel's help "this campaign would not have been carried through so successfully."

In 1919, he organised demonstrations against the Rowlatt Acts which perpetuated restrictive laws that had been enacted during the Great War. These laws permitted government to deny due process. Patel also sold prescribed literature and published *Satyagraha Patrika*.

It was during the Bardoli *satyagraha* of 1928 that he became famous and earned the title *Sardar*. This campaign, like that of Kheda, was over the issue of land revenue. In Bardoli taluka the assessment had been increased by 22 percent in some villages and to as much as 60 percent in others.

Once again, non-payment of taxes was the strategy, and once again, those who participated in the campaign were subjected to brutality, arrests and confiscation of property. And once again, it was successful as the government was forced to give into the pressure of 80,000 non-tax-paying peasants.

An ardent follower of Gandhi, he took part in one way or other in every major agitation, like the Salt March, boycott of the Simon Commission, civil disobedience, etc. He was jailed a number of times, but that served to strengthen his determination to fight British imperialism. At the 1931 session of the Indian National Congress he was elected its president and presided over its 46th session.

The session ratified the Gandhi-Irwin Pact which provided for the release of political prisoners by the British and suspension of the civil disobedience campaign by the Congress. The way was now clear for Gandhi to proceed to London for the celebrated Round Table Conferences.

It failed, and in the agitation that followed both Gandhi and Patel, along with many other leaders, were imprisoned. From January 1932 until May 1933, Gandhi and Patel were together in Yeravada Jail. Later Patel spent a year in Nasik Jail.

When the Congress accepted the Government of India Act of 1935 as a trial, Patel, as chairman of the Congress parliamentary sub-committee, guided and controlled the activities of the Congress governments in the seven states where they had majorities and had formed governments. But this was short-lived because the viceroy, at the outbreak of World War II, declared without consulting the Congress that India was at war with Germany.

The Congress governments in the provinces resigned, and 8 August 1942 the Quit India resolution was adopted by Congress, and Patel, along with several other leaders, was arrested.

When the war was over and Britain was preparing to grant independence to India, Patel was one of the chief negotiators. Then when independence finally came, 15 August 1947, Patel was made deputy prime minister and given responsibility for the home, states, and information and broadcasting portfolios.

The Iron Man of India

His greatest contribution to the country was the integration of the Indian states. In less than a year he managed to reduce the number of states from 562 to 26 administrative units. He was also the chief architect of the merger of Hyderabad with the Indian Union. He foresaw the necessity of a strong Indian military force and was responsible for the reorganisation of the services. It is because of all this that he is described as the "Iron Man of India."

He died 15 December 1950, leaving behind a son, Dahyabhai Patel and a daughter, Maniben Patel.

— P.N. Chopra

Suggested Further Reading

Ahluwalia, B.K.
    Sardar Patel : a life. — New Delhi : Sagar, [1974]
    xiv, 294 p. ; 23 cm.

SARVEPALLI RADHAKRISHNAN
(1888-1975)

The second president of the Republic of India was a philosopher and diplomat who distinguished himself both inside and outside India.

Sir Sarvepalli Radhakrishnan was born 5 September 1888 in Tirutani, Chittoor district, in the Madras presidency. (The district is now in Andhra Pradesh.) He came from a middle class Telugu Brahman family and was educated in Christian schools: Lutheran Mission School, Tirupathi (1896-1900), Vellore College, Vellore (1900-04) and Madras Christian College (1904-08). At the age of 18 he was married to Sivakammama.

His career began with a lecturership at Presidency College, Madras, and by 1918 he had become professor of philosophy at Mysore University, a post he held until 1921, when he was appointed by King George V, professor of philosophy at the University of Calcutta. He taught there for ten years, until 1931, and again from 1937 to 1944. In the interval, from 1931 until 1936, he was vice-chancellor of Andhra University.

He was vice-chancellor of Benares Hindu University from 1939 to 1948 and of Delhi University from 1948 until 1962, at which time he was elected president of India.

Greeted Warmly by Stalin

Radhakrishnan's diplomatic service began with his appointment as leader of India's delegation to the United Nations Educational, Scientific and Cultural Organization (1946-52). He served as chairman of the executive board of UNESCO for 1948-49. From 1949 to 1952 he was Indian ambassador to the U.S.S.R. and had the signal honour of being greeted warmly by Joseph Stalin.

On his return from Russia he was elected vice-president of India and served during the presidency of Rajendra Prasad.

He retired from the presidency of the republic, and from politics, in 1967.

Radhakrishnan is best known for his philosophical writings, a complete list of which would constitute a respectable bibliography. Here are a few of his more noteworthy works: *Indian Philosophy* in two volumes (1923-27), *The Philosophy of the Upanishads* (1924), *An Idealist View of Life* (1932), *Eastern Religions and Western Thought* (1939) and *East and West : Some Reflections* (1955).

He received many honours in his career. He was knighted in 1931, and he was awarded over 100 honorary degrees from universities all over the world: Iran, Nepal, Ireland, U.S.S.R., U.S.A. and Italy, not to mention Cambridge and Oxford.

In 1952, the Library of Living Philosophers published an enormous volume entitled *The Philosophy of Sarvepalli Radhakrishnan*.

Radhakrishnan believed that the highest aim of life was to attain, in steps, *Brahmachari* (one who lives and moves about and believes in Brahma), *Brahmajñani* (one who knows Brahma, or the Absolute) and *Brahmavadin* (one who speaks or writes about Brahma). In his first book (which was based on his master's thesis and published in 1908), *The Ethics of Vedanta and Its Presupposition*, he stated:

> Philosophy in India is not an abstract study, remote from the life of man ... The Civilization of India is an effort to embody philosophical wisdom in social life.

Radhakrishnan was opposed to the caste system and made many speeches, both as vice-president and president, in which he stated his wish for all Indians to rid their minds of caste distinctions.

Nehru once said of him:

> He has served his country in many capacities. But above all he is a great Teacher from whom all of us have learned much and will continue to learn. It is India's peculiar privilege to have a great philosopher, a great educationist and a great humanist as her President. That in itself shows what kind of men we honour and respect.

Radhakrishnan died in 1975.

Suggested Further Readings

Radhakrishnan, Sarvepalli, Sir, 1888-1975.
     An idealist's view of life. — London : Allen and Unwin, [1932]
     352 p. ; 22 cm. — (Hibbert lectures ; 1929)
Samartha, Stanley J.
     Introduction to Radhakrishnan : the man and his thought. — New Delhi : Y.M.C.A.
     Publishing House, [1964]
     xi, 110 p. ; 19 cm.

VENGALIL KRISHNAN KRISHNA MENON
(1897-1974)

India has produced many men of admirable qualities. Krishna Menon was one of them.

He was born 3 May 1897, at Paniankara in Calicut. His father was Komath Krishna Karup, a successful lawyer, and his mother was Lakshmikutty of Vengalil House. She was an accomplished musician and scholar, and it may have been from his parents that Krishna Menon got his obstinacy and arrogance.

He began his education at the Tellichery Municipal School. From there he went to the high school of the Brennan College and later the Native High School of Calicut. This was followed by Zamorin's College in Calicut in 1915 and the B.A. examination at Presidency College in Madras in 1918.

He attended Madras Law College for a short time and then studied at the National University in Adyar. While at Adyar he became acquainted with Annie Besant and the theosophical movement and got interested in social work. Before leaving for England, he founded the "Twenty-Nine Club" and the "Social Service League" in Cochin and was Boys' Scout commissioner for Malabar-Cochin.

He went to London in 1924, and obtained a teacher's diploma the following year. He taught history for a year at St. Christopher's School in Hertfordshire before entering London School of Economics, taking his B.Sc. degree in economics in 1927 with first class honours. He got his M.A. degree from University College, London, in 1930 and his M.Sc. degree from London School of Economics in 1934. In that year he was called to the Bar from the Middle Temple. He remained in England until 1952 when he was called home for government service in India.

Influenced by Laski

During his years in England Krishna Menon met and was greatly influenced by Harold Laski who imparted socialist ideas to him and persuaded him that socialism would be just the thing for India once independence came. He became a fire-breathing socialist and made acquaintance with a number of Labour Party leaders and in 1929 founded the India League in London to work for independence. Among his friends and colleagues during this time were Peter Freeman, Reginald Sorensen, Bertrand Russell, Stafford Cripps, Aneurin Bevan and J.B.S. Haldane.

In 1932, Krishna Menon met Jawaharlal Nehru, and the two became life-long friends. Krishna Menon never bothered to build a power base for himself because he knew he could always count on the support of Nehru.

He parted with the British Labour Party in 1941 because it would not support India's claim to independence while the war was on. In 1946 he supported the Cabinet Mission's proposals and urged the Congress to accept them also.

In 1947, he was appointed Indian high commissioner in London and several times led the Indian delegation to the United Nations. His uncompromising position vis-à-vis Kashmir was a reflection of India's uncompromising position there. On one occasion he was asked why he opposed a plebiscite to let the people of Kashmir decide their own fate. His answer was concise — and honest:

"We'd lose."

He was elected to the Lok Sabha in 1952, 1957 and 1962. His popularity was waning as the 1962 election was approaching; so, as defence minister, he persuaded Nehru to do something dramatic to bolster it.

At this time the controversy over Goa had been brewing for some years. Portugal had declared its enclaves in India to be "*provincias,*" as opposed to "*colonias,*" which meant that invasion of Goa, Daman and Diu would be tantamount to invasion of Portugal itself. Goa was, according to Prime Minister Salazar, an "integral part" of Portugal. On the other hand, since Goa was located on Indian soil, Prime Minister Nehru considered it an "integral part" of India. The issue was decided when Indian troops "liberated" Goa in December 1961.

Krishna Menon was re-elected in 1962.

His biggest fiasco, and the one for which he will not soon be forgotten, was his policy of friendship with Communist China. The so-called *Panchshila* ("Five Principles") were to be the cornerstones of Sino-Indian friendship. These cornerstones were smashed when Chinese armies crossed over the Himalayan ranges and occupied Indian territory. At this writing they are still occupying it.

Public pressure was too great for Nehru. He was forced to let his beloved friend go.

Vengalil Krishnan Krishna Menon lived out the remaining years of his life in well-earned disgrace and died in 1974.

He had a brilliant mind, but it was warped by faulty presuppositions. His open and unreasoned hatred for the United States did nothing to improve Indo-American relations at a time when they should have been improved. He thought socialism was best for India. He may have been right about that.

He also thought India could live in peace with a giant Red neighbour next door.

He was wrong about that.

— Henry Scholberg

Suggested Further Readings

George, Thayil Jacob Sony.
  Krishna Menon : a biography. — London : Cape, 1964.
  272 p. ; 23 cm.

Goyal, Sita Ram.
  In defence of Comrade Krishna Menon. — New Delhi : Bharati Sahitya Sadan, [1963]
  272 p. ; 22 cm.

JAWAHARLAL NEHRU
(1889-1964)

After many years of political apprenticeship to his father, Motilal Nehru, to Mahatma Gandhi, Sardar Patel and other Congress leaders, Jawaharlal Nehru became the first Prime Minister of an independent India. He held that office continuously until his death in 1964.

Especially after Patel's death in 1950, Jawaharlal came into his own as a politician. He attempted to dominate the Congress Party as well as India's national and international political agenda. While allowing great autonomy on the level of state politics, he succeeded in leaving his stamp on the federal centre of Indian government. His impact was so great that for years after his death large numbers of Indians believed that only one of his descendants was capable of holding the office he commanded for so long.

At the height of his power one of his critics said of him that he was "English by education, Muslim by culture and Hindu by accident of birth." Though a piece of political polemic, the statement does contain some keys to understanding Nehru, his life and work.

Nehru's kinship group, the "Kashmiri Pandits," were for at least a century and a half, fixtures of the cosmopolitan culture of north India created under the auspices of the Mughuls and their successors. This tradition, that of the "Urdu speaking elite," was a mix of both Muslim and Hindu elements. For example, the first portion of his given name is derived from the Arabic word for "gem:" *jawhar*. His father, Motilal, was a student of Persian and Urdu. His Muslim contemporaries often described Motilal as "one of us in all save religion."

The Nehru Jacket

The Nehru jacket was the *sherwani*, a garment based on the everyday court dress of Mughul nobles. Throughout his life, when not using English, Jawaharlal spoke Urdu rather than the highly Sanskritised Hindi which came into vogue after independence.

Motilal was a convinced Anglophile. He visited England several times and when, in later life, he opposed the British politically, he retained a deep love of English literature, political ideals and institutions.

Jawaharlal Nehru was born in Allahabad 14 November 1889. Motilal hired British tutors for him, and when he was 15, his father took him to England and enrolled him in one of the country's premier public schools, Harrow. Jawaharlal did very well there, displaying the capacity for hard work which characterised his entire life.

After less than two years at Harrow, Jawaharlal entered Trinity College, Cambridge. There he read the natural sciences. Though his subsequent career left him little time to pursue that interest, as prime minister one of his great delights was to chair various scientific advisory committees. Most importantly, throughout his life he retained many of the positivist habits of mind common among British academic scientists of his era.

Jawaharlal's father had hoped that his son would enter the prestigious Indian Civil Service. He was only temporarily disappointed when Jawaharlal decided to enter one of London's Inns of Court and seek admission to the Bar. Jawaharlal became a member of the Inner Temple and was called a barrister, which gave him automatically the right to practise before any court in India. In 1912, he returned to Allahabad with the thought of working alongside his father at the High Court.

In the last years of the nineteenth century and the first decade of the twentieth, Motilal made a reputation as a winner in the court. His income was soon well over Rs.100,000 per year. When he was building his practice, Motilal remained on the fringes of leadership in the Indian National Congress Party. He held seats on one or two important committees, but devoted most of his time to acquiring the fortune which would eventually finance his own as well as his son's political career.

In England, Jawaharlal became involved in the politics of the Indian student community. He was much more radical than his father who remained a staunch moderate. Still, the relationship between father and son was unusually close. While Motilal was a popular and convivial man, he seemed to have few close friends. For much of their life together, his wife was a semi-invalid who suffered from time to time, potentially mortal attacks. Motilal opened up to his son while the latter was still in his teens and treated him like a confidant. As a boy Jawaharlal had few playmates and grew up to be a lonely young man.

Charming, Even Irresistible

He venerated and perhaps feared his father. He responded to his father's openness in kind, but Jawaharlal seemed to feel completely at ease only in the presence of women. His own wife, Kamala, died at a relatively young age, but ladies always seemed to find Jawaharlal charming, even irresistible.

With the end of the First World War both father and son threw themselves into the political life of the Congress Party and the struggle for independence. Motilal rose to become an influential member of the Congress inner circle. Jawaharlal took his turn at doing mundane political tasks, but his father's power soon brought him into prominence.

The Nehrus' relationship with Gandhi was a strange mix of respect, forbearance and tension. Gandhi employed the symbolism and language of popular Hinduism, while the Nehrus were both religious sceptics. Gandhi wanted an independent India based on the supposed virtues of India's pre-industrial village life. Jawaharlal, a committed but non-dogmatic socialist, saw the future in terms of industrialisation and working class democracy.

After Motilal's death on 6 February 1930 Jawaharlal seemed to offer the Mahatma the same mixture of awe and discomfort he had had for his father. As for Gandhi, whose relationship with his own children was never close, he apparently adopted towards Jawaharlal the attitude of an indulgent father. He did not agree with Jawaharlal, but he constantly supported him. By the end of the 1930s Gandhi made it clear that Jawaharlal was his choice to lead India when independence actually arrived.

Like most of the other Congress leaders, Jawaharlal spent time in prison. He used that time well. Always an avid, though unsystematic reader, Jawaharlal deepened his knowledge of Indian history and devoted much time to pondering over the great issues which confronted the nationalists. His own writings bear the mark of his extensive reading and deep thought.

With the end of the Second World War the nationalists began the intensive and frustrating negotiations which would lead not only to independence, but also partition. Nehru once again disagreed with Gandhi by accepting the split between India and Pakistan. As he said, "We have to cut off the head to get rid of the headache."

When Gandhi, in a desperate attempt to stave off partition, offered Jinnah the prime ministership of a united India, Nehru refused to go along. Throughout this time Nehru managed to impress favourably the last viceroy, Lord Mountbatten. He was particularly close — some contend intimate — with Lady Mountbatten. In any event, Mountbatten's account of the last days of the British *raj* gives Jawaharlal more than a fair share of compliments.

Prime Minister Nehru

As Prime Minister of independent India Jawaharlal was at first hemmed in by the power of Patel. After the latter's death in 1950 Jawaharlal was able to perfect the Nehru style. In terms of domestic politics, this meant his control of the national centre. The Congress Party had always been loosely organised. Jawaharlal allowed that factionalisation to persist in the individual states and tolerated non-Congress governments in some of them, but otherwise his views became Party policy. Nehru tried to press for centrally controlled industrial growth and social reform.

On the international scene he was a leading founder of the Non-Aligned Movement. He tried to maintain good relations with all major world powers, while attempting to gain recognition for the rights of the developing world. Some Europeans and Americans condemned him as a Communist stooge, but hindsight demonstrated that he was a perceptive critic of cold war politics.

Many of Jawaharlal's hopes were shattered when China took advantage of a long-standing border dispute to invade India. The Indian army was unprepared for the engagement and suffered a humiliating defeat. Jawaharlal accepted military aid from the United States and reluctantly agreed to drastic increases in his government's military budget. He also found that despite his best efforts, India's growing population erased any gains in the economy.

When he died on 27 May 1964, he was overworked, frustrated and more than a little embittered. In time his daughter, Indira Gandhi, and his tage of a long-standing border dispute to invade India. The Indian army was unprepared for the engagement and suffered a humiliating defeat. Jawaharlal accepted military aid from the United States and reluctantly agreed to drastic increases in his government's military budget. He also found that despite his best efforts, India's growing population erased any gains in the economy.

When he died on 27 May 1964, he was overworked, frustrated and more than a little embittered. In time his daughter, Indira Gandhi, and his grandson, Rajiv Gandhi, succeeded him as prime ministers, but little of his descendants' political careers could have given him some satisfaction that his hopes had been realised.

— **Gregory C. Kozlowski**

Suggested Further Readings

Nanda, Bal Ram.
    The Nehrus : Motilal and Jawaharlal. — London : Allen and Unwin, [1962]
    357 p. : ill., ports. ; 22 cm.

Nehru, Jawaharlal, 1889-1964.
    The discovery of India. — New York : John Day, [1946]
    xi, 595 p. ; 22 cm.

Nehru, Jawaharlal, 1889-1964.
    Jawaharlal Nehru's speeches, 1946-1964. — New Delhi : Publications Division,
    Ministry of Information & Broadcasting, 1958-68.
    5 v. : ill., ports. ; 26 cm.

Nehru, Jawaharlal, 1889-1964.
    Toward freedom : the autobiography of Jawaharlal Nehru. — New York : John Day,
    1941.
    xvi, 445 p. : plates, ports. ; 23 cm.

LAL BAHADUR SHASTRI
(1904-1966)

This brave little man rose from humble beginnings to become the second prime minister of independent India and a giant among men. He was born Lal Bahadur, the son of Sarda Prasad Srivastava, a lower middle class Kayastha school teacher who later served as a revenue officer.

Lal Bahadur's place of birth was Mughalsarai, Benares district, United Provinces, and his date of birth was 2 October 1904. His father died when the child was less than two years old and Lal Bahadur lived with his mother in her parents' house until he was ten, at which time he went to live with his maternal uncle in Benares and attend Harishchandra High School there. He stayed in school until he was 17, and then joined the non-cooperation movement and was imprisoned for a brief time.

He was married in 1927 to Lalita Devi of Mirzapur and would accept nothing more in the way of a dowry than a spinning wheel.

gress Committee from 1935 to 1937.

He was elected to the U.P. legislative assembly in 1937 and again in 1946. In '36 be was made the chief minister's parliamentary secretary, and in the following year he was appointed minister of police and transport.

The Aliyalur Railway Accident

In 1951, he served as secretary of the All India Congress Committee and as minister of railways and transport in the central cabinet. In 1956, he accepted responsibility for the Aliyalur railway accident and resigned.

But he returned to the cabinet in 1957, holding several portfolios: minister of transport and communications, minister of commerce and industry, and home minister.

His big moment came in May 1964 when he was called upon to fill the shoes of Jawaharlal Nehru who died 27 May of that year. Shastri was prime minister only 19 months, but in that short time he showed the kind of courage, decency and strength of character that would be missing in his successors.

His country had two wars with Pakistan: one in the Rann of Kutch and the other in Kashmir. The Indian army beat back the former, and the latter was subjected to negotiation in Tashkent under the auspices of the Soviet Union.

He died 11 January 1966, a few hours after he and President Ayub Khan had signed the Tashkent Declaration. In recognition of his service to his nation he was posthumously awarded the *Bharat Ratna*. One of his biographers put it this way:

> He wanted freedom and prosperity for all. He believed in a constant search for areas of agreement in the working of democracy. Pragmatism rather than dogma appeared to be the guiding principle of the Cabinet under his leadership as Prime Minister, but one objective was constantly kept in mind. As he himself put it: Socialism is our objective. He was always conscious of the problems of poverty and unemployment. He laid stress on strengthening the defence of the country and in honouring the man behind the plough. He did not want to take national unity and solidarity for granted, or be complacent about this sensitive issue.

Lal Bahadur Shastri was short of physical stature, but gigantic of moral character. He was humble, devout and honest and should serve as an example to the fat, corrupt, white-clad, Swiss bank account-laden scoundrels who contaminate the body politic of India today.

There may never be another like him, and that is the tragedy of India.

Suggested Further Readings

Brecher, Michael.
   Succession in India : a study in decision-making. — London : Oxford University
   Press, 1966.
   xii, 269 p. : tables ; 23 cm.

Mankekar, D. R.
   Lal Bahadur : a political biography. — Bombay : Popular Prakashan, [1964]
   vi, 168 p. : group ports. ; 23 cm.

INDIRA GANDHI
(1917-1984)

Indira Gandhi was born 19 November 1917 in her grandfather's house in Allahabad. He was Motilal Nehru, a wealthy lawyer whose ancestry was Kashmiri Brahman. His only son and Indira's father was Jawaharlal Nehru.

Indira's family heritage was one of privilege, both through traditional Indian high caste status and English education. From infancy politics was central to her world. Although given much affection in the household, her childhood was disturbed.

Known as "Indu," she was an only child with few companions and often lonely. She described her childhood as "insecure," and she was described by others as solemn. Her parents and grandparents were jailed frequently by the British during her childhood and adolescence. At the age of four she encountered the British police while they were confiscating valuables at Anand Bhavan, the family home. The story is that she flew at them and threatened them with a knife. Joan of Arc was her childhood heroine, and biographers have speculated that her later ideas of persecution and martyrdom stem from this period.

Anand Bhavan was given to the Congress Party to aid in the struggle for independence in 1929. Indira's father was Congress president and in jail then. Worried about his daughter's education, he began writing her letters full of history lessons, affection and exhortation to be brave. They were later collected and published as *Glimpses of World History*, and Indira regarded them as more valuable than all her other schooling.

Smuggling Messages and Making Flags

She was eager to participate in the freedom movement, and at 12 founded the *Vanar Sena* (Monkey Army), styled after Hanuman's army in the *Ramayana*. It was a children's organisation designed to serve the Congress effort by auxiliary duties such as smuggling messages and making flags.

Indira's early education was inconsistent, and she was never to be a scholar like her father, although she was an avid reader. Throughout this early period Indira's mother was fighting tuberculosis of which she died in

1936 in a sanatorium in Switzerland. Feroze Gandhi, a Congress worker, had been a family friend and was devoted to Kamala Nehru in her illness. After her death he followed Indira to London.

In London, Indira studied for entrance exams to Oxford and in 1938 was admitted to Somerville College, Oxford. She had several bouts of illness as a student, leading to a stay in Switzerland to convalesce. Upon returning to London in 1940, she encountered the blitz and did relief work for a short while.

The following year she returned to India, accompanied by Feroze Gandhi, and they intended to marry. Feroze was a Parsi of moderate means, and Jawaharlal was hesitant about the match because of the wide difference in their backgrounds. Indira was adamant, however, and the marriage took place in 1942.

Later that year Indira tried to address a prohibited nationalist meeting in Allahabad but was arrested and jailed for nine months. Feroze had also been jailed, and they were reunited in August 1943. Indira gave birth a year later to a son, Rajiv.

The family moved to Lucknow where Feroze managed the *National Herald*, the newspaper which had been founded by Jawaharlal. In late 1946, Indira made frequent trips to Delhi where her father was acting as head of the interim government. It was there that she gave birth to her second son, Sanjay, in December 1946.

Despite poor health, Indira travelled from Mussoorie to Delhi during the riots of Partition in 1947. She exhibited courage by twice confronting mobs to save victims from communal anger. She also did relief work in the Muslim quarters of Delhi at the request of Mahatma Gandhi shortly before his death.

Soon after Nehru became prime minister, Indira and her children moved in with him; and she became his official hostess at Teen Murti, the official residence. Until Nehru's death in 1964 she managed the household with its many domestic and foreign visitors and frequently travelled with her father.

Her career with the Congress Party really began in 1955 when she was nominated to the Congress Working Committee. After a few years of increasing responsibility, in 1959 she was elected to the Congress presidency. As the Party president, she came into conflict with her father, the prime minister.

Feroze Gandhi suffered a heart attack in 1959 and died of a second attack in 1960. His death was a shock to Indira. In the next few years Mrs. Gandhi became more visible in politics, travelling frequently abroad and promoting causes such as anti-communalism in India and anti-colonialism abroad.

The Syndicate

In the struggle after Nehru's death a group of five powerful Congress leaders, known as the Syndicate, chose the new prime minister, Lal Bahadur Shastri, and Indira became his minister for Information and Broadcasting.

When Shastri died in Tashkent in January 1966 following the war with Pakistan the previous year, the Syndicate made Indira Gandhi prime minister.

In the election of 1967 she did well in her own district, but the Congress Party lost ground. Also some of the Syndicate members were defeated; so she now had a freer hand in choosing her cabinet. The battle for Party domination, however, was not over. During the next two years there were skirmishes between Indira and factions in the Party representing the conservative and leftist wings. The old party bosses were now sorry that they had chosen Indira in the first place.

The Congress Party crisis came to a head in 1969, the issue being the selection of a new president of India to fill the vacancy caused by the death of Zakir Husain. Mrs. Gandhi's choice was defeated by the Party committees, and she realised that her job was at stake. She acted quickly to propose leftist reform measures which would raise her popularity with the Indian public, thereby outflanking the internal opposition.

First, she removed Morarji Desai as finance minister, and, having done so, she pushed a presidential ordinance nationalising the banks of India. This decision was rewarded with mass popular support. The battle lines had the Syndicate, Desai and their allies, Jan Sangh and Swatantra, on one side, and Indira with the left of the Congress and the two Communist parties on the other. Her candidate, V.V. Giri, was approved for president.

By the end of 1970 Mrs. Gandhi decided to hold elections early and asked the president to dissolve parliament. An alliance of conservative parties campaigned against her with the slogan *"Indira hatao"* ("Remove Indira"). Her campaign promised radical social reform, and her slogan was *"Garibi hatao"* ("Remove Poverty").

Indira and her Party won an astounding two-thirds majority in the Lok Sabha for carrying out her election promises.

Foreign affairs, however, demanded attention first. West Pakistan had invaded East Pakistan after an election result that was unpalatable to West Pakistan. Refugees were streaming over the border into India and were to reach 10,000,000 before the war was over, creating an impossible drain on India's resources. India felt isolated diplomatically as the United States was tilting toward both Pakistan and China against India. In August 1971, Mrs. Gandhi signed a treaty of friendship with the Soviet Union. This was reassuring to India, and the Soviet veto in the Security Council saved India from United Nations sanctions once the war began.

The Bangladesh War

India sided with East Pakistan when the two-week long war broke out. Pakistan surrendered unconditionally 16 December 1971, and Mrs. Gandhi rode on a wave of popularity. However, despite legislative and popular support, she was having trouble fulfilling her promise to end poverty, and trouble was brewing.

The economic crisis of 1972-75 was fueled by the crop failures of 1972-73, the international oil crisis and the inflationary aspect of the Bangladesh War. Prices rose by 22 percent from 1972 to 1973, and government resorted to deficit spending. Food distribution programmes intended to aid the poor were rife with corruption and black marketeering. Instead of poverty being swept away, the gap between the rich and the poor was increasing.

Popular discontent was also increasing, and the central response was repression. Industrial strikes were becoming common place, and Mrs. Gandhi's handling of the massive railway strike of 1974 was not well received. Further damage to Mrs. Gandhi's popularity came with scandals of bribery and corruption within her own party. Perhaps most damaging was her support of Sanjay Gandhi's Maruti auto plant which was a model of bungling inefficiency and monetary waste.

In 1974, a seasoned Gandhian, Jayaprakash Narayan (J.P.) galvanised the discontent against the government. J.P., as he was known, started a movement in Bihar and Gujarat which aimed to lower prices and rid the country of corruption. The method to be used was mass civil disobedience. In early 1975 Congress began losing by-elections, the most spectacular being in Gujarat.

In the midst of this turmoil the Allahabad high court in June delivered a verdict which stunned the country; Mrs. Gandhi was found guilty of corrupt election practices during her 1971 election to parliament. Her election was annulled, and she was barred from public office for six years.

By this time Mrs. Gandhi felt that she was the irreplaceable leader of India, and she used the formidable machinery of the state to keep herself in power. On 26 June 1975, the nation woke up to a surprise. During the previous night all the leaders of opposition and some within her own party were arrested. An arranged power outage kept newspapers from appearing in the morning. She had persuaded the president to declare an emergency in the country. The reason she gave for the emergency was that a "plot" existed against the authority of the government. These charges were never substantiated.

During the emergency, which lasted two years, civil rights and democratic processes were severely restrained, and some felt that Indira was on the road to dictatorship. It is estimated that almost 35,000 people were jailed without trial under the Maintenance of Internal Security Act, and 72,000 were arrested under the Defence of India Regulations. Some were tortured and died in prison. Demonstrations were banned and wages frozen, and state governments which opposed Mrs. Gandhi were taken over.

Sanjay, now his mother's chief advisor, was responsible for some of the worst excesses of the emergency. Slum clearances were carried out to beautify Delhi and other cities at his behest, with great hardship to the slum dwellers. He was also a vigorous promoter of the sterilisation efforts of the family planning programme, and the demand for high numbers of sterilisations led to administrative abuses, including involuntary sterilisations.

In January 1977, Mrs. Gandhi suddenly announced elections for March. With uncharacteristic unity the opposition acted quickly to create the Janata Party, and in the election it handed Mrs. Gandhi a stunning defeat.

The Unifying Factor

Hatred for Indira Gandhi was the only unifying factor the Janata Party had. After three years of bungling, corruption and incompetence, Janata was defeated in the election of 1980, and Indira became prime minister for the second and last time.

Communal problems were developing for her government in Assam and Kashmir, but the most severe problem was that of the separatist movement in the Punjab where militant Sikhs were resorting to terror. In the spring of 1984, Mrs. Gandhi sent 70,000 Indian Army troops to surround the Golden Temple at Amritsar and demanded that the terrorists inside it should surrender. They refused and Operation Bluestar was under way. When it was over, 800 to 1,000 within the Temple had been killed, including Bhindranwale, the leader, and 200 to 300 Indian troops had died.

Four months later, 31 October 1984, Mrs. Gandhi was assassinated by two of her security guards, both Sikhs.

Her son Rajiv was sworn in as prime minister that evening.

— **Diane Clayton**

Selected Further Readings

Masani, Zareer.
    Indira Gandhi : a biography. — New York : Crowell, 1976.
    341 p. : ill. ; 24 cm.

Sahgal, Nayantara.
    Indira Gandhi : her road to power. — London : Macdonald, 1982.
    xv, 260 p. ; 24 cm.

CHAPTER 11

AFGHANISTAN, BANGLADESH, NEPAL, PAKISTAN & SRI LANKA

Afghanistan:
Ahmad Shah Durrani
Dost Muhammad
Sher Ali
Abdul Rahman Khan
Bangladesh:
Mujibur Rahman
Nepal:
Prithvinarayan Shah
Mahendra Bir Bikram Shah

Pakistan:
Muhammad Iqbal
Muhammad Ali Jinnah
Liaquat Ali Khan
Ayub Khan
Zulfikar Ali Bhutto
Zia-ul-Haq
Sri Lanka:
Solomon W.D.R.Bandaranaike
Ananda Kentish Coomaraswamy

*B*ritannia ruled the Indian subcontinent for almost 200 years, from 1757 when Clive won the Battle of Plassey, until 1947 when Lord Mountbatten came out to sever the chains that bound a single colony and numerous little principalities to the mother country. It was at this fatal juncture that a colossal mistake was made: the creation of a geographical and political monstrosity they called Pakistan.

It was a monstrosity bound together only by religious fervour. In the east was a Bengali-speaking population which outnumbered the multi-lingual peoples of the west; yet the nation was to be ruled by the west and have one of the western languages, Urdu, imposed on the east. The two unequal components of this marriage made in hell were separated by 1,600 kilometres of the inhospitable soil of India. The marriage ended in a fiery divorce and a new nation, Bangladesh, was born in freedom, but was ultimately nurtured in military dictatorship.

The unfinished business of Kashmir has haunted the relations between India and Pakistan. At this writing, the brutality with which the agitation in Kashmir is being suppressed exceeds anything witnessed during the days of British *raj*.

This chapter relates the life stories of some of those who participated in this sad history.

There was Jinnah, the *pater patriae* whose genius and strong will won him the dubious title "Creator of Pakistan" but who died thirteen months after his goal had been achieved. There was Liaquat Ali Khan who, like Jinnah, did not live to see the full consequence of what they had created.

And they were followed by Ayub Khan, Zulfikar Ali Bhutto and Zia-ul-Haq, all dictators who were capable only of paying lip service to the ideals of democracy.

On the other side was Bangladesh whose erstwhile hero, Mujibur Rahman, turned villain and died the death of tyrants.

Also included in this chapter are three neighbours, all of whom have figured and still figure in the affairs of the subcontinent.

Afghanistan was very much in the politics of British India, particularly in the nineteenth century, and very much in the politics of Pakistan during the 1980s when Russia bestowed on it the blessings of communism. Both Nepal and Sri Lanka have had a running feud with India, a feud coloured by blood and punctuated by agonised cries of sorrow.

AFGHANISTAN

AHMAD SHAH DURRANI, AMIR OF AFGHANISTAN
(1722?-1752)

Ahmad Shah Abdali, who later took the name Durrani, was born around the year 1722 in Multan. He was of the Sadozai clan and the second son of Muhammad Zaman Khan, the chief of the Abdali tribe of Afghans.

When Nadir Shah of Persia invaded and conquered Afghanistan in 1738, Ahmad Shah was taken prisoner and made mace-bearer for Nadir Shah. He rose in the ranks, and by 1747, when Nadir Shah was assassinated, he had command of the Abdali cavalry battalion.

Following the assassination, he and a group of Uzbeks attacked the Persian army, but were driven off. He then marched on Kandahar which he captured. He also captured a convoy of treasure which was on its way to the Persian camp.

His troops elected him *Amir*, and he took the title *Durr-i-Durran*, meaning "Pearl amongst Pearls" or "Pearl of the Ages." He invaded India for the first of several times in January 1748 with 12,000 veteran troops and captured guns, horses and a great deal of wealth, but was repulsed by Mir Mannu and Ahmad Shah, heir-apparent to the Mughul throne, at the battle of Manpur near Sirhind, north of Patiala.

Then in 1750, he invaded India again and this time defeated Mir Mannu, who had been appointed governor of the Punjab, won from the new Mughul emperor, Ahmad Shah, all of India west of the Indus, plus the revenues of four districts in the Punjab.

Later in that year he captured Herat, and in 1751 Nishapur and Meshed in Khurasan. He won Badakhshan and Balkh in 1751.

Concerned because the Punjab revenues were not forthcoming, he invaded India a third time in December 1751, and defeated Mir Mannu a second time. During this invasion he also conquered Kashmir and forced

Ahmad Shah to cede to him territory as far east as Sirhind. He also set up Mir Mannu as his governor in Lahore. Mir Mannu died in 1753, and the Punjab fell into a state of anarchy; so in 1756-57 Durrani invaded India a fourth time.

This incursion may have been his most devastating for India. The inhabitants of Delhi, Mathura and Brindaban were put to the sword and Hindu temples desecrated. Durrani was forced to return to Afghanistan because of an outbreak of cholera among his troops. He left his son, Timur Shah, as governor of the Punjab after marrying him off to a member of the imperial family.

The next invasion was brought about by the invasion of the Marathas in the Punjab and their expulsion of Timur Shah. Durrani came down from Kabul and, after joining forces with Afghans from Rohilkhand, met the Marathas at the battlefield of Panipat and defeated them 14 January 1761.

Durrani invaded the Punjab in 1764 because the Sikhs had taken over the province and expelled its governor, Khwaja Abid. This time the invasion was limited to a fortnight because Durrani's troops were in mutiny for not having received their pay regularly.

He attempted a final invasion in 1769, but was once more driven back to Kabul by the Sikhs who by this time had a firm hold on the Punjab.

(According to an article in the *Indian Historical Quarterly* (December 1934), there are English records indicating that Durrani made a final invasion of the Punjab in 1769.)

He died in 1772 and was succeeded by his son, Timur Shah. The dynasty lasted until the early part of the next century.

R.C. Majumdar says of Durrani's last invasion:

> Though Ahmad Sháh Abdálí had to return hurriedly from India, his invasion affected the history of this country in several ways. Firstly, it accelerated the dismemberment of the tottering Mughul Empire. Secondly, it offered a serious check to the rapidly spreading Marátha imperialism. Thirdly, it indirectly helped the rise of the Sikh power.... Lastly, the menace of Afghán invasion kept the English East India Company in great anxiety, both during the lifetime of Ahmad Sháh Abdálí and for some time after his death.

Suggested Further Reading

Singh, Ganda.
   Ahmad Shah Durani : father of modern Afghanistan. — London : Asia Publishing House, [c1959]
   xvi, 457 p. : ill., ports. ; 23 cm.

DOST MUHAMMAD KHAN, AMIR OF AFGHANISTAN
(1791?-1863)

Dost Muhammad, born some time between 1789 and 1793, was the 20th of 21 (according to some, 22) sons of Payindah Khan who was chief of the Barakzais and brother of Fateh Khan, the *Barakzai* ("Mayor of the Palace") of Mahmud Shah of the Durranis. Following his father's execution in 1799, Dost Muhammad went to live with his Kazilbash mother's relatives and then with his eldest brother, Fateh Khan, the *Vizir* of Mahmud Shah, ruler of Herat.

The two brothers were commanded in 1816 to defend Herat against an invading army from Persia. While at Herat Dost Muhammad insulted one of the princesses by robbing her of her jewels. Mahmud's son, Kamran, took it upon himself to avenge this insult; so he went to Herat, captured Fateh Khan and blinded him. Dost Muhammad had escaped to Kashmir, but when he and his 20 (or 21) brothers learned of this, and of the subsequent torture and death of Fateh Khan, they revolted against Mahmud Shah and his son and drove them out of Afghanistan.

The brothers then divided up Afghanistan amongst themselves, and Dost Muhammad, being the most talented of the group, got the *créme de la créme*: Kabul, Ghazni and Jalalabad. In 1826, he declared himself *Amir* of Afghanistan.

However, he was surrounded with troubles on all sides. In the north were revolts in Balkh, in the south one of his brothers was opposing him in Kandahar, in the west Mahmud and Kamran were plotting against him, backed by Persia, and in the east the Sikhs had captured Peshawar, with the help of Dost Muhammad's brother, Sultan Muhammad Khan, and were supported by Shah Shuja, the grandson of Ahmad Shah Durrani.

Assuming the title *Amir-ud Mumini* ("leader of the faithful") and declaring *jihad* his troops advanced on Peshawar in 1836 but were defeated by Ranjit Singh.

Dost Muhammad sent a congratulatory letter in May 1836 to the new governor-general, Lord Auckland, asking for help against Persia and the Sikhs. Lord Auckland replied that he did not wish to interfere in the affairs of other states.

However, in the following year a British delegation headed by Captain Alexander Burnes showed up in Kabul seeking Afghan help against Russian threats. Dost Muhammad had asked for, but failed to get, British help in his conflict with the Sikhs; so he showed his contempt for this mission by cordially receiving a Russian envoy, Captain P. Viktevitch.

The British delegation was thereupon withdrawn and the First Afghan War followed in 1839. The British enjoyed initial success, and installed Shah Shuja on the throne of Afghanistan. Dost Muhammad escaped to Balkh and later to Bukhara where he was imprisoned. However, he broke out of prison in 1840, raised an army and attacked the British at Parwandara. For reasons which have not been explained, he surrendered to the British without a fight (even though he enjoyed a strong position) and was sent a prisoner to Calcutta.

The British succeeded in keeping Shah Shuja on the throne in Kabul, but his reception by the Afghan people was less than enthusiastic. The presence of British troops on Afghan soil was even less enthusiastically received, and ultimately the British were forced to back out of the country after a loss of 15,000 men and 15 crores of rupees.

Dost Muhammad was released, and he returned to Kabul in 1842. He gave aid to the Sikhs during the Second Sikh War (1848-49) but after that stayed out of Indian affairs and consolidated power in his own kingdom. He signed treaties of friendship with the British in 1855 and 1857, incorporated Kandahar in his realm in 1856, recovered his lost provinces in the north and recaptured Herat in 1863. During the Indian Revolt of 1857 the British were grateful for his neutrality.

Before he died in Kabul 9 June 1863, he appointed Sher Ali, his third son, to succeed him.

Dost Muhammad Khan had to fight to gain the throne of a divided country. After he gained it, he had to fight to keep it. In the last 20 years of his life he strengthened his hold on his country, and left Afghanistan a strong, united and viable kingdom.

It would be for his sons and grandson to tear it apart and then unite it again in the generations after his death.

Suggested Further Reading

Mohan Lal, Munshi.
   Life of the amir Dost Mohammed Khan of Kabul ... . — New York : Oxford University Press, 1978.
   2 v. : front., ports. ; 23 cm.
   Reprint of 1846 edition.

SHER ALI, AMIR OF AFGHANISTAN
(1820-1879)

Sher Ali, *Amir* of Afghanistan, was born in a period of relative tranquility, but his career was marked as a period of intense rivalry and turmoil.

His date of birth has been listed as 1820 or 1825. He was born in Kabul, the fifth (and third surviving) son of Dost Muhammad who had sixteen sons. Before he died in 1863, Dost Muhammad nominated Sher Ali as his successor.

Sher Ali at once proclaimed himself *Amir*; however, there were other claimants to the throne: his elder brothers, Muhammad Azam and Muhammad Afdal, and Afdal's son Abdul Rahman.

In 1866, Abdul Rahman captured Kabul after the battle of Shaikhabad and later drove Sher Ali from Kandahar where he had taken refuge. In 1867

Afdal died; whereupon Abdul Rahman shifted his loyalty to his uncle, Azam. Sher Ali's elder son, Yakub, defeated both Abdul Rahman and Muhammad Azam in 1868, and Viceroy Lord Lawrence, who throughout the fratricidal struggle in Afghanistan had maintained a policy of "masterly inactivity" (neutrality), at once recognised Sher Ali as *Amir*.

He was invited to India in 1869 by the new viceroy, Lord Mayo, for a *durbar* at Ambala, but returned to Kabul disappointed in the treatment he had received from the British. Instead of being assured of British support in the event of an attack by Russia, which at that time was making threatening moves near Afghanistan's northern border, Lord Mayo simply stated that the government of India would "view with severe displeasure any attempts on the part of your rivals to disturb your position."

The remainder of Sher Ali's career was taken up with his pre-occupation with India to the south and Russia to the north. In 1970, General Kaufmann, the Russian governor-general of Turkestan, began corresponding with Sher Ali. When Kaufmann occupied Khiva in 1873, Sher Ali once again appealed to the British in India for help, but once again was turned down.

The British further alienated Sher Ali and the Afghans when they arbitrated the claims of Persia and Russia over Seistan, Sher Ali maintaining that the British had shown disfavour towards Afghanistan during the negotiations. Further alienation occurred when Sher Ali nominated his son, Abdullah Jan, as his successor and asked the British to recognise him as such. The British refused to do so.

Sher Ali moved closer to friendship with Russia, and a Russian mission under General Stolietoff was received in Kabul. In response to this the British sent a mission to Afghanistan, but it was turned away at the border.

This action gave Viceroy Lord Lytton an excuse to invade Afghanistan, and the Second Afghan War commenced. The British captured the three great passes leading into Afghanistan and occupied Kabul. Sher Ali fled to Mazar-i-Sharif and pleaded for Russia to help him, but the Russians advised him to make peace with the British.

Before he could do so, he died at Mazar 21 February 1879.

He was succeeded to the throne by his son Yakub Khan, but Yakub Khan did not sit on the throne very long.

ABDUL RAHMAN KHAN, AMIR OF AFGHANISTAN (1844-1901)

Abdul Rahman Khan was the son of Muhammad Afzal Khan, the nephew of *Amir* Sher Ali and the grandson of *Amir* Dost Muhammad. He was born in Kabul in 1844, and not much is known of his childhood. (His name is variously rendered "Abdurrahman Khan," "Abdal-Rahman Khan," "Abdur Rahmán," etc.)

When he was ten, his father was appointed provincial governor of Mazar, and he went with him there.

On the outbreak of civil war in 1863 between his father and his uncle, Muhammad Azam Khan, on the one side and his other uncle, Amir Sher Ali, on the other side, he took his father's side. He escaped to Bukhara when his father was imprisoned in 1864, gathered a force, defeated Sher Ali at the Battle of Shaikhabad and took Kabul in May 1866.

When his father died in 1867, he became commander-in-chief of his uncle Azam Khan's forces. On 3 January 1869 he was defeated at Tanak Khan by his cousin, Yakub Khan, Sher Ali's son, and escaped to Samarkand where he was granted an allowance by Russia which was looking to bring Afghanistan into its sphere of influence.

He spent the next ten years in Samarkand, but during the Second Afghan War and following the death of Sher Ali (in 1879), he returned to Afghanistan and received a hearty welcome from the people.

At a conference in Kabul 22 July 1880, the British, who were in possession of the city then, declared Abdul Rahman *Amir* of Afghanistan.

The British left Afghanistan, and Abdul Rahman showed himself to be an able, if at times cruel, leader. He was also a statesman of no mean ability, which he proved by maintaining friendly relations with both England and Russia.

Once he had established his authority, he proceeded to settle border disputes. An agreement in 1887 established the border between Afghanistan and Russia. Then in October-November 1893 he negotiated with Sir Henry Mortimer Durand, the border between Afghanistan and India: the Durand Line.

Unlike his predecessors who were constantly contending with one warring faction after another, Abdul Rahman was able, once he had consolidated his position, to concern himself with bringing about internal administrative reforms.

He brought in English experts to set up factories to manufacture commodities for the people, but he maintained a policy of not allowing too many foreigners into the country. During his reign the first modern hospital was built in Afghanistan. He died 1 October 1901 and was succeeded by his son, Habibullah Khan.

Suggested Further Readings

Wheeler, Stephen.
   The Amir Abdur Rahman. — London : Bliss, Sands & Foster, 1895.
   xvi, 251 p. : ill., map ; 20 cm.

BANGLADESH

SHEIKH MUJIBUR RAHMAN
(1920?-1975)

Sheikh Mujibur Rahman, the "liberator" of Bangladesh, was born in the village of Tangipur, district Faridpur, in eastern Bengal. His date of birth has been given as 17 March 1919, 17 March 1920 and 22 March 1922. He was the elder of two sons born to his parents who also had four daughters.

His father, Sheikh Lutfur Rahman, worked at the civil court as a *sarastadar* and owned over 100 bighas of agricultural land to which he retired after completing government service.

According to one of his biographers, Mujib started taking part in "agitations" when he was in school as a child, and on one occasion spent seven days in prison. He attended school at Gopalganj for a couple of years and then transferred to a Christian mission school from which he matriculated in 1942.

There were two great influences in Rahman's early life: his father and Hasan Shahid Suhrarwardy, an activist who visited Gopalganj in 1939. He was also influenced by Mahatma Gandhi and Netaji Subhas Chandra Bose.

Following matriculation from the mission school, Rahman went to Calcutta to attend Islamia College, living in Baker Hostel off Dharmatala Street (now Lenin Sarani).

Beginning in 1943 Rahman was a councillor in the Bengal Muslim League, and when the time for the election campaign of 1946 came, Suhrarwardy put him in charge of Faridpur district.

He graduated from Islamia College in 1947, the year of independence, partition and the creation of Pakistan, and enrolled himself as a law student at Dacca University in the capital of East Pakistan.

Language soon became a major issue which separated East Pakistan from West Pakistan. Jinnah in 1948 paid a visit to Dacca University and addressed a convocation, during which he called for Urdu to be the one national language of all Pakistan — to which Rahman and his friends shouted:

> No! No! We want Bengali! Bengali is our demand! We want Bengali as the state language of Pakistan!

As a law student he founded the East Pakistan Muslim Students League and became involved in the language movement, organising strikes, demonstrations and meetings to further the cause of the Bengali language. The University authorities at one point expelled him, but shortly after that his expulsion was revoked. Later he was arrested by the Amin Nurul government and imprisoned for six days on 11 September 1948, being held in solitary confinement.

He was expelled a second time, but told his expulsion would again be revoked on condition that he sign a bond of good behaviour. He refused and later was imprisoned a second time by the Amin Nurul government. Altogether Rahman spent about nine years behind bars after the creation of Pakistan.

In 1948, Rahman called a Muslim League council meeting in Dacca. He was convinced that the Muslim League was not representing the will of the majority of East Bengalis. The meeting was not recognised by Chaudhuri Khaliqassaman, chief of the Pakistan Muslim League; so Rahman and his supporters called a conference at Naranganj which ultimately resulted in the birth 23 June 1949 of the Awami League, Pakistan's first opposition party. Its first president was Maulana Bhashani and Shamsul Haq its first secretary. Rahman was elected joint secretary, even though he was in prison at the time. After his release and after Haq was forced to quit because of illness, Rahman became general secretary.

In the election of 1954 the Awami League joined a Popular Front in opposition to the Muslim League and won a spectacular victory. A.K. Fazlul Haq was named chief minister, and Mujibur Rahman was not given a post in the government, despite his backing by Suhrarwardy. Later, however, when Haq found himself in troubled political waters, he added ten Awami League members to his cabinet, and Rahman was given the posts of minister of commerce and industries and of anti-corruption departments.

The coalition government did not last long. It was dismissed by the central government in Karachi after a series of riots broke out in the Chittagong Hill Tracts.

When Ayub Khan came to power in 1958, martial law was declared and political parties banned. However, in the election of 1964, the Awami League came to life and joined a Combined Opposition Party, supporting Miss Fatima Jinnah, sister of the founder of Pakistan, in her ill-fated campaign against Ayub Khan.

Then, in the election of December 1970, promulgated by President Yahya Khan (who had come to power in 1969), the Awami League under Rahman, now its undisputed leader, won 167 seats in the 313-seat national assembly. Nevertheless, both Yahya Khan and Prime Minister Bhutto refused to allow Rahman to form a government and they put him on trial for treason.

The issue of secession was submitted in December 1971 to the highest tribunal known to man: war. In the brief conflict the Pakistan army was crushed by the so-called *Mukti Bahini* (Freedom Army), with not a little help from the Indian army. Bangladesh was born. Rahman was released from prison and, on his return to Dacca, received a tumultuous welcome as the leader of a new nation, Bangladesh — Bengal Country.

He was elected prime minister, and all parties, except the Awami League, were banned. In January 1972, he had himself declared president with virtual dictatorial powers.

His reign did not last long. He and his family were murdered 15 August 1975 in a coup d'état, and the hero of the Bangladesh revolution was succeeded by a litany of generals and dictators.

In the beginning he was undoubtedly a sincere democrat, believing in the power of the people. But if there is a moral to his life's story, it is that absolute power corrupts — absolutely.

Suggested Further Reading

Bhatnagar, Yatindra.
    Mujib — the architect of Bangla Desh : a political biography. — [Delhi : Indian School Supply Depot, 1971]
    299 p. : ill., port. ; 22 cm.

NEPAL

PRITHVINARAYAN SHAH
(1723-1775)

Prithvinarayan Shah forged what had been a miscellaneous collection of petty Himalayan states and satrapies into the modern kingdom of Nepal.

He was born in January 1723, the son of Narabhupal, the king of Gorkha, which at that time was one of the *chaubisi rajya** of western Nepal. His mother was the second queen of Gorkha and daughter of the king of Palpa.

In about 1737 Prithvinarayan married the daughter of Hemkarna Sen, the king of Makwanpur. In the years just before and after his marriage, his travels in Nepal included a lengthy visit to Bhadgaon (Bhaktapur) in the Kathmandu Valley, whose prosperity he grew to admire and covet. One of his first acts after he ascended the throne in 1742 was an abortive attack on Nuwakot, a strategic stepping stone en route to the Kathmandu Valley.

Following this unsuccessful adventure, he went on pilgrimage to Benares where he acquired a second wife, the daughter of Abhiman Singh who later helped him acquire rifles.

After concluding a treaty with Lamjung to the west, he was ready in 1744 to mount another assault, successful this time, on Nuwakot.

For the next 15 years Prithvinarayan avoided major battles and concentrated instead on conquests of small towns and villages near the Kathmandu Valley, thus consolidating his hold on the approaches to the Valley. After two unsuccessful attacks, the fortress town of Kirtipur finally fell to Prithvinarayan's forces in 1767.

By this time the king of Kathmandu, Jaya Prakash Malla, was becoming increasingly nervous about the growing strength of the Gorkha forces. At his request the East India Company sent a force under Kinloch to break Prithvinarayan's blockade of the Valley, but the Company troops were badly

---

*   Twenty-four kingdoms.

defeated. The subsequent conquest of the three kingdoms of the Valley was then assured. Kathmandu fell after a four hour fight in 1768, Patan a matter of days later, and Bhadgaon in 1769.

Prithvinarayan's armies continued to add territory to the west and east in the early 1770's, and by the time he died, 10 January 1775, the kingdom of Nepal had been shaped into more or less its present form.

His military strength resulted from his practice of allowing members of different ethnic groups (Magars, Gurungs, etc.) to share equally the rewards of high military rank. His government was austere, and he kept important posts in the hands of a few loyal families. His legacy included an implacable opposition to corruption and bribery, a tradition of tolerance and respect for the different cultures, religions, and languages that comprised Nepal, and a strong army.

His influence continues today as his direct descendant, King Birendra, rules from the throne in Kathmandu.

— James F. Fisher

Suggested Further Readings

Stiller, Ludwig F.
   Prithwinarayan Shah in the light of Dibya Upadesh. — Ranchi : Catholic Press, 1968.
   viii, 74 p. ; 23 cm.

Stiller, Ludwig F.
   The rise of the House of Gorkha. — New Delhi : Manjusri, 1973.
   xvi, 390 p. : ill., maps ; 23 cm.
   (Bibliotheca Himalayica ; v. 14)

MAHENDRA BIR BIKRAM SHAH
(1920-1972)

Mahendra Bir Bikram Shah was born in Kathmandu 11 June 1920.

He became king of Nepal in 1955 at the death of his father, King Tribhuvan. The Shah Dynasty has ruled Nepal since 1769 when it was founded by Prithvinarayan Shah (q.v.). King Tribhuvan had participated in the successful 1950 revolt against the hereditary prime minister (all from the Rana family) which had effectively ruled Nepal since 1846.

Mahendra grew up a virtual prisoner in the royal palace. He had few contacts with the outside world and was educated by tutors.

After ascending the throne in 1955, he continued the experiments, begun by his father in 1951, in democratic governments formed by various political parties then vying with each other for leadership of the country. The longest lived of these, led by Prime Minister Tanka Prasad Acharya in 1956-57, lasted only 18 months. Despite the political instability of the 1950's, under Mahendra's rule Nepal proceeded to establish diplomatic relations with many nations, join the United Nations and the non-aligned nations movement, attract foreign aid and tourists, and establish new government departments and reform old ones.

The Nepali Congress Party won an overwhelming victory in the 1959 general elections (the first held in Nepal). But the leader of the Party, B.P. Koirala, was a powerful leader who at times threatened the power of the Crown. In December 1960 Mahendra abolished the constitution, jailed Prime Minister Koirala and his ministers, and ruled the country directly. Claiming that Western style parliamentary democracy was unsuited to Nepal's conditions, in 1962 he proclaimed a new constitution, advocating a "partyless Panchayat democracy." The economic counterparts to this political innovation were the establishment of the *sajha** movement and the institution of land reform, neither of which was effectively implemented.

Mahendra continued to rule Nepal through the Panchayat system, expanding the development of roads and education, until his death 31 January 1972.

He was succeeded by his son Birendra.

— James F. Fisher

Suggested Further Readings

Chauhan, Ranbir Singh.
 The political development in Nepal, 1950-1970. — New Delhi : Associated Pub.
 House, 1971.
 x, 336 p. ; 22 cm.

Gupta, Anirudha.
 Politics in Nepal. — Bombay : Allied Publishers, 1964.
 xvi, 332 p. : maps ; 22 cm.

PAKISTAN

MUHAMMAD IQBAL
(1877-1938)

The poet-philosopher of Pakistan, Muhammad Iqbal, was born in Sialkot 9 November 1877. One of his biographers, Iqbal Singh, gives his date of birth as 22 February 1873, and *Dictionary of Indian History* has it down as 1876. However, there appears to be little dispute that he was born in Sialkot.

He was able to trace his genealogy far back enough to know that he was a descendant of Sapru Brahmans from Kashmir and that his forebears had converted to Islam at some point during the seventeenth century. In one of his verses he wrote:

---

* Cooperative.

Look well at me, for in India you will not find another Man of Brahman descent who is versed in the mysteries of Rüm and Tabriz.

Iqbal's father, Sheikh Nur Muhammad, was a devout Muslim who owned a small business and spent much time in the company of local clergymen. His first son was sent to a Christian Mission school as was young Muhammad later on. At one point the father had second thoughts on this and considered withdrawing Muhammad from it and sending him to the local mosque. However, the lad's Arabic and Persian teacher, Mir Hassan, persuaded the father that the boy's training should be in a school, not a mosque.

During his adolescence Iqbal began writing poetry under the tutelage of Hassan. By the time Iqbal completed his studies at the Mission School it had been raised to the status of a college, and he went to the Government College at Lahore in 1895 for further study.

While at Lahore Iqbal was readily accepted in literary circles and often gave readings of his poetry. At the same time he was influenced by two forces that were at work in India at the time: the Aligarh Movement and the Indian National Congress. Iqbal also became active in the *Anjuman-i-Himayat-i-Islam* ("Society for the Aid of Islam").

He graduated from Government College with distinction in English literature and Arabic and went on to get his M.A. degree in philosophy in 1899. Soon after that he was appointed a lecturer in philosophy at Oriental College, Lahore, and later he taught at Government College, his *alma mater*. After teaching for six years, Iqbal, on the advice of his friend and mentor Sir Thomas Arnold, sailed for Europe.

He studied philosophy at Trinity College, Cambridge, where he was fascinated by the works of Hegel, Bergson and Nietsche. And it was in London that he began writing poems in Persian. Although he continued to write in Urdu, Persian became the principal language of his poetic expression.

After England, Iqbal travelled to Germany, on Sir Thomas' advice, and studied at Munich and Heidelberg where he was enthralled by the works of Schiller, Kant, Schopenhauer and Goethe. Iqbal believed woman's place was in the home and in *purdah*, so it came as a shock to him that his three professors at Heidelberg in language, poetry and philosophy were *Fräuleins* Wegnast, Senechal and Schat.

Ultimately, he got his doctorate from Munich on the strength of his thesis, *The Development of Metaphysics in Persia*.

While at Cambridge Iqbal did what many Indian students had done: he studied law; so that by the time he was ready to return to India, he was admitted to the Bar. That was in 1908.

He joined Government College, Lahore, with a professorship in philosophy, but after two and a half years he resigned because he could not fully express himself while in the employ of the British government.

He was knighted in 1922 for his brilliance in poetry, and in 1930 as president of the Muslim League he issued a call for Muslims of India to campaign for a country separate from India. He did not use the term "Pakistan" because that term was not invented until 1933, but the year 1930 and Iqbal's speech can be identified with the genesis of the Pakistan ideal.

Iqbal died in Lahore 21 April 1938 without living to see his dream turn into reality. One can only conjecture, what kind of poetry Muhammad Iqbal would write today if he could see what has happened to his dream.

— **Henry Scholberg**

Suggested Further Readings

Beg, Abdullah Anwar.
  The poet of the East : the life and work of Dr. Muhammad Iqbal. — Lahore : Sh. Md.
  Ashraf, [1961]
  xx, 323 p. : port. ; 25 cm.

Munawwar, Muhammad.
  Iqbal : poet-philosopher of Islam. — Islamic Book Foundation, [1982]
  207 p. ; 22 cm.

Nadvi, Abulhasan Ali.
  Glory of India. — Lucknow : Academy of Islamic Research and Publications, [1973]
  220 p. ; 23 cm.

Singh, Iqbal.
  The ardent pilgrim : an introduction to the life and work of Mohammad Iqbal. — London,
  etc : Longmans, Green, [1951]
  vi, 246 p. : front. port. ; 19 cm.

MUHAMMAD ALI JINNAH
(1876-1948)

Muhammad Ali Jinnah was born Christmas Day 1876 in Karachi. There is some dispute about his date of birth because the register of his school in Karachi recorded it as 20 October 1875; however, he himself insisted on Christmas Day 1876.

(His first name is usually spelled "Mohamed," but the editors here are using "Muhammad" as the preferred spelling of that name throughout this book.)

He was the son of Jinnah Poonjah, a hide merchant, and little is known of his early years. In 1882 he was enrolled at the Sind Madrasah Islam in Karachi which he left in 1886 to attend Gokul Das Tej Primary School in Bombay but to which he returned the following year. He left the *Madrasah* in 1891 to enter Christian Missionary Society High School, Karachi.

The following year (or in 1893) he left for England to study business administration at the Graham Shipping and Training Company, London; however, he later decided to join Lincoln's Inn because "on its main entrance, the name of the Prophet was included in the list of great law-givers of the world."

He remained in London until 1896 at which time he returned to Karachi and started legal practice at the Karachi Bar Council. In 1897, he enrolled as an advocate at the Bombay High Court and was the only Muslim barrister in Bombay. By 1903 he had joined the Bombay Municipal Corporation as legal adviser, and in 1905 he went with Gopal Krishna Gokhale to England to plead for Indian independence in the English elections, representing the Bombay Presidency Association.

The succeeding years were years of heightened political activity for Jinnah. In 1907, he was elected vice president of the Indian Mussalman Association and in December of that year attended the Indian National Congress session in Surat, siding with the moderates in the Congress. The following month he pleaded the case of Bal Gangadhar Tilak in the Bombay High Court, and in 1910 he was elected as the Muslim member of the Imperial Legislative Council where, in February, he sided with Gokhale's amendment to the Press Bill.

In 1913, he was elected president of the Muslim League, and in 1916 he negotiated the so-called Lucknow Pact with Congress leaders whereby separate electorates were secured for Muslims.

Jinnah worked tirelessly for Hindu-Muslim unity, but broke with Gandhi over the latter's policies of trying to achieve independence through *satyagraha*. He also became convinced that Muslims would not get proper representation in a Hindu-dominated political structure.

His distrust of Congress and Gandhi came to a head following the Round Table Conference of the early 1930s, and he withdrew from politics to practise law in London. This period of his life was not long-lasting. In 1934 he returned to India and gradually accepted and promoted the concept of Pakistan as a separate nation to be governed by a Muslim majority.

The 1937 elections resulted in Hindu majorities in all the provinces, and in 1940 the Muslim League under his unquestioned leadership adopted the creation of Pakistan as its goal.

During the years that followed he steadfastly held to this goal despite pressures from Hindu leaders, British statesmen and some of his own Muslim colleagues for compromise.

The Constituent Assembly of Pakistan, of which Jinnah had been elected president, passed a resolution 12 August 1947 making it official and conferring on Jinnah the title *Quaid-i-Azam* which means "Supreme Leader." (He had unofficially acquired this title around 1940.)

Then, on 14 August 1947 Pakistan, a geographical and political anomaly in which a western minority ruled an eastern majority, was created, and Jinnah was its first governor general.

He died 11 September 1948 to be succeeded in the years since by an unending parade of dictators who have paid only lip service to the high political ideals Muhammad Ali Jinnah had espoused all his life.

— Henry Scholberg

Suggested Further Readings

Ahmad, Nazir.
   Quaid-i-Azam : father of the nation. — Lahore : Qaumi Kutub Khana, [1968]
   vii, 134 p. : ports. ; 18 cm.

Ahmad, Riaz.
   Quaid-i-Azam : a chronology. — Karachi : Quaid-i-Azam Academy, 1981.
   161 p. ; 23 cm.

Ahmad, Riaz.
   Quaid-i-Azam's role in South Asian political crisis, 1921-1924. — Rawalpindi : Alvi, 1989.
   x, 286 p. ; 23 cm.

Allana, Ghulam Ali.
   Quaid-i-Azam Jinnah : the story of a nation. — Lahore : Ferozsons,, [1967]
   537, v p. : ill. ; 23 cm.

Bolitho, Hector.
   Jinnah : creator of Pakistan. — 1st ed. — London : Murray, [1954]
   x, 244 p. : ill. ; 23 cm.

Latif, Syed Abdul.
   The great leader. — Lahore : Lion Press, l947.
   200 p. ; 19 cm.

LIAQUAT ALI KHAN
(1895-1951)

He was called *Quaid-i-Millet*, which means "Leader of the Country," and he was Pakistan's first prime minister.

Liaquat Ali Khan was born 1 October 1895 in Karnal. He was the son of a landowner named Rukn-ud-Daulah Shamsher Jang Nawab Rustum Ali Khan and educated at Muslim Anglo-Oriental College (later Aligarh Muslim University) and Allahabad. In 1919, he went to England and entered Exeter College, Oxford, from which he took his degree in 1921. He later completed his term at the Inner Temple and was called to the Bar in 1922.

On his return to India in 1923 he devoted his time to social, political and educational activities, rather than practising law. In 1926, he was elected to the United Provinces Legislative Council, and he stayed in that position until 1940. He was elected deputy president of the Council and was head of the Democratic Party in the Council. In 1940, he was elected to the Central Legislative Assembly and became the deputy leader of the Muslim League Party, Muhammad Ali Jinnah being its leader.

When Jinnah reorganized the All-India Muslim League in 1936, Liaquat was elected its honorary general secretary and remained in that post until 1947 when he became prime minister of Pakistan. In the ten years preceding independence, Liaquat was Jinnah's right hand man and stayed in the background, leaving the public appearances and public speaking to Jinnah.

In 1946, he was appointed a member of the viceroy's executive council and leader of the Muslim League in the Indian interim government. He was the first Indian finance minister, and the budget he presented was called "a poor man's budget."

When a conference was called in London with His Majesty's government, four Indian leaders were summoned to attend it. Liaquat was one of the four, and 15 August 1947 he became the first prime minister of the Dominion of Pakistan.

Jinnah was governor-general of Pakistan, and it fell to Liaquat Ali Khan as prime minister to build the nation, guiding both domestic and foreign policy. He stated his beliefs quite eloquently once when speaking to an American audience:

A question I am sometimes asked is: What is the ideology of Pakistan as a State? I will try and tell you this in a few very simple but very clear words. We Muslims believe in God and His supreme sovereignty. We believe in fundamental human rights, including the right of private ownership and the right of people to be governed by their own freely chosen representatives.

We believe in equal citizenship for all, whether Muslim or non-Muslim, equality of opportunity, equality before law. We believe that each individual, man or woman, has the right to the fruit of his or her own labours. Lastly, we believe that the fortunate amongst us, whether in wealth of knowledge or physical fitness, have a moral responsibility towards those who have been unfortunate. These principles we call the Islamic way of life. You may call them by any name you like.

Jinnah died before the first year of Pakistan's independence had ended; so the responsibility of governing the country fell entirely on Liaquat's shoulders. He carried the responsibility well.

The nagging international problem for both India and Pakistan was that of Kashmir. Here was a princely state which was not surrounded by either India or Pakistan, but lay squarely between them. Its ruler was Hindu, but its population predominantly Muslim.

India's prime minister, Jawaharlal Nehru, was a Kashmiri Brahman and was not about to let the state go to Pakistan. On the other hand, Pakistan insisted that a plebiscite be held in Kashmir, allowing the people to determine their own destiny.

The matter was submitted to the United Nations, and the state was divided, the eastern half going to India and the western half to Pakistan.

It is to Liaquat's credit and due to his strenuous efforts that war between India and Pakistan was averted.

He was addressing a gathering in Rawalpindi 16 October 1951 when an assassin, Said Akbar, an Afghan national from Khost in Afghanistan, fired two shots and killed him.

His last words were:

Khuda Pakistan ki hifazat kare. ("May God preserve Pakistan.")

Pakistan would not have an effective leader until the appearance of Ayub Khan in 1958.

Suggested Further Reading

Zia-ud-Din Ahmad, ed.
        Quaid-i-Millat Liaquat Ali Khan : leader and statesman. — Karachi : The Oriental Academy, [1970]
        xi, 295 p. : ill., ports. ; 22 cm.

AYUB KHAN
(1907-1974)

Ayub Khan was the second son of a non-commissioned officer in the British Indian army. He was born 14 May 1907 at Rehana. Belonging to a Pathan family, he was brought up in the traditions of devout Muslims devoted to good family life and fond of children. After his school education, he was enrolled at Aligarh Muslim University where, due to his family's army connections and also his own good scholastic record, he succeeded, even before his graduation, in being chosen for Sandhurst.

Trained as a soldier, his military career was marked with distinction. During World War II he saw service in the North-West Frontier Province, rising there to command a battalion of the famous 15th Punjab Regiment. After the war, he had in a little over four years, promotions to various ranks, leading to his appointment as the first ever non-white commander-in-chief of the Pakistan army. Holding himself to that position since 1951, he took a significant part in political manoeuvring which resulted in the formation of the Baghdad Pact and the Southeast Asia Treaty Organization (SEATO).

He was drawn into the vortex of his country's internal politics much against his will, first under the presidency of Ghulam Muhammed, and then under his successor, Major-General Iskander Mirza. Called upon by the former to intervene and take over the country, he steered clear of the tempting suggestion by holding himself to his "belief that I could serve the cause of Pakistan better from the place where I was."

Again during a subsequent emergency that followed the suppression of the Constituent Assembly in 1954, he stood by the government of General Mirza who, senior to him by about seven years, had ousted Ghulam Mohammed and taken over as president.

Appointed defence minister by General Mirza, Ayub Khan shared the latter's dislike of politics in general and politicians in particular.

It is no wonder that in the intervening circumstances marked with the reckless moves and measures of the office-hungry politicians, Ayub gave the country a new political dimension by the inevitability of a military *coup d'e'tat*. He was sworn in as president of Pakistan 28 October 1958, and General Mirza was given a one-way ticket to London.

It would seem to be one of Pakistan's many paradoxes that in the 10 years following the bloodless revolution of 1958, the army played a far smaller role in the country's political life than it did before. Within a few weeks of the take-over the army was off the streets, back in its barracks and field stations where it stayed most of the period until widespread political unrest challenged Ayub Khan's authority at the end of 1968. Behind the imposing facade of military rule, President Ayub's was essentially a civilian government.

As president of Pakistan, Ayub Khan ruled with thoughtful care and benevolence unexpected of a military dictator. He was not a believer in the Bismarckian code of political conduct based on the application of sheer force and a policy of blood and iron.

Ayub Khan built the country's assets in a number of ways. His policy in that respect expressed its force and vigour in terms of large and increasing investments in the fields of education, banking, trade, commerce, industry, transport, communications, railways, airports, agriculture, dams, bridges, hydro-electric schemes, nuclear power stations, sports, art, crafts, and, last but not the least, architecture with a beautiful capital at Islamabad, besides numerous satellite towns, minars, mausolea and museum galleries.

He made several attempts to redress the lot of the peasantry while he tried to safeguard and protect also the rights of Muslim women by, despite the vehement protests of the Muslim fundamentalists, innovative modifications bearing on the Islamic personal law pertaining to marriage and divorce.

Building up the country's foreign relations by trade agreements and political alliances with a number of Muslim, non-Muslim and European states, he availed himself of the intermediacy-offer of the Shah of Iran to have good neighbourly relations with Afghanistan as well as India, with particular reference to the Pakhtoonistan issue and Indus Water Dispute.

Notwithstanding his manifold achievements, the seeds of his eventual fall from power lay in his own first act in having introduced a system of what he termed Basic Democracy. This new system had provision for the election of 120,000 basic democrats to be drawn mostly from working and the lower middle classes. These basic democrats were to choose the president and the legislature to rule a nation of 125,000,000 people.

Growing disenchantment with Ayub's regime had been swelling since 1965 when the Kashmir issue and dispute with India had led Pakistan to a war ending with his accepting of a cease-fire, unacceptable and unpopular with many of those inside and outside the army.

Finally, with the crisis of a threatened secession on the part of East Bengal, Ayub Khan surrendered the reins of authority to General Yahya Khan because he did not want to preside over the disintegration of his country. Shortly after that the Bangladesh War broke out.

Ayub Khan died near Islamabad 19 April 1974.

History will remember him as a considerate, thoughtful and de Gaulle-like distinguished military ruler of his times.

— **Mohd. Ikram**

Suggested Further Readings

Ahmad, Mohammed.
  My chief. — Lahore : Longmans, Green, [1960]
  111 p. : ill. ; 22 cm.

Khan, A.A.
  The despot. — [Rawalpindi : Freedom Printing Press, 1968]
  211 p. ; 22 cm.

ZULFIQAR ALI BHUTTO
(1928-1979)

The son of Sir Shah Nawaz Bhutto, a wealthy Sindhi landlord, Zulfiqar Ali Bhutto grew up in Bombay and was educated there at Cathedral and John Cannon School and the J.J.School of Arts before leaving India in 1947 for the United States to study in California, first in southern California, and then in northern California, graduating from the University of California at Berkeley.

After an hiatus in Pakistan where he married Nasrat Sabunchi (his second wife), he studied jurisprudence at Christ Church, Oxford, graduating in 1952, and he was called to the Bar at Lincoln's Inn in 1953. On return to Pakistan he taught constitutional law at Sind Muslim Law College, and he practised at the high court in Karachi.

In 1957, he was a member of two delegations to the United Nations in New York, and in 1958 he represented Pakistan at the U.N. in Geneva. A member of the Muslim League, he entered Iskander Mirza's cabinet as minister of commerce, retaining the position when Ayub Khan took over in October 1958. Appointed minister of information and national reconstruction in January 1960, he was given the Kashmir affairs and the fuel, power and natural resources portfolios in April of that same year. In 1959, and 1960 he led Pakistan's delegation to the United Nations and in December 1962 he headed the Pakistan team for six rounds of talks with India on bilateral relations.

After Muhammad Ali Bogra's death in January 1963 he became minister for external affairs and continued as foreign minister after the 1965 general election. In 1966, he separated from Ayub Khan over the Tashkent Agreement and was removed from his position as general secretary of the Muslim League in March and dropped from the cabinet in June.

Due to the split with Ayub he established his own Pakistan People's Party in 1967. It was a period of unrest in Pakistan; student demonstrations broke out 5 November 1968 after the illness of Ayub Khan, and a student was shot 7 November. Bhutto sided with and addressed the demonstrators; as a result he was arrested 10 November and charged with inciting disaffection. He was jailed and remained in prison for some months until Yahya Khan imposed martial law. Appointed minister of commerce by Yahya, he introduced the Bonus Voucher Scheme to boost Pakistan's exports.*

In the army-supervised elections of December 1970 Bhutto's P.P.P. was victorious in West Pakistan while in East Pakistan Mujibir Rahman's Awami League swept the field. Secessionist fever rose in East Pakistan, and the army took over East Bengal, leading to war with India 3 December 1971. On 7 December Bhutto was appointed deputy prime minister and foreign minister.

Following the defeat of Pakistan by India, Yahya stepped down, all authority was handed over to civilian rulers, and Bhutto became president of Pakistan 20 December 1971.

Bhutto withdrew Pakistan from the Commonwealth in 1972 and instituted land reform (with further land reforms in 1977), and signed the Simla Agreement in July with Indira Gandhi, improving relations with India.

In 1973, he nationalised some 32 basic industries and promulgated a new constitution. In 1974, he hosted the Islamic Summit Conference in Lahore, recognising Bangladesh for the first time. He called for elections in March 1977, and his party won 154 of 200 seats in the National Assembly. Amidst cries of rigging and electoral corruption the opposition refused to take part in political life.

As civil disobedience increased, the army under Zia-ul-Haq staged a coup in July and Bhutto was arrested, but quickly released on bail. He was rearrested under a martial law order on the charge that, on his orders, the federal security force had murdered Ahmad Khan Kasuri, the father of one of Bhutto's opponents. He was put on trial in October 1977, found guilty, and condemned to death. He appealed against the verdict to the supreme court, but by a verdict of 4-3 his appeal was denied, and the conviction and penalty upheld.

Amidst widespread appeals for clemency from people all over the world, he was hanged 4 April 1979.

Zulfiqar Ali Bhutto was outwardly a gregarious man full of bonhomie and joie de vivre, and there is no doubt he enjoyed the finer things of life. But this masked the sensitive and thoughtful person underneath. He was well-read, articulate, and a promising party leader who at first attracted

---

* He abolished the Scheme himself in 1972.

the idealists and independent-minded. But he was also a man who needed to be the centre of attention: he could brook no rivals and countenance no criticism.

As his power increased, he became more dictatorial; and he removed all potential rivals from positions of authority in his government and in his party: it was his nature to regard his party and the democratic system as instruments of power, not of policy. He was the consummate politician. He could be very kind, and he could be cruel. This much-loved (and much-feared) mercurial figure will long be remembered in Pakistan both for his faults as well as for his great charisma.

— **Roger Loug**

Suggested Further Readings

Schofield, Victoria.
    Bhutto : trial and execution. — London : Cassell, 1979.
    xiii, 250 p., plates : ill., ports. ; 23 cm.

Taseer, Salmaan.
    Bhutto : a political biography. — New Delhi : Vikas. 1978
    208 p., plates : ill. ; 23 cm.

ZIA-UL-HAQ
(1924-1988)

Born at Jullundur in northwest India 12 August 1924, Zia-ul-Haq was one of three sons of Akbar Ali, a clerk in a government office in the Punjab. On the partition of India in 1947, his family fled to Pakistan and settled in Peshawar.

After his early education at a local Islamic school, Zia was reckoned bright enough to be sent for further studies at the prestigious St. Stephen's College, Delhi.

At the outbreak of World War II he was attracted by a recruiting poster with the impressive figure of a tank commander wearing a black beret and grinning out of a turret. He made up his mind for an army career. Availing himself of a war-time officers' training scheme, he joined the British Indian army. Commissioned into an armoured unit, he first clipped on his pips and wore his tank commander's beret as a second lieutenant in May 1946. During the last three months of the war he saw service in Burma, Malaya and Java. At the time of partition he was serving on the North-West Frontier which prompted his family's decision to migrate to Pakistan.

After the creation of Pakistan and his promotion as a brigadier, Zia was seconded to Jordan and acted as a military adviser at Amman in 1971 in connexion with the furtherance of King Hussein's policy of crushing the Palestine Liberation Organization.

New prospects for further promotion opened up for him on his return, coinciding as it did with the aftermath of the Bangladesh War. The Pakistan army at that time seemed quite bereft of generals since so many had been disgraced and ousted as a result of their abject fall and surrender in East Pakistan. His promotion in the circumstances was as much rapid as it was inevitable. He was made major-general in 1971 and lieutenant-general in 1975.

The next year, 1976, saw his instantaneous rise to full power and military command. It came under the regime of Zulfiqar Ali Bhutto, the first democratically elected prime minister of Pakistan. Looking for someone to replace General Tikka Khan as chief of the army staff, Bhutto's eyes fell on Zia-ul-Haq, and Zia was appointed by him to that post.

New opportunities for further rise awaited Zia in 1977 when Bhutto had to turn to his chief of the army staff to help bring peace and order in the country. Bhutto's sweeping victory at the polls in the general election, having been disputed and denounced as fraudulent, had led to a wide-spread political conflagration with violence and turbulence all over the land. In the circumstances, Zia-ul-Haq felt himself duty bound to intervene, and did so with the imposition of martial law.

He subsequently arrested Bhutto. This detention order, as well as the proclamation of martial law and the regulations thereunder were, later on in November, challenged in a *habeas corpus* petition from Bhutto's wife. The Supreme Court, however, dismissed the petition.

Not long afterwards, criminal charges for the murder of a political opponent were brought against Bhutto. After a prolonged judicial trial, Bhutto was condemned to be hanged 14 August 1979. Despite appeals from around the world, Zia did not commute the sentence.

Ruling Pakistan, first as Chief Martial Law Administrator and then as its president for 11 years, Zia was as ruthless as had been Oliver Cromwell in the merciless exercise of military powers and enforcement of a Puritanical code of conduct during the Protectorate. As many as 11,000 political opponents and others were locked up with severe sentences under the military courts, while breaches of Islamic law were punished with public hangings and floggings.

Zia survived two army coups against his rule and rode out the international opprobrium provoked by his grim resolve to hang and eliminate Bhutto. And so he would emerge time and again safe and sound from under the thick and toxic smoke of ever increasing misgivings about his intents and policies because of his repeated repudiation of his promises for restoration of democracy and civilian rule.

His title, Chief Martial Law Administrator (CMLA), had come to mean "Cancel My Last Announcement."

At a time when the course of his headstrong and ruthless actions had made Zia a pariah and embarrassment to his Western backers, Russia, like some Angel of Mercy, appeared at the scene one fine morning in 1979. For this day of days synchronised luckily for him with what would be known as the Russian invasion of Afghanistan.

Overnight all changed for good for Zia. Far from being the international oddity, General Zia-ul-Haq, in the words of an American news agency became "the doughty defender of Western interests and the last bulwark against Communistic expansion to the warm waters of the Gulf." The United States, having lost the Shah of Iran to Ayatollahs, saw Pakistan under Zia as the new front line bastion against Russian expansion.

Zia backed the *Mujahideen* in Afghanistan, and in so doing reaped billions of dollars in American aid. His career and life ended abruptly in a plane crash 17 August 1988.

It might be reckoned as a measure of Zia's shrewdness and skill as a political operator that he started by being under-estimated and ended by being over-estimated. Nothing would seem to have behooved him so well in his political life as the manner of leaving it. For, by the providential character of his exit, fate went too far to redeem the unprincipled errors of his career as a seemingly soft-minded yet inwardly hard-hearted politician.

Over and above all else, Zia's end removed mercifully the vendetta between Bhutto's family and the hangman of Zulfiqar Ali Bhutto

— **Mohd. Ikram**

Suggested Further Reading

Sawney, R.G.
     Zia's Pakistan : implications for India's security. — New Delhi : ABC, 1984.
     xv, 200 p. ; 22 cm.

SRI LANKA

SOLOMON WEST RIDGEWAY DIAS BANDARANAIKE
(1899-1959)

Solomon West Ridgeway Dias Bandaranaike, known among family members as "Sonny," was the fourth prime minister of Ceylon.* He was born at the family home, Horagolla, Veyangoda, 8 January 1899, the only son of Maha Mudaliar Sir Solomon Dias Bandaranaike, a wealthy Christian landowner who had supported the British and was amply rewarded for that support.

Young Solomon was first educated by a tutor, a Cambridge graduate. Later, at the age of 16, he entered St. Thomas College in Colombo and then finished his education at Christ Church, Oxford, being called to the Bar at the Inner Temple in 1925.

He returned home, entered politics, renounced his Christian faith and became a Buddhist. In 1927 at a by-election to the Colombo municipal

---

* Since all the events in the life of Bandaranaike occurred before the country was named Sri Lanka, the term Ceylon is employed here.

council he defeated a prominent labour leader and during that same year was elected secretary of the Ceylon National Congress (CNC) which was agitating for constitutional reforms. In 1931 when adult suffrage was initiated in Ceylon, Bandaranaike was elected unopposed to the State Council, representing the Veyangoda constituency, and in 1936 he was made minister of local administration.

He founded the Sinhala Maha Sabha (SMS) in 1937 to give himself a power base with the Sinhalese Buddhist intelligentsia.

In 1947, as a prominent member of the United National Party (UNP), he entered the House of Representatives and was appointed minister of health and local government.

Bandaranaike was an effective speaker but was constantly attacked in the press as a "drummer boy." He had a sharp tongue which he often used to insult his opponents. On one occasion a Trotskyite leader referred to him as "the famous son of a famous father;" whereupon Bandaranaike countered that the Trotskyite was "the obscure son of a still more obscure father."

In 1951, he resigned from the government and from the UNP and the following year founded the Sri Lanka Freedom Party (SLFP) and returned to government in the capacity of leader of the opposition.

In 1956, after forming a united front with four leftist parties under the banner of People's United Front (PUF), he won a landslide election and was named prime minister. He defeated the UNP under Sir John Kotelawala.

A salient feature of the campaign was 10,000 Buddhist monks going door-to-door, singing the praises of Solomon West Ridgeway Dias Bandaranaike.

The PUF advocated a neutralist (*i.e.*, leaning toward the U.S.S.R.) foreign policy and Sinhalese Buddhist nationalism. Britain released her naval bases in Ceylon, and Ceylon stayed inside the Commonwealth of Nations.

Problems occurred for Bandaranaike when he installed Sinhala as the official language of Ceylon and the economy began to falter. He had to steer a devious course between the leftist militants and the conservatives in his coalition in order to stay in power.

During his term of office, in addition to getting Britain to release her naval bases and making Sinhala the official language of the country, Bandaranaike revived Ayurveda as a system of medicine under a commissioner, inaugurated a provident fund scheme for all workers, founded two Buddhist monastic universities, nationalised the Colombo port and the omnibus services of the country, rescued farmers from the clutches of absentee landlords and established diplomatic reciprocal missions in the U.S.S.R., China and other Communist bloc countries.

Finally, he was assassinated by a Buddhist monk, Talduwe Somarama Thero. The shots, six in all, were fired 25 September 1959, and Bandaranaike died the following day.

In 1960, his widow, Sirimavo Ratwatte Dias Bandaranaike, became the world's first woman prime minister.

One of his biographers, Vijaya Samaraweera, said of him:

> Bandaranaike sought and achieved greater visibility for Ceylon through his role in the non-aligned movement, but his successes in foreign policy were not matched domestically.

The extent to which Bandaranaike may be held responsible for the current troubles between Tamils of Indian origin and ethnic Sinhalese may have to be assessed by future historians.

Suggested Further Reading

Gooneratne, Yasmine.
   Relative merits : a personal memoir of the Bandaranaike family of Sri Lanka. — New
   York : St. Martin's Press, [c1986]
   272 p. : ill., geneal. tables ; 23 cm.

ANANDA KENTISH COOMARASWAMY
(1877-1947)

Sir William Rothenstein, the great English portrait artist, said of him: "Today, if India takes her due rank as a first class artistic power, it is in large measure owing to Ananda Coomaraswamy."

Ananda Kentish Coomaraswamy was born in Colombo, Ceylon (present Sri Lanka) 22 August 1877. He came from a distinguished family, his father being Sir Muthukumaraswami Mudaliar and his mother an English lady from Kent, Elizabeth Clay Beely. Sir Muthukumaraswami was a great scholar in his own right, a member of the Ceylonese legislative council, a friend of Disraeli, and he had the singular distinction of being the first Asiatic to be knighted.

He died when Ananda was two years old; so it was natural that his English mother would take him to England for his education. At the age of 12 he joined Wycliffe College in Stonehouse. He had difficulties at first because of his foreign background, but his intellectual gifts soon became obvious, and when he was 15, he was made house monitor and a year later prefect and curator of the club house.

A classmate described his school days thus:

> Coomaraswamy was respected by the boys of Wycliffe College, partly on account of his scholastic ability, but no less by his powers in kicking up his leg, level with or above his head .... He had his ordinary share of teasing by his school mates, based in part on his being of different nationality and colour. This, however, could only be done in safety when

out of reach of his arms and legs. In his first years at school his temper was a very quick one .... He left school with the affectionate regard of his contemporaries who have followed his distinguished career with the greatest interest and little surprise.

After completing inter-arts in 1895, Coomaraswamy joined University College, London, from which he took his D.S. degree in geology and shortly after that was appointed director of the Mineralogical Survey of Ceylon.

Coomaraswamy was pained to notice that young people in his country were turning their backs on Ceylonese culture and opting instead for Western learning. Thus he and his friends initiated a programme of national education and the teaching of national history and culture and of the Sinhalese and Tamil languages.

As part of this campaign he published a monumental work entitled *Medieval Sinhalese Art*.

He wanted to extend his knowledge and appreciation of oriental art and spent some time studying in India. With his intellectual background and his fluency in numerous languages, English, French, German, Pali and Hindi, he was the ideal person to make a serious study of art as interpreted by both Eastern and Western scholars. (He also had a working knowledge of Italian, Spanish, Dutch, Persian, Tamil and Sinhalese.)

In 1910, he collected, during a tour of north India, a massive quantity of Indian art which he offered to the government on the condition that a suitable museum for it be built in Benares, indicating his willingness to serve as curator of it.

The government turned him down; so he approached the trustees of the Museum of Fine Arts in Boston, U.S.A., and they agreed to accept the collection and build a worthy gallery to house it.

Coomaraswamy was appointed keeper of the collection and a research fellow in Indian, Persian and Muhammadan art at Boston. After 16 years he was made curator of the section on Indian and Far Eastern Art and remained in that position most of his life.

He was now free to publish, which he did with a vengeance. His works include: *Aims of Indian Art, Indian Drawings and Paintings, Visvakarma* and *Dance of Siva*.

In his *History of Indian and Indonesian Art* he traced the influence of Indian art as it spread from India to Central, East and Southeast Asia. He wrote several books on Buddhist art and displayed an unsurpassed interpretation of Buddhist iconography with: *Buddha and the Gospel, Elements of Buddhist Iconography and Buddha, The Gospel of Buddhism* and *Nature of Buddhist Art*.

Coomaraswamy was not a man given to the creature comforts of modern living. He once said:

Life is larger than bath tubs, radios and refrigerators. I am afraid, the higher standard of living, the lower the culture.

Nor was he a seeker after publicity or notoriety. After retiring, he planned to settle "perhaps at the foot of the Himalayas or in Tibet, some spot where I shall be least accessible."

However, his dream was never realised. He died at his home in Needham, Massachusetts, 9 September 1947, a little more than two weeks after his 70th birthday.

Coomaraswamy once described Indian art in these words:

This vigorous archaic outline is the basis of its language. Wiry, distinct and sharp as that golden rule of art and life desired by Blake: sensitive, reticent and tender, it perfectly reflects the severe self-control and sweet serenity of Indian life.

Suggested Further Readings

Bagchee, Moni.
    Ananda Coomaraswamy : a study. — Varanasi : Bharat Manisha, 1977.
    xvii, 205 p., [4] leaves of plates : ill. ; 22 cm. — (Bharata Manisha research series ; 9)

Jag Mohan.
    Ananda K. Coomaraswamy. — New Delhi : Publications Division, Ministry of Information and Broadcasting, 1979.
    xiii, 118 p., [1] leaf of plates : port. ; 21 cm. — (Builders of modern India)

Raja Singham, S. Durai, ed.
    A garland of flowers : homage of Ananda K. Coomaraswamy. — Kuantan : 1948-1952.
    2 v. : ill., port. ; 19 cm.

CHAPTER 12

THE RELIGIOUS LEADERS

Gautama Buddha	Raja Rammohun Roy
Mahavira Vardhamana	Swami Dayanand Saraswati
Sankaracharya	Ramakrishna Paramahamsa
Ramanuja	Swami Vivekananda
Chaitanya	Sister Nivedita
Guru Nanak	Mother Teresa
Guru Gobind Singh	

*O*ne is struck with a sameness when one studies the lives of the great religious leaders who have come out of the Indian sub-continent. Almost to a man they bore a striking resemblance to Jesus of Nazareth.

Several of them began their ministries at around the age of 30, notably Gautama Buddha, Mahavira, Ramanuja, Guru Nanak. Most of them turned their backs on worldly possessions, were concerned with the poor and the helpless and were opposed to class distinctions.

India is famous for its caste system, which, though outlawed, still permeates Indian society. Yet men of the stature of Gautama Buddha, Mahavira and Dayanand Saraswati taught and preached against it.

Most of these religious reformers and innovators, though of South Asian heritage, could have an appeal to the Western mind. (Exceptions would be Mahavira who went about wearing nothing but the sky and Sankaracharya who put a curse on those who taunted him when he was performing funeral rites for his mother.)

All of the persons in this chapter hailed from South Asia, and all were men, with the exceptions of Sister Nivedita (Margaret Noble) who was British and Mother Teresa who was born of Albanian parents, but became an Indian citizen. Mother Teresa has remained a loyal daughter of the Roman Catholic Church. Sister Nivedita, on the other hand, accepted the universal gospel preached by Vivekananda.

It is fitting that a chapter should be devoted to the great and the near-great of India's spiritual past.

GAUTAMA BUDDHA
(c.566-c.486 B.C.)

Gautama Buddha, was born in about 566 B.C. in present day Nepal. He was the son of Suddhodana, Raja of Kapilavastu, and Maya, a princess of Devadaha. The family was of the clan of Sakhya of the Kshatriya caste.

The story of his birth, like many of the stories of his life, are based on legend and tradition, inasmuch as no written record of his life appeared until over 200 years after his death.

Raja Suddhodana was married to Maya and her sister, Prajapati, but neither sister had produced a son. Then one night Maya had a strange dream. In the dream four kings raised her and her bed and took her away. Then their queens bathed her and put her on a couch with her head to the east. Next a white elephant appeared, encircled her bed three times, struck her in the side with his trunk and entered her womb.

In the morning she told her husband about the dream, and he summoned his most learned Brahmans, all of whom agreed that this meant she would give birth to a famous son. If he stayed in the palace, he would become a mighty king, they said; but if he renounced the world, he would become one of its wonders.

When Maya's time was near, she insisted on going to her village at Devadaha for the birth. But before she arrived, she delivered her son at a wood known as Lumbini Grove. The forest rejoiced at the birth, and Maya and her child were carried to Devadaha where she died seven days later. The child was named Siddhartha, and he was brought up by Prajapati.

Although a prince, he early on showed mystical and spiritual leanings. At the age of five he was sent to a school intended only for the sons of nobility and run by a learned Brahman. Siddhartha was popular with his schoolmates, but his popularity caused his cousin, Devadatta, to become jealous.

This came to a head one day when Siddhartha and his Brahman friend, Udayan, were walking in the palace garden. A flock of wild geese was flying overhead, and as the boys were admiring it, one of the geese fell at their feet, wounded by an arrow. Siddhartha picked it up, removed the arrow and nursed it back to health. The goose had been shot by Devadatta. When Devadatta learned that Siddhartha had healed the wounded goose, he demanded that it be given back to him. Siddhartha refused, claiming that since he had healed the bird, it belonged to him.

Devadatta spread rumours to the effect that Siddhartha was not fit to become the ruler of a warlike race since the hunt, not the healing of wounded animals, was the true sport of kings. As soon as the Raja heard this, he had Siddhartha take training in riding, archery and horsemanship.

When the time came for Siddhartha, now 16, to prove his manliness, a challenge was issued to all the nobles of the kingdom. A contest was held, and the victor, Siddhartha, won the hand of Yasodhara, the sister of Devadatta.

Siddhartha, after a time tired of the pleasures of the palace, his wife, and his son, Rahula, and at the age of 29 renounced all and became a *sannyasi* (ascetic) to seek the supreme peace of *nirvana* (the state of a snuffed out candle).

When he left the palace and his family, he was tempted by Mara, the spirit of evil, to return to a life full of the worldly pleasures, an event reminding one of Jesus who was tempted by Satan for 40 days and 40 nights following his baptism.

Buddha, like Jesus, resisted the tempter, and reached the bank of the Anoma River. There he took off his jewels and gave them to his servant, telling him to return with them to the palace. He then gave his fine clothes to a poor man passing by and walked to Rajgriha, the capital of Magadha. There were hills nearby and caves where Brahmans lived. Siddhartha attached himself to two of the Brahmans, Alara and Udraka, and under their guidance for six years he tried self-mortification as a means of achieving *nirvana*.

Finally, he left them and walked to the Nairanjara River where, exhausted, a maiden offered him a bowl of rice milk intended for the village gods. He sat down under a pipal tree and meditated. He fell soon into a deep trance-like sleep. When he awoke the next morning, he felt refreshed and realised that he had attained what he had been searching for: Enlightenment. He had achieved it not through self-mortification, but through Self-Knowledge.

Thus he became known as Buddha, the "Enlightened One," and *Tathagatha*, the "One Who Has Attained the Truth." He gathered about him 60 followers, and they helped him spread his message. For 45 years he went about north India preaching. At one point he converted the Raja of Magadha, Bimbisara, and this caused his fame to spread. His aging father sent messengers to bring him home, but the messengers would be converted and remain with Buddha. Finally, his father went to him himself and brought him back to the palace.

Rahula, Buddha's son, became a monk, and Yasodhara, Buddha's wife, became a nun, as did Buddha's mother after the king died.

When Buddha was 40 years old, Devadatta, his childhood enemy, who had founded a rival order, attempted to assassinate him. This failed, and Devadatta died shortly after that. On his death, his monks joined Buddha's order.

Like many founders of religious orders, Buddha did not leave the Hindu religion into which he was born. It is not likely that he suspected his teachings would form a distinct religion that would spread throughout India and to other parts of the world. The essentials of his religion, Buddhism, are found in the Noble Eight-Fold Path: 1. Right Belief, 2. Right Aims, 3. Right Speech, 4. Right Actions, 5. Right Means of Livelihood, 6. Right Endeavour, 7. Right Mindfulness, 8. Right Meditation.

Buddha did not believe in blood sacrifices or the caste system. His doctrine was ethical, rather than theological.

In his old age he said to Ananda, his personal attendant for many years:

You may think that the Word ends when the teacher goes, but it is not so. The law and the rules that I have laid down will be your teacher.

Then, addressing a crowd of monks, he spoke his last words:

Decay is inherent in all component things; work out your salvation with diligence.

He was 80 years old when he died.

Suggested Further Readings

Books on Gautama Buddha and Buddhism, if set on shelves side by side, would form a
     library.
Here are a few suggested for the avid searcher:

On Gautama Buddha:
Ikeda, Daisaku.
     The living Buddha : an interpretive biography. — New York : Weatherhill, 1976.
     x, 148 p., 4 leaves of plates : ill. ; 24 cm.

Oldenberg, Hermann, 1854-1920.
     Buddha : his life, his doctrine, his order. — London : Williams & Norgate, 1882.
     viii, 454 p. ; 23 cm.

Thomas, Edward J.
     The life of Buddha as legend and history. — 3rd ed. — [London?] : Routledge &
     Kegan Paul, 1949.
     xxiv, 299 p., 4 leaves of plates : ill. ; 22 cm.

On Buddhism:
Rahula, Walpola.
     What Buddha taught. — 1st ed. — Bedford : Gordon Fraser Gallery, 1959.
     xvi, 103 p. : front., plates ; 22 cm. — (Gordon Fraser Gallery gift books)

Ranasinghe, C.P.
     The Buddha's explanation of the universe. — Colombo : Lanka Bauddha Mandalaya
     Fund, [1957]
     414 p. ; 19 cm.

Silachara, Bhikku.
     The noble eight-fold path. — Madras : Theosophical, 1944.
     vii, 194 p. ; 19 cm.

MAHAVIRA VARDHAMANA
(599?-527? B.C.)

Mahavira Vardhamana, the 24th and last of the Jain prophets, or *tirthankaras*, was the son of Siddhartha, a Jñatrika chief of Kundapura, and Trisala, a Kshatriya princess who was the sister of Chetaka, a powerful ruler of Vaisali.

His dates have been given as 599-527 B.C. by some scholars, and 540-468 B.C. by others. The problem here is that there are two distinct Jain traditions, Digambara and Svetambara, which add to the confusion. What is generally agreed is that he died at the age of 72.

What is more important than the exact dates of his birth and death is what he did with his 72 years and the influence he may have had on history.

According to the Svetambara tradition, he married a princess named Yasoda, but left her when he was 30 for a life as a naked ascetic. He wanted to leave for this life style when, at the age of 28, his parents died, but he was dissuaded by his brother, Nandivardhana, to remain due to the bereavement caused by the deaths of his parents.

Mahavira (which means Great Hero) was gifted with three kinds of wisdom: *mati, sruta,* and *avadhi.* The fourth kind, *manahparyaya* he received on the eve of his renunciation, and the fifth and last, *kevala,* came to him after his *sadhana* (search for *samadhi,* complete meditation) of about 12 years.

To demonstrate his total rejection of material things, he went about stark naked and did not even possess a bowl for collecting food. He would eat it out of his hands. His naked body was the object of attacks by worms, gnats, mosquitoes, bees and wasps. Because of the horrible sight of his body, people would drive him away, beating him with sticks and throwing stones at him.

He showed complete reverence for all forms of life: earth bodies, fire bodies, wind bodies and vegetable bodies. His entire being was devoted to gaining absolute self-control of body, speech and mind.

During the second monsoon of his *sadhana* he found himself at Nalanda where he met Gosalaka Makhaliputta whose motives for associating with Mahavira were less than altruistic. He hoped to become famous; so he used some of the occult secrets he had learned from Mahavira to gain a following of his own. He defamed Mahavira, but the truth finally triumphed, and when Gosalaka died, he confessed that Mahavira was the *jina* (victor).

Finally, after 12 years of *sadhana,* Mahavira attained *kevala* outside the city of Jrimbhikagrama in the field of Syamaka under a tree on the bank of the Rijupalika River. It was 10th day of the bright half of the month of Vaisakha. "Thus," his biographer, Dr. A.S. Gopani, tells us, "he saw everything and knew everything."

Shortly after this Mahavira learned that a sacrifice was being organised by a Brahman named Somilacharya. He rushed to the place and addressed the people, telling them that the road to final liberation was through right vision, right knowledge and right character.

He told them about *ahimsa* (the doctrine of non-violence), and 11 Brahmans who had brought their pupils became converts to Mahavira's cause. They, then, were the *ganadharas,* his spiritual heirs. Mahavira continued to preach and teach and gathered a huge following, which contained among its ranks members of royal families.

He passed his last monsoon at Pava where, in the fourth month on the 15th day in the dark half of Kartika, he died at the age of 72.

He had preached that all persons, regardless of caste or sex, can attain perfection. Animal sacrifice is to be replaced by sacrifice of the brute self. "Mortify the flesh to develop the spirit," he preached.

The Svetambara Jains believe that Mahavira's teachings are contained in 14 texts called *purvas*. At the end of the fourth century B.C. a number of Jains migrated to Mysore under the leadership of Bhadrabahu. Those who remained behind at Pataliputra convened a council in which 12 *angas* were composed which they considered the Jain canon.

On their return from the south the migrants refused to accept the new canon. They are known as Svetambara Jains. Those who remained behind are Digambaras, the naked ones who wear nothing but the sky.

If Plutarch, the Greek biographer of antiquity, had known about Buddha and Mahavira, he surely would have written a chapter in his *Lives* comparing the two men. Both came from royal families, both married well, and both left their wives: Buddha at 29 and Mahavira at 30 years of age. Both men preached a message of peace, respect for life and right living.

But they differed in that Buddha saw no value in self-mortification. He tried it, but it failed for him.

The appeal of their doctrines differed greatly in that Buddha's doctrine spread to other parts of the world: Sri Lanka, Tibet, China, Japan, Southeast Asia; and Mahavira's doctrine stayed in India where the Jains live.

Suggested Further Readings

Lalwani, Kastur Chand.
    Sramana Bhagavan Mahavira : life & doctrine. — Calcutta : Minerva, 1975.
    xi, 206 p. ; 22 cm.

Nathamal, Muni.
    Shraman Mahavir : his life & teachings. — Calcutta : Mitra, 1976.
    333 p. ; 23 cm.

SANKARACHARYA
(788?-820)

Sankaracharya was born in a Nambudiri Brahman family in Keladi in present day Kerala. His father was Sivaguru and his mother Aryamba. Unlike other great ancient Indian philosophers and religious leaders (Buddha, Mahavira, Ramanuja) who lived eight or more decades, Sankara died at a relatively early age. He was born between 780 and 788 and died in 820 A.D. He was born on the fifth day of the bright half of Vaisakha and was given the name Sankara by a numerology known as *Katapayádi Sankhya*.

According to the tradition of his followers, Sankara is the incarnation of the god Paramesvara who came into the world to arrest the decline of *dharma* (virtue, religion).

Another tradition has it that his childless parents prayed for a son at the Siva temple in Tiruchur and were told by Lord Siva that he would be born as their son and thus fulfill his own mission to Vedic religion and the Vedantic philosophy which had been undermined by atheistic creeds and sanctimonious practices. This is a reference to Buddhism which was going through a period of decadence at this time. When Aryamba was asked if she would prefer her son to be stupid but have a long life, or be bright and have a short one, she tearfully requested the latter.

Sankara is considered one of the leading religious thinkers of Indian history. One of his biographers, P. Sankaranarayanan, goes even further:

> Among the Master Minds, Sages and Saviours of the World, Sri Sankara holds a place rarely equalled and never excelled by any other in any country at any time.

While still a young boy Sankara's father died, and the beautiful child grew under his mother's tutelage. One day when he was eight years old, he went to bathe in a nearby river, but a crocodile caught hold of his feet. The boy cried out to his mother for help and informed her that the only way for him to save his life would be to die symbolically then and there by taking *sannyasa* (monastic vows).

Standing in the water, Sankara uttered the *mantra* of entrance into the *sannyasa* order, was granted another eight years, and, coming ashore, begged his mother to let him become a *sannyasi* (ascetic). His mother grieved that she would not be able to bring up her child in her own household, but he consoled her, saying:

> All those who offer me *bhiksha* hereafter will be my mothers. My disciples will be my sons. I shall delight myself consorting in private with my spouse of meditation on the Supreme Being.

Promising to be at his mother's bedside when the hour of her death came, Sankara went forth in search of a *guru* from whom to gain knowledge, wisdom and understanding. On the banks of the Narmada River he found his *guru*, Sri Govinda Bhagavatapada.

After receiving training from him, Sankara travelled to Benares to confer with great scholars from all parts of India, and while he was at Benares, he wrote his commentaries on the *Upanishads*, the *Bhagavad Gita* and the *Brahma Sutras*.

There is a tradition that one day Vishnu's alter-ego, Vyasa, was engaged in a dialectical debate with Sankara on the commentaries. The debate dragged on for some time until one of Sankara's followers said, "Who can decide between the contestants when one is the *avatar* of Vishnu and the other is the *avatar* of Siva?"

Finally Vyasa indicated he appreciated the manner in which Sankara had remained true in his interpretation of the *Brahma Sutras* and granted him another 16 years of life.

Sankara travelled about India extensively and established *maths* (monasteries) which are still going strong in Conjeeveram, Tamil Nadu; Sringeri, Mysore; Dwaraka, Karnataka; Puri, Orissa; and Badrinath in the Himalayas.

True to his promise, Sankara was at his mother's side at her death. Although a *sannyasi* was forbidden to perform funeral rights, he proceeded to do so in the face of taunts of his kinsmen in Keladi. When she was dead, he hacked her body to pieces and consigned it to flames which he produced by incantation. He then put a curse on Keladi by which no *sannyasi* was to accept *bhiksha* while in that town.

Sankara died at the age of 32, his life having been divided into four parts: the first eight years ending with the incident with the crocodile, the second eight with the debate with the *avatar* of Siva. The final segment ended with his death either in Kanchi, Kashmir or Kedarnath.

Sankaracharya, as he came to be known, was a leading exponent of *advaita* (pure monism). He believed in the supremacy of Brahman and that to recognise the truth of Brahman is to attain release.

Pandit Nehru said of him:

He was evidently a man who was intensely conscious of his mission, a man who looked upon the whole of India from Cape Comorin to the Himalayas as the field of his action and as something that held together culturally and was infused by the same spirit, though this might take many external forms. He strove hard to synthesize the diverse currents that were troubling the mind of the day and to build a unity of outlook out of that diversity. In a brief life of 32 years, he did the work of many long lives and left such an impression of his powerful mind and rich personality on India that it is very evident today.

Suggested Further Readings

Buch, Maganlal Amritlal.
    The philosophy of Shankara ... — Baroda : [Widgery, 1921]
      276 p. ; 19 cm. — (Gaekwad studies in religion and philosophy ; 6)

Joshi, Shanti.
    The message of Sankara. — Allahabad : Lokbharti, [1968]
      196 p. ; 22 cm.

RAMANUJA
(1037?-1137)

According to one tradition Ramanuja was born in 1017, according to another in 1037, and according to history he died in 1137. One is then left to choose between having him die at the age of 120 or at the age of 100. The age of 100 is more reasonable.

Ramanuja was born in Bhutapuri (modern Sriperumbudur), not far from Kanchi (Conjeeveram). His father, Kesava-Somayaji, was a Tamil Brahman scholar and the grandson of Yamuna who was a philosopher, poet, saint and administrator who ruled the Srivaishnavas from Srirangam. Yamuna was a master of dialectic who tried to stem the rising tide of monism by controverting the theories of *maya* (illusion) and *avidya* (ignorance) which are basic to *advaita*.

Yamuna's grandfather, Nathamuni, in turn, had been the author of two lost works on Yoga and the collector of 4,000 hymns of the Alwars. It is not surprising, therefore, that Ramanuja should be a precocious student, ready to be steeped in philosophy and religion.

He was a handsome child, and under his father's tutelage he received traditional education, both religious and secular. He was married when he was 17. His father died soon after that, and Ramanuja moved with his wife and mother to Kanchi where he studied *advaita* under a professor, Yadavaprakasa, who had distinguished himself by criticizing Sankara.

Ramanuja studied for six years under Yadavaprakasa, but relations between master and student became strained as Ramanuja disputed some of his master's interpretations of the *Brahma Sutra*.

Then one day Yadavaprakasa organized a pilgrimage to Kasi (Varanasi) for his class. On the way Ramanuja learned that his own life was in danger; so he abandoned the pilgrimage and made his way back to Kanchi.

He resumed his studies under Yadavaprakasa later, and by the time he was 22 his reputation had spread to the extent that it came to the notice of Yamuna, his grandfather. Yamuna chose Ramanuja to be leader of the Vaishnava order and summoned him to Srirangam to confront him with this decision. Ramanuja responded, but when he reached the outskirts of Srirangam, what confronted him was the funeral procession of his grandfather.

Discouraged and disheartened, Ramanuja returned to Kanchi to further his studies. However, after a few years he found that his studies were hampered by his domestic life. His mother had died, and since he had made the great renunciation (as Buddha and Mahavira had done before him, also at about the age of 30), he made provision for his wife, and took up the life of a *sannyasi* (ascetic) at the Vishnu temple in Kanchi.

He was soon recognised as the outstanding leader of the sect, and, egged on by followers of the late Yamuna, he moved to Srirangam to take over the order.

He had a three-fold task before him. One, he had to establish his own position as being in the succession of inspired teachers; two, he had to organise the ritual of the many Vishnu temples and make them true spiritual centres; and, three, he had to provide the order with philosophical literature which would challenge the precepts of Sankara's famous works.

He had little or no trouble with the first task because he was universally accepted as a brilliant thinker, teacher and spiritual leader. The second task required hard work and travel which he accomplished by making extensive tours to the centres where his people had settled.

The third task was more demanding. He studied the works (many of which are no longer extant) of Bodhyayana, Guhadeva, Dramidacharya, Tanka, Kapardin and Bharuchi and wrote his most famous work, *Srí Bháshya*, an extensive commentary on the *Vedanta Sutras*. He is credited with having written at least eight other treatises, among which were: *Vedanta Samgraha*, deriving this doctrine from the *Upanishads*; *Vedanta Sara* and *Vedanta-Dipa*, summarizing his *Sri Bháshya*; *Gita-Bhashya*, a commentary on the *Bhagavad Gita*, emphasizing *bhakti* (piety), and *Nityam*, a manual of eternal duties. All his works were written in Sanskrit. They gave Ramanuja's expression of *vishishtadvaita* (the ultimate oneness of the differentiated).

Ramanuja's influence grew so that eventually he was able to count 12,000 disciples, 700 *sannyasis* and 74 select leaders in his entourage. But there was trouble with the ascension to the throne of the Chola Empire of Kulottunga I (1070-1122). Desiring unity in the realm, the emperor insisted that all Srivaishnavas swear under oath that there was no god greater than Siva.

Ramanuja and his followers fled to the hills of Mysore where a new power, the Hoysalas, was emerging under the leadership of Vishnu-vardhana. Ramanuja and his followers were granted refuge by the Hoysalas for a period of 20 years. On the death of Kulottunga I in 1122, Ramanuja returned to Srirangam where he remained until his death in 1137, at the ripe age of 100 or, as some prefer, 120.

Every Vishnu temple resounds with this benediction:

*Rámánujarya divyájñá vardatamahbi vardhatám.**

— **S. Ramakrishnan**

Suggested Further Readings

Ramanuja.
  Rámánuja on the Bhagavadgita. — 2nd ed. — [New Delhi] : Motilal Banarsidass, 1968.
  xiii, 187 p. ; 25 cm.

Srinivasachari, P.N.
  The philosophy of Visishtadvaita. — Madras : Adyar Library, 1978.
  648 p. ; 23 cm. — (The Adyar Library series)

---

* "May the divine commands of Ramanuja ever gain strength."

CHAITANYA
(1486-1533)

Chaitanya, also known as Gauranga ("The Fair One"), was the Bengali mystic who inspired an influential religious movement in Bengal and neighbouring regions known as Bengali or Gaudiya Vaishnavism, or the *Chaitanya Sampradaya*.

The life of Chaitanya can be told in many details. There are several biographies of him in Bengali and Sanskrit written in the sixteenth or early seventeenth centuries by people who were his contemporaries and either knew him personally or were in close touch with his nearest companions. Probably the most important among those works is Krishna Kaviraj's *Chaitanyacharitámrita* ("The Nectar of the Life of Chaitanya"), composed about 1600 A.D., which is both a lengthy biography and a compendium of the faith. It is also a masterpiece of pre-modern Bengali literature.

Already during his lifetime his admirers came to consider him the *avatar* of Vishnu Krishna, the Supreme Lord. Later some of his followers claimed he was the joint *avatar* of both Krishna and his sweetheart Radha. The biographies of Chaitanya were modelled to a large extent after the *puranas* that described the lives of gods and so were filled with various miraculous events and universal mythic motifs. (Some influence of Islamic and even Christian holy traditions might also have been there.) Modern scholars extract from these sacral narrations, the hard core of more or less reliable facts.

Chaitanya was born in 1486 to a high caste Brahman family at Navadvip (present day Nadia), the famous centre of traditional Hindu learning in Bengal. His father had come there from Sylhet, and his mother's ancestors are said to have come from Orissa. By that time Bengal and north India had been for almost three centuries ruled by Muslims. Many Bengalis had been converted to Islam; the rest could hardly escape its influence. The life of Chaitanya almost coincides with the rule of the Hussain Shahi Dynasty in Bengal (1496-1538) whose founder, Ala-ud-Din Hussain Shah, has come down through history as an efficient and rather liberal ruler and a patron of architecture and literature.

It was provincial governors of Hussain Shah who commissioned the earliest Bengali versions of the *Mahábhárata*. If we are to believe the biographers of Chaitanya, Hussain Shah on one occasion himself expressed his faith in Chaitanya and guaranteed his protection. Two of Hussain's highest officials, Brahmans who had converted to Islam, were reconverted by Chaitanya into his faith and later became his leading theologians of Gaudiya Vaishnavism. One of the closest companions of Chaitanya, named Haridas, had been a Muslim (probably with a Sufi background).

For Chaitanya there was no difference between Muslim and Hindu, "for" (he could have said with the Apostle Paul) "the same Lord is Lord of all and bestows his riches upon all who call upon him." (Romans X:12 RSV)

In his early years Chaitanya must have received traditional Hindu education. In due time he himself started teaching Sanskrit and was married first to Lakshmipriya who died of snake bite shortly after their marriage, and then to Vishnupriya. At the age of 22 he went to Gaya to perform the funeral rites for his late father and must have had there an overwhelming religious experience which made him a *bhakta* (fervent devotee) of Krishna.

Back at Navadvip he became a charismatic leader of the Vaishnava minority there and started the practice of the *samkirtanas*, the collective singing of the divine name, as the ritual of worship. The majority of Hindus at Navadvip were Shaktas, worshippers of Shakti, and were hostile to Chaitanya. A rumour was circulated that Chaitanya was the Brahman predicted to become king of Gaud (Bengal). The hostile Hindus reported this to the local *Qazi* (Muslim magistrate), implying that Chaitanya should be punished. The conflict, somewhat reminiscent of that between Jesus and Pilate, was resolved peacefully through a kind of civil disobedience demonstration organised by Chaitanya.

But in 1510, at the age of 24, the rebel left Navadvip and became a *sannyasi* under the name Krishna-Chaitanya, *i.e.* "One whose Consciousness is Krishna", commonly abridged as Chaitanya. For six years he travelled throughout India, proclaiming his devotion to Krishna, and in 1516 settled in Puri, Orissa (then an independent Hindu kingdom) by the temple of Jagannath. There he lived until the end of his life in 1533, ever immersed in reveries and ecstasies about Krishna while he himself was worshipped as an *avatar* by more and more people.

Chaitanya hardly ever articulated any detailed doctrine. His message was mainly emotional and personal, expressed through his ecstatic behaviour. Only eight stanzas in Sanskrit are attributed to him. They describe and prescribe in a rather general way the devotion to Hari-Krishna as the Supreme Lord. Among Chaitanya's followers there were several "lines" which interspersed his legacy in somewhat different ways and composed a massive body of doctrinal texts, largely in Sanskrit.

The most prolific and influential of the "line" of Vrindavan were *Gosvámis* (pastors) who, inspired by Chaitanya, rediscovered and restored Vrindavan as the sacred place of Krishna's childhood and youth. In Bengal itself among various "lines" and "deviations" there were some contaminated with Tantric traditions. The Chaitanya movement as a whole has effected a deep impact on Bengali culture and, in particular, on Bengali literature. Apart from rich hagiographical and doctrinal literature, Bengal Vaishnavism has produced even richer poetic traditions. One of the modern heirs of this tradition was Rabindranath Tagore.

In modern Bengal attitudes towards Chaitanya and his movement are varied and often ambiguous. Sometimes the movement is charged with baneful, "effeminating" influences on Bengal society and culture; it is claimed that the erotic symbolism of Chaitanya's *Krishna-bhakti* can too easily descend from spiritual heights down to the lowest moral depths. Followers of Chaitanya may, of course, retort that any high ideal can be debased.

For an historian, the Chaitanya movement is part of a religious reformation that swept over north, northwest and northeast India in the fifteenth to seventeenth centuries. It is worth noting that Chaitanya was a contemporary and, to a certain extent, a counterpart of Guru Nanak. A very important catalyst of this reformation was, no doubt, Islam.

In Chaitanya's case the impact of Islam may be seen in the very shift from the hereditary, non-proselytising and caste-bound religious message meant for proselytising. But, like most other varieties of the *bhakti* movement in India, the Chaitanya movement has turned into a *sampradaya, i.e.* just one more faction in the pluralistically structured Hindu society.

In the nineteenth century, under British rule, the prestige of Gaudiya Vaishnavism in Bengal was declining; then a vigorous revitalisation movement was launched. An offshoot of this movement is the International Society for Krishna Consciousness founded by Abhayacharan De in 1966 in New York. The ISKCON is an attempt to realise and actualise, on a world scale, the universalist potential of Chaitanya's legacy.

— **Sergei Serebriany**

Suggested Further Readings

Chakravarty, Sukumar.
> Chaitanya et sa théorie de l'amour divin. — Paris : Les Presses Universitaires de France, 1933.
> xv, 185 p. ; 23 cm.

De, Sushil Kumar.
> Early history of the Vaisnava faith and movement in Bengal from Sanskrit and Bengali Sources — Calcutta : K.L. Mukhopadhyaya, 1961.
> ix, 703 p. ; 22 cm.

Dimock, Edward C.
> The place of the hidden moon : erotic mysticism in the Vaisnava-sahajiyá cult of Bengal. — Chicago : University of Chicago Press, 1966.
> xix, 299 p. ; 22 cm.

Eidlitz, Walther.
> Krsna-Chaitanya : Sein Leben under seine Lehre. — Stockholm : Almqvist & Wiksell, 1968.
> 561 p. ; 24 cm.

Kennedy, Melville.
> The Chaitanya movement : a study of Vaishnavism in Bengal. — Calcutta, etc. : Assn. Press, 1925.
> v, 270 p. ; 26 cm.

Majumdar, Ashoke Kumar, 1916
> Chaitanya : his life and doctrine : a study in Vaisnavism. — Bombay : Bharatiya Vidya Bhavan, 1969.
> xv, 392 p. ; 26 cm.

Sen, C.D.
> Chaitanya and his age. — Calcutta : University of Calcutta, 1922.
> xxxiii, 417 p. ; 22 cm.

GURU NANAK
(1469-1539)

Guru Nanak was born 15 April 1469 in the village of Talwandi south-west of Lahore. (According to the oldest extant biography of Nanak, he was born in April, though later biographers put this date in November of the same year.) He was of the household of Mehta Kalu, a revenue official, in what may be considered a dark age for the Indian sub-continent. This was a time when his motherland was being incessantly invaded by Afghan or Mughul hordes, and neither life nor honour was safe for anyone.

The country was torn by sectarian strife, principally between the subject race of the Hindus, who constituted the overwhelming majority of the population, and the minority races of Islam. Hindus were further divided and sub-divided by caste and blind superstition. Almost half of the Indian humanity, the women, and one fourth of the low caste Hindus were condemned and ostracised as Untouchables for whom life was nothing short of a perpetual hell.

Nanak, the Guru, came to fight these evils, at first single-handedly, and then, supported by an expanding band of followers, to create not only a spiritual, but also a socio-political revolution in the sub-continent.

Muhammad Iqbal, the great poet-philosopher, believed that after the Buddha, Nanak's name was the most celebrated in proclaiming the message of "one man" under one God.

A Shop-Keeper

Nanak did study the three R's for a time, but refused to farm or keep a shop, as was usual for the Hindu Khatri tribe to which he belonged, though after he married at the comparatively young age of 14 or so and had two sons, he agreed to work for about 16 years as a store-keeper for a Muslim Nawab, Daulat Khan Lodhi of Sultanpur in the district of Kapurthala.

As soon as his sons could look after themselves, Nanak took leave of the household (at the age of around 30), and for 20 years thereafter toured the entire country and even went abroad, preaching his gospel.

Several stories of his life reveal his revolutionary thinking in both spiritual and social matters. When in his adolescent years he was asked to wear the customary sacred thread which the three higher caste Hindus had to wear to become "twice born" (but which privilege was denied to women and Untouchables), he declined the invitation, saying:

> If compassion were the cotton and contentment the thread and chastity the knot and truth the twist, I would wear the sacred thread. But why should I wear a thread which, as time passes, is soiled or broken, and goes not along with us into the beyond? Our hands that rob and kill wear not such a thread nor our feet which rush out to commit evil nor our tongues which slander others nor our eyes which covet another's beauty or riches. O Brahman, thy mind is blind, though thy name is wisdom!

Later he protested in the same way about discrimination against women:

Why call women evil, who give birth to kings, prophets and all? Who is it who has to deal not with a woman, as mother, wife, or daughter? Is there a man without a woman, save God?

The first utterance he made on declaring his prophethood at the age of 27 was:

There is no Hindu, no Mussalman.

By this he meant that both are alike in the eyes of God, and mankind should not be divided on the basis of creed. He was equally vehement in his denunciation of caste:

Before God, caste is an evil. Do the flowers have caste, or butter, or silk, or a devotee of God?

In a verse he said:

Nanak is with the lowliest and the lost and the least of these. What has he to do with the high and mighty?

The Travels of Guru Nanak

Guru Nanak travelled for over 20 years on foot through India from Kashmir to Cape Comorin and from the Punjab to Assam. He also visited Sri Lanka, Afghanistan, Mecca, Baghdad, Mesopotamia, Turkey, Tibet and Nepal.

He took along with him a Muslim drummer, Mardana by name, to fight the prejudices against the mixing of castes and creeds. While Mardana played on the rebec, Nanak sang to diverse audiences his own poetic compositions. His message was:

There is but one God, whose name is Truth. He is the creator of all, without fear, without hate, the Immortal Being. He is self-existent and not incarnated. He is our Illuminator and is gracious to all.

Guru Nanak's methods of teaching were simple, dramatic and telling. At Hardwar on the banks of the Ganges River, the Hindu place of pilgrimage, he saw men throwing water towards the east in order to propitiate their dead ancestors, believed to be abiding in the region of the sun.

The Guru had a hearty laugh and started throwing water towards the west.

"What are you doing, you ignorant one?" they asked.

"I have my farms in the Punjab, to the west of here," he replied. "As it hasn't rained for some time, I wanted to throw some water westwards, so that my farms are irrigated."

"How can that be? How can your water reach that far, in the Punjab, and help irrigate your farms?" they inquired in amusement.

"If your offerings can reach your dead in the high heavens, why can't mine reach even the Punjab, only a few hundred miles away?" he answered.

During his journeys the Guru stayed always with the poor and the outcastes, tended the sick (including the lepers) and argued with the *Qazis* and Brahmans on matters of spirit or social habits. He also preached against political slavery and the bloody orgies of conquering hordes, and it is said that he courted imprisonment at the hands of Babar, the first Mughul emperor of Hindustan.

. Guru Nanak ended his tours at the age of about 50 and for about 20 years thereafter settled down in the Punjab on the banks of the Ravi River in a village called Kartarpur which he had founded and where he took to farming along with his followers. He converted it into a sort of commune. Anything that the farm yielded was distributed through a community kitchen to all who lived there or to visitors and wayfarers. (This tradition continues to this day, each Sikh temple having a free kitchen attached to it.)

At the age of 69, Guru Nanak selected a devotee, Lehna (later known as Guru Angad) who had served him and the community with supreme devotion, as his successor.

Guru Nanak breathed his last 22 September 1539.

— **Gopal Singh**

Suggested Further Reading

Singh, Gopal, 1917-
     Guru Nanak. — New Delhi : National Book Trust, [1967]
     xi, 134 p. ; 18 cm. — (National biographical series)

GURU GOBIND SINGH
(1666-1708)

Guru Gobind Singh, the tenth and last Guru of the Sikhs, was in many ways a person unique in the annals of man. Born 26 December 1666 at Patna, he lived only a brief span of 42 years, mostly in Anandpur — a city his father had founded in the Siwalik Hills of the Punjab.

He was assassinated by an Afghan fanatic at Nandur in the Deccan 7 October 1708, but he left such a deep impression on the life and history of his demoralised and disintegrated nation that it continues to move millions of people to this day.

The son of a martyr (the ninth Guru, Teg Bahadur, who was martyred by Aurangzeb) and great grandson of a martyr (the fifth Guru, Arjan Dev, who was martyred by Jahangir), Guru Gobind Singh was born at a time when the oppression of the Mughul regime, notably under Aurangzeb, had made the religious and socio-political life of the majority of Hindu and Sikh people as well as of the majority of the various liberal though minority Muslim sects (like the Shias and Sufis), extremely vulnerable and discriminatory.

Until then the Guru Nanak's house had, for almost two centuries, fought against socio-spiritual superstitious cant, idol-worship and caste, and had emphasised the unity of humankind under one God, irrespective of creed or sex, colour or station.

A Secular Challenge

But now a new secular challenge had to be met for the sheer survival of the majority of the people of India and to restore to them their lost honour and human dignity. The Guru, therefore, resolved to revolutionise the structure and aims of his community and even to take up arms in defence of the weak, not only of his own faith, but of the others also, as was the tradition of Guru Nanak's house.

In the armed conflicts that followed, the Guru had to sacrifice, besides his numerous followers, his four sons (two of whom were killed in battle, the other two being bricked up alive by the Nawab of Sirhind). He thereby infused a new death-daring spirit in a whole people and aroused in them a new passion for liberty, equality and fraternity. He was obliged to fight four or five battles in the Siwalik Hills against the Rajput vassals of the Mughul emperor and against the Mughul forces themselves between 1686 and 1704.

Though victorious in most of the battles, the Guru refused to build an empire or to acquire an inch of anyone's territory. His maxim in battle seems to have been: only that battle succeeds in which no one is defeated!

He had to fight both Hindus and Muslims, yet the oppressed among both also fought along side of him. The Guru saw to it that in the heat of the moment, his movement did not become sectarian or anti-Islamic. He refused to inculcate hatred against the religious persuasion of any of his adversaries. "The Hindu temple and the Muslim mosque cry out to the same God," he said.

It is a fact of history that although Aurangzeb had given the Guru every conceivable cause for grievance against his house, the Guru helped the emperor's pious eldest son, Bahadur Shah, win the battle of succession in 1708.

Though a matchless warrior, the Guru remained a saint at heart. "If there is one God," he said, "then there is one man."

His conversion of the hitherto peaceable Sikhs into the militant *Khalsa* at Anandpur in 1699 is an event of such world significance that Arnold Toynbee has called it the precursor and forerunner of Lenin's Communist party two centuries later: an idealistic minority fighting with the weapons of the adversary in the name and for the sake of the majority, obliterating all distinction of caste, nationality, status and sex. However, Toynbee has failed to pinpoint the essential difference in outlook and even methodology of the two world revolutionaries.

Open diplomacy and shared democracy were indeed the hall-marks of Guru Gobind Singh's *Khalsa* and not secret manoeuvre for power or self-perpetuation of an imposed system, however good the intentions or quicker the end results. The means, according to the Guru, determined the quality of the ends.

Guru Gobind Singh did not believe in idol worship nor in any gods or goddesses, incarnations or chosen messiahs and mercilessly decried superstition and ritual in their name as spurious and false. The God of Guru Gobind Singh is, however, no abstraction, but involved with and deeply concerned about the welfare of His creation. That is how weapons of all kinds are lauded in his works, and yet the emphasis is on their employment always for the Good Cause, and never for evil or for the subjugation of others. "One must overpower one's self, and not others," said the Guru.

The Adi Granth

God, according to the Guru, is not only the Giver of Grace, but also a Holy Warrior and Punisher and Destroyer of Evil.

The Guru's works are assembled in his book, *Dasam Granth*, compiled about 26 years after his death.

Guru Gobind Singh abolished succession and anointed not his own *Daswen Padshah ká Granth* ("The book of the Tenth Sovereign"), but the *Adi Granth* (compiled by the fifth Guru, Arjan Dev, in 1604) as the visible embodiment of the Gurus.

Such was the Guru's concern against man-worship that though looked upon as a Prophet and even the incarnation of God, he decried this vehemently among his followers. He said:

> He who calleth me God will burn in the fires of hell. I am but the servant of the Supreme Being, come to witness His Play.

— **Gopal Singh**

Suggested Further Reading

Ahluwalia, Rajendra Singh.
     The founder of the Khalsa.— Chandigarh : Guru Gobind Singh Foundation, [1966]
     113 p. : ill., col. port. ; 23 cm.

RAJA RAMMOHUN ROY
(1772 or 74-1833)

Rammohun Roy was one of the key figures of modern Indian culture — a social and religious reformer, an educationist and politician.

He was born in 1772 or 1774 at Radhanagar, Bengal, and died 27 September 1833 at Bristol, England.

The formative years of Rammohun Roy coincided with the stabilisation of the British power in Bengal and its spreading over almost all the rest of the sub-continent.

Rammohun Roy's life spanned a clear-cut period of modern Indian history: from the Regulating Act of 1773 and the governor-generalship of Warren Hastings till the Charter Act of 1833 and the reforms of William Bentinck. Rammohun Roy was probably the most eminent of those Indians who not only accepted and responded positively to the new political and social developments, but also tried actively to participate in them and to comprehend their implications both for India and the world.

Rammohun Roy's ancestors were Bengali Brahmans who served under Muslim Nawabs of Bengal and were, to use the words of Jawaharlal Nehru in his *Discovery of India*, "products of mixed Indo-Muslim culture."

The family name "Ray" (anglicised as "Roy") is a contraction of the title "Ra-a-rayan" (in Persian, "prince of princes") which was granted by a Nawab to Rammohun Roy's great-grandfather. So Rammohun Roy inherited a tradition of cross-cultural mediation, if not cross-cultural synthesis. (Even within his family there was a sort of religious pluralism, the father being a Vaishnava and the mother a Shakta.) Rammohun Roy carried this tradition further, as it were, striving later in his life to embrace in a broader synthesis not only Hinduism and Islam, but Christianity and modern Western culture as well.

In his younger years, following family tradition, Rammohun Roy studied Persian and Arabic, perhaps to qualify himself for government service. He must have been well acquainted with the Koran, Muslim theology and philosophy (including what is inherited from Greek antiquity), as well as with classical Persian poetry, permeated as it was with Sufi ideas. Later he studied Sanskrit as well and must have acquired a sound knowledge of the *Shastras* and sacred texts of Hinduism. He seems to have taken interest in Buddhism as well, though it is difficult to say to what extent he was familiar with Buddhist traditions.

Essentially Rammohun Roy was a "self-made man." He is said to have begun his study of the English language in about 1796. From 1803 to 1815 he worked as an assistant to several officials of the East India Company, improving his financial position and deepening his knowledge of English and modern Western culture.

In 1803 or 1804 Rammohun Roy published (in Murshidabad, the former capital of the Nawabs) a tract in Persian, *Tuhfat-al-Muwahhidin*,* in which he argued that all religions had a common kernel of truth (a monotheistic "natural religion"), falsified in each of the "extraneous attributes" (like idolatry, etc.).

In 1815, Rammohun Roy retired and settled in Calcutta, then the capital of the British dominions in India, and his years in Calcutta (1815-1830) were filled with manifold activities. He went on publishing tracts on religious

---

* "A gift to monotheists"

problems, in Bengali, English, Hindustani and Sanskrit. The first one was the *Vedanta Grantha* (1915), a Bengali commentary of Badarayana's *Vedanta-sutras*. The *Vedanta Sara* (1816) contained Rammohun Roy's interpretation (in Bengali) of Vedanta philosophy. About the same time he published English versions of the two tracts. In 1816-1819 Rammohun Roy brought out, with his own introductions, his Bengali translations of five major *Upanishads*, as well as English translations of some of them. Rammohun Roy was the first to translate *Upanishads* (and the *Vedanta Sutras*) into Indian vernacular. In this respect he may be compared to Luther and other figures of the Reformation who translated Christian scriptures into European vernaculars.

Like Luther, Rammohun Roy also reinterpreted his translations. He claimed that "true Hinduism" as expounded by the *Vedas* (and particularly by *Upanishads*) was monotheistic and did not authorise "idolatry" and other customs of contemporary Hinduism. Rammohun Roy was not the first to express such ideas in print. He had predecessors like H.T. Colebrooke, one of the leading scholars at the Asiatic Society in Calcutta, and Ramram Bose, a Bengali pandit at Fort William College. But Rammohun Roy was the first to propagate these ideas to the Hindu community in Calcutta and Bengal at large. Radhakant Dev and other Hindu scholars contested Rammohun Roy's interpretation of Hinduism and heated polemics followed.

Still more heated were the debates about the custom of *sati*.* Rammohun Roy wrote more than one tract on this problem, arguing that the self-immolation of widows was not *prescribed* by sacred texts as a sacred duty, but only *offered* as an act of free choice. Rammohun Roy's arguments contributed to Lord Bentinck's decision to ban the custom of *sati* in 1829. In his other works Rammohun Roy defended the civil rights of Hindu women — the rights of property, of inheritance, etc.

In 1820, Rammohun Roy published a book in English entitled *The Precepts of Jesus; Guide to Peace and Happiness, Extracted from the Books of the New Testament Ascribed to the Four Evangelists*. Like Thomas Jefferson before him and Leo Tolstoy after him, Rammohun Roy made an attempt to present the Gospels only in their ethical and spiritual aspects, omitting all "miraculous relations" and theological peculiarities of Christianity. Again a long controversy followed — this time mostly with Baptist missionaries stationed at Serampore. In 1820-1823 Rammohun Roy wrote three long "Appeals to the Christian Public," stating more and more explicitly his views on Christ and Christianity. He highly praised the ethical teachings of Jesus, but refused to accept his divinity and redemption.

It may be assumed that Rammohun Roy's approach to Christianity was predetermined to some extent by his acquaintance with Islamic theology. The views of Rammohun Roy proved to be akin to those of Western Unitarians with whom he corresponded.

His works were republished and his name became known in England, continental Europe and the U.S.A. Thus Rammohun Roy was the first Hindu to participate in transcontinental intellectual exchange in modern times.

---

* The burning of widows in the funeral pyres of their husbands.

In 1828, Rammohun Roy, with a group of friends, founded the Brahmo Samaj, "The Society of Worshippers of Brahman." It was described as a "place of public meeting, of all sorts of descriptions of people, without distinction,... for the worship and adoration of the Eternal, Unsearchable, and Immutable Being who is the Author and Preserver of the Universe ...." After being re-founded by Debendranath Tagore in the 1840's, the Brahmo Samaj influenced considerably the intellectual, social and religious life of India.

Rammohun Roy was an outstanding journalist and a man of letters, one of the first Indians to found and edit newspapers (in Bengali and Persian). In 1823, when the governor-general passed a restrictive Press Ordinance, Rammohun Roy with some friends appealed first to the Supreme Court and then to the King in Council, defending very forcefully the freedom of press in India and thus, according to R.C. Dutt, "starting that system of constitutional agitation for political rights which his countrymen learned to value so much."

A great problem in those days was whether public money should be spent on sponsoring education along traditional lines (Hindu and Muslim) or on introducing Western type education. Rammohun Roy favoured the later. He himself founded schools with English as the medium of instruction and supported the founding of the famous Hindu College (in 1817). In 1823, in protest against the establishment of a government-supported Sanskrit college in Calcutta, Rammohun Roy wrote a letter to the governor-general advocating the introduction of Western learning and Western sciences to Indians, and thus he anticipated the famous *Minute on Education* of T.B. Macaulay.

In the meantime Rammohun Roy contributed to the development of his mother-tongue as a vehicle of modern culture. Apart from his prose works already referred to (which have prompted some of his admirers to call Rammohun Roy "the Father of Prose Literature in Bengal,") he wrote a grammar of the Bengali language, published in English in 1826 and in Bengali in 1833. He wrote also a number of religious poem-songs in Bengali. As in the field of religion, so in the field of learning, Rammohun Roy stood for a synthesis of all that was valuable in various traditions.

In 1830, fulfilling his old dream, Rammohun Roy sailed for England and was one of the first Hindus to violate the traditional ban on overseas travels. The Mughul emperor, Akbar II, appointed him his official envoy (conferring on him the title "Raja") to defend his financial interests before the British crown. In England Rammohun Roy was received with great honours as an unofficial ambassador of India. He was present at the coronation of William IV, given a dinner by the directors of the East India Company and greeted by Jeremy Bentham as an "intensely admired and dearly beloved collaborator in the service of mankind."

While in England, Rammohun Roy lived a very active public life. He closely watched the House of Commons' work on the renewal of the East India Company's Charter and submitted to a special committee his detailed recommendations on ways to improve the government of India. He presented to the House of Commons his memorandum about the *sati* problem and witnessed the rejection by the Privy Council of an appeal (from some orthodox Hindus of Calcutta) against the Lord Bentinck's decree that abolished the custom.

Rammohun Roy was very excited with the passing of the Reform Bill in 1832. He even considered the idea of being elected to Parliament. In 1832 Rammohun Roy visited France and was received by King Louis Philippe.

After losing his savings in a bank failure, he died among English friends in Bristol.

Rammohun Roy was a man of what we would now call "a global consciousness." Living in Calcutta, he took lively interest in events happening far away. Thus, in 1821 he felt "depressed" by the news of the defeat of the revolution in Naples. In 1823, he gave a dinner to celebrate the liberation of Spanish colonies in South America. In 1830, he was elated with the victory of the revolution in France. In 1831, in his letter to the then Foreign Minister of France, the famous (and infamous) Prince Talleyrand, Rammohun Roy wrote:

> It is now generally admitted that not religion only but unbiased common sense as well as the accurate deductions of scientific research lead to the conclusion that all mankind are one great family of which numerous nations and tribes existing are only various branches. Hence, enlightened men in all countries feel a wish to encourage and facilitate human intercourse in every manner by removing as far as possible all impediments to it in order to promote the reciprocal advantage and enjoyment of the whole human race.

Further in that letter Rammohun Roy put forward the idea of a "World Congress" — the later League of Nations or the United Nation Organisation.

Indian opinion about Rammohun Roy often was and still is divided. For some, Rammohun Roy is "the Father of Modern India" or "Inaugurator of the Modern Age in India " (Tagore) or even "A Prophet and Precursor of Coming Humanity" (Brajendranath Seal).

But it is exactly Rammohun Roy's cosmopolitan outlook, as well as his critical attitude towards traditional Hinduism, that made him unacceptable to some Indians. Even Mahatma Gandhi on one occasion called Rammohun Roy a "Pigmy" compared to Shankara (although he never retracted that remark).

Rammohun Roy was one of the first products of that complex cultural synthesis which began evolving in India at the beginning of the nineteenth century and which still evolves there. As long as this process itself remains a matter of debate and controversy, Rammohun Roy too will remain a controversial figure, an object of both pride and criticism.

— **Sergei Serebriany**

Suggested Further Readings

Chakravarti, Satis Chandra, ed.
  The father of modern India : commemoration volume of the Rammohun Roy Centenary
  Celebrations, 1935. — Calcutta : Office of the Rammohun Roy Centenary Celebrations,
  1933.
  xxxviii, 572 p. : ill., ports. ; 24 cm.

Collet, S.D.
  The life and letters of Raja Rammohun Roy. — 3d ed. — Calcutta : Sadharan Brahmo
  Samaj, [1962]
  xii, 502 p. : ill., facsims., ports. ; 23 cm.

Singh, Iqbal.
  Rammohun Roy : a biographical inquiry into the making of modern India. — Bombay:
  Asia Publishing House, 1958.
  v. : port. ; 23 cm.
  Contents: v. 1. The first phase. — V. 2 & 3. Middle and last phase, 1984.

SWAMI DAYANAND SARASWATI
(1825?-1883)

Swami Dayanand Saraswati, the founder of the Arya Samaj, was born in Tankara, Morvi State, Kathiawar during the third decade of the nineteenth century. His year of birth is not known with any certainty and has been variously given as 1824, 1825, 1827, etc. He died in 1883.

His father, Krishnaji Tiwari, a Shaivite and Audichya Brahman, was a land-owner, a money-lender and a tax-collector for the state.

Dayanand was betrothed during his teens, but when his father tried to marry him off at the age of 21, Dayanand protested, broke with his father and left home, never to return.

He had studied Sanskrit at the village school until he was 14, and after that he studied under a Brahman in a nearby village.

Following his departure from home, he wandered about for 20 years, searching for the Truth. He became familiar with Islamic thought and at one point, in Ajmer, encountered Christians and was dismayed by their doctrine of original sin.

He became a *sannyasi* (ascetic) and took the name Saraswati from one of his teachers. It was in Mathura between 1860 and 1863 that he learned a great deal about classical Sanskrit literature from Virganand, a blind teacher.

His life as a missionary began in 1865 when he started writing and publishing pamphlets. His most important work was *Satyarth Prakash*. He also travelled extensively. He was in Calcutta (1872-73), and Poona and Bombay (1875).

He was anxious to dispute with anyone, Brahman, Muslim or Christian, concerning religion. A celebrated debate was held in Benares in 1869 during which Dayanand argued with a number of Brahman pandits that there was no basis for idol worship in the *Vedas* and challenged his adversaries to prove otherwise. After the debate the Brahmans claimed victory, but several journals (*The Pioneer, The Christian Intelligencer, The Hindoo Patriot* and the *Tattvabodhini Patrika*) gave the win to Dayanand.

Dayanand met Keshub Chandra Sen at a meeting in Calcutta where Dayanand spoke in Sanskrit. Keshub Chandra told him to stop going about in a loin cloth and, to be more effective, to speak in the language of the people, rather than Sanskrit.

In 1875, Dayanand established the first Arya Samaj, the principles for which were finally given shape at Lahore in 1877. While in Rajputana Dayanand made converts of at least two Rajput princes: Maharaja Nahar Singh of Shahpur, Maharaja Pratap Singh of Jodhpur.

However, Dayanand's militancy made him enemies, and he died in Ajmer 30 October 1883, it is commonly believed, of poison which had been administered to him in Jodhpur.

Dayanand was a reformer who sought wisdom not from meditation or self-mortification, the means used by earlier reformers, but from the *Vedas*.

In the *Vedas* he found no basis or justification for: the caste-system, polytheism, child marriage, astrology, idol worship or incarnation.

On the positive side, he believed in equality for women, a system of national education, the use of Indian-made goods, uplift of the depressed classes, Hindi as a national language and the importance of performing social work.

The ideals of Dayanand and the Arya Samaj which he founded were not very dissimilar to the ideals of Raja Rammohun Roy and the Brahmo Samaj which Rammohun Roy founded. A conference was held in Calcutta in 1869 with representatives of both orders in an attempt to find unity and common ground. It failed, and each group went its separate way.

Whereas, Rammohun Roy appealed to the intelligentsia, Dayanand appealed directly to the people. Both the Arya Samaj and Brahmo Samaj became important factors in the political, religious and social life of India.

One of the most important contributions of Dayanand was the *Suddhi* movement, a programme of conversion of non-Hindus back to Hinduism. This movement, designed to unify India and to counter Christian missionary activity, is still active.

Following Dayanand's death his work was continued by Lala Hansraj, Guru Dutt, Lala Lajpat Rai and Swami Sraddhananda.

Suggested Further Readings

Dayanand Saraswati, 1824?-1883.
  Satyartha-prakash — 5th ed. — [Calcutta : Banga-Assam Arya Pratinidhi Sabha],
  1947.
  689 p. ; 25 cm.
  In Bengali.

Singh, Chhajju.
  Life and teachings of Swami Dayanand Saraswati. — Lahore : "Addison" Press, 1903.
  2 v. ; 17 cm.
Sharma, Brij Mohan.
  Swami Dayanand (his life and teachings). — Lucknow : Upper India Publishing House,
  1933.
  163 p. : ports. ; 19 cm.

RAMAKRISHNA PARAMAHAMSA
(1836-1886)

During the nineteenth century India was passing through various kinds of crises — social, economic, political, cultural and religious. Politically overthrown by the British, French and Portuguese, she was rapidly coming under the sway of Western civilisation. The new conquerors brought the local rulers, leaders and intellectuals under their control by offering them limited power or titles. Foreign languages and culture were then introduced, while Christian missionaries spread Western education and began converting Indians to Christianity. This strong Western influence cast a spell over the country and shook people's faith in India's ancient culture and religion.

Gradually, in order to counteract the Western influence, a few socio-religious reform movements were founded. In 1828 Raja Rammohun Roy established the Brahmo Samaj. After his death in 1833 this movement was guided by Debendranath Tagore and Keshab Chandra Sen. The Arya Samaj was founded in 1875 by Dayananda Saraswati, and about the same time other orthodox Hindu organisations were also formed to preserve India's spiritual heritage.

During this period of India's history Ramakrishna was born 18 February 1836 in Kamarpukur, a village 100 kilometres northwest of Calcutta in West Bengal. His father, Khudiram Chatterjee, and mother, Chandramani, were very devoted to God, and both had visions about their son before he was born. Ramakrishna grew up in Kamarpukur and was sent to the village school where he learned to read and write. When he was six or seven years old he had his first experience of Cosmic Consciousness. After his father's death in 1843, Ramakrishna became more indrawn and meditative, and he soon lost interest in mere "bread-earning education."

Ramakrishna moved to Calcutta in 1852 to assist his elder brother Ramkumar, who was conducting a school and performing ritualistic worship in private homes for a living. On 31 May 1855 Ramkumar officiated at the dedication ceremony of the Kali temple in Dakshineswar, which had been founded by Rani Rasmai, a wealthy woman of Calcutta, and in time he became a priest in the temple.

Ramakrishna now began his spiritual journey in earnest. While performing the worship of the Divine Mother, he questioned:

> Are you true, Mother, or it is all a fabrication of my mind — mere poetry without reality? If you do exist, why can't I see you?

As days passed, Ramakrishna's yearning for God became more and more intense, and he prayed and meditated almost 24 hours a day. One day he became desperate. As he described it:

> In my agony I said to myself, "What is the use of this life?" Suddenly my eyes fell on the sword that hangs in the temple. I decided to end my

life with it then and there. Like a mad man I ran to it and seized it. And then — I had a marvelous vision of the Mother and fell down unconscious.

After this, it was not possible for Ramakrishna to continue the worship in the temple. His relatives thought that he had become mad, so they brought him back to Kamarpukur and arranged his marriage. In 1859, he was married to Sarada Mukherjee, a young girl from the neighbouring village of Jayurambati. Ramakrishna returned to Dakshineswar in 1860 and again plunged into *sadhana*.

Bhairavi Brahmani, a Tantric nun, came to Dakshineswar soon after Ramakrishna's return and initiated him into Tantra *sadhana*. Later he practised *vatsalya bhava** under Jatadhari, a Vaishnava monk, and then *Madhura bhava***. Again, in 1864 he was initiated into *sannyasa*** by Totapuri, a Vedantic monk, and he attained *nirvikalpa samadhi**** — in which the aspirant realises his oneness with Brahman, the Ultimate Reality.

In 1866, Ramakrishna practiced Islam under the guidance of a Sufi named Govinda Roy. He later told his disciples:

I devoutly repeated the name of Allah, and I said their prayers five times a day. I spent three days in that mood, and I had the full realisation of the *sadhana* of their faith.

Furthermore, in 1874 he had a vision of the Madonna and the Child Jesus in the parlour of Jadu Mallick's garden house in Dakshineswar. A few days later, while walking in the Panchavati, he saw a foreign-looking person walking toward him. The man had a beautiful face with large, brilliant eyes. As Ramakrishna pondered who this stranger could be, a voice within said:

This is Jesus Christ, the great *yogi*, the loving son of God, who was one with his Father, and who shed his heart's blood and suffered tortures for the salvation of mankind.

Jesus then embraced Ramakrishna and merged into his body.

Ramakrishna met many well-known people of his day, including Debendranath Tagore, Dayananda Saraswati and Bankim Chandra Chatterjee. In 1875 he met Keshab Chandra Sen, leader of the Brahmo Samaj, and as a result many people learned about the saint of Dakshineswar through Keshab's writings in the Brahmo journals.

People now came in large numbers and from all over to Ramakrishna, and he talked to them about God for as much as 20 hours a day. Finally, in the middle of 1885 the physical strain resulted in throat cancer. When his disciples tried to stop him from teaching, he said:

---

    * The attitude of a parent towards the Divine Child.
    ** The attitude of the lover towards the Divine Mother.
    *** Monastic vows.
**** The culmination of spiritual practices.

I do not care. I will give up 20,000 such bodies to help one man.

He trained his disciples to spread his message, and he made Swami Vivekananda their leader. On 16 August 1886 Ramakrishna died at a garden house in Cossipore, a suburb of Calcutta.

During Ramakrishna's time the religious leaders were trying to protect India's religion and culture either through a compromise with Christianity or through reform. But Ramakrishna had the Oneness of existence through different religions, and thus his life itself was a demonstration of the harmony of religions. He not only strengthened the Hindus' faith in their own religion and culture, but he also dissuaded people from becoming narrow and bigoted in their religious outlook. He said:

It is not good to feel that one's own religion alone is true and all others are false. God is one only, and not two. Different people call on Him by different names: some as Allah, some as God, others as Krishna, Shiva and Brahman. It is like the water in a lake. The Hindus call it *jal*, the Christians water and the Muslims *pani*.

The rigidity of the caste system was stifling Indian society, and reformers tried to eradicate it. But Ramakrishna pointed out:

The caste system can be removed by one means only, and that is love of God. The lovers of God do not belong to any caste.

Besides this, Ramakrishna also felt deeply for the poor and for suffering humanity. He knew that a person could not think of God with an empty stomach, so he trained his disciples to serve human beings as veritable manifestations of God. Later, Swami Vivekananda carried out this idea in the philanthropic activities of the Ramakrishna Mission.

Mahatma Gandhi once said:

The story of Ramakrishna Paramahamsa's life is a story of religion in practice. His life enables us to see God face to face.

To the sceptics and atheists, Ramakrishna would say:

God really exists. You don't see the stars in the daytime, but that doesn't mean that the stars do not exist. There is butter in milk. But can anyone see it by merely looking at the milk? You cannot realize God by a mere wish. You must go through some mental disciplines.

Moreover, he declared to all:

The goal of human life is to realize God.

— **Swami Chetanananda**

Suggested Further Readings

Isherwood, Christopher.
    Ramakrishna and his disciples. — New York : Simon & Schuster, 1965.
    348 p. : ill., map, port. ; 24 cm.

Ramakrishna, 1836-1886.
    The gospel of Sri Ramakrishna. — New York : Ramakrishna-Vivekananda Center, 1942.
    xxiii, 1063 p. : plates, ports. ; 24 cm.

Rolland, Romain, 1866-1944.
    The life of Ramakrishna. — Calcutta : Advaita Ashrama, 1965.
    x, 302 p. : port. ; 19 cm.

Sadanananda, Swami.
    Sri Ramakrishna : the great master. — Madras : Sri Ramakrishna Math, 1970.
    2 v. : plates, ports. ; 26 cm.

SWAMI VIVEKANANDA
(1863-1902)

"If you want to know India, study Vivekananda. In him everything is positive and nothing negative," said the great poet Rabindranath Tagore. Vivekananda's life was the personification of his own message, a message in which science and religion, reason and faith, the secular and the sacred, the modern and the ancient, and the East and the West become unified.

Swami Vivekananda (Narendranath Datta), the greatest patriot-saint of modern India, was born 12 January 1863 in Calcutta at a time when British influence was at its peak. His father, Vishvanath Datta, was a lawyer and greatly drawn to Western culture, while Vivekananda's mother, Bhuvaneswari Devi, was very orthodox and religious, and she trained her children in the traditional Indian manner. Thus, Vivekananda was brought up with a familiarity with both Western and Eastern cultures. As a young boy he was quite precocious and seemed to possess indomitable energy; yet he showed a love of meditation even then. Pointing to a line on the palm of his hand, he would say to his friends:

I shall certainly become a monk. A palmist has predicted it.

Vivekananda was a brilliant student and attended the University of Calcutta from which he graduated in 1884. His studies did not satisfy him, however. Although he had a deep interest in history, philosophy, literature and contemporary Western thought, he wanted something more. In his search for truth he met different religious leaders, and he became a member of the Brahmo Samaj, a socio-religious reform movement of India, but nothing satisfied him.

In 1881, he met Ramakrishna at the temple garden of Dakshineswar and asked him, "Sir, have you seen God?

Ramakrishna immediately answered:

Yes, I have seen God. I see him as I see you here, only more clearly. God can be seen. One can talk to him.

This reply was the turning point of Vivekananda's life.

Ramakrishna knew what Vivekananda's mission in life was, and he trained him accordingly. Vivekananda learned from his Master the spiritual heritage of *Vedanta*, the synthesis of knowledge and devotion, the harmony of religions, the true purport of the scriptures, and the worship of God in human beings.

When Ramakrishna was on his death bed at the Cossipore garden house, Vivekananda asked him for the experience of *nirvakalpa samadhi*. But Ramakrishna scolded him, saying:

> Shame on you! You are asking for such an insignificant thing. I thought that you would be like a big banyan tree and that thousands of people would rest in your shade. But now I see that you are seeking your own liberation.

Nevertheless, within a few days Vivekananda experiences this *samadhi*.

Ramakrishna died 16 August 1886, and soon after his disciples established a monastery at Baranagore under the leadership of Swami Vivekananda. Thus, the Ramakrishna Order came into existence. They took for their motto: "To work for one's own liberation and to dedicate oneself to do good to the world."

In 1887, Vivekananda left the monastery to live for a while as a wandering monk. He travelled over almost all India, mostly on foot, and was thus able to have first hand experience of the lives of the people. Seeing the pitiable living conditions of the masses, he was at time moved to tears, and he remembered Ramakrishna's saying, "Religion is not for an empty stomach." He tried to draw the attention of local rulers to the conditions of the masses, but he could not get much response.

Later, he expressed his feelings:

> May I be born again and again, and suffer thousands of miseries so that I may worship the only God that exists, the only God I believe in, the sum total of all souls — and above all, my God the wicked, my God the miserable, my God the poor of all races, of all species, is the special object of my worship.

While travelling in India, Vivekananda heard about the Parliament of Religions, which was to be held in Chicago in September 1893. Many Indian rulers and influential people asked him to attend and represent Hinduism, and he finally agreed. He left Bombay for Chicago 31 May 1893, travelling via Japan and the Pacific. His very first lecture at the Parliament created a stir, and he became widely known and sought after as a lecturer. From 1893 to 1896 he preached the ancient spiritual message of India in various parts of the U.S.A. and Europe.

---

* The highest Vedantic experience.

When Vivekananda returned to India in 1897, he was given a reception unprecedented in the nation's history. He was welcomed as a national hero, and wherever he went people swarmed to see him and hear him speak. While lecturing throughout India, he greatly inspired and united the people by renewing in them a sense of pride in their national heritage. He reminded the Indians of the teachings of their scriptures:

> Strength is what the *Upanishads* speak to me from every page. Be not weak. Will sin cure sin, weakness cure weakness? Stand up and be strong.

> Arise! Arise! And stop not till the goal is reached.

> The national ideals of India are renunciation and service. Intensify her in those channels and the rest till take care of itself.

As a student of history Vivekananda knew that no great work could be done without an organisation. Therefore, on 1 May 1897 he established the Ramakrishna Math and Mission in Calcutta and delineated its aims and ideals, which are purely spiritual and humanitarian in nature. Property was purchased at Belur (across the river from Calcutta), which became the headquarters of the Order. Two other centres — one in Mayavati, Himalayas, and the other in Madras — were also started by him. Besides this, he founded three journals to propagate the message of *Vedanta*.

After a short time Vivekananda's health began to fail because of constant work. At the request of his American friends and disciples, he left for the West on 20 June 1899 with Sister Nivedita (Margaret Noble) and Swami Turiyanananda. The sea voyage and rest improved his health, and again he preached the religion of *Vedanta* to the West. Travelling through Europe, he prophesied:

> Europe is on the edge of a volcano. Unless the fires are extinguished by a flood of spirituality, it will blow up.

Vivekananda returned to India in December 1900.

An editor and his Punjabi friend once came to interview Vivekananda, and the conversation drifted to the duty of the rich to provide food, education, and so on, to the poor. The Punjabi visitor, however, expressed his disappointment that the Swami did not talk about religion. Vivekananda gravely replied:

> Sir, as long as even a dog of my country remains without food, to feed and take care of him is my religion, and anything else is either non-religion or false religion.

He reminded the Indians:

> He who sees Shiva in the poor, in the weak, and in the diseased, really worships Shiva; and if he sees Shiva only in the image, his worship is but preliminary.

Vivekananda's impact on India has been immense. Mahatma Gandhi said:

> I have gone through his works very thoroughly, and after having gone through them, the love that I had for my country became a thousandfold.

Vivekananda's writings inspired many of India's freedom fighters. Moreover, the Ramakrishna Mission, which he established has grown to be an international organisation, with philanthropic and spiritual activities in India and abroad.

Vivekananda died 4 July 1902 at the Belur monastery. Once he said to his followers:

> My ideal, indeed, can be put into a few words, and that is: to preach unto mankind their divinity and how to make it manifest in every moment of life.

— **Swami Chetanananda**

Suggested Further Readings

The Life of Swami Vivekananda / by his Eastern and Western disciples. — Calcutta : Advaita Ashrama, 1979-81.
  2 v. : ill. ; 23 cm.

Rolland, Romain, 1866-1944.
  The life of Swami Vivekananda and the Universal Gospel. — Calcutta : Advaita Ashrama, 1965.
  xii, 382 p. : port. ; 18 cm.

Vivekananda, Swami, 1863-1902.
  The complete works of Swami Vivekananda. — Calcutta : Advaita Ashrama, 1970-73.
  8 v. ; 22 cm.

SISTER NIVEDITA
(1867-1911)

Among the Indian leaders who promoted the new ideal of national consciousness, unity, renaissance and political freedom between the founding of the Indian National Congress in 1885 and the gaining of independence in 1947, Sister Nivedita was the most influential spokeswoman. She was Irish by birth, so her absorption in the mainstream of Indian life and thought was a remarkable manifestation of her love for her adopted motherland.

Her contact with India was for 14 years, but within that short period the impact of her thought and work in education, art, culture and politics was tremendous. Mahatma Gandhi hailed her as one of the makers of modern India. Her appreciation and tender concern for everything Indian, and her selfless service and sacrifice made her work rich and varied, and it earned for herself a place among the immortals.

Margaret Elizabeth Noble (sister Nivedita) was born 28 October 1867 at Dungannon, County Tyrone in Ireland, the eldest daughter of Rev. Samuel Richmond Noble and Mary. Her father left Ireland to become a Congregational minister at Great Torrington in Devonshire. Due to poverty and hard work, he died at 34. Margaret Elizabeth, then only 10, brought up her younger sister, May, and brother, Richmond, with the help of her mother. At 17, when she finished her education, she became a teacher at the Congregational College in Halifax. From 1884 to 1891 she taught at schools in Keswick, Wrexham, Chester and Liverpool.

She finally started her own school at Wimbledon in 1892. Educational reformers like Pestalozzi and Froebel influenced her, and by the early 90s her talents were recognised. She was a good journalist and speaker and joined the Sesame Club where she met Shaw, Huxley and Yeats. She wrote in furious defence of the poor people, the independence of women and Irish home rule.

Truth, morality and sincerity were the bases of her work. But her religious and spiritual ideas had yet to attain stability during her intellectual growth. She was influenced by the various ecclesiastical systems: the Congregationalists, the Unitarian movement and the Broad Church School of the Church of England. Buddha and his doctrine also attracted her. For some time she turned to the study of the natural sciences. Nothing satisfied her, and she suffered mental anguish in her search for Truth and felt uncertain about her future.

In 1895, she met Swami Vivekananda. His rational and humanistic teachings of the *Vedanta* philosophy, his plea for a better understanding between India and the Western world and his synthesis of religion and science threw new light on her spiritual experience. She was attracted towards the universal principles of *Vedanta*, and she accepted Vivekananda as her Master before she left England in 1896.

She worked for the *Vedanta* movement in England till she left for India in January 1898. Because of her complete dedication Vivekananda gave her the name "Nivedita" (the Dedicated One).

The Swami had emphatically announced that the aims and ideals of the Order were purely spiritual and humanitarian and not connected with politics. Nivedita's mind had, however, gradually turned towards India's political emancipation; so, after his death, she resigned from the Ramakrishna Order. But till the end of her life she was bound to it by ties of mutual affection and respect.

Vivekananda believed that his foreign disciples should know India and understand its ideals and aspirations, and so he travelled in north India with Nivedita and others, pointing out every place of interest with passionate enthusiasm. Soon Nivedita understood that "the ignorance of the Western people about India bordered on illiteracy." Later, in her articles, she revealed to the astonished Westerners pictures of the real soul of India and its potentialities. Nivedita had come to India primarily as an educator to give practical shape to Vivekananda's plans for women's education. She experimented in a school in a small house in Calcutta for some months, trying to harmonise Indian traditions with Western ideals. She closed the school in 1899 to go to the West to collect funds.

She returned in 1902 and reopened the school. In 1903 she added a women's section to train young women in arts, crafts and the basic three R's. Her school still teaches and trains.

Nivedita lived simply in Indian style in her small house. She had no difficulty in mixing with her poor neighbours, and she served them with love and motherly care, indifferent to her own health and comfort. Her selfless service during plagues, famines and floods in Bengal was highly appreciated. Rabindranath Tagore rightly called her the "Mother of the People."

Nivedita was deeply involved in the revival of Indian art which she regarded as an essential part of national regeneration. She was against the teachings of Western methods of composition in the government art schools in Calcutta, Bombay and Madras. They afterwards changed their initial practice. E.B. Havell, Abanindranath Tagore and Ananda Coomaraswamy were her allies in this crusade. Together they refuted the theory that Indian art had its origin in Greek art. As she was an intrepid defender of India, the English papers dubbed her "A Champion of India" and "A Traitor to her Race." Nivedita was unconcerned.

India was now her motherland. She was angry when she saw that by law and practice the British government thwarted every effort of Indian leaders to bring about national regeneration and gain political freedom. Her house was visited by moderate as well as radical Indian statesmen, scientists, scholars, poets, artists and students. Many English and American men and women of distinction, including Lady Minto, the viceroy's wife, visited her. She never directly participated in any movement. She inspired Indian youth, who looked upon her as the "philosopher of romantic nationalism and aggressive Indianism."

On 11 October 1911 Nivedita died in Darjeeling at the age of 44. During her close contact with the Indian people, they came to love their "Sister" with devoted admiration amounting to veneration. Public recognition of her eminence was given by the people when they put up a tablet on her memorial built in the Hindu cremation ground in Darjeeling which proclaims to this day:

> HERE REPOSES SISTER NIVEDITA
> WHO GAVE HER ALL TO INDIA

Works

Of her major works, *Kali the Mother* (1900) and *Cradle Tales of Hinduism* (1901) were favourably received. *The Web of Indian Life* (1904) aroused great controversy in the West, for it depicted the Indian people differently from what was portrayed in missionary propaganda. *The Master as I Saw Him* (1910) was acclaimed a masterpiece. *The Northern Tirtha: a Pilgrim's Diary* (1911), later entitled *Kedar Nath and Badri Narayan: a Pilgrim's Diary*, and

Notes of Some Wanderings with Swami Vivekananda (1913) are narratives of travel and partly autobiographical.

Aggressive Hinduism (1901), *Glimpses of Famine and Flood in East Bengal in 1906* (1907), *Shiva and Buddha* (1919), *Lambs among Wolves* (1901) and *An Indian Study of Life and Death* (1905) are minor works.

Nivedita's contributions to journals and newspapers were endless. A few of these were published in book form after her death: *Studies from An Eastern Home* (1913), *Footfalls of Indian History* (1915), *Religion and Dharma* (1915), *Civic and National Ideals* (1911) and *Hints on National Education in India* (1914).

Besides these there are innumerable articles and lectures, biographical sketches and reviews not yet published in book form. Nivedita was a prolific letter writer. Her letters, now published in two volumes, reveal her intimate personal outlook of life and work.

— **Pravrajika Atmaprana**

Suggested Further Readings

Noble, Margaret Elizabeth, 1867-1911.
   The complete works of Sister Nivedita / ed. by Pravrajika   Atmaprana. — Madras :
   Ramakrishna Math, 1968-73.
   4 v. ; 22 cm.

Chakravarty, Basudha.
   Sister Nivedita. — New Delhi : National Book Trust, 1975.
   84 p. ; 18 cm. — (National biographical series)

MOTHER TERESA
(1910-1997*)

Mother Teresa of Calcutta, founder of the Order of the Missionaries of Charity, is widely regarded as a living saint.

She was born Agnes Gonxha Bojaxhiu in Skopje, Albania, 26 August 1910 of a merchant family. She had one sister and one brother. Her childhood was a happy one in the minority Roman Catholic community. As a school girl, she joined a Catholic association for children, the Solidarity of Mary, and became enthusiastic about mission work. A group of Jesuit missionaries from Yugoslavia who were serving in Bengal wrote home accounts that inspired the devout girl. The writings of Pope Pius XI and the institution of the Feast of Christ the King were also early influences.

At the age of 18 Agnes volunteered for the Bengal Mission with the Loreto Sisters. She went to Loreto Abbey, Rathfarnham, Dublin, for a short period of English language instruction before departing for her novitiate in Calcutta. She arrived in India in 1929 and was sent to Darjeeling for further training in English and to prepare for becoming a teacher.

---

* At the time of going to the printer for final printing of the book, we heard the sad news of Mother Teresa's demise — *Publishers.*

Her First Vows

In May 1931, she took her first vows of poverty, chastity and obedience. She took the religious name Teresa after St. Teresa of Lisieux who was a French missionary in Indochina and the patroness of missionaries. Sister Teresa then went to Calcutta for a long and successful period of teaching. She taught geography and history at a high school for girls in Entally, Calcutta, which was run by the Loreto Sisters.

After learning Bengali, Sister Teresa began teaching in that language at St. Mary's, a school for local girls within the large compound at Entally. On 14 May 1937 she took her final vows in Darjeeling. She eventually became the principal of St.Anne, an affiliated order of Indian nuns who taught at the school.

An early exposure to the life of Calcutta's slums was provided to Sister Teresa through the Solidarity of the Blessed Virgin, the same organisation which had been so important to the young Agnes. This group of young Indian girls reported to her the distressing conditions that they witnessed while visiting families in the slums.

"The Poorest of the Poor"

Her intense involvement with the poor, however, came during a train journey to Darjeeling. She was travelling there on annual retreat 10 September 1946 when she heard a call from God, "a call within a call," as she describes it. The message was to give up her life at Entally and live in the slums, "to serve Him in the poorest of the poor." She requested exclaustration, the freedom from strict enclosure, from her spiritual advisor and her archbishop. Appeals to the Mother General of Loreto and to Pope Pius XII followed. She was granted a probationary year of exclaustration from the papal nuncio at Delhi.

In August 1948, Sister Teresa left the Loreto Convent. She spoke of it later as being the most difficult step of her life. She began wearing a simple white *sari* with a blue border. After a short nursing course with the Medical Mission Sisters in Patna she moved back to Calcutta to begin her work, alone.

In a *basti* in Moti Jihil, Sister Teresa began a school for children in Bengali. By mid-1949 she had ten followers, former students from St. Mary's who also lived with her in the apartment of a faithful parishioner. The group was supported by small gifts as well as some actual begging. Support for Sister Teresa's work within the diocese increased, and she applied to Rome to begin a new congregation, the Missionaries of Charity.

A fourth vow was added to the usual three vows of poverty, chastity and obedience: "to give wholehearted and free service to the poorest of the poor," shaped the unique direction of what was to become a large and successful religious organisation.

The new congregation was recognised in October 1950, and Sister Teresa became Mother Teresa of the Missionaries of Charity. In 1953 they moved into permanent quarters at 54A Lower Circular Road, Calcutta, which became the Mother House for the international endeavours that followed the initial efforts. Their own rules of poverty have remained strict. Each nun is allowed to possess two *saris*, rough underwear, a pair of sandals, a crucifix that is worn on the left shoulder, a metal bucket for washing and a thin mat for sleeping.

Through the years the group expanded, opening other schools and orphanages for Calcutta children, medical and food dispensaries and fixed and mobile centres for leprosy treatment.

Hostel for the Dying

The best-known of Mother Teresa's Calcutta efforts is her Hostel for the Dying. In 1954 Mother Teresa had brought dying destitutes to local hospitals, only to have them rejected. She asked the municipal authorities for a house to care for those dying on the streets. A building, which she named Nirmal Hriday, was given to her in Kalighat. Early Hindu opposition to the operation of a Catholic institution so near the sacred Kali temple soon gave way to admiration for her loving care of those who were rejected by all others and beyond medical hope. After the dying are picked up or brought to Nirmal Hriday, they are washed, fed, and given whatever medical attention is possible.

They are allowed their final wishes according to their faith, with Hindus receiving Ganga water, Muslims being read to from the Koran and Christians receiving last rites.

Central to this work for the dying destitutes is Mother Teresa's advocacy of considering each human to be Jesus, and therefore worthy of selfless love. Above the crucifix in every chapel of the Missionaries of Charity are the words, "I thirst." This comes from the Gospel of Matthew which she recites:

> I was hungry, and you gave me no food, I was thirsty, and you gave me no drink, I was a stranger, and you did not welcome me, naked and you did not clothe me, sick and in prison, and you did not visit me.

By 1962 Mother Teresa's work had been recognised by the Government of India which awarded her the Padmasri for her service to the people of India. In 1963 a new branch was established for men, the Missionary Brothers of Charity. In 1964 the Pope donated the car used by him for his visit to India to Mother Teresa. She raffled it off to raise money for her work.

Shortly thereafter the Missionaries of Charity became a Society of Pontifical Right. This gave the Society the right to work anywhere in the world. By this time there were over 300 nuns, and teams had established centres for medical aid in several locations throughout India.

The first invitation to work outside of India came from Venezuela in 1965. A team of four nuns was initially sent out to establish a centre to provide shelter for the homeless, education and medical aid. This began the remarkable expansion of the Missionaries of Charity. Accustomed to abject conditions in Calcutta and committed to a life of poverty, they were welcomed into communities throughout the Third World, and later to the developed nations. Everywhere they focussed on the "poorest of the poor" in cultural context. Soup kitchens, shelters for women and unwed mothers, homes for the dying, prison ministry, nursing homes, refugee shelters, religious education programmes and other schools for the destitute were established. By 1989 there were over 2,500 professed Sisters in over 80 countries around the world and five novitiates for the training of new nuns.

The Nobel Peace Prize

Public recognition of this work has come from many quarters. India, her adopted country, was the first to recognise Mother Teresa with the *Padmasri* in 1962. She received the John F. Kennedy International Award in 1971, the first Pope John XXIII Peace Prize in 1971, the Jawaharlal Nehru Award for International Understanding in 1972, the Templeton Prize for Progress in Religion in 1973, the Food and Agricultural Organization's Ceres Medal in 1975, and honorary degrees from colleges and universities worldwide. In 1979 she travelled to Oslo to accept the Nobel Peace Prize and deliver the Nobel lecture. The Government of India commemorated this event by issuing a Mother Teresa stamp in 1980.

Her attitude towards all the accolades has been that it was Christ's work, not hers, that was rewarded.

One of the outstanding qualities of Mother Teresa's religious philosophy is her willingness to accept and incorporate Hindu and Muslim ideas that are compatible with Christianity. As well as permitting the dying of all faiths to have their own ceremonies in the Home of the Dying, she has adapted verses from the *Bhagavad Gita* for prayer. When the Missionaries of Charity celebrated their 25th anniversary in 1975, 18 religious congregations participated with their own ceremonies.

Mother Teresa is not without her critics, however. Her stance has always been non-political, and many Catholics working for social change and justice are frustrated by her silence on these issues. They feel that by dealing with the causes of social ills as well as the human wreckage, her effectiveness would be increased. Her long-standing campaign against artificial measures of birth control and abortion has also troubled proponents who see a rising population rate as a chief contributor to the conditions which she seeks to allay. She has also adamantly opposed the priesthood for women. When questioned about this, she says:

No one could have been a better priest than Our Lady, and she remained only the handmaiden of the Lord.

In the fall of 1989 Mother Teresa suffered a severe heart attack, and a pacemaker was installed. In the spring of 1990 she announced her resignation as superior general of the Missionaries of Charity. Her order rejected her decision later in the year, however, and in a recent ballot unanimously re-elected her to a further six-year term.

— **Diane Clayton**

Suggested Further Readings

Egan, Eileen.
   Such a vision of the street. — New York : Doubleday, 1985.
   432 p. ; 23 cm.

Le Joly, Edward.
   Mother Teresa of Calcutta. — San Francisco : Harper and Row, 1983.
   345 p. : ill. ; 25 cm.

Spink, Kathryn.
   The miracle of love. — San Francisco : Harper and Row, 1982.
   256 p. ; 22 cm.

"Mother Teresa". A film by Jeanette Petrie with narration by Sir Richard Attenborough.
   1986. 82 minutes.

CHAPTER 13

THE WRITERS

Kalidasa	Bankim Chandra Chatterjee
Andal	Michael Madhusudan Dutt
al-Biruni	Mirza Ghalib
Amir Khusrau	Francisco Luís Gomes
Ibn Batutah	Rudyard Kipling
Kabir	Premchand
Tulsi Das	C. Subramania Bharati
Abul Fazl	Sarojini Naidu
Mirabai	Rabindranath Tagore
Warris Shah	

*G*reater India has produced many writers, and the lives of some, but by no means all, of them are sketched here. In the Early Period are al-Biruni and Ibn Batutah who could be considered outsiders because they were born beyond the borders of South India, and in the Modern Period is Rudyard Kipling, an Englishman. In his time he was called Anglo-Indian which meant "an Englishman who is domiciled in India."

We have arranged the writers in the Early Period in chronological order, but this did not seem appropriate for those of the Modern Period because many of their lives overlap each other. Nevertheless, it is appropriate to conclude this chapter with the redoubtable Rabindranath Tagore, India's famous modern poet and Renaissance Man and winner of a Nobel Prize for Literature.

Ancient India gave the world more great writers than those listed above, but they will be found in other chapters where they seemed to fit better. Chanakya belongs to the period of the Mauryas, Brahmagupta with the scientists, etc.

Lost in the Vedic period is Valmiki, author of the *Rámáyana*, the great Indian epic, followed by Kalidasa the dramatist, a glittering gem of India's Golden Age — the Gupta Period.

Then one day came a visitor from Khiva, arriving in India on the eve of the present millennium. He wrote on many subjects, but his most famous work was his *Ta'rikh al-Hind*. Another Muslim writer was Amir Khusrau, a poet of the Delhi Sultans, followed by Ibn Batutah from Tangiers, whose history of the Delhi Sultanate is one of the best sources for that period.

These are rivalled by Hindu writers who produced some of the finest literature of medieval India: Tulsi Das, Andal and Kabir. They are followed by Abul Fazl, the chronicler of Akbar.

The Modern Period gave us writers, most of whom had to deal with subjects like social reform and nationalism. They did not confine themselves to one language, either. They wrote in English, Bengali, Punjabi, Persian, Urdu, Hindi and even Portuguese. Kipling described the India he saw, and some say he was anti-Indian, but this is not everyone's observation.

Writers like Dutt, Subramanya Bharati and Warris Shah had a profound effect on the development of their respective regional languages and literatures, and writers like Iqbal, Naidu, Gomes, Ghalib and Chatterjee cried for social and political justice.

KALIDASA

Kalidasa is one of the greatest names in the history of Sanskrit literature, but Indian tradition has not preserved any biography of him. Two hundred years of modern scholarship have failed to unearth any solid facts about him and his life.

The name itself may denote more than one person. Many works in Sanskrit are ascribed to the name "Kalidasa." But it is clear that all of them cannot belong to the same author. As early as the tenth century A.D., Rajasekhara wrote about three different Kalidasas. Evidently, with time, as "Kalidasa" became a synonym for poetic glory, many lesser poets signed their works with that famous name — quite a common thing in the history of Indian literature.

The begetter of this fame and glory, the first and original Kalidasa, is now considered to be the author of only six (or, at most, seven) works: three plays and three (or four) poems.

The *Rtu-Samhara* ("The Circle of the Seasons") is a sequence of about 150 stanzas (divided into six cantos) which describe the six seasons of the Indian year (along with various amorous ideas and feelings appropriate to each season). The attribution of this poem to the Kalidasa is a matter of controversy among scholars, a compromise viewpoint taking it to be a work of his younger years. In any case, the poem has the distinction of being the first Sanskrit literary work submitted to printing in the original (in 1792 in Calcutta by William Jones).

His *Meghadúta* ("The Cloud Messenger"), a poem of more than 100 exquisite stanzas, is a soliloquy of a *yaksha* (semi-divine being) who fancies that a cloud will bring a soothing message from him to his wife, tormented as he himself is by their separation. This poem, translated by now into many languages of the world, is one of the most popular and valued gems of Sanskrit literature. It was very often translated, commented upon and imitated, both in Sanskrit and in other Indian languages.

The *Kumara Sambhava* ("The Birth of Kumara") is a *mahákávya* (great poem) in eight cantos. Cantos nine to seventeen are believed to have been added by a later and lesser known poet. It tells the story of the love and marriage of Siva and Parvati, the parents of Kumara, or Skanda, the god of war.

The *Raghuvamsa* ("The Dynasty of Raghu"), also a *mahákávya* (in nineteen cantos, probably incomplete), tells the story of kings, descendants of the legendary Raghu, including the famous Rama, the hero of the *Rámáyana*. The poem is considered by many to be the greatest work of Kalidasa. In Indian tradition the poet was sometimes called "Raghukar," the maker of the *Raghu(vamsa)*.

The play *Málavakágnimitra* (*i.e.* "Málaviká and Agnimitra") presents one of the love stories of the king Agnimitra (identified with an historical character who ruled in the second century B.C.). Attributing this play to Kalidasa is also questioned, or else it may be considered his early work.

The play *Vikramorvasiya* ("*Urvasiya* Obtained by Valour") also presents a story of love: between a mortal man and a celestial woman, Purúravas, and Urvasi. These characters first appear in one of the hymns of the *Rigveda*, and the story of their frustrated love had been retold before Kalidasa more than once in the *Mahábhárata*, the *Puránas* and other works.

Also from the *Mahábhárata*, *Puránas* and other works has been taken the plot of the famous play *Abijñána-Shakuntala* ("Shakuntala Recognised"), now more commonly called simply *Shakuntala*. It is a story of love between King Dushyanta and Shakuntala, a daughter of a celestial nymph. Their love blossoms, then is frustrated, but in the end triumphs. Its fruit, Bhárata, is a legendary ruler of India from whose name the country got her Sanskrit name.

William Jones' English translation of *Shakuntala* in 1789 was one of the first direct translations from Sanskrit into a European language. It was soon retranslated into several other European languages and greatly impressed European minds. Thus, in Germany *Shakuntala* was enthusiastically greeted by Goethe and Schiller, Herder and Von Humboldt. Since then in the West, Kalidasa is best known as the author of *Shakuntala*.

His dating is a matter of guesswork. Though some Indian scholars put him before the beginning of the Christian era, the most plausible date seems to be the fifth century A.D. An inscription early in the seventh century praises Kalidasa as a famous poet, and so does the poet Bana in the same century. From the works listed above we may infer that their author lived (and probably was born) in north India, maybe in Ujjaini, so vividly described in *Meghadúta*. We may also infer that he was a Brahman, well versed in various branches of learning, and worshipped Siva, though not in a narrow, sectarian way.

Apart from such inferences, we have only legends. They portray Kalidasa as one of the "nine gems" in the court of Vikramaditya (a kind of Indian King Arthur), or as the court poet of King Bhoja, another hero of legends. There is a story that Kalidasa was a blockhead in his youth, but got his exceptional talent and learning through the grace of the goddess Kali; hence the name Kalidasa, "a slave of Kali." Another legend says that Kalidasa was a friend of King Kumaradasa of Sri Lanka and was murdered by a wicked courtesan. Such stories obviously belong more to folklore than to history.

It seems as if Kalidasa and his traditions have deliberately withheld from us all specific data about his transient human personality in order that we might read his work as permanent expressions of him or sometimes even as expressions of universal human condition.

— **Sergei Serebriany**

Suggested Further Readings

Balakrishnan, Purasu.
> Glimpses of Kalidasa. — Bombay : Bharatiya Vidya Bhavan, 1971.
> v, 112 p. ; 19 cm. — (Bhavan's Book University. Rupee series ; 17)

Panda, Pitambar.
> Kalidasa in his own words. — [Balasore? : 1960]
> 158 p. ; 23 cm.

ANDAL

Andal (or Goda), a Tamil bhakti saint, was one of the 12 Vaishnava Alvars or poet-saints. Vaishnavism flourished in Tamil Nadu between the seventh and ninth centuries A.D., and prominent in this movement were the 12 Alvars noted for their divinely-inspired songs or *prabhandhas*. Alvars, whose dates are uncertain, emphasised not so much metaphysics as personal experience of the deity. She is thought to have lived in the ninth century A.D.

She is considered one of the Alvars and the only woman saint. According to legend, the baby Andal was found in a tulsi bush by Perialvar of Srivilliputtur, a fervent devotee of Vishnu. Being childless, he adopted her and brought her up in an atmosphere of deep piety for the deity Ranganatha, enshrined in the town of Srirangam, Tamil Nadu.

Andal refused offers of marriage so as to devote herself entirely to God, and she spent days and nights before the idol, vowing to marry none other than her Lord Vishnu.

Whenever her father instructed her to place a fresh garland on the deity Ranganatha in the temple as part of the daily puja, she would wear the garland herself, before placing it around the idol, thus symbolising a marriage ceremony. Perialvar was horrified when he eventually discovered this practice, for it was sacreligious to offer a deity a "polluted" garland.

He put a stop to it; however, Ranganatha appeared in a vision to him, taking offence at his action because it pleased him that Andal's desires should be fulfilled since she was none other than an incarnation of Lakshmi, his consort.

The legend concludes by describing how one day in the presence of a crowd of people Andal ascended the plinth of the deity at the Srirangam temple, embraced the idol and miraculously merged into it.

Like the other Alvars, Andal was a devotional poet of a very high order, portraying ecstasy and rapture in her ardent piety for Vishnu. Of her two works, *Nacciyar Tirumoli* and *Tiruppavai*, the latter is more famous.

Nacciyar Tirumali, a poem in 143 stanzas, is an exquisite lyric expressing the sentiment of *viplalambha sringara*, or "love in separation" — separation from her divine lover.

Tiruppavai, in 13 stanzas, has become one of the foremost and most popular Vaishnava hymns in the southern part of India. In this poem Andal, as one of the *gopikas* of Lord Krishna, sings his praises, recounts his deeds of valour and various manifestations of his power. She exhorts the *gopikas* to observe all the required rituals to achieve their objective of uniting with Krishna. The word *Tiruppavai* is derived from "tiru" meaning sacred and *pavai* meaning vow, or woman.

Among the Vaishnavaites with whom this is an important work, it is usual to recite early in the morning one stanza each day for 30 days during the month of Markali (15 December to 12 January). In modern day Tamil Nadu it is common for young unmarried girls to piously recite the entire *Tiruppavai* daily for the 30 days of Markali as part of their prayers for suitable husbands.

On a literary level *Tiruppavai* is a wonderful poem of rare beauty with an ingenious mix of rhyme, metaphor and various layers of interpretations from the highly philosophical to the mundane granting of wishes.

Thus Andal is remembered and glorified each year as the human/divine maiden whose *Tiruppavai* was a ritual offering or oath to Vishnu. She has been defined as consort of Vishnu, and there is a great temple dedicated to her at Srivilliputtur.

— **Usha T. Bhasker**

Suggested Further Readings

Antal.*
>The divine song of Goda : English translation of Andal's Tiruppavai. — Madras : Higginbothams, 1967.
>63 p. ; 18 cm.

Gopalakrishna Naidu, G.T.
>The holy trinity, the three saintly ladies of ecstatic mysticism : comparative studies of Divine Mother Sarada Devi, Sri Mira Bai & Sri Andal. — Coimbatore : Mercury Book Co., 1974.
>viii, 58 p. ; 19 cm.
>Includes quotations in Tamil and English; prefatory matter in English or Tamil.

Simha, Seshadriiyengar Lakshmi Nara.
>Tiruppavai of Goda : our lady saint Andal's Krishna poem. — Bombay : Ananthacharya Indological Research Institute, 1982.
>46 p. ; 23 cm. — (Ananthacharya Indological Research Institute series ; no.12)
>Includes English translation of Andal's Tiruppavai.

Further data may be found in K. Zvelebil's *Tamil Literature* which is in volume 10, fascicle 1 of *A History of Indian Literature* published by Harrassowitz, Wiesbaden, in 1974.

---

* Some libraries spell her name 'Antal'.

AL-BIRUNI
(973?-1048)

One of the greatest scholars of the medieval period of world history was Abu al-Raihan Muhammad ibn Ahmad al-Biruni, better known as al-Biruni (which means "the Master"). Sometimes his name is spelled "Alberuni."

He was born in the town of Birun, Khwarizm province (modern Khiva) 3 Dhul 362 A.H. (which corresponds roughly to 4 December 973 A.D.) and died in Ghazni (Afghanistan) 3 Rajab 440 A.H. (13 December 1048 A.D.)

(*Editor's note:* There appears to be a discrepancy here. According to the Christian calendar, he lived to be 75, but according to the Hegira calendar, 78. The latter calendar is based on lunar months and Hegira years.)

He was brought to India some time after 997, during the reign of Sultan Mahmud of Ghazni, as either a prisoner or hostage, and lived in the Punjab for a number of years. He returned to Khwarizm where, because of his great erudition, he was appointed a councillor at court. In 1017 Mahmud invaded the country and took a number of hostages to his court in Ghazni. Among the hostages was al-Biruni.

He travelled to and from India many times during a space of 40 years, and it is said that his works exceeded a camel load.

His most famous work, or that which would be of interest to scholars of India, was his *Ta'rikh al-Hind* ("History of India"). Other famous works include *al-Athar al-Baqiyyah* ("Chronology of Ancient Nations"), *al-Tahfim* ("Elements of Astrology"), *al-Qanun al-Mas'udi* ("The Mas'udi Canon") and a treatise on astronomy which he dedicated to Mahmud and for which he received an elephant load of silver coins. He also wrote *Kitab al-Saydalkah*, a *materia medica*.

Beale's *Oriental Biographical Dictionary* states that in addition to his scholarly pursuits he was adept in the magic art and relates this story:

> One day Sultán Mahmúd ordered him [al-Biruni] to deposit with a third person a statement of the precise manner in which the monarch would quit the hall where he then was sitting. The paper being lodged, the king, instead of going out by one of the numerous doors, caused a breach to be made in one of the walls, by which he effected his exit; but how he was amazed, when, on the paper being examined, there was found in it a minute specification of the precise spot through which he penetrated!
>
> Hereupon the prince denounced the learned man as a sorcerer, and commanded him to be instantly thrown out of a window. The barbarous sentence was presently executed; but care had been taken to prepare beneath a soft cushion, into which the body of the sage sank without sustaining any injury.
>
> Abú-Raihán was then called before the monarch, and was required to say whether by his boasted art he had been able to foresee these

events, and the treatment through which he had that day passed. The learned man immediately desired his tablets to be sent for, in which there were found, regularly predicted the whole of these singular transactions.

Al-Biruni was conversant in Turkish, Persian, Sanskrit (which he learned when he arrived in India), Hebrew, Syriac and, of course, Arabic, in which he wrote his many books. He knew little or no Greek, but was familiar with Greek mathematical and scientific texts through Arabic translations. (His Third Book of *al-Qanun al-Mas'udi* was hailed by M.A. Kazim of Aligarh Muslim University as "the first Compendium of Trigonometry.")

Al-Biruni's mother tongue, about which he wrote somewhat disparagingly, was Khwarizmian, a Persian dialect with strong Turkish elements in it. He wrote a history of his mother country, but the manuscript is lost and known about only through quotations.

A Shi'ite Muslim according to some and a Sunni according to others, al-Biruni tended towards agnosticism. He was a contemporary of Ibn Sina (Avicenna) and corresponded with him regularly. Though lodged in a Muslim court much of his life, he was fascinated by Hindu literature and philosophy.

He read the *Bhagavad Gita* with delight, studied Patanjali and was familiar with the *Puranas*. He also translated some Sanskrit works into Arabic.

Speaking of Hindu lore, he wrote in his *Ta'rikh al-Hind*:

I found it very hard to work my way into the subject, although I have a great liking for it, in which respect I find myself quite alone in my time, and I do not spare either trouble or money in collecting Sanskrit books from places where I supposed they were likely to be found, and in procuring for myself, even from remote places, Hindu scholars who understand them and are able to teach me.

In astronomy al-Biruni made accurate calculations of longitude and latitude and agreed with the theory of the rotation of the earth. In geography he stated that the Indus Valley had once been a sea basin. And in physics he explained natural springs by the laws of hydrostatics.

Suggested Further Reading

Iran Society, Calcutta.
Al-Bírúní commemoration volume : A.H. 362- A.H. 1362. — Calcutta : [1951]
xxviii, 303 p. : facsim. ; 25 cm.
In English, Italian, French, Arabic and Persian.

AMIR KHUSRAU
(1253?-1325?)

Turk Allah (God's Turk), or as he is also known, *Tuti-i-Hind* (the Parrot of India), was born in Patiala circa 651 A.H. (circa 1253 A.D.), the son of Amir Mahmud Saif-ud-Din Shamsi, a Turk who was most probably a slave-officer in the court of Sultan Iltutmish of Delhi. Amir Mahmud was of the Lachin tribe and had come to the Punjab and settled in Patiala.

Khusrau was orphaned at an early age and reared by his maternal grandfather, Imad-ul-Mulk, a high-ranking nobleman and former Rajput who had converted to Islam.

Khusrau was one of the most celebrated poets of mediaeval India and to his credit are 99 poetical works, among them: *Tuhfat-ul-Saghír, Shatt-ul-Hayát, Ghurrat-ul-Kamál, Baqiq Naqiah, Hasht Bahisht, Sikandar Namah* and *Risala Nasr*.

As a talented poet, Khusrau sought and acquired patronage in the royal court and was first employed by Sultan Kaiqubad for whom he wrote a long poem entitled *Qirán-ul-Sadain* ("The Conjunction of Two Auspicious Stars").

Following the death of Kaiqubad in 1290, he continued in the service of Jalal-ud-Din Khilji whom he praised in his *Miftáh-ul-Futúh* ("The Key to Victories").

Khusrau was at his most prolific during the reign of Ala-ud-Din Khilji. During his period he wrote *Khazáin-ul-Futuh* ("The Treasury of Victories") and *Àshiqah*, the love story of Khidr Khan and Dewal Rani.

The Parrot of India was not shy about paying eloquent tribute to those who may have been undeserving. His *Nuh Sipehr* ("The Nine Spheres") was written in honour of Mubarak Shah Khilji who was known to be a vainglorious drunkard.

But he was happy during the last years of his life with the reign of Ghiyas-ud-Din Tughluq whom he considered to be a just ruler, and in his honour he wrote his famous *Tughluq Namah*, one of the best first-hand sources for the history of this period. Khusrau received 1,000 tankas monthly from Ghiyas-ud-Din.

According to his biographer, Saleem Kidwai, "Khusrau was the first poet in India to compose war and court epics in Persian. As a prose writer he was remarkably eloquent; as a poet he was a master of all forms of verse: *rubáis* (quatrains), *qasídahs* (odes), and *ghazals* (lyrics). A superb lyricist, Khusrau confidently mixed Persian and Hindi metaphors with striking results."

Amir Khusrau owed much of his popularity and success to the Sufi saint, Shaikh Nizam-ud-Din Auliyah of the Chishti order. The Chishtis gave a somewhat liberal interpretation to Islam, and much of their activities and energies were devoted to music, dance and poetry and other cultural activities, in direct conflict with the orthodox *ulema* of the period. Khusrau was never actually initiated into the order, but Nizam-ud-Din appreciated his music and poetry.

In addition to his talents as a Persian prose writer and poet, Khusrau wrote in Hindi and was the inventor of several *ragas* and musical instruments, including the sitar.

He died circa 725 A.H. (circa 1325 A.D.)

Kidwai says of his subject:

Khusrau also embodies the contradictions arising from his situation. As a courtier dependent on the political survival of the Muslim rulers, he vocalizes an intense and often crude hatred for the Hindus, identifying in them the main threat to his class. But as a poet inspired by the ideology of the Chishtíyah, he displays a touching sensitivity and respect for the religion and culture of India. For this reason Khusrau represents a fine example of the evolving synthesis between the Islamic and the indigenous cultures of the Indian sub-continent.

Suggested Further Readings

Habib, Muhammad.
   Hazrat Amir Khusrau of Delhi. — Lahore : University of the Panjab, 1962.
   iii, 262 p. ; 25 cm. — (Panjab University oriental series)
   Reprint of 1927 edition.

Mirza, Muhammad Wahid.
   The life and works of Amir Khusrau. — Lahore : University of the Punjab, 1962.
   262 p. ; 22 cm.
   Reprint of 1927 edition.

IBN BATUTAH
(1304-1368)

He was the greatest Arab traveller of the middle ages. His biographer, Herman F. Janssens, calls him, quite simply, *"Le Voyageur de l'Islam."*

Of the tribe of Luwata, he was born in Tangiers in 1304. He is known as Ibn Batutah (spelled various ways), and he came from a family of *qazis* (judges) and was educated accordingly. In 1325, at the age of 21, he set out on a pilgrimage to Mecca. This was done with a dual purpose: to fulfill his religious duties and to improve his education by studying with famous scholars. However, he appears to have acquired the wanderlust which would impel him to live the life of a traveller.

Leaving Tangier, he journeyed to Mecca by caravan, going via Alexandria, Cairo, Damascus and Medina. Having reached Mecca, he determined to travel the classical lands of Islam "never, so far as possible, to cover a second time any road" that he had once travelled. Thus he went through southern Iraq and southwestern Persia to Baghdad, and from there he went from Tabriz and northern Mesopotamia and then back to Mecca via Baghdad.

He had apparently, even at this young age, acquired a scholarly reputation because, on leaving Mecca for Kufa, he was under the direct protection of the commander of the pilgrim caravan. He spent two or three years in Mecca before setting out on his third voyage. This one, with a group of followers, took him to Yemen via the Red Sea and from Aden down the coast of East Africa to Mogadishu, Mombasa and Kilwa, then up again along the southern coast of Arabia to Oman and the Persian Gulf.

He made a third pilgrimage to Mecca in 1332, but he was being beckoned by India. He had heard of Sultan Muhammad bin Tughluq and of how generous he was with foreign scholars. But he could find no India-bound ships; so he travelled instead to Asia Minor and visited Constantinople where his account of the Ottoman Empire, then in its infancy, provided future historians with a valuable record.

He finally made his way to India going the northern route: Khiva, Samarkand, Balkh and Afghanistan, reaching the Indus River in 1333.

Ibn Batutah was fascinated by India, and about one-fourth of his book, *Rehlah*, is devoted to his impressions of the life there. He won the favour of Muhammad bin Tughluq and was appointed chief *qazi* of Delhi. He painted Muhammad bin Tughluq in a series of anecdotes which evoke a rather cruel despot. In order to accede to power, Ibn Batutah tells us, Muhammad bin Tughluq had eliminated his father and brothers. Once on the throne he "was inclined to spill blood. It rarely happened that there was not a dead body at the door of the palace. This sovereign punished little faults the same way that he punished big ones. Every day they led into the audience chamber certain individuals in chains, their arms chained to their necks and their feet chained together. Some were killed, others were tortured and beaten."

Later Ibn Batutah recounts that Muhammad bin Tughluq had, among the servants in each house, spies who reported to him the least utterances of their masters.

Ibn Batutah also had about 20 pages of horror stories about persons who had displeased the Sultan, many of whom were skinned alive, stuffed, stoned, decapitated, boiled alive or impaled. Some victims had the hairs of their beards pulled out one by one. Others he forced to swallow dung. Ordinarily, those who had displeased him were trampled by elephants. One day he had the flesh of an enemy, who had previously been skinned alive, cooked in rice, after which he forced the man's wives and children to eat him off a plate.

On a whim, Muhammad bin Tughluq would decimate entire provinces, and when one day someone distributed in Delhi a pamphlet which he considered seditious, he forced all the inhabitants to leave their houses and move to Daulatabad, 40 days distant from the capital. Ibn Batutah says the Sultan "commanded a blind man to be dragged from Delhi to Daulatabad. This unhappy man fell to pieces during the journey and nothing of him arrived in Daulatabad but one leg."

When Muhammad bin Tughluq was assured that Delhi was abandoned, he mounted a terrace of the palace, viewed the city where there were no fires, no smoke and no lights and said:

Now my heart is satisfied and my spirit is at peace.

Not all of Ibn Batutah's account of India is of the Sultan's atrocities, however. Much of it describes the administration of the realm and the life of the people.

R.C. Majumdar says:

The work of the African traveller, Ibn Batutah, is also of great impor- tance for the history of this period. He came to India in September, A.D. 1333, and was hospitably received by the Delhi Sultán, who appointed him Chief *Qazi* of Delhi, which office he continued to hold till he was sent as the Sultán's ambassador to China in July, A.D. 1342. His account bears on the whole the stamp of impartiality and is remarkable for profuseness of details.

Ibn Batutah remained in Delhi for about nine years (1333-1342), at the end of which he was sent as an ambassador to the court of the Mongol emperor of China, taking a rather circuitous route to get there. He went first to central India, then down the Malabar coast to Calicut and after that to the Maldive Islands where he spent 18 months as a *qazi*. He next went to Ceylon where he made a pilgrimage to "the footprint of Adam" at Adam's Peak.

Since the sailing season for China had not arrived, Ibn Batutah used his waiting time profitably by touring Bengal and Assam, and later he sailed for Sumatra en route to China.

The Muslim ruler of Sumatra provided him with a junk which took him to China. He did not stay in China long, leaving there for the West in 1347. His stay in Fez did not last long, and soon he was off to Andalusia in Granada, and later two crossings of the Sahara Desert. He finally settled in Fez where the Sultan of Morocco ordered him to dictate his memoirs to his secretary, Ibn Juzayy.

He died in Fez in 1368, leaving behind one of the best records scholars have of Asia during the Middle Ages.

Suggested Further Readings

Ibn Batutah, 1304-1368.
    The travels of Ibn Battúta A.D. 1325-1354. — Cambridge : Published for the Hakluyt Society at the University Press, 1971.
    xvii, 269 p. : ill., plans ; 23 cm. — (Works issued by the Hakluyt Society. 2d ser. ; 110)

Janssens, Herman F.
    Ibn Batouta : *"le voyageur de l'Islam"*. — Bruxelles : Office de Publicité, 1948.
    113 p. : map ; 20 cm. — (Collection Lebe'gue)

KABIR
(1440?-1516?)

Kabir, north Indian mystic and poet, is one of the great names in the religious and literary history of India. Information about his life has come down to us mostly in the form of legends, transmitted orally or fixed in written sources — Hindu as well as Muslim. Though Kabir himself hardly intended to establish any new creed or any separate sect, he came to be revered by several north Indian sects either as the founder of the *Kabír Panth* or as one of the founding teachers of the Sikh *Dádú Panth* sect.

For a historian Kabir belongs to the line of the *Sant* poets of North India, mystics-cum-preachers, who are part of the broader Bhakti movement, a pan-Indian phenomenon which has many different manifestations at various times and places.

Kabir must have lived in the fifteenth century A.D., probably in its second half. Legends make him a contemporary and a victim of the Delhi Sultan Sikandar Lodi. Geographically, Kabir is associated with Benares where he seems to have lived most of his life, though he might have been born and have died in the town of Maghar not far from Benares.

In his poems Kabir called himself a *juláhá* (weaver), and modern scholars assume that he was born to a family of low-caste Muslim weavers, probably recent converts to Islam. But according to a legend, Kabir was the miraculously born son of a Brahman virgin widow who put the infant into a basket and set it afloat on a pond. The child was picked up and adopted by a Muslim couple. A *qazi*, invited to give a name to the child, opened the Koran and the first word he saw there was *Kabír*, meaning "great." Most probably this legend was circulated by Hindu admirers of Kabir who did not like him to be a low-born Muslim.

The same tension is reflected in the famous legend about Kabir's death. Hindus and Muslims argued about what to do with the saint's corpse, but when the shroud was removed, they found only a heap of flowers. It was divided into two parts: one was buried and the other cremated.

The posthumous fate of Kabir's poetry is more complicated. Kabir is believed to have been illiterate. His verses (as songs or as pithy distichs) passed into the oral traditions of north, northwest and northeast India and were recorded from the lips of people as recently the twentieth century. His poetry has been preserved also in at least three different written traditions: that of the Sikhs, that of the *Kabír Panth* and that of the *Dádú Panth* in Rajasthan.

In the *Adi Granth*, the holy book of the Sikhs, we have the oldest fixation of Kabir's poems, postdating the author by at least 100 years. The scripture of the *Kabír Panth*, believed to contain only texts of Kabir, is called the *Bíjak* ("Account Book"). The scripture of the *Dádú Panth* is called the *Pañch Vani* ("Words of the Five," *i.e.* the five *gurus* of the sect: Dadu, Kabir, Namdev, Raidas and Haridas).

The latter two sets of scriptures might have been compiled in the seventeenth century. All in all, there are several thousand poems of various kinds ascribed to Kabir. Various traditions differ from each other both linguistically and, to some extent, in terms of the religious ideas expressed in them. There are only about 40 poems common to all three of them.

It is quite clear that the historical Kabir did not compose all the poems ascribed to him. As it often happened in India, many later texts composed by others stick to the famous name in the course of centuries, somewhat like snow sticks to an initially small snowball when it rolls down a slope. We may never know exactly what poems were composed by the historical Kabir, though future research may shed more light on the transmission, transformations, and various interpretations of texts ascribed to him.

Hence, the difficulty of defining the contents and meaning of Kabir's thoughts is apparent. Only more or less plausible reconstructions can be attempted. But, in any case, the insights of Kabir are hardly reducible to exact verbal definitions. Historically, we may discern in his sayings many influences and strands. A tradition connects Kabir through his alleged teacher Ramananda, with Ramanuja, and this is supported by Vishnava-Ramaite motifs in the texts of Kabir. Other lines of continuity go back to the *Upanishads* and Buddhist thought, including Buddhist tantrism, and to the legendery teacher Gorakhnath and his Saiva-yogic *Nátha-panth*.

Hardly less important is the influence of Islamic monotheism, especially in its Sufi form. Some contribution of Christianity may also be there. But all this is not to deny a striking individuality of Kabir's spiritual quest which can be felt (even if not defined) in spite of the uncertainly of the textual tradition. Kabir's message is iconoclastic; he fights against religious hypocrisy and blind orthodoxy (both Hindu and Muslim) and strives to achieve an immediate personal experience of the true reality, of the Absolute which has neither a form nor *nirguna* (attributes).

In twentieth century India Kabir was and is often looked upon as a synthesist of Hinduism and Islam, as "an apostle of Hindu-Muslim unity." But it might be better to say that Kabir tried to go *beyond* both creeds and *beyond* any inherited, conceptual and institutionalised religion.

Kabir the poet was one of the first in north India to use a vernacular as a medium of expression. He is one of the greatest names in the tradition of Hindi literature. Many poems of Kabir sound strikingly modern and often inspire translations into today's Western poetic idioms.

— **Sergei Serebriany**

Suggested Further Readings

Kabir.
One hundred poems of Kabir / tr. by Rabindranath Tagore. — London : Indian Society, 1914.
xxvii, 67 p. ; 23 cm.

Keay, Frank Ernest.
Kabir and his followers. — Calcutta, [etc.] : Assn. Press, 1931.
156 p. : ill. ; 19 cm. — (The religious life of India)

TULSI DAS
(1532?-1623)

Tulsi Das, the sixteenth and early seventeenth century north Indian religious poet, was one of the greatest creative geniuses of Indian culture.

Indian tradition has not preserved any biography of Tulsi Das apart from pious legends which can hardly be mistaken for solid facts. There is very little reliable information about Tulsi Das' life. Nevertheless, the temporal and spatial coordinates of his early existence can be grasped more definitely than, for example, that of Kalidas or even that of Kabir.

Modern scholarship, sifting the contradictory evidence of tradition, most often assumes 1532 to be the year of Tulsi Das' birth, but sometimes 1543 is considered more probable. The year of his death is generally taken to be 1623. These dates are more or less conjectural, but we can be sure enough that Tulsi Das lived and composed his works during the second half of the sixteenth and early part of the seventeenth century and that he was a contemporary of Akbar and Jahangir. Popular legend alleges that Tulsi Das was in touch with some poets of Akbar's court.

The place and the circumstances of Tulsi Das' birth are not exactly known. As were most old Hindu authors, he was rather reticent about himself, but from his works it is usually inferred that he was born somewhere in the eastern part of the Hindi-speaking area, into a Brahman family. In his *Kavitávalí* he writes that his parents were very poor and did not welcome his birth. According to some legends, his parents for astrological reasons had to abandon him in childhood. His later life is associated mostly with Ayodhya, the city of Rama, and with Benares where the poet is believed to have stayed and died.

About 20 works are ascribed to Tulsi Das, but modern scholars take only about a dozen to be really his. The most famous work of Tulsi Das, indeed his *magnum opus* is *Rámacharitamánasa* ("The Holy Lake of Rama's Life,") an epic poem of about 20,000 lines. In the text itself a date is mentioned which corresponds to 1574 A.D., though it is not quite clear whether it signifies the beginning or the completion of the poet's work. In any case, according to tradition, it took Tulsi Das only two and a half years to write this long epic poem.

The work is a retelling of the story of Rama which had been told by Valmiki in his classical Sanskrit *Rámáyana*, but modern scholars have shown that Tulsi Das based his epic not so much on Valmiki's work as on other, more philosophical and esoteric Sanskrit versions of the Rama story. The *Rámacharitamánasa* (sometimes called Tulsi Das' *Rámáyana*) is both a great work of poetic art and a great achievement of religious synthesis. For an historian of literature it is one of the greatest poems ever written in the new Indo-Aryan language (Hindi) of north India.

On the pan-Indian scale, the work is one of those recastings of the Rama story which are the masterpieces of Indic literature. On the other hand, Tulsi Das' epic, written in a literary dialect called Awadhi, follows, in a way, the tradition of Sufi allegorical romances written in this dialect by north Indian Muslims since the late fourteenth century.

In his own time and space Tulsi Das was not a solitary literary giant, either. The sixteenth century is often called the Golden Age of Hindi Literature. Together with Tulsi Das to this century belong such outstanding literary figures as: Mirabai, a Hindu princess who became an ardent devotee of Krishna; Malik Muhammad Jayasi, the author of the allegorical Sufi romance *Padmávat*; Dadu, the Muslim who, following Kabir and somewhat like Akbar, tried to find new ways beyond all inherited religions; Surdas, the legendary author of the *Súrságar*, a huge compendium of Krishnaite devotional poetry in Braj *bhasha*; Keshavdas, a great master of Braj poetry, and Abdur Rahim Khan-i-khanan, a general of Akbar and a famous patron of poets, artists and scholars who himself, under the name of Rahim, wrote poems in three languages.

The age of Akbar was the time of various attempts at cultural syntheses. In his *Rámáyana*, Tulsi Das offers a synthesis of various Hindu traditions and trends: the devotion of Rama on the one hand and to the cults of Siva and Krishna on the other; the more popular spirit of *bhakti*, and the high brow philosophical monism of *Advaita Vedanta*. For Tulsi Das Rama is at once the Person, the Saviour from the chains of rebirths, and the Absolute, the Essence of all that is. (Some Western scholars claim to have discerned the influence of Christianity in Tulsi Das.)

It must be this Catholic and syncretic outlook, expressed with great poetical skill *in a vernacular*, that has made the epic of Tulsi Das virtually a scripture for millions of people in north India. In the twentieth century it was one of the favourite books of Mahatma Gandhi. The *Rámáyana* of Tulsi Das is sometimes compared with the *Bible* or the *Koran*, but at least not less appropriate would be a comparison with *La Divina Commedia* of Dante, also an attempt at a religious-cum-philosophical synthesis in the form of poetic narration.

Several other works of Tulsi Das, composed in Braj, are also worth mentioning. The *Krishna Gítávalí* ("Collection of Songs about Krishna") is the story of Rama retold once more in a sequence of short *padas* (poem-songs). The *Vinaya Patriká* ("Letter of Petition") is a collection of laments and prayers addressed to Rama. The *Kavitávalí* ("Collection of Poems"), one of the latest works of Tulsi Das, contains, among other things, some remarks of the poet on himself and his time.

Tulsi Das and his works have attracted the attention of scholars, both in India and in the West, probably more than any other pre-modern author of Hindi literature. But still a lot remains to be done to make his real stature as a religious poet known to the work at large.

— **Sergei Serebriany**

Suggested Further Reading

Handoo, Chandra Kumari.
    Tulasidása : poet, saint and philosopher of the sixteenth century. — Bombay : Orient
    Longman, [1964]
    xxii, 300 p. : ill. ; 22 cm.

ABUL FAZL
(1551-1602)

Abu al-Fazl ibn Mubarak (popularly known as Abul Fazl) was the informal secretary, confidant and historian of Akbar. His *Akbar Namah*, the official history of Akbar's reign, ranks among the finest historical works in Persian.

Abul Fazl's family originally belonged to Yemen from where one of his forefathers, Shaikh Musa, migrated to Siwistan. Abul Fazl's grandfather, Shaikh Khizr, decided to settle at Nagaur (in Rajasthan) where Abul Fazl was born 14 January 1551.

A precocious child, he completed his education of the traditional and rational subjects, particularly Greek philosophy, at the age of 15. His father, Shaikh Mubarak, who was himself an erudite scholar, saw to it that his son acquired insight in all branches of knowledge. Mubarak came to Agra and set up a *madrasah* of higher learning. Having incurred the displeasure of other *ulema*, he had to live through difficult days, and his family was hunted from pillar to post. It was through the intercession of Mirza Aziz Koka that Mubarak and his son, Faizi, entered the court of Akbar, and a new phase in their careers began.

In 1574, Abul Fazl, who was initially reluctant, presented himself at the court with a commentary on some verses of the *Koran*. The emperor appreciated the present, and Abul Fazl found a foothold in the court. Slowly and gradually he wormed his way into the confidence of the emperor and in course of time became a spokesman of his unexpressed desires and ambitions. Until his assassination, which took place 22 August 1602 at the instigation of Prince Salim, he remained the most trusted noble of Akbar who sent him on difficult diplomatic missions and conducted delicate diplomatic correspondence through him.

Abul Fazl established his intellectual eminence at the court by his intelligent participation in the debates of the *Ibadat Khanah* (prayer hall which Akbar had constructed for religious discussions) and discredited the conservative group of the *ulema* led by Makhdum-ul-Mulk and Abdun Nabi.

It was at the *Ibadat Khanah* that Abul Fazl came into contact with the religious leaders of different faiths — Hindus, Jains, Buddhists, Zoroastrians, Christians, etc. — which widened his intellectual horizon and developed his interest in comparative religious studies.

Abul Fazl had intellectual links with the Nuqtawi movement of Persia. According to the author of *Tárikh-i-'Alam Ara-i-Abbasi*, his letters were found with the Nuqtawi leaders of Iran.

Abul Fazl was very liberal and cosmopolitan in his views. He believed in the basic oneness of human society, looked down upon denominational differences and preached a humanitarian approach in all matters. For him *Sul-i-kul* (peace with all) was the ideal principle of social relationship. In an inscription which he wrote for a temple in Kashmir, he highlighted the essential unity of religious approaches.

Abul Fazl was a member of Akbar's *Dín-i-Iláhi*. He invested Akbar with almost every prophetic attribute.

His minionism, however, pricked his conscience, and in a letter addressed to Abdur Rahim Khan-i-Khanan he confessed that opportunism and selfishness had debased his character.

Abul Fazl occupies an unrivalled place in the history of Persian literature as a historian and as an epistle writer. His letters, in which powerful style is combined with vigorous thought, are models of excellence. As a historian his monumental work, *Akbar Námah*, with *Ain-i-Akbari* as its supplement, ranks among the most remarkable works in the East. A whole secretariat of scholars assisted him in the collection of material for his chronicle. His concept of history was vast, and he surveyed the historical landscape from all angles. In his *Ain-i-Akbari* one finds a glimpse of mediaeval society in all its aspects, political, cultural, literary and economic. What has infinitely enhanced the value of his work is the statistical information that he has supplied about various professions, geographical locations, agricultural products, etc.

Abul Fazl followed a florid and grandiloquent style in his chronicle perhaps because he felt that the achievements of a ruler like Akbar should be presented in a style as grandiose and awe-inspiring as the emperor himself.

— **K.A. Nizami**

Suggested Further Readings

An autobiographical account may be found in *Ain-i-Akbari*. For modern assessments: see Azra Alavi's *Socio-Religious Outlook of Abul Fazl* (2d ed., 1938) and Z.U. Ahmad's *Abul Fazl* (1975).

Also
Nizami, Khaliq Ahmad.
On history and historians of medieval India. — New Delhi : Munshiram Manoharlal, 1983.
276 p. ; 23 cm.

MIRABAI
(c.1498-c.1564)

The birth date and death date of Mirabai are matters of dispute, and several pages could be devoted to a discussion of them. The earliest birth date given is 1440, but the distinguished writers Usha Nilsson, A. J. Alston and Hermann Goetz contend she was born in 1498.

According to Dr. Goetz, she was born at Kudaki near Merta, a small fortress-city about 60 km. northeast of Ajmer. Her father was Ratan Singh Rathor, the son of Dudaji Rao who had created the kingdom of Merta. Mirabai's mother died in 1503 when Mirabai was five years old, and the little girl was sent to live with her grandparents. She was educated at home and received her musical training there.

Much of her life is wrapped in mystery and legend, but a few facts may be gleaned, some of them from her poetry. In 1516, she was married to Bhoj Raj, the eldest son of Rana Sanga of Mewar. It is said that at the wedding she circumambulated an idol of Krishna (given to her by a mendicant) instead of her husband, claiming afterwards that Krishna, not Bhoj Raj, was her real husband.

Five years later her terrestrial husband, the crown prince of Mewar died, probably of battle wounds. Since Mirabai had never gotten around to consummating the marriage, she was not required to commit *sati*.

The Worship of Krishna

Instead she devoted her life to the worship of Krishna and to composing songs dedicated to him. The years from 1522 to 1527 were productive ones for Mirabai. It is believed that during this period she composed her *Raga Govinda* and *Govinda ki Tika*.

Other works attributed to Mirabai, but not necessarily written by her, include *Narasi ji ro Mahera*, *Mirabai ka Malar Raga*, *Satbhana*, *Sorath ke Pada*, *Garbe Gita* and *Mira ni Garbi*.

Following the Battle of Khanua in 1527 in which Babar, the Mughul Emperor, defeated Rana Sanga, Mirabai's life changed dramatically. After the death the following year of Rana Sanga, Mirabai was forced to live in the Chittorgarh palace of Ratan Singh II, her most bitter enemy.

It was not that he disapproved of her religious feelings. He considered her an enemy because of her connexion with Merta, and he believed that the travelling mendicants with whom she was associating were spies.

In 1536, she made a tour of Saurashtra, settling in Dwarka in 1537. She found a Krishna temple in ruins there and, it is said, was instrumental in having it rebuilt. She also engaged in missionary activity among the lower castes.

In 1546, Udai Singh sent a deputation to Dwarka, requesting Mirabai to return to Chittorgarh. She refused; whereupon, the delegates engaged in a fast. In response to this she agreed to consult the deity and entered the temple of Ranchhodji.

The next morning the temple was opened, and, low and behold, she was no where in sight. But they found her clothing in the arms of the Krishna idol. This gave rise to the legend that she died then and there and became one with Krishna, but Goetz maintains she only disappeared.

The next ten years of Mirabai's life are a mystery, but it is believed she may have spent them in southern and eastern India. She turned up in north

India in 1560, or before that, and appeared at the court of Raja Ramachandra Baghela at Bandhogarh.

By now she was an established poet, and it is said that she may have met and been interviewed by the Emperor Akbar.

In her last years she tried to bridge the gap between Hinduism and Islam but failed, as have so many others. She died somewhere between 1563 and 1565.

Her Hindi poems extolling Krishna are still read and loved by the people of north India. In the concluding paragraph of his biography, Goetz writes:

That Mira has survived all these distortions is the best sign of her greatness. She belongs to the greatest figures of mankind. And I, personally, know only one other similar person, Jesus, the Christ, shrouded in the presence of his Divine Father, as she in that of her Divine Husband, pure, loving, and misunderstood and misinterpreted like her.

Suggested Further Readings

Goetz, Hermann.
    Mira Bai : her life and times. — Bombay : Bharatiya Vidya Bhavan, 1966.
    46 p. ; 18 cm. — (Bhavan's Book University, rupee series)

Mirabai c.1498-c1564.
    The devotional poems of Mirabai / translated [from the Hindi] with introduction and notes, A.J. Alston. — Delhi : Motilal Banarsidas, 1980.
    x, 144 p. 22 cm.

Mirabai, c.1498-c.1564.
    Songs of Meera : lyrics in ecstacy / [translated from the Hindi by] Baldoon Dhingra. — New Delhi : Orient Paperbacks, c1977.
    136 p. ; 18 cm.

Mirabai, c.1498-c.1564.
    The songs of Mirabai / Pritish Nandy translates. — New Delhi : Arnold-Heinemann Publishers (India), [1975]
    71 p. : ill. ; 23 cm.

Nilsson, Usha S.
    Mira Bai. — New Delhi : Sahitya Akademi, [1969]
    70 p. ; 23 cm.

WARRIS SHAH

Warris Shah, the author of the most celebrated Punjabi romance *Hir and Ranjha*, made this *kissa* (literary account) of perennial appeal, and this romance, in turn, made him immortal. Warris's *Hir and Ranjha* has always been, and will always be, regarded as a classic of the Punjabi language, and is certainly one of the great masterpieces of world literature. The ballad of *Hir and Ranjha* is the one and only composition of Warris.

Some scholars assign to him authorship of some *siharfis* (poems of thirty stanzas in which each stanza begins with a letter of the Persian script also in alphabetical sequence, starting with *arif*) to Warris, but this assertion has not been generally accepted and therefore remains a conjecture.

Amar Var (1768-1848), a romantic stalwart and a critic and literary figure himself, writes that he has spent over 50 years in writings and producing several works; whereas, Warris could produce only one *kissa* of *Hir and Ranjha*. It is logical to conclude that Warris wrote only one piece.

His own life account is shrouded in mystery, except for a few facts listed in the *kissa* itself. No two scholars agree on Warris's dates of birth or death. He was born at Jandiala Sher Khan, a village in the Sheikhapura district (now in Pakistan), and his father was Mian Bulsher Shah (according to some versions Qutb Shah) who was a Sayyid, a priestly class of Muslims. The date of the composition of *Hir and Ranjha* as given by Warris himself is 1180 A.H. which is the equivalent of 1766 A.D. Some scholars give his date of birth as 1735.

Warris got his education from Ustad Makhdum (Hafiz Ghulam Murtaza). He was, in all probability, a classmate of Bulhe Shah, who is regarded as the greatest mystic poet of the Punjabi language. After his education in Kasur Warris seems to have visited Pakpattan, and it was somewhere in that area, as tradition would have us believe, he fell in love with Bhag Bhari, a beautiful Brahman woman. The love affair seems to have ended unhappily for him. It was perhaps this suffering that gave him the inspiration to write his masterpiece.

The story of *Hir and Ranjha* is very simple. Hir was the daughter of Chuchek, the Sial chief of Jhang. Ranjha, youngest of the eight sons of Maujau of his clan of Jats, fed up with the treatment meted out to him by his brothers and sisters-in-law, leaves home, crosses the Chenab River (associated in Punjabi folklore with many romances) and falls in love with Hir. Hir takes Ranjha home to her father for employment as a cattleherd. The love affair between them becomes known to Hir's parents. Hir's father marries her to Saida, son of the Khera chief of Rangpur. Hir does not surrender to her husband, and in her misery succeeds in winning the sympathy of her husband's sister, Sehti. With her help Hir elopes with Ranjha who comes to her house in the guise of a faqir.

They are caught by the Kheras and brought to the *qazi* for judgement. The *qazi* orders the custody of Hir to the Kheras. After this judgement Rangpur catches fire, and the misfortunes are attributed to the sighs of the lovers.

Hir's marriage is annulled. She returns to her parents at Jhang, and Ranjha goes to his house with the object of making preparation to marry Hir. Hir is, however, poisoned by her parents and dies.

Ranjha, after hearing this sad news, goes to Hir's tomb. Unable to control himself, he falls dead on the tomb of his beloved.

There are other versions of this ballad of *Hir and Ranjha*, notable among them are the ones by Damodar and Muqbil. Their story, however, ends in comedy. *Hir and Ranjha* leave for Makka after they marry.

Warris's version, however, is the most celebrated one and remains un-surpassed in beauty in the Punjabi language. George Grierson, Charles Usborne and Richard Temple, all appreciated Warris for his supreme com-mand and rich vocabulary of Punjabi. Usborne says that this is the best book for the students of Punjabi. Rabindranath Tagore once said:

> The language which has been the medium of expression for Nanak and Warris can never be poor.

Whenever the singing of recitation of *Hir and Ranjha* by Warris takes place in India, Pakistan, or any part of the world, the hearts of Punjabis become intoxicated and that intoxication breaks all the barriers of race, colour, caste, geographic areas, religion, etc.

It is rightly said that as long as there is *Bhangra* Punjabi folk dance and *Hir and Ranjha* of Warris, Punjabi culture can never disintegrate.

— **Om P. Sharma**

BANKIM CHANDRA CHATTERJEE
(1838-1894)

Bankim Chandra Chatterjee, who was born in a Calcutta suburb 26 June 1838 and died 8 April 1894, is considered by many as the greatest modern Bengali literary figure next to Rabindranath Tagore. His essays on social, philosophical and religious problems were no less brilliant and in-fluential. An often quoted statement by historians is that "Bankim Chandra was the greatest figure of the second phase of the Bengal Renaissance as Rammohun Roy was of the first."

Perhaps no other writer has so vividly and accurately recaptured In-dian history in his novels as did Chatterjee. In his immensely popular *Ananda Math*, which has been translated into Telugu, Kannada, Malayalam, Hindi and Urdu, Bankim Chandra portrayed the heroic struggle, in the 1770's, of a band of selfless patriots to free their Indian motherland from British rule. So effective was the novel as popular history, that one of its songs, *Bandemataram*, or "Hail to the Mother," has become a national hymn and inspired a generation of militant Hindu nationalists to sacrifice all for their motherland.

Other historical novels ranged in time from the last days of the Sena Dynasty in Bengal before the Muslim occupation in 1200 (*Mrinalini*), to the Mughul era under Aurangzeb in the late seventeenth century (*Durgeshnandini*). Historians are amazed at Bankim's depth of understand-ing about the age he has chosen to depict and of his consistently remark-able mastery of details. His historic consciousness was also quite evident outside of his fiction. In his *Krishna Charitra*, or "Life of Krishna," Bankim sought to historicise the human Krishna much as Western biblical scholars were then historicising Jesus.

Bankim Chandra's Renaissance spirit of Hindu modernism was reflected in novels which dealt with contemporary social issues. In *Krishnakanta's Will*, for example, humanism, rationalism and the potentialities of individual freedom were all manifested as positive goals for Hindus to achieve. Interestingly enough, though Bankim was not a Brahmo advocate of women's equality, he selected as his apotheosis of modernism in the novel a heroic woman, Brahmar, whose superhuman struggle against her tragic fate has won the admiration of countless Bengalis since the book was written.

In another novel, *Rajini*, he exposed the evils of kulin polygamy. In *Chandrasekhar* he drew sympathy to the plight of two lovers from childhood who could not marry because their relationship was prohibited under the orthodox Hindu Law of Affinity. In one novel, *Rajani*, Bankim satirised an egocentric Bengali male who remained callously indifferent to the sufferings of widows, child brides, kulin wives and illiterate women crying out for emancipation.

In 1872, Bankim Chandra started his provocative *Bangadarshan*, a cultural journal modelled on Addison's *Spectator*, which contained scholarly and other intellectual articles on Bengali language, religion and philosophy. It was in this journal that Bankim's most influential essays appeared side by side with his serialised fiction.

Other members of the intelligentsia were encouraged to contribute. The impact of *Bangadarshan* was to widen the appeal of Hindu modernism beyond the demanding ethical and intellectual constraints of the Brahmo Samaj.

— **David Kopf**

Suggested Further Readings

Sen Gupta, S.C.
    Bankim Chandra Chatterjee. — New Delhi : Sahitya Akademi, 1977.
    ix, 60 p. : plates, ill. ; 22 cm. — (Makers of Indian Literature)

For further readings, T.W. Clark's chapter on Bankim Chandra Chatterjee in *The Novel in India* (Berkeley : George Allen & Unwin Ltd., 1970) is still probably the best literary analysis by a western scholar with a deep understanding and love of the Bengali language.

The English translation of Vera Novikava's *Bankim Chandra Chattopadhyay* (Calcutta : National Publishers, 1976) is the best "social analysis" of Bankim's literature by a Russian.

In India S.C.Sen Gupta's *Bankim Chandra Chatterjee*, indicated above in the Makers of Indian Literature series, is strongly recommended as a biography.

MICHAEL MADHUSUDAN DUTT
(1824-1873)

Madhusudan Dutt was the son of Raj Narayan Dutt, a pleader in the *Sadr* (high) court. His mother was Jahnavi, and she gave birth to Madhusudan 24 January 1824 in Sagardari, Jessore district, eastern Bengal, on the banks of the Kapotaksha River.

In 1833, he entered junior school at Hindu College where he distinguished himself by reciting Shakespeare at a prize-giving ceremony. In 1841 he entered senior school at the College and obtained a junior scholarship there. He wrote some poems in English and won a gold medal for an essay he wrote on women's education.

When he learned his father wanted him to marry, he ran to the Old Mission Church, embraced Christianity, was baptised 9 February 1843 and took the name Michael.

Since Christian students were not allowed to read at Hindu College, he transferred to Bishop's College at Sibpore where he studied Greek, Latin and Sanskrit. In spite of his clash with his father, his father underwrote his expenses from 1843 until 1848. When the money stopped coming in, he went to Madras and taught at the Male Orphan Asylum, Blacktown.

There he met Rebecca Mactavys and married her.

His literary career was on its way when he started publishing poems in the *Madras Circulation* under the nom de plume of Timothy. He also worked on the editorial staff of the *Madras Circulation*, the *General Chronicle* and the *Spectator*.

He published his first long poem, "The Captive Ladie," in 1849. This was a turning point in his life. He sent the poem to J. E. Drinkwater Bethune, president of the council of education, and Bethune was so impressed with it that he told Dutt to write in Bengali and enrich his own literature.

In 1852, he took an appointment as a teacher at Madras University High School. The death of his father in 1855 was a great blow to him. The following year he left his wife and married a Frenchwoman, Emilia Henrietta Sophia, and moved with her to Calcutta.

In Calcutta he first served as a judicial clerk to the junior police magistrate and later as an interpreter in the Calcutta police court.

The most productive period of his life occurred between the years 1859 and 1862. During this time he produced three dramas, two satirical sketches and four poetical works.

The dramas were *Sharmistha Natak* (1859), *Padmavati Natak* (1860) and *Krishnakumari Natak* (1861). The first two were based on Indian classical themes, and the third was modeled after Shakespeare.

His sketches, *Budo Shaliker Ghade Ron* (1860) and *Ekei Ki Bale Sabhyata* (1860), satirised orthodox hypocrites.

He ventured into the unknown with his poems. His *Tilottama Sambhava Kavya* (1859) introduced his Bengali readers to blank verse in their language for the first time. His *Meghnadbadh Kavya* (1861) was the first modern epic in Bengali. *Rajangana Kavya* (1861) struck a tender note. Finally, *Virangangana Kavya* (1862) was based on *Heroides* (1862) by the Roman poet Ovid.

In 1862, Dutt sailed for England, and the following year his wife and children joined him there. He had a daughter, Sarmishta, and two sons (Albert Napoleon and Frederick Milton) by his second wife, and one son (Mactavys) by his first wife.

They moved to Paris and settled at Versailles for a time, but they ran short of funds, and Dutt borrowed Rs. 8,000/- from Vidyasagar — which he ultimately paid back.

While in France he wrote *Chaturdaspadi Kitababali* (a book of a hundred sonnets) which was published in 1866. These were the first sonnets in the Bengali language.

He was called to the Bar in 1866 and returned to India. In 1867 he was admitted as an advocate of the Calcutta high court. His only prose work, *Hector Badh*, was published in 1867.

He was a great poet, but a less than great lawyer and a poor money manager. He ran up huge debts, and was forced to move to Hugli where he lived in poverty in the Uttapara Library. In 1873 both he and his wife became severely ill. He was summoned to the General Hospital, Calcutta, in June. His wife died 26 June. When he learned of it, he recited "Tomorrow and Tomorrow" from Macbeth.

He died 29 June 1873 and was buried the following day in Lower Circular Cemetery according to Anglican rites.

"Madhusudan was a child of the Bengali Renaissance in the true sense of the term," wrote his biographer, Debipada Bhattacharya. "He imbibed within him deep respect for Classical studies both Eastern and Western, spirit of revolt against orthodoxy, sympathy for progressive social changes like remarriage of widows, female education, etc. .... Under his advice actresses were first introduced in the Bengali Theatre ... Madhusudan was born a rebel and died a rebel."

Suggested Further Reading

Bose, Amalendu.
    Michael Madhusudan Dutt. — New Delhi : Sahitya Akademi, 1981.
    94 p. ; 23 cm. — (Makers of Indian Literature)

MIRZA GHALIB
(1797-1869)

Mirza Asadullah Khan Ghalib was born in Agra 27 December 1797 and died in Delhi 15 February 1869.

Of Seljuk, Turkish stock, he was proud of his heritage. His father's father came to India from Transoxiana some time between 1759 and 1806. Ghalib's father was Abdullah Beg Khan Bahadur and was first in the service of Nawab Asaf-ud-Daulah of Oudh. Later he served Nawab Nizam Ali Khan of Hyderabad, and still later he entered the service of Rao Raja Bakhtawar Singh, the Raja of Alwar. He was killed in a battle in 1803, and his brother, Nasrullah Beg Khan Bahadur, took charge of Ghalib who was then five years old. Three years later Nasrullah Khan died, and Ghalib and his siblings were left in the care of their mother's side of the family.

Not much is known of Ghalib's mother except that she was from a distinguished family in Agra.

Like Mozart, Ghalib's creative juices started flowing at a very early age. It was when he was about eight that he began writing poetry. None of his early poems is extant except an Urdu *masnavi** he had placed in the mouth of a kite:

My friend has tied a string around my neck
And leads me everywhere it pleases him.

His early years were spent in Agra, and he was educated in the manner expected of well-to-do Muslim children. He learned Arabic, Persian, philosophy, medicine, etc., but it was at Persian that he excelled. By the time he was 11, he was writing poems in Persian.

At the tender age of 13 he married Umrao Begam who was at the tender age of 11. This was in 1810, and shortly after that he moved to Delhi to live, but he loved Agra and frequently returned there for extended visits.

It was in Delhi that he joined a community of poets and developed his thinking on religious matters. Although his family was of Sunni persuasion, he tended away from it and became more of a Shia. He had little respect for traditional views of religion and felt free to criticise God from time to time.

He never paid much attention to the Islamic injunction concerning the consumption of alcoholic beverages. He would take a little wine at bedtime, but never drank it to excess. There is a story that an acquaintance once informed him that God does not answer the prayers of a wine-bibber, to which Ghalib said: "If a man has wine, what else does he need to pray for?"

There is another story that during the Revolt of 1857 he was questioned by an English colonel as to his religion. He is supposed to have said he was half-Muslim. When questioned about this, he said: "I drink wine, but I don't eat pork."

Ghalib's life in Delhi was a happy one as long as money was pouring in. This ceased when his uncle, Nasrullah Beg, died in 1806. At this point, Ahmad Bakhsh, Nawab of Loharu, intervened with the British authorities to provide for Ghalib and his family.

On the death of Ahmad Bakhsh, legal problems about Ghalib's stipend arose; so in 1827 he journeyed to Calcutta, then the capital of British India, to settle the matter with British authorities. He was there two or three years and loved Calcutta for its greenery and its weather.

(One wonders what he would think of the putrified stink hole Calcutta has become today!)

Naturally, Ghalib joined the literary community of Calcutta; however, the literary community of Calcutta did not like Ghalib's Persian poetry, and Ghalib did not like the Persian poetry of Indian poets — with the exception of Amir Khusrau.

---

* A poem in rhymed couplets.

Ghalib in November 1829 returned to Delhi without having solved his financial problems. He was now over Rs. 40,000 in debt and in constant threat of imprisonment. What saved him was that authorities tended to look with a kindly eye towards prominent men, which is what Ghalib was at this time in his life.

In 1831, Ghalib was granted a pension of Rs. 62.5 per month. Finally, in 1847 he gained admission to the court of the Mughul emperor, Bahadur Shah II, and was commissioned to write a history in Persian prose of the Mughul Dynasty for which he received a stipend of Rs. 600 a year.

His income was further enhanced in 1854 when he was made *ustad*[*] and was granted an annual salary of Rs. 400, and later, from Nawab Vajid Ali Shah of Oudh, Rs. 500 a year.

It was during the Indian Revolt of 1857 and the siege and capture of Delhi by the British that Ghalib suffered great hardships. By now he was old and deaf. In a letter to a friend he wrote:

> Here in the city with my wife and sons, I am swimming in a sea of blood. I have not stepped over my threshold. Neither have I been caught, thrown out, imprisoned, or killed.

In another letter are these words which tell much about Ghalib's feelings towards both the Indian and British side of the conflict:

> Don't think that my grief is only for myself. Of many British whom these filthy natives have murdered, some were my benefactors, some my patrons, others my close comrades, and still others my students. Even among Indians I have lost relatives, friends, students and lovers. Now every one of them is gone. It is so terribly difficult to mourn for a single relative or friend. Think of me who has to mourn for so many. My God! So many of my friends and relatives have died that if now I were to die, not a single soul would be left to mourn for me.

And in *Dastambu*, one of his most famous works, he wrote:

> May the sockets of my eyes be filled with dust if during this tragic time I have seen anything but weeping.

Ghalib wrote *Dastambu* ("A Posy of Flowers") during the siege of Delhi, but it does not reveal his real feelings at the time. These can be ascertained from letters he wrote during the period, some of which have been quoted above.

Ghalib hoped to be named by Queen Victoria the *Poet Laureate of India*, which explains his reticence to be critical of British conduct during the Revolt. His hope was never realised.

The years following the Revolt were difficult ones for Ghalib. His health was failing, and his financial health was not good, either.

---

[*] The poet to whom one submits one's verse for correction.

Mihr-i-Nimroz, the history of the Mughul Dynasty which Bahadur Shah II had commissioned Ghalib to write was published before the Revolt of 1857. *Dastambu* came out in 1858 and was presented to Queen Victoria. The next year *Qate-i-Burhan*, an attack on Indian lexicographers of Persian, was written. It was not published until 1862. *Ud-i-Hindi*, a collection of Ghalib's letters, was published in 1868.

Many of his works, in both Urdu and Persian, have been published since his death and are available in the many libraries which collect material in those languages.

In February 1869, a day or two before he died, Ghalib was asked by a friend how he was. Ghalib replied:

Why ask me how I am? Wait a day or two and then ask my neighbours.

Ghalib was one of the great poets of India. His independent spirit, his sense of humour and his literary excellence established his place in the history of world literature. It is sad that his true greatness was not universally recognised until he breathed his last breath.

Suggested Further Readings

Ghalib, Mirza Asadullah Khan Bahadur, 1797-1869.
   Ghalib, 1797-1869 / tr. and ed. by Ralph Russell and Khurshidul Islam. — London :
   Allen and Unwin, [1969-
   v. : front. ; 25 cm.
   Contents: v. 1. Life and letters.

Gilani, Arifshah C. Sayyid.
   Ghalib : his life and Persian poetry. — Karachi : Azam Books Corp., [1962]
   xiv, 296 p. ; 28 cm.

Spear, Percival.
   Twilight of the Mughuls. — Cambridge, Eng. : Cambridge University Press, 1951.
   x, 269 p. : plates, fold. map ; 23 cm.

FRANCISCO LUÍS GOMES
(1829-1869)

(*Note*: This is a revision of a paper entitled "The Writings of Francisco Luís Gomes" which was delivered at the Second International Seminar on Indo-Portuguese History and later published in its proceedings: *Indo-Portuguese History: Old Issues, New Questions.*)

Francisco Luís Gomes was at once a child of the French Revolution and of the Church. He was a romanticist who loved liberty and a moralist who judged the world around him against the ethical standards of his Roman Catholic faith.

He was born 31 May 1829 in Navelim, Goa. His father, Francisco Salvador Gomes, was a physician and civic leader.

In 1850, at the age of 21, or in 1846 at the age of 17 (depending on which biography one reads), Francisco Luis, a precocious child by any standards, graduated from the Medical College in Nova Goa and started practising medicine and involving himself in civic affairs as his father had done.

Finally, in 1860, he stood for election to the Portuguese *Cortes* from the constituency of Margão. He served in the *Cortes* until his death 25 September 1869 at the age of forty years, three months and twenty-five days.

It was during his incumbency in the *Cortes* that his principal works were published. Their first editions are listed here in chronological order.

His first major works were in Portuguese: *A Liberdade da Terra e a Economia Rural da India Portugues* (1862) and his only novel: *Os Brahamanes* (1866).

His next two were in French *Essai sur les Teéories de l'Economie Politique et de ses Rapports avec la Morale et le Droit* (1867) and *Le Marquis de Pombal : Esquisse de sa Vie Publique* (1869).

One sees by these titles a versatile man: economist, novelist, agriculturist, political scientist, lawyer, biographer and historian.

These are his major works. In addition, we have some of his speeches in the *Cortes*, some letters to his friend, the poet Lamartine and articles he wrote for various journals. His first published work was a thirty-four-page pamphlet entitled *De la Question du Coton en Angleterre et dans les Possessions Portugaises de l'Afrique Occidental* (1861). His unpublished works include an account of a voyage from Goa to Bombay and a Konkani grammar dedicated to Joaquim Heliodoro da Cunha Rivara.

His most famous speech in the *Cortes* was his maiden speech delivered 18 January 1861, just three days after he had taken his seat in the Chamber of Deputies. A member from Madeira had made a speech in which he argued that since Great Britain did not permit colonial representation in its Parliament, Portugal ought not to feel obligated to permit colonial representation in the *Cortes*.

In his rebuttal Gomes paid tribute to England as a great nation which "was the first to unfurl the constitutional flag," but went on to urge that Portugal not imitate the motives of England for refusing native representation in her Parliament. He then pointed out that the great Pombal had insisted there be no legal distinction between the natives of Goa and those of Portugal.

Next he called the attention of the members to the fact that he himself represented a civilised and educated constituency, and he believed that it had a right to be fairly represented in the law-making assembly of Portugal.

Was Francisco Luis Gomes a forerunner of the Indian Independence Movement? Perhaps. In his letter to Lamartine he wrote:

I ask for India liberty and light.

What did he mean by "light"? Understanding? The ability of rulers to rule with enlightenment?

Was he the forerunner of the Goan Independence Movement? In his lifetime he worked for political and social reform in Goa, but he never actually pleaded for independence from Portugal.

If he had lived a hundred years later, he might well have.

— **Henry Scholberg**

Suggested Further Readings

George, Evagrio, 1925-1975.
  Eminent Goans. — Panjim : Goa Cultural and Social Centre, 1970.
  17 p. : ill. ; 23 cm. (The biography of Gomes appears pp. 5-13.)

Newman Fernandes, Inacio P.
  Dr. Francisco Luis Gomes, 1829-1869. — Avedem, Goa : Coinia Publications, 1969.
  116 p. ; 24 cm.
  In English, French, Portuguese and Konkani (Roman script).

RUDYARD KIPLING
(1865-1936)

Rudyard Kipling was born 30 December 1865 in Bombay. He died in London 18 January 1936 and is buried in Westminster Abbey — an honour reserved for the very few.

His father, John Lockwood Kipling (1837-1911), was a prominent author in his own right, and his mother, Alice Macdonald (1837-1910), came from a family which would later produce a prime minister, Stanley Baldwin.

Little "Ruddy" was sent home to England at the age of six, according to a custom of Anglo-Indian* parents, in order to get a proper English upbringing. For five years he remained in Southsea at the home of Captain and Mrs. Holloway ("Uncle Harry" and "Aunty Rosa"). It was an unhappy period of his life, and he wrote about it in *Baa, Baa, Black Sheep*.

From 1878 to 1882 he attended the United Services College at Westward Ho! It was here that be began to develop some of the literary skills which would later make him famous. *Schoolboy Lyrics*, a product of this period, was published privately in Bombay in 1881.

He returned to India in 1882 and joined the staff of the *Civil and Military Gazette* in Lahore, followed by a two-year stint with the *Pioneer* of Allahabad.

Upon his return to England (via Japan and the United States) in 1889, he found that his reputation as the author of *Departmental Ditties* and *Plain Tales from the Hills* had preceded him, and he was soon being mentioned as a possibility for *Poet Laureate* — an honour he never wanted and one he never officially got.

The succeeding years would see a flood of works from the pen of Rudyard Kipling: *The Light that Failed* (1890), *Life's Handicap* (1891), *The*

---

* The term Anglo-Indian is taken here to mean what it meant in the nineteenth century: Englishmen living in India.

Naulakha and *Barrack-room Ballads* (1892), *Many Inventions* (1893), *The Jungle Book* (1894), *The Second Jungle Book* (1895), *The Seven Seas* (1896), *Captains Courageous* (1897), *The Day's Work* (1898), *Stalky & Co.* and *The White Man's Burden* (1899), *Kim* (1901), *Just So Stories* (1902), *The Five Nations* (1903), *Traffics and Discoveries* (1904) and *Luck of Pooks' Hill* (1906).

In 1907, he won the Nobel prize for literature, but his output continued with: *Actions and Reactions* (1909), *Rewards and Fairies* (1910), *Songs from the Books* (1912), *Letters of Travel* (1913), *A Diversity of Creatures* (1917), *The Years Between* (1919), *Land and Sea Tales* and *The Irish Guards in the Great War* (1923), *Debits and Credits* (1926), *Brazilian Sketches* (1927), *A Book of Words* (1928), *Thy Servant a Dog* (1930), and *Limits and Rewards* (1932).

His unfinished autobiography, *Something of Myself,* was published posthumously in 1937. Actually, some of his works were autobiographical — but in fictionalised form. *Baa, Baa, Black Sheep,* for example, told of his life at Southsea, and *Stalky & Co.* of his career at Westward Ho!

Kipling was a much-travelled man. In addition to the trips to and from England and India which have already been mentioned, he saw much of the world and recorded many of his impressions. He visited South Africa, New Zealand and Australia, and his last visit to India was in 1891.

The following year he married Caroline Balestier, a descendant of the Huguenots and of the American patriot, Paul Revere. The couple were married 18 January 1892 and in February sailed for America and their honeymoon, much of which was spent in Yokohama. On their return from Japan they settled in the bride's home town of Brattleboro, Vermont, in a house which they rented for $10 per month. They did not get along well with their neighbours.

In 1895, Kipling was invited to the White House in Washington and met President Cleveland with whom he was not impressed. Later he met Theodore Roosevelt, who was yet to become president, and the two got along famously.

The Kiplings returned to England in 1896 and in 1899 made their last visit to the United States. Their eldest child, Josephine, died there of whooping cough at the age of five.

From 1900 through 1908 they spent each January-March in South Africa, and in 1913 Kipling travelled to Egypt.

Tragedy struck the Kiplings once again when their son, John, was reported wounded and missing and presumed dead in France in 1915. He was 18.

Kipling made a voyage to Brazil in 1927, following it with *Brazilian Sketches,* and to the West Indies in 1930.

Much has been made of Kipling's attitude towards India. He has been regarded as everything from a friend of India to a hater of India. It is not the purpose here to explore all the shades of opinion that exist between these two poles, but a few observations might not be inappropriate.

If the conclusion is that he did not like Indians, one may gain some small comfort from the fact that he was not always favourably impressed with the French or the Americans, either.

His loyalty to the British Empire has been used as an indication that he looked down upon the Indians "(the white man's burden)," but it must be remembered that his attitude was the product of his upbringing and of Anglo-Indian attitudes in the nineteenth (and even twentieth) century.

His most-quoted line is:

Oh, East is East and West is West, and never the twain shall meet.

Many people take this to mean that Kipling was somehow full of prejudice against the East but are not aware that this line is followed by a comma and that the next three lines read:

Till Earth and Sky stand presently at God's great Judgment Seat;
But there is neither East nor West, Border, nor Breed, nor Birth,
When two strong men stand face to face though they come from the
ends of the earth.

One would be hard put to accuse Kipling of prejudice after reading "Lispeth" from *Plain Tales from the Hills*. It is the story of a *Pahari* girl who fell in love with an Englishman. She had been converted to Christianity, but the missionaries in the story thought "that it was wrong and improper for Lispeth to think of marriage with an Englishman."

It is a sad story. Lispeth was lied to by the Englishman with whom she had fallen in love and by the missionaries who had looked after her parents had died. The Englishman finally went home, and Lispeth returned to her hill people and to the religion of her forebears.

The issue of Kipling's feelings about India may be debated until the End of Time, but there is a quatrain of his which cannot be overlooked:

You Lazarushian-leather Gunga Din!
Tho' I've belted you an' flayed you,
By the livin' Gawd that made you,
You're a better man than I am, Gunga Din!

Suggested Further Readings

Carrington, Charles E.
    The life of Rudyard Kipling. — New York : Doubleday, 1955.
    xxi, 433 p. : ill., ports. ; 22 cm.

Kipling, Rudyard, 1865-1936.
    Something of myself. — London : Macmillan, 1937.
    vii, 237 p. : front. ; 20 cm.

Rao, K. Bhaskara.
    Rudyard Kipling's India. — Norman : University of Oklahoma Press, [c1967]
    ix, 190 p. ; 24 cm.

MUNSHI PREMCHAND
(1880-1936)

Premchand was born of a Kayastha family 31 July 1880* at Lamahi near Benares. His father was Munshi Ajaiblal Srivastava, a clerk, and the child was named Dhanpat Rai. His mother died when he was seven, and his father remarried. The stepmother did not get along well with the step child. He wrote under two pseudonyms: first it was Nawab Rai, then Premchand — the name by which he is best known, and the one that will be used throughout this sketch.

Premchand's early education was in a *madrasa* where he learned Urdu and Persian under a *maulavi*. Later he went to the Mission High School in Gorakhpur where he passed the matriculation examination in the second division. He failed the intermediate examination three times because he was weak in mathematics. He was married when he was 15, much against his wishes, and began his teaching career when he got a job tutoring an advocate's son for Rs. 5 per month.

He was hired as a teacher at the Mission School in Chunar in 1899 at Rs. 18 per month but was fired the following year for differences with school authorities. He then took a job as fifth master at the District School in Bahraich at Rs. 20 per month. Two months later he found himself transferred as first master to the District School in Partabgarh.

In 1902, he enrolled at the Training College in Allahabad and in 1905 passed the junior class examination as a teacher. He was appointed headmaster at the Training College Model School and finally, in 1910, passed his intermediate examination when proficiency in mathematics was no longer required.

A Second Marriage

His first wife attempted suicide in 1905, after which she returned to her parents' home. He married a second time the following year, this time to a child widow, Sivarani Devi, who wrote a book about him after he died entitled *Premchand Ghar Men* ("Premchand at Home"). There were two sons of the second marriage: Sripat Rai and Amrit Rai.

He became a teacher at Gorakhpur in 1919 after passing his B.A. with English, Persian and History.

Premchand's literary career began during his early teaching years. He was friends with Munshi Dayanarayan Nigam, editor of *Zamana*, an Urdu journal, and published a critical essay in that journal in 1904. At that time he was writing in Urdu and using the earlier of his two pseudonyms, Nawab Rai.

In 1908, he published *Soz-i-Vatan* ("The Dirge of the Nation"), inspired by the protest movement against the partition of Bengal in 1905. The district judge found it seditious, and all copies were destroyed.

---

* Library of Congress has him born in 1881 and spells his name Premacanda.

Premchand loved to read and was captivated by many foreign writers, including: Tolstoy, Chekhov, Gorki, Guy de Maupassant, Romain Rolland, Hardy, Thackeray and George Eliot. Some of his stories bear a striking resemblance to some of these writers. For example, his *Kausala* in which a woman dupes her stingy husband into buying her a necklace for Rs. 600 reminds one of de Maupassant's *The Necklace*. (In fact, in 1926 he was accused of plagiarising the works of Thackeray, Tolstoy and Hardy.)

Not given much to travel, Premchand spent most of his life in the Benares region. He did a short, unpleasant stint in Bombay as a screen writer, writing the scenario and dialogue for *Mazdur* and actually making a cameo appearance in it. Occasionally he journeyed to Lucknow or Delhi. In 1934, he toured the west and south, addressing the Rashtra Bhasha Sammelan in Bombay and the Hindi Prachar Sabha in Madras. Then in 1935 he presided over the Progressive Writers Conference in Lucknow.

During the 30s he edited *Jagarak*, a fortnightly and the *Hans*, the latter of which was proscribed because of its nationalist leaning.

A Prolific Writer

Premchand wrote many short stories and about 20 novels: *Asrar-i-Maabid* (his first novel), *Bazaar-i-Husn, Durgadas, Ghaban, Godan* ("The Gift of a Cow," his most famous novel), *Hamkurma-o-Hamsavab, Karmabhumi, Kayakalpa, Kishna, Mangalsutra, Nirmala, Pratijna, Premashram, Rangabhumi, Rangamanch, Ruthi Ram, Samaryatra, Sevasadan* and *Varadan*. Some of these novels can be described as novellas, and some were written originally in Urdu, followed later by Hindi versions, examples being *Gaudan* (Urdu) which is better known as *Godan* (Hindi) and *Jalva-i-Isar* which was published later as *Varadan*.

Of the novels, only one, *Godan* has been translated into English. In 1968, it came out as *The Gift of a Cow*, translated by Gordon C. Roadarmel, and earlier (in 1958) under its Hindi title, a translation by P. Lal and Jai Ratan.

Premchand is perhaps most famous internationally for his short stories, many of which have been translated into English. Of these, the best known is *Shatranj ke Khiladi* ("The Chess Players"). It is described by Robert O. Swan as "his best historical story" whose intention is "to ridicule the sham values of nawabs, two of whom watch without a tremor of conscience as the English army overruns their land. Their only passion is for playing chess, and they watch with complete indifference while their king is marched off into captivity."

In 1977, Satyajit Ray, the famous Bengali film director, enlarged the story and made it into a colour film.

In addition to his short stories and novels, Premchand wrote many articles and translated into Hindi some of the works of Tolstoy, Anatole France, Galsworthy, Maeterlinck and George Eliot. He also translated Nehru's *Letters from a Father to his Daughter*. Added to his other works are four plays: *Karbala, Prem ki Vedi, Ruhani Shadi* and *Sangram*.

Premchand died 7 October 1936 after an illness of four months.

Premchand had a profound effect on modern Hindi literature. In her centenary bibliography of his works (listed below) Usha Tripathi says of him that "through his transformation of the traditional novel he established a new school of realism in fiction."

Naravane in his biography (also listed below) writes:

Premchand was the first writer in Hindi to understand the potentialities of the novel. He realised that of all genres the novel alone was capable of reflecting the various aspects of Indian life in a broad sweep.

Suggested Further Readings

Naravane, N.S.
   Premchand : his life and work. — [New Delhi] : Vikas, [1980]
   viii, 291 p., [1] leaf of plates : port. ; 23 cm.

Rai, Amrit.
   Premchand : a life / Amrit Rai ; translated from the Hindi by Harish Trivedi. — New Delhi : Peoples Publishing House, 1982.
   ix, 413 p., [1] leaf of plates : port. ; 23 cm.

An excellent sampling of Premchand's writing may be found in the following:

Premchand, 1880-1936.
   Twenty four stories / by Premchand ; translated by Nandini Nopany & P. Lal. — New Delhi, Vikas, [1980]
   xvi, 191 p., [1] leaf of plates : port. ; 23 cm. — (Vikas Library of Modern Indian Writing ; 1)

A brief bibliography listing first editions of his works in the India Office Library & Records is:

Tripathi, Usha.
   Premchand (1880-1936) : a reading list commemorating the centenary of his birth / Usha Tripathi. — London : India Office Library & Records, 1980.
   21 p. : port. ; 21 cm.

C. SUBRAMANIA BHARATI (PARATIAR)
(1882-1921)

Subramania Bharati was born at Ettayapuram in Tirunevelli district 11 December 1882. His father, Chinnaswamy Iyer was a scholarly Brahman who was attached to the Ettayapuram Zamin. Iyer was interested in Western technology and installed the first textile mill at Ettayapuram.

Subramania's mother died when he was barely five, and his father died when Subramania was in his adolescence.

Quite early in life Subramania showed extraordinary talent for Tamil literature and was awarded the title of *Bharati* by the Raja of Ettayapuram. He joined the Zamin's service in 1897, and in that year he married Chellammal.

After his father's death in 1898 Subramania went to live with his aunt Kuppammal in Benares. He studied Hindi and Sanskrit while in Benares, and when the time came, he passed the entrance examination for the University of Allahabad.

He returned to Ettayapuram, but was not happy there, so he took a teaching post in Tamil at Madurai Setupati High School.

Later he joined the staff of the Tamil daily *Swadeshamitram* where his job was to translate into Tamil news from English newspapers. He became interested in politics and covered the Indian National Congress sessions in Benares (1905) and Calcutta (1906). He met Sister Nivedita, his political *guru*, who encouraged him in his involvement in politics and concern for the emancipation of women.

Refuge in Pondi

Bharati was closely associated with the extremists in the Indian National Congress, and soon found himself in trouble with the British authorities. In 1908 he took refuge in Pondichéry, the French settlement on the Coromandel Coast. He remained there ten years, living in poverty, all the while writing brilliant prose and poetry.

When he emerged from Pondichéry, he was promptly arrested by British authorities, but he was soon released and allowed to return to his desk at *Swadeshamitram*. He died in 1921 after being hit by a temple elephant at Triplicane.

Bharati gave India a huge corpus of Tamil poetry. It may be divided into four parts: patriotic poems which showed the influence of Shelley's love of liberty, devotional songs which showed his deep religious convictions, miscellaneous poems which dealt mainly with social reform, and his three great poems: *Kanna Pattu* which praised Krishna, *Panchali Sapatham*, an epic in five cantos, and *Kuyil Pattu*, a fable about a nightingale, a monkey, a bull, a prince and a poet.

Bharati also wrote a number of essays and short stories as well as a novel, *Chandrikayan Kathai*. His English writings are contained in *Agni and Other Poems and Translations* and *Essays and Other Prose Fragments*, both published in 1937.

Subramania Bharati was the father of modern Tamil style. He was among the first to speak of India as a national entity. This sentiment may be found in a simple quatrain:

> She has thirty crores of faces,
> But her heart is one;
> She speaks eighteen languages,
> Yet her mind is one.

Suggested Further Readings

Subramania Bharati, C., 1882-1921.
　　Poems of Subramania Bharati : a selection, in an English verse rendering, with an
　　introduction and notes / Prema Nandakumar. — New Delhi : Sahitya Akademi, c1977.
　　232 p. ; 22 cm. — (UNESCO collection of representative works: Indian series)

Vijaya Bharati, S., 1939-
　　Subramania Bharati : personality and poetry. — New Delhi : Munshiram Manoharlal,
　　1975.
　　viii, 183 p., [1] leaf of plates : ill. ; 22 cm.
　　A revision of the author's thesis, Annamalai University, 1967.

Editor's Note: Subramania Bharati's name can be and has been spelled in a number of vari-
ant ways: Subrahmanya, Subramanya, etc. In some libraries and bibliographies it may
be found under Bharati, S ... Library of Congress has decided to go from the confusing
to the ridiculous, and now enters it under "Paratiar."

SAROJINI NAIDU
(1879-1949)

Sarojini Naidu, poet, orator and politician for Indian national freedom
and the rights for women, was closely associated with Gandhi who gave
her the familiar epithet of "The Nightingale of India."

She was born 13 February 1879, the eldest daughter of eight children of
Agorenath Chatterjee and Varada Sundari who were Bengali Brahmans.
Her father was a brilliant chemist (and alchemist) and was the first Indian
to obtain a doctorate in science. He founded and served as the first principal of the Nizam's College in Hyderabad. Sarojini's family culture was intellectual and liberal, and the family was active in the Brahmo Samaj. Her
mother, a poet in her own right, wrote songs in Bengali and was an accomplished singer.

Sarojini, whose first language was Urdu, learned English very early.
All her poetry and most of her oratory were in English. At the age of 15 the
Nizam awarded her a scholarship to study in England. She was first at
King's College, London, and later at Girton College, Cambridge. Although
she returned to India without a degree, she came back having impressed
English literary figures with the beauty of her poetry.

In 1898, she married a non-Brahman doctor from Andhra who was ten
years her senior, Govindarajalu Naidu. She settled in Hyderabad in the
home that was to be known as the "Golden Threshold." She had four children and a happy family life. She continued to write poetry, and her first
volume was published in London in 1905.

Called *The Golden Threshold*, the volume was introduced by Arthur
Symons, her mentor. He said about her lyrical poems, "it is for the bird-like
quality of song, it seems to me, that they are to be valued." And about
Sarojini: "It was her desire for beauty that made her a poet: her nerves of
delight were always quivering at the contact of beauty."

Her next volume, called *The Bird of Time,* was published in 1912. This from the introduction by Edmund Gosse: "She is the most brilliant, the most original, as well as the most correct of all the natives of Hindustan who have written in English."

But Sarojini's interests were turning away from poetry to politics. Her first serious cause was women's rights. As early as 1904 she had met women's reformers at an Indian National Congress session. She quickly connected the religious image of *Bharat Mata,* or Mother India, with contemporary efforts to raise the status of women. Further, she used the imagery of *Bharat Mata* to argue that the restoration of women's rights was a necessary condition for Indian freedom.

While addressing a conference in 1906 on education of Indian women, she accused men of denying women their natural rights and charged, "Restore to women their ancient rights, for as I have said, it is we, and not you, who are the real nation builders, and without our active cooperation at all points of progress, all your congresses and conferences are in vain."

Gopal Krishna Gokhale, who was her political mentor from 1907 to 1914, influenced her towards liberal and humanist politics. She developed a second important cause from this period, that of Hindu-Muslim unity. In 1911 she addressed the Muslim League and was happy when it passed a constitution seeking Hindu unity there. A unique event occurred in 1915 which illustrates her causes of rights for women, Indian nationalism and Hindu-Muslim unity. At an Indian National Congress meeting she read a poem to Kali, the Hindu goddess, and dedicated it to Jinnah, the leader of the Muslim League!

In 1914, she met Gandhi in London and became his close friend. She served with him many years on the Congress working committee, was a chief lieutenant in the Salt March campaign and accompanied Gandhi to the second Round Table Conference in 1931.

Another volume of poetry, *The Broken Wing,* was published in 1917 when Sarojini was 38. Regarding her poetry, praise had been high early on. English newspapers said, "Her poetry seems to sing itself," and, "Her simplicity suggests Blake." She was admired for the luxuriance of imagery, and for her technical skill in cadences. In 1917 three of her poems were included in *The Oxford Book of Metrical Verse.* However, her style was sentimental and rapidly seen as old-fashioned. Critics charged her with "slushy" and "intellectually thin" verse. She discontinued the serious writing of poetry in this period.

But by 1917, her contributions as a politician and orator were just beginning. She had met the Nehru clan the previous year, and grew to call Jawaharlal her brother. Her visibility grew as a proponent of women's suffrage. She pressed this issue with the British government, speaking with Edwin Montagu on the subject, and also was able to pass a resolution on equal voting for men and women at a Congress session in 1918.

With her poetic vision, command of English and fire for Indian independence, she was becoming an orator of renown. She toured the country widely, speaking before schools and organisations on the topics of independence, women's rights, Hindu-Muslim unity and the status of Indian indentured servants of South Africa.

The year 1925, marked the height of her political career. Elected to the presidency of the Indian National Congress at Cawnpore, she gave a fiery inaugural speech in which she again employed the imagery of *Bharat Mata*. She pledged to "set my Mother's house in order" and "reconcile the tragic quarrels that threaten the integrity of her old joint family life of diverse communities and creeds."

The next few years were frantic ones for Sarojini. She gave speeches all over the country on independence and Hindu-Muslim unity, and also helped found the All-India Women's Conference, the umbrella women's rights organisation. In 1928, she travelled to the United States and Canada as Gandhi's representative, and received a tremendous reception.

In 1930, she was involved in Gandhi's Salt March. When he was arrested, she took over the campaign and supervised 25,000 volunteers who non-violently protested at the Darshana Salt Works. She was arrested in mid-May.

The next year she went to London with Gandhi as a representative to the second Round Table Conference. She was known for her good humour and high spirits, qualities that Gandhi appreciated. Looking for him at the conference table in London, she asked, "Where is our little Mickey Mouse?" At the same conference she told a delegate pressing for a second chamber, "Why not a third, and lethal one for certain politicians."

Sarojini also shared a lengthy imprisonment with Gandhi in 1942-43. At independence in 1947 she was appointed governor of Uttar Pradesh and worked hard to stem communal violence there. When Gandhi died in 1948, Sarojini said he had been "my master, my leader, my father."

Her own death was 3 March 1949. She had struggled with heart disease for many years and was 70 years old. Her eulogy was delivered in parliament by Nehru:

> Here was a person of great brilliance ... Her whole life became a poem and a song. And she did that amazing thing: she infused artistry and poetry into our national struggle. Just as the Father of the Nation had infused moral grandeur and greatness into the struggle, Mrs. Sarojini Naidu gave it artistry and poetry and that zest for life and that indomitable spirit which not only faced disaster and catastrophe, but faced them with a light heart and with a song on her lips, a smile on her face ...
>
> She was indeed a pillar of fire and then again she was like cool running water, soothing and uplifting and bringing down the passion of her politics to the cooler lives of human things. So it is difficult to speak about her except that one realises that here was a magnificence of spirit and it is gone ...

— **Diane Clayton**

Suggested Further Readings

Alexander, Meena.
    "Sarojini Naidu : Romanticism and Resistance." in *Ariel*,
    v. 17:4, October 1986, pp. 49-61.

Baig, Tara Ali.
    Sarojini Naidu. — New Delhi : Ministry of Information and Broadcasting, 1974.
    iv, 175 p. : ill. ; 21 cm. — (Builders of Modern India)

Sengupta, Padmini.
    Sarojini Naidu : a biography. — Bombay : Asia Publishing House, 1966.
    xi, 359 p. : ill. ; cm.

RABINDRANATH TAGORE
(1861-1941)

Rabindranath Tagore, Bengali poet, playwright and author, was one of the most outstanding and famous South Asians of the twentieth century. His place in modern history is often compared to that of Gandhi. First and foremost, he was a poet, recognised in his lifetime as a classicist of Bengali literature (and even as the greatest genius of its whole history). Tagore was a multifaceted personality who expressed himself in the arts and in other fields of human activity: music, painting, education, social work and even, sometimes, politics.

After he was awarded the Nobel Prize for literature in 1913, he became a kind of world public figure, a cultural ambassador of India to other countries, almost a symbol of India, both for herself and for the rest of the world. The world fame of Tagore, reaching its height in the 1920s, later had ups and downs. In South Asia, especially in Bengal, Tagore is sometimes turned into an icon, an object of both worship and iconoclasm.

Tagore is a representative figure of Indian culture: in his personality, life and work he exemplifies and embodies the development of his country's culture during almost a century. His life span is almost equally divided between the nineteenth and twentieth centuries. Born in Calcutta 7 May 1861 only a few years after the Sepoy Revolt, Tagore grew up and lived the first half of his long life through the heyday of the British Indian Empire. He was moulded by the Victorian epoch.

But during the second part of his life Tagore witnessed the progressing crisis of the Empire and died in Calcutta 7 August 1941 only a few years before Indian independence.

The origins of Tagore are in themselves exemplary and symbolic. His ancestors claimed to have descended from one of those semi-legendary north Indian Brahmans who, according to tradition, were invited to Bengal in the eighth century to restore a Hindu culture "corrupted by Buddhism." But later some descendants of that Brahman caste disgraced themselves in the eyes of orthodox Hindus by too close contacts with Muslim rulers of

Bengal and became a kind of outcaste under the derogatory term *Pirali*
Brahman and were thus forced to seek unconventional, unorthodox ways
of living. Tagore inherited from his *Pirali* ancestors a conscience of being
both elitist and outcaste.

By the end of the seventeenth century ancestors of Tagore settled in
present day Calcutta and started profitable transactions with Europeans.
As Tagore once put it: "Our ancestors came floating to Calcutta upon the
earliest tide of the fluctuating fortune of the East India Company. The code
of life for our family became composed of three cultures, Hindu, Muslim
and British." Thus cultural synthesis was also part of the poet's family
traditions. Hindu neighbours addressed *Pirali* Brahmans as *Thakur* (Lord).
The British pronounced it "Tagore." The appellation, *Thakur* or Tagore,
became with time the family name.

Tagore's grandfather, Dwarkanath Tagore (1794-1846), was one of the
richest men in Calcutta, a landlord, entrepreneur and philanthropist. A
friend of Rammohun Roy, the founder of the Brahmo Samaj, Dwarkanath
was one of the first to violate the traditional ban on overseas travels and
died in London. His son, Debendranath (1817-1905), inherited not so much
his father's wealth and business, as Rammohun's work for religious
reform. For many years the *Maharshi*, as Dwarkanath was called, was the
leader of the Brahmo Samaj.

Rabindranath, Devendranath's 14th child, was the most famous of the
Tagores, but some of his brothers and sisters were also quite outstanding.
The eldest brother, Dwijendranath (1840-1926), was a poet, philosopher and
musician. The next brother, Satyendranath (1842-1923), was the first
Indian to enter the Indian Civil Service and was a social reformer.
Jyotindranath (1848-1925), was also a man of many talents: musician, painter,
playwright, author and translator from English and French. One of Tagore's
sisters, Svarnakumari Devi (1855-1932), was the first successful woman
novelist in Bengal.

In the younger generation of the family there were also several noted
figures, the most famous being the brother painters Gagendranath (1867-
1938) and Abanindranath (1871-1951).

Tagore was born and grew up in the ancestral home at Jorasanko where
the Tagores lived as a huge joint family. It was at home that the boy got
most of his early education, imbibing various influences. A great (if not
dominating) influence was his father, an earnest non-conformist religious
seeker and stern traditionalist in social matters. Next in importance was
the influence of Jyotindranath. Tagore's mother died in 1875, and
Jyotindranath's wife, Kadambari Devi, became almost a substitute mother
for him and the fosterer, together with her husband, of Tagore's early creative endeavours.

It was in the same 1875 that Tagore made his first public appearance as
a poet, both in person and in print. In 1878-80 he undertook an abortive
educational trip to London. In the early 1860s his first book of poems, first
dramas, a book of essays and a novel were published.

By the end of 1883 the family arranged a marriage for him with an eleven year old daughter of a provincial Brahman, one of the junior officers of the family estate. Mrinalini Devi, as Tagore renamed her, was his devoted wife for almost 20 years and bore him five children. Soon after the marriage, in 1884, Kadambari Devi committed suicide. The reasons have never been disclosed, but it was undoubtedly a very traumatic experience for Tagore and is reflected again and again in his works.

There were other painful losses during Tagore's long life. His wife died in 1902. Then, one by one, he lost three of his five children. His only grandson, Nitindranath, died in 1932, 20 years of age. The death of Tagore's father in 1905, though more natural, was also a traumatic landmark for the poet.

During the second half of his life Tagore must have been rather lonely, though his eldest son, Rathindranath, and his wife, Pratima Devi, as well as other relatives and friends (some of them European and American) were faithful companions in Tagore's travels and various undertakings.

The life of Tagore has by now been well researched and described in many external details, but the inner life of the poet is very much a closed book because he was reticent about himself and preferred to pose as a mouthpiece of eternal verities and universal humanity rather than as an interpreter of his own human and creative person.

Tagore's creativity was extraordinary. His literary output consists of about 50 books of poetry, a dozen novels, more than 100 short stories, about 50 plays, several books of letters and recollections and several hundred essays. He wrote about 2,000 songs which now may be the most popular part of his legacy. One of his songs has been made the national anthem of India. Another song is the national anthem of Bangladesh.

Past 65, Tagore started painting, expressing some otherwise suppressed aspects of his self, and from the late 1920s until the end of his life he produced almost 3,000 paintings which, though well received both by specialists and the general public, seem hard to classify in terms of Western art criticism.

Nor is it quite proper to describe Tagore's literary works in terms of conventional Western literary criticism. Their nature and value can be adequately understood only in the context of Bengali and Indian literary history. Tagore was an heir of the Vedic and classical Sanskrit literary traditions. He synthesised in his creative work ancient pan-Indian and regional Bengali traditions with a considerable amount of Western influences and did it in such a great way as to create a new classic for his people.

Tagore's importance for the Bengalis may be compared with that of Goethe for Germans or with that of Pushkin for Russians. Buddhadev Bose (1908-1974), an eminent Bengali poet, once wrote: "Rabindranath is our Chaucer and our Shakespeare, our Dryden and our equivalent to the English translation of the Bible. To describe him in terms of English literature, one must name quite a number of authors, for he compressed in one man's lifetime the development of several centuries. He has created language, both prose and verse ... He has done all, all that can be done with the written word."

Not less important was Tagore's contribution in the sphere of ideas. It would be misleading to call him a philosopher, but in many a work Tagore expressed the ideas which were and still are topical for South Asia and for the world. Tagore's generation had to explain the British domination over the subcontinent and to work out the ideal of post-colonial India. Meeting this challenge, Tagore evolved an elaborate philosophy of Indian history and culture. According to him, India was destined to be a meeting ground of various cultures, and her task, indeed her genius, was to evolve out of them a harmonious whole, which would be a nucleus of a future global cultural synthesis.

On the political side Tagore hoped that India would not follow the Western way of developing separate egoistic national states and would pass straight from being a "non-nation" to what may be called a "post-national" stage.

To implement these ideas, Tagore founded in 1918 a university called Visva Bharati which name may be translated as "universally Indian" or "Indian as universal". The university grew out of the school he founded in 1901 at Shantiniketan ("The Abode of Peace"), a place near Calcutta. Tagore was an ardent educationist and gave a lot of time to teaching.

From 1912 until the early 1930s Tagore was also an ardent traveller. He undertook quite a number of trips to Europe (including Russia), both Americas, China, Japan, Southeast Asia and Iran and Iraq, not to mention trips within India.

Within India Tagore was often a lonely non-conformist in conflict with the prevailing zeitgeist. Thus, in 1905 he at first took an active part in the Swadeshi movement in Bengal, providing it with enthusiastic songs, but soon afterwards, disgusted with unscrupulous politics and terrorism, he withdrew from the movement and was condemned by many as a traitor.

Tagore was one of the first in India to greet Gandhi in 1915 and the first to call him *Mahatma*. But in the 1920s and 1930s on several occasions he initiated severe polemics with Gandhi, criticising the latter's ideas on non-cooperation. Gandhi, however, responded reverentially, and the two retained mutual respect until the end. Nor were Tagore's relations with the British always smooth and easy. In 1919 after the Jallianwalla Bagh massacre Tagore wrote a letter to Viceroy Lord Chelmsford resigning from the knighthood conferred on him in 1914.

Tagore is often compared with figures of the European Renaissance. Sometimes one speaks of the Bengali and/or Indian Renaissance with Tagore as its greatest figure. It is thought-provoking to compare the cultural changes that took place in India in the nineteenth and twentieth centuries with the European Renaissance. But any such comparison is beyond the scope of this essay. The scope for further thinking on Tagore as a great representative figure of his culture and age, is limitless.

For the Bengalis, Tagore will forever remain one of the creators of their language. For other South Asians he is not only a great man of letters and the creator of enchanting songs, but also a man of ideas and ideals that mostly have not come true on the subcontinent but remain relevant and inspiring. For the world Tagore is all that and also a great pioneer of mutual understanding between people and cultures, of the global intercultural cooperation which has become a *conditio sine quo non* for the survival of mankind.

— **Sergei Serebriany**

Suggested Further Readings

Banerjee, Hiranmay
The humanism of Tagore : special lectures. — [Mysore] : Prasaranga, University of Mysore, 1968.
69 p. ; 18 cm.

Bhattacharya, Vivek Ranjan.
Tagore : the citizen of the world. — Delhi : Metropolitan Book Co., [1961]
118 p. : ill. ; 19 cm.

Kripalani, Krishna.
Rabindranath Tagore; a biography. — New York : Grove, [1962]
417 p. : ill., front. port. ; 22 cm.

CHAPTER 14

THE SCIENTISTS

Ancient:	**Modern:**
Aryabhata	Sir J.C. Bose
Brahmagupta	Sir C.V. Raman
Susruta	Sir P.C. Ray
	Ramanujan

The Ancient Period

There were many great Indian scientists in antiquity: Dírghatamas, the discoverer of the Vedic Era; Bharadvája, who presided over the first medicinal plants symposium; Atryea Punarvasu, the first great teacher of systematic medicine; Kanada, the first expounder of realism, law of causation and atomic theory; Medháthithi, the first to extend numerals to billions; Lagadha, the first to rationalise astronomy; Látadeva and Srísena, who introduced Greek astronomy to India, and Baudháyana, the first great geometrician.

We have chosen three great scientists, each of whom added to man's knowledge of the world: Aryabhata, Brahmagupta and Susruta.

The Modern Period

For the modern period we have chosen four scientists who are more closely identified with the twentieth century: Sir Jagadis Chandra Bose (1858-1937), the plant pathologist; Sir Chandrasekhara Venkata Raman (1888-1970) who worked in X-ray and radio-activity; Sir Prafulla Chandra Ray (1861-1944), the discoverer of mercurous nitrite; and Srinivasa Ramanujan, the great mathematician.

These are only a few of the illustrious Indian scientists of recent memory who made their mark and helped mankind make its "giant leap forward."

Suggested Further Readings

Jaggi, Om Prakash.
    Scientists of ancient India and their achievements. — Delhi : Atma Ram, 1966.
    viii, 258 p. ; 19 cm.

Prakash, Satya.
    Founders of sciences in ancient India. — New Delhi : The Research Institute of Ancient Scientific Studies, [1965]
    iv, 675 p. ; 25 cm.

Singh, Jagjit.
   Some eminent Indian scientists. — Delhi : Publications Division, Ministry of Information
   and Broadcasting, [1966]
   131 p. : ill., ports. ; 21 cm.

ARYABHATA

Aryabhata, astronomer and mathematician, was born in Kusumapura near Pataliputra (modern Patna). Not much is known of his life: where he was educated, whether he had a wife and children, when he died, and all the other data that go to make a proper biography.

His name is sometimes spelled "Aryabhatta," but the spelling in the title above is generally accepted. He revealed his date of birth by stating "60 *yugas* of 60 years, and three *yugapádas* have gone by while he has been of 23 years." This places his date of birth at 3577 Kaliyuga Samvat, or 476 A.D.

There was a second astronomer of the name Aryabhata who lived in the tenth century A.D. To differentiate the two, they are called Aryabhata I and Aryabhata II. The present concern is Aryabhata I.

He wrote his first treatise, *Aryabhatíya* (also known as *Arya-Siddhánta*), at the age of 23. This was lost, but a revision of it was written later. The revision was published in Sanskrit by J.H.C. Kern in Leiden in 1874. A French translation appeared in 1879, and a definitive translation into English was made by Walter Eugene Clark, professor of Sanskrit at Harvard University, and published by the University of Chicago Press in 1930.

The *Aryabhatíya* is, according to Clark, "the earliest preserved Indian mathematical and astronomical text bearing the name of an individual author, the earliest Indian text to deal specifically with mathematics, and the earliest preserved astronomical text of the third or scientific period of Indian astronomy" — assuming it is genuine.

The edition brought out by Professor Kern contained the commentary of Paramadishvara entitled *Bhatadípiká*. There was another commentary called *Bhattaprakása*. The manuscripts of both of these commentaries were in Malayalam.

The *Aryabhatíya* is written in verse couplets and divided into four chapters called *padas:*

1. The *Gitika Pada* has 10 verses which the author calls Dashagítikásútra. "One who knows these verses, one who knows the movements of planets and *naksatras*, goes much beyond them and attains the Absolute Brahman." This is the shortest of the four *padas*.

2. The *Ganita Pada*, of 33 verses, deals with mathematics and reveals that the work was composed in Kusumapura. Subjects covered include *varga* (squares), *ghana* (cubes), *vargamúla* (square-roots), *ghanamúla* (cube-roots), area of a triangle and volume of a prism, area of a circle and volume of a sphere, area of a *visamacaturasa* (quadrilateral), circumference of a circle, jívá (Rsine or radius plus sine), determination of the Rsine of the zenith

distance, *báhu* (the base of the right-angled triangle), and *kotí* (the upright of the right-angled triangle), *karna* (hypotenuse of the right-angled triangle), trairáshika (rule of three), *vyasta* (reverse rule of three) and *kuttákára-ganita* (the theory of pulveriser).

In the *Gitika Pada* large numerals are represented by using vowels in the Sanskrit alphabet:

a   1
i   100
u 100^2 or 10,000
r 100^3 or 1,000,000
lr 100^4 or 100,000,000
e 100^5 or 10,000,000,000
ai 100^6 or 1,000,000,000,000
o 100^7 or 100,000,000,000,000
au 100^8 or 10,000,000,000,000,000

For the lower numbers *vargas* in the Aryabhata system are represented by consonants, and the remaining eight *vargas* among the vowels represent 30-100.

Aryabhata also gives the Pythagorean theorem by demonstrating in one of his verses that in a right-angled triangle the square of the *bhujá* (base) added to the square of the *kotí* (perpendicular) equals the square of the *karna* (hypotenuse).

He calculated pi to equal 3.1416, and he was read by Brahmagupta, another famous mathematician-astronomer, who came along two centuries later and not always agreed with him.

3. The *Kálaktriyá Pada*, with 25 verses lists the time units: 1 *varsa* = 12 *masa* (months); 1 *mása* = 30 *divasa* (days).

4. The *Gola Pada* has 50 verses and is devoted to astronomy. It discusses the páta (ascending nodes) of the planets and the shadow of the earth movement on *arka-apanamandala* (the path of the sun). This is the longest of the chapters and the one for which Aryabhata is most famous. He maintained that the earth is the centre of the universe, that it revolves on its axis and that the asterisms are stationary. Later astronomers disagreed with him on these points.

In the preface of *Aryabhatíya*, Clark states:

The names of several astronomers who preceded Aryabhata, or who were his contemporaries, are known, but nothing has been preserved from their writings except a few brief fragments. The *Aryabhatíya*, therefore, is of the greatest importance in the history of Indian mathematics and astronomy.

Suggested Further Readings

Aryabhata.
> The Aryabhatíya of Aryabhata : an ancient Indian work on mathematics and astronomy. — Chicago : University of Chicago Press, [1930]
> xxix, 90 p. ; 20 cm.

Aryabhata.
> Aryabhatiya of Aryabhata : with a commentary of Bhaskara I and Somesvara / critically edited with introd. and appendices of Kripa Shankar Shukla. — New Delhi : Indian National Science Academy, 1976.
> cxviii, 219 p. : ill. ; 25 cm. — (Aryabhatíya critical edition series ; pt. 2)
> In Sanskrit; introd. in English.

BRAHMAGUPTA
(c.598-c.665)

More is known about the life of Brahmagupta, mathematician and astronomer, than about Aryabhata and many of the other notable savants of ancient India. In his *Brahmasphutasiddhanta* (generally referred to by the initials BSS) he writes:

> In the reign of Vyághramukha, a great king of Cápa Dynasty, when 550 years of the Saka era had passed, Brahmagupta, son of Jisnu, at the age of 30, composed BSS to please the good mathematicians and astronomers.

We are thus able to place his date of birth at circa 598 because Saka 550 is the approximate equivalent of 628 A.D. We also know that he was born in Bhillamala in north India.

The noted Arab scholars and scientists of the eleventh century, considered him the most distinguished mathematician of India.

BSS, a treatise which deals with algebra, arithmetic and mensuration, was not Brahmagupta's only work. In 665 A.D. he wrote *Khandakhádyaka*, an astronomical treatise.

But Brahmagupta is perhaps best known in the West for having "invented zero". One of his biographers Dr. O.P. Jaggi, called him the man "who gave zero its status." Dr. Jaggi writes:

> Strange though it may seem to us the concept of zero and its use in various ways was not well known to earlier mathematicians. In the chapters on algebra ("*Kuttakadhyaya*") Brahmagupta, for the first time, dealt with zero and its operation. He showed that zero subtracted from a negative or positive or zero would furnish a negative, positive or zero respectively. Zero multiplied by a negative, a positive or a zero would also furnish zero.

It is interesting to note that Aryabhatta, who predates Brahmagupta by over 100 years, compiled a list of numerals to be represented by Sanskrit consonants and vowels, but in that list the zero is lacking.

Brahmagupta, in his chapter *"Ganitadhayaya"* in BSS, deals with 20 operations of arithmetic: 1. *samkalita* (addition), 2. *vyavakalita* (subtraction), 3. *ganana* (multiplication), 4. *bhágahára* (division), 5. *varga* (square), 6. *vargamúla* (square-root), 7. *ghana* (cube), 8. *ghanamúla* (cube-root), 9-13. *panca-játi* (five standard forms of fractions), 14. *trairáshika* (rule of three), 15. *vysta-trairáshika* (inverse rule of three), 16. *pañca-ráshika* (rule of five), 17. *sapta-ráshika* (rule of seven), 18. *nava-ráshika* (rule of nine), 19. *ekádasha-ráshikam* (rule of eleven) and 20. *bhánda-pratibhánda* (barter and exchange).

In the subject of astronomy Brahmagupta sometimes agreed and sometimes disagreed with Aryabhata and other astronomers who preceded him. He believed the earth and sky were round, contradicting the *Puranas* which claimed that the earth was flat. He disagreed with Aryabhata who maintained that the earth rotated on its axis.

Al-Biruni, who admired Brahmagupta as a mathematician, was not impressed with his talent for astronomy. He wrote:

> But look at Brahmagupta, who is certainly the most distinguished of their astronomers. He shirks the truth and lends his support to imposture.

Jaggi explains this by stating that denial of accepted Brahmanical theories "was tantamount to sacrílege of religion."

This brings to mind the difficulties another astronomer had 1,000 years later when his views conflicted with those of the Church.

His name was Galileo.

Suggested Further Readings

Brahmagupta.
    Algebra, with arithmetic and mensuration from the Sanskrit of Brahmagupta and Bhascara / translated by Henry Thomas Colebrooke. — London : Murray, 1817.
    lxxxiv, 378 p. ; 30 cm.
    Reprinted by Dr. Martin Sandig, Wiesbaden, Germany in 1973.

Brahmagupta.
    The Khandakhádyaka (an astronomical treatise) of Brahmagupta, with the commentary Bhattotpala / edited and translated by Bina Chatterjee. — Calcutta : World Press, 1970.
    2 v. ; 23 cm.
    Vol. 1 is in English; vol. 2 in Sanskrit.

Prakash, Satya.
    A critical study of Brahmagupta and his works ..... — New Delhi : The Indian Institute of Astronomical & Sanskrit Research, [1968]
    iii, 344 p. ; 25 cm.

Mukherjee, Kalinath.
    Popular Hindu astronomy. — [Calcutta : N. Mukherjee, 1969]
    xxviii, 218 p. : fold., ill. ; 23 cm.

SUSRUTA

Susruta, India's greatest surgeon of antiquity, is believed by some to have lived around the sixth century B.C., and by others around the last one or two centuries before the Christian era. There is also debate about the date of his famous work *Susrutasamhita*. Some place it in its present form, as revised by Nagarjuna, in the later part of the fourth century B.C. Others put it in the seventh century A.D.

Another controversy which scholars love to debate is whether Indian medicine influenced Greek medicine, or vice versa. There are similarities between Susruta and Hippocrates. To quote Dr. Satya Prakash in his *Founders of Science in Ancient India*:

From the very apparent similarity which exists between the contents of this *Samhitá* and the aphorisms of Hippocrates, one is apt to conclude that the ancient Indians drew their inspiration in the healing art from the medical works of the Greeks. But the reverse may be said of the Greeks as well because such an assertion is supported by historic facts, and confirmed by the researches of the scholars of the West. According to all accounts, Pythagoras was the founder of the healing art amongst the Greeks and the Hellenic peoples in general. This great philosopher imbibed his mysteries and metaphysics from the Brahmans of India.

Dr. Prakash quotes such well-known authorities as Weber and Pococke to support his thesis. It is not the purpose here to engage in this fascinating debate except to say that it would be a worthy project for a scholar knowing both Greek and Sanskrit (and medicine) to take this on as a project of serious research.

There is a legend that Susruta led a group of sadhus to the hermitage of the incarnation of Dhanvantari, the physician who was incarnated on earth. Susruta approached him and said:

We behold mankind smitten by many pains and hurts in illnesses of their bodies and minds, we see them cast down by sickness coming to them from outside or originating from their inner being. Though they are protected by divine patrons, they cry out as if they had none. This troubles us and we would hear for the sake of all creatures thy sacred Doctrine of Longevity. Instruct us, that we may learn to heal the illnesses of those who desire well-being and that we prolong our own lives. On this knowledge rests all weal in this world and in the next. For this we have approached the Venerable one as his pupils.

To which the Venerable one replied:

Welcome, my children, we all, without further examination, are worthy to receive the teaching. I will teach you the science of surgery in conformity to facts, knowledge, theories and analogy. Be attentive.

Susruta, a descendant of the Vedic sage, Vishvamitra, wrote a book of surgery entitled *Susrutasalyatantra*. It was revised and *Susrutasamhita* is its present version.

Susruta not only practised surgery, but taught it as well. He taught his pupils to practise with their surgical instruments on inanimate objects long hours before using them on patients. Thus they made incisions on vegetables, dead animals and eventually on dead humans before going to work on live humans.

Susruta maintained that "the physician who is learned only in book knowledge, but is unacquainted with the practical methods of treatment or the one who knows the practical details of the treatment but from self-confidence does not study the books is unfit to practise his calling. Such a person deserves to be killed by a king."

(*Editorial note*: This last statement does not sound very Hippocratic. Let us assume Susruta was speaking in hyperbole.)

Rhinoplastic surgery was not unknown to Susruta. Here is how he affixes a new nose where the old one was cut off:

(*Editorial note*: It is not recommended to read this while eating lunch.)

Now I shall deal with the process of affixing an artificial nose. First, the leaf of a creeper, long and broad enough to fully cover the whole of the severed or slipped off part should be gathered and a patch of living flesh equal in dimension to the preceding leaf, should be cut from the region of the cheek and turned back and swiftly adhered to the severed nose which had been made raw already. Then the cool-headed physician should steadily tie it up with a decent bandage. Then two small pipes should be inserted into the nostrils to facilitate respiration and to prevent the adhesioned flesh from hanging down. After that the adhesioned part should be dusted with the powder of licorice, red sandal-wood and the extract of Indian barberry. The nose should be enveloped in cotton and several times sprinkled over with the refined oil of pure sesamum. Clarified butter should be given to the patient to drink and he should be anointed with oil and also treated with purgatives. Adhesion should be deemed complete after the incidental ulcer has been perfectly healed up. Otherwise, the nose should be again sacrificed and bandaged in the case of semi or partial adhesion. The adhesioned nose should he elongated where it would fall short of its natural and previous length or it should be surgically restored to its natural size in the case of the abnormal growth of its newly formed flesh. The mode of bringing about the adhesion of severed lips is identical with what has been described in connection with the severed nose with the exception of the insertion of pipes.

Another interesting technique of Susruta was that of using ant heads as stitching material. It was discovered that ordinary string was not suitable when performing abdominal surgery; so a method was devised whereby the intestinal wound would be joined by letting big black ants cut the ends of the intestines which had been brought nearer together. The body of the ant would then be cut off, leaving the mandibles as clamps, to which the body of the patient was receptive.

Susruta also made studies and wrote on midwifery, surgical instruments, the influence of seasons and winds on health and the classification of animals, worms and leeches. He was also interested in medical botany, medicinal alkalies and metals and their compounds.

There can be no doubt that Susruta had a profound influence on the development of medical knowledge. Some of his techniques are in use to this day.

SIR JAGADIS CHANDRA BOSE
(1858-1937)

It has been said of Jagadis Chandra Bose that he proved that plants have feelings.

He was born on the last day of November 1858 in Mymensingh, Bengal, the son of Bhagwan Chandra Bose whose ancestral home was Rarikhal in Vikrampur, Dacca district. The father was a government official in Faridpur who founded a vernacular school there to which he sent his son at the age of five. He was keen to have his children learn their mother tongue before they learned English.

Even as a boy, Jagadis showed an interest in plants and animals, and he learned much from his father. He also enjoyed folk plays and stories from the *Ramayana* and *Mahabharata*.

At 11 he went to Calcutta to enrol in St. Xavier's School and College, passing the entrance examination for the University of Calcutta in 1875 and the B.A. in science (B) group in 1879.

At St. Xavier's, Bose was influenced by Fr. Eugene Lafont, S.J., a leading scientist, who aroused his interest in experimental physics.

On graduation in 1879, it was decided to send Bose to England to further his studies, and his mother, Banasundari Devi, sold her jewellery. Bose wanted to study medicine, but he became ill from malaria which he had contracted during a hunting trip in Assam. Finally, in 1880 he left for England to take up medical studies in London. However, his health was still poor, and his anatomy professor persuaded him to give up medicine, which required very hard work, and to study science instead.

So in January 1881, he obtained a scholarship and enrolled in Christ's College, Cambridge, for scientific studies. Among his teachers were Michael Foster (physiology), Francis Balfour (embryology), Francis Darwin (vegetable physiology), Sidney Vines (botany) and Lord Rayleigh (physics).

Bose took his Cambridge degree in the natural sciences tripos (physics, chemistry and botany) in 1884 and also gained a B.Sc. from London at about the same time.

On his return to India in 1884 he brought with him a letter of introduction to Lord Ripon, the viceroy. The letter was from Professor Fawcett, the British postmaster-general, who was a close friend of Jagadis Chandra Bose's brother-in-law, Ananda Mohan Bose, India's first wrangler.

Lord Ripon received Bose cordially and promised him a job commensurate with his abilities in the imperial educational services. Sir Alfred Croft, the director of public instruction in Bengal, was not amenable to the idea of a Indian person being handed a lofty position; so he offered him a minor post in the provincial educational service instead. Bose refused it, but when Lord Ripon noticed that the appointment had not been gazetted, he intervened; and Bose was appointed assistant professor of physics at Presidency College, Calcutta.

It was the custom in those days to pay Indian teachers two-thirds of the salary of European teachers. He wrote a letter of protest to the authorities. It was ignored, and for three years he refused to accept his salary.

In spite of not receiving pay, Bose continued his teaching duties. Finally, after three years he received full pay in a lump sum. He used the money, plus some of his saving and part of his salary over the next six years, to retire the family debts. This worked a hardship on Bose and his wife, Abala Das, whom he had married in 1887. They lived in Chandernagore, and he commuted to Calcutta, crossing the river by rowboat.

Around 1894 Bose began research on electric waves. He was inspired by the work of Heinrich Rudolf Hertz, the German physicist who had established beyond doubt the electromagnetic nature of light. Bose published articles on his work in leading scientific journals, and on the basis of these was awarded the D.Sc. from London University in 1896.

Bose's research falls into three main groups: the property of electric waves, response in the living and the non-living, and the physiological properties of plant tissues and the similarity of their behaviour with that of animal tissues.

In the study of electric waves, Bose invented and built a small apparatus by which he could demonstrate the optical properties of reflection, refraction, selective absorption, interference, double refraction and polarisation and so forth.

Of living and non-living entities, he showed how animal and vegetable tissues responded to electrical stimulation as well as to stimuli due to heat, drugs, chemicals, etc., and how similar stimuli could bring about responses in non-living substances.

His investigation of plant responses showed that plant tissues undergo change in shape under the action of electrical stimuli just as animal muscles do, and he proved that conducting impulses in plant tissues follows the same laws that apply in animal tissues.

At first, Bose was not well-received by the British scientific community which disputed many of his findings; however, by 1916, the year after his retirement from Presidency College, he was knighted in recognition of his many accomplishments. In 1920 he was elected to the fellowship of the Royal Society of London and in 1928 to the corresponding membership of the Vienna Academy of Science.

While carrying out his research, Sir Jagadis produced several inventions: the Resonant Recorder which measured intervals up to 1/1,000 of a second, the Oscillating Recorder for recording very faint pulsations of leaflets, the Photo-Synthetic Recorder (called "Bubbler") for sap movement experiments, the Compound Lever Crescograph which can magnify 5,000 times, and the Diametric Contraction Apparatus which shows diametric expansion and contraction in plants under cold, heat, poison or stimuli.

Sir Jagadis had many publications to his credit, three important ones of which are *Response in the Living and Non-Living, Plant Response,* and *The Motor Mechanism of Plants.*

He died 23 November 1937 in Giridih, Bihar.

One of his biographers, Dr. J.C. Ghosh, said of him:

He was the first Indian scientist of eminence who tried to align his scientific investigations to the natural Pantheistic view of Nature ... Future historians may find the introduction of this standpoint an important contribution of the Indian mind to the scientific conception of Nature.

Suggested Further Readings

Basu, Sachindranath., 1915-
    Jagadis Chandra Bose. New Delhi : National Book Trust, 1970.
    v, 83 p. ; 18 cm. — (National biography series)

Geddes, Patrick, Sir, 1854-1932.
    The life and work of Sir Jagadis C. Bose. — London : Longmans, Green, 1920.
    xii, 259 p. : front., ill., plates, diagrs. ; 24 cm.

Gupta, Manoranjon.
    Jagadish Chandra Bose : a biography. — Bombay : Bharatiya Vidya Bhavan, 1964.
    xv, 135 p. : front. port. ; 19 cm.

SIR CHANDRASEKHARA VENKATA RAMAN
(1888-1970)

Sir Chandrasekhara Venkata Raman has the distinction (at this writing 1996) of being the only scientist from India to win a Nobel Prize.

When he received the award in Stockholm, he gave a demonstration of the Raman Effect (the experiment which had made him famous) on a number of liquids, one of which was alcohol. After the ceremony and during a cocktail hour, a friend reproached him for refusing an alcoholic drink:

You delighted us in the morning with a demonstration of the Raman Effect on alcohol. Why not continue the pleasure by a reciprocal exhibition of the alcoholic effect on Raman?

It is not known how the story ends, but Raman, being a teetotaler, probably declined the challenge.

He was born 7 November 1888 in Trichinopoly, the second son of R. Chandrasekhara Iyer who at that time was a pupil teacher in a high school, working towards a bachelor's degree. The father was the first of his family to break with tradition and seek Western learning. The mother, Parvathi Ammal, belonged to a family of "Sanskrit Pandits," and it is said of her father that he once walked from Trichinopoly to Calcutta to study *Nyaya**.

Soon after Raman's birth, his father obtained his degree in physical sciences and was appointed to a position as lecturer at the Trichinopoly S.P.G.College. However, the pay was not good; so he took a job at Hindu College in Vizagapatam, and it was in Vizagapatam that Chandrasekhara Venkata Raman grew up.

He finished his high school education at the age of 12, passing the matriculation examination from the University of Madras in 1900. In 1902, he passed the first arts exam from Hindu College, Vizagapatam, and enrolled at Presidency College, Madras, from which he received his B.A. degree in physics. At the degree examination in 1904 he was the only first class that year in science and received the University Gold Medal for physics. He also received prizes for writing English essays.

While working towards his M.A. degree at the University of Madras, he wrote a paper entitled "The Unsymmetrical Diffraction Bands due to a Rectangular Aperture." It was published in the *Philosophical Magazine* in London in 1906. The following year, Raman was awarded his M.A. degree with the highest distinction.

Because there were no suitable job openings in India for physicists at this time, Raman took the Indian Finance Service examination in February 1907 and won first place. He was given a post as assistant accountant-general in the finance department, serving successively in Calcutta, Rangoon, Nagpur and again in Calcutta.

During his first stint in Calcutta, he learned by chance of the British Association for the Cultivation of Science, founded by Dr. Mahendra Lal Sarkar. Raman made the acquaintance of Dr. Sarkar's son, Amrit Lal (who was secretary of the Association), and was granted permission to work in the laboratories.

His work came to the attention of Dr. Asutosh Mukherjee, vice-chancellor of the University of Calcutta who offered him the Palit Chair of Physics. The pay was less than what he was getting as a finance officer, but he took the job, effective 1917.

---

* In Indian philosophy, the Problem of Knowledge.

In his remarks at the laying of the cornerstone of the University's College of Physics, Dr. Mukherjee said:

For the chair of physics created by Sir Tarkanath Palit, we have been fortunate enough to secure the services of Mr. Chandrasekhara Venkata Raman, who has greatly distinguished himself and acquired a European fame by his brilliant researches in the domain of physical science, assiduously carried on under the most adverse circumstances amidst the distraction of pressing official duties. I rejoice to think that many of those valuable researches have been carried on in the laboratory of the Indian Association for the Cultivation of Science, founded by our late illustrious colleague, Dr. Mahendra Lal Sarkar, who devoted a lifetime to the foundation of an institution for the cultivation and advancement of science in this country. I shall fail in my duty if I were to restrain myself in my expression of the genuine admiration I feel for the courage and spirit of self-sacrifice with which Mr. Raman has decided to exchange a lucrative official appointment for a University professorship, which, I regret to say, does not carry even liberal emoluments. This one instance encourages me to entertain the hope that there will be no lack of seekers after truth in the Temple of Knowledge which it is our ambition to erect.

On the death of Amrit Lal Sarkar in 1919, Raman was elected secretary of the Association. He continued in the dual role (professor of physics and Association secretary) until 1933.

In 1924, he was elected a fellow of the Royal Society of London, and in 1928 he received the Matteucci Medal of the Italian Society of Sciences. In 1929 he was knighted, and the following year awarded both the Hughes Medal of the Royal Society and the Nobel Prize for physics.

During his lifetime he received many other honours: honorary doctorates from the Universities of Paris, Glasgow and Freiburg, as well as several Indian universities; the Franklin Medal from the Philadelphia Institute in 1951, Bharat Ratna in 1954 and the International Lenin Prize in 1957. He was an honorary fellow of the Royal Philosophical Society of Glasgow, the Zurich Physical Society, the Deutsche Akademie of Munich and the Hungarian Society of Sciences. He was also an honorary member of the Indian Mathematical and Chemical Societies and the Indian Science Congress, a corresponding member of the Soviet Academy of Sciences and foreign associate of the Académie des Sciences of Paris.

From 1933 to 1948 he was director of the Indian Institute of Science in Bangalore, and in 1948 he founded, and was director of, the Raman Research Institute in Bangalore. He also founded the Indian Institute of Physics in 1933 and in 1934 the Indian Academy of Science, of which he remained president until his death.

The experiment which won the greatest fame for Raman was that in which he produced what came to be known as the Raman Effect. For a number of years he and his associates had been studying and experimenting with the diffusion of light in liquids and other transparent substances. In the words of his biographer, Professor J.C. Ghosh, "the final step was taken by Raman in February 1928 when he used the light of the mercury lamp for these experiments, and found in the spectrum of the light scattered by various substances, new lines or bands not present in the incident beam of light. These new lines or bands are now known as the Raman lines or bands, and the spectrum containing them as the Raman spectrum of the substance studied."

A reviewer in a British scientific journal wrote:

The discovery of the Raman Effect in 1928 opened a view of research which has almost paralleled the early history of work in X-rays and radio-activity.

During the period 1933-48 numerous important studies were made by Raman and his associates, including: the diffraction of light by ultrasonic waves, the theory of atomic vibrations in crystals and the lattice structure of diamonds. Raman was also interested in the study of music and natural history.

His wife, Lokasundari Raman, was a constant companion and source of help and inspiration to him in his studies.

Chandrasekhara Venkata Raman published many books on his research. Among them: *Molecular Diffraction of Light, Mechanical Theory of Bowed Strings, Physics of Crystals and Diffraction of X-rays, Theory of Musical Instruments* and his last monograph, *The Physiology of Vision*.

He believed that scientific research could play a part in overcoming poverty in the world, but he did not agree that poverty could be alleviated by spending huge sums to put men on the moon.

Time may prove him right.

Suggested Further Reading

Bhagavatam, S.
 Professor Chandra Venketa Raman : his life and work. — Hyderabad : Andhra Pradesh
 Akademi of Sciences, [1972]
 103 p. : port. ; 19 cm.
 Science and culture. Vol. 37, May 1971. (Raman number)

SIR PRAFULLA CHANDRA RAY
(1861-1944)

Popularly known as Acharya P. C. Ray, Prafulla Chandra Ray was born 2 August 1861 in Raruli-Katipara, Khulna district (now in Bangladesh) in a Kayastha zamindar family.

His grandfather acquired a great deal of landed property. His father, Harish Chandra, gave his son a liberal education, teaching him that, contrary to modern Hindu custom, beaf-eating was very much the practice in ancient India.

Until the age of nine, Prafulla Chandra was educated in his father's school. In 1870 his family moved to Calcutta where he enrolled in Hare School. Unfortunately, his school days at Hare were cut short by a violent attack of dysentery which forced him to leave school. He spent his convalescence by reading and studying at home, following which he attended Albert School where he was the best student.

He passed the entrance exam in 1879 and entered Metropolitan Institution and attended chemistry classes at Calcutta's Presidency College. In 1882 he won a Gilchrist scholarship and in 1882 enrolled in Edinburgh University from which he graduated with a B.Sc. in 1885 and a D.Sc. in 1887.

His studies toward his B.Sc. were interrupted for a time when he submitted an essay entitled "India, Before and After the Mutiny" for an essay contest. It was said that in the essay "he indulged in many bitter diatribes against British rule" but the essay was judged *Proxime accesserunt.** However, Ray learned an important lesson: he found he was good at writing.

His studies at Edinburgh resulted in his being awarded a special scholarship by the Gilchrist Foundation and the Hope Prize Scholarship for 1887-88.

On his return to India in 1888 Dr. Ray joined the faculty of Presidency College, Calcutta, as a lecturer in chemistry with a salary of Rs. 250 per month. He had learned during his sojourn in Europe that a professor's reputation and salary depended more on externals like publishing and research than on teaching; so he engaged in publishing and research.

He was fascinated by *ayurveda*, the ancient Indian medicine, and, with the help of the French chemist, Marcelin Berthelot, found many manuscripts on the subject, and in 1902 published his *History of Hindu Chemistry* in two volumes.

In 1906, he made a name for himself by discovering mercurous nitrite, a compound of unusual stability. For his work in the field of nitrites and leadership in promoting scientific study in India he was knighted in 1919 and elected president of the Indian Science Congress in 1920.

In 1892, he found the time and money (a few hundred rupees from his saving) to found the Bengal Chemical and Pharmaceutical Works which laid the foundation of the Indian chemical industry. The company in 1902 had a capital of Rs. 200,000; in 1944 it had a capital of Rs. 2,000,000 and 5,000 employees.

In 1904, he was sent by the government to England to study research laboratories there, and in 1912 as a representative of the University of Calcutta to attend the Congress of the Universities of the British Empire.

Following 28 years at Presidency College, Sir Profulla retired in 1916. However, he found work as director of the chemical laboratories in the College of Science at the University of Calcutta.

---

* Close, but no cigar.

Although most of Ray's achievements are in chemistry and entrepreneurship, he is also remembered for his part in the Bengal famine of 1922. During this terrible period he raised several lakhs* to help the suffering. A correspondent for the *Manchester Guardian* wrote:

> In these circumstances, a professor of chemistry, Sir P. C. Ray, stepped forward and called upon his countrymen to make good the Government's omission. His call was answered with enthusiasm. The public of Bengal, in one month gave three lakhs of rupees, rich women giving their silk and ornaments and the poor giving their garments. Hundreds of young men volunteered to go down and carry out the distribution of relief to the villages, a task which involved a considerable amount of hard work and bodily discomfort in a malarious country. The enthusiams of the response to Shri P. C. Ray's appeal was due partly to the Bengali's natural desire to scare off the foreign Government, partly to genuine sympathy for the sufferers, but very largely to Sir P. C. Ray's remarkable personality and position. He is a real organiser and a real teacher. I heard a European saying: "If Mr.Gandhi had been able to create two more Sir P.C. Rays, he would have succeeded in getting Swaraj within this year."

But Acharya was not interested in politics. He met both Gandhi and Gokhale, but he was more interested in the uplift of the masses and in the fight against untouchability than in the issue of self-government for India.

He died 16 June 1944, and perhaps the greatest tribute of all came from Tagore:

> It is stated in the *Upanishads* that the One said: I shall be many. The beginning of creation is a move toward self-immolation. Acharya Prafulla Chandra has become many in his students and has made his heart alive in the hearts of many. And that could not have been at all possible had be not unreservedly made a gift of himself. The power of creation having its inception in self-sacrifice is a divine power. The glory of this power in the Acharya will never be worn out by decreptitude. It will extend further in time through the ever-growing intelligence of youthful hearts; by steady perseverance they will win new treasures of knowledge.

Suggested Further Reading

Ray, Prafulla Chandra, Sir, 1861-1944.
    Life and experiences of a Bengali chemist. — Calcutta : Chuckervertty, Chatterjee, 1932.
    2 v. viii, 557 p. : plates, fold facsims. ; 23 cm.

---

* One lakh = 100,000.

SRINIVASA RAMANUJAN AIYANGAR
(1887-1920)

Nearly 25 years ago India honoured one of the most romantic figures in the history of modern mathematics, Srinivasa Ramanujan Aiyangar, when it issued a stamp to cherish his memory.

Ramanujan was born in Erode 22 December 1887. After receiving his early education at Town High School, Kumbakonam, and at Government College, Kumbakonam, he went to Trinity College, Cambridge, in 1914 as a research scholar. He became a fellow of the Cambridge Philosophical Society 18 February 1918 and was the second Indian to become a fellow of the Royal Society and (at age 30) one of the youngest fellows in the entire history of the Royal Society. He was elected "for his investigations in Elliptic Functions and the Theory of Numbers."

On 13 October 1918 he was the first Indian to be elected a fellow of Trinity. However, he was taken ill shortly after that and returned to India in 1919. He died in Kumbakonam of tuberculosis 26 April 1920.

Ramanujan's work on Rieman's Zeta Function has been applied to the Theory of Pyrometry, the investigations of the temperature of furnaces. His work on the Partition of Numbers resulted in two applications: new fuels and fabrics like nylons.

The Hardy-Ramanujan Paper

In 1917, a paper by Ramanujan and his mentor, Prof. G.H. Hardy, triggered a new discipline: the Probabilistic Number Theory. It dealt with the roundness of numbers, the measure of which is given by prime factors. This paper, which contained a hint of Probability, was projected in a Probabilistic perspective by Paul Turan in 1934. The reason for the delay in publishing this work was that the significance of the Hardy-Ramanujan work could have been grasped only by one who had expertise in Probability as well as in Number Theory.

An account of the birth of the new discipline has been given by Professor Marc Kac:

> Fortunately for me and possibly for mathematics, Paul Erodos was in the audience, and he immediately perked up. Before the lecture was over, he had completed the proof which I could not have done, not having been versed in Number Theoristic Methods, especially those relating to the sieve*. With Erodos' contribution it became clear that we have had a beginning of a nice chapter of Number Theory.

A great discovery was made at Cambridge University when the "lost" notebook of Ramanujan was found. The following account was given by Professor George Andrews:

---

* The sieve is a mathematically elegant tool in Number Theory which owes its origin to the great Alexandrian geographer and mathematician Eratosthenes.

In the spring of 1976 I visited the Trinity College Library of Cambridge University.... In one box of materials from Watson's I found a number of items written by the famous Indian mathematician Srinivasa Ramanujan. The most interesting item in this box was a manuscript of more than one hundred pages in Ramanujan's distinctive handwriting, which contained over six hundred formulae listed one after another without proof.

It is my contention that this manuscript or notebook was written during the last year of Ramanujan's life after he returned to India from England. My evidence for this is all indirect.

Professor Andrews visited Madras in October 1981, and during this visit he was asked to comment on the applications of Ramanujan's work. He replied that Professor Rodney Baxter of Australian National University in Canberra had solved the Hard Hexagon Model in Statistical Mechanics in 1979. Andrews added:

Baxter received the Boltzmann medal for this achievement in 1980. Crucial to his solution were the numerous formulae discovered by Ramanujan. The most famous of these formulae are the celebrated Rogers-Ramanujan Identities.

Andrews wondered how Ramanujan would have done if he had the advantage of computers to work with. "Sometimes when studying his work," he stated, "I have wondered how much Ramanujan could have done if he had MACSYMA or SCRATCHPAD or some other symbolic algebra software package. More often I get the feeling that he was such a brilliant, clever, and intuitive computer himself that he really did not need them."

Strange Contrasts

Ramanujan's life is full of strange contrasts. He had no formal training in higher mathematics, and yet according to professor Hardy, he was, "in terms of natural mathematical genius, in the class of Gauss and Euler."

Moreover, Ramanujan was on terms of personal friendship with every one of the first 10,000 integers, although his life could only be regarded as an unfinished symphony. The story of his promenade through the Numbers Theory reads like a romance, and paradoxically enough it constitutes a tragedy too deep for tears.

It is fortunate, however, that recent developments initiated by Andrews, Baxter, and Professors Richard Askey and Berndt and others have focussed renewed interest in the memory of this great mathematician.

These contemporary developments reinforce the value of an opinion expressed in 1951 by Sir Chandrasekhara Venkata Raman, India's only Nobel Prize winner in physics:

Ramanujan is, in my opinion, without question the greatest man of science India has produced in recent times.

Suggested Further Reading

Ranganathan, Shiyali Ramanrita, 1892-1972.
   Ramanujan : the man and the mathematician. — Bombay, New York : Asia Publishing House, [1967]
   138 p. : ill., facsims., ports. ; 23 cm. — (Great thinkers of India ; 1)

CHAPTER 15

THE SCHOLARS

Sir Syed Ahmad Khan	Sir William Jones
Krishna Mohan Banerjee	Madan Mohan Malaviya
Sir Richard Burton	Friedrich Max Mueller
Johann Georg Buehler	Sir Asutosh Mukherjee
Körösi Csoma Sandor	Ishwar Chandra Vidyasagar

*I*ndia has produced many great scholars, and many great scholars have been drawn to India. In this chapter are sketched the lives of ten of these men: five of them were Indian, and five European.

The European Scholars

To say that Friedrich Max Mueller was drawn to India is only fifty percent true. He never set foot in India; however, he was so absorbed in Indological studies that his name will forever be associated with India. It was he who secured for Georg Buehler a position at Elphinstone College, and it was Buehler who made a great name for himself as a encyclopaedist and gatherer of Sanskrit manuscripts.

Csoma belongs in a class by himself. A studious Hungarian, he knew 17 languages, published a Tibetan grammar and dictionary and was elected an honorary member of the Asiatic Society of Bengal.

Sir Richard Burton may be thought of more as an adventurer and searcher for the source of the Nile than a scholar, but he was an anthropologist and linguist who knew Arabic well enough to join a caravan and make a pilgrimage to Mecca — and get away with it.

Sir William Jones is remembered as the founder of the Asiatic Society of Bengal, but he was the first Englishman to know Sanskrit, and his knowledge of Hindu law was legendary.

The Indian Scholars

Sir Asutosh Mukherjee, Rev. Krishna Mohan Banerjee, Madan Mohan Malaviya, Ishwar Chandra Vidyasagar and Sir Syed Ahmad Khan might be thought of as educators rather than as scholars.

Sir Syed founded the Anglo-Oriental College which became Aligarh Muslim University. Sir Asutosh is most often associated with the University of Calcutta, an institution he reformed and turned into one of the great schools of learning in the East.

Rev. Banerjee brought out the first Bengali encyclopaedia and was an outstanding educator. Vidyasagar, whose name means "Lake of Wisdom," was an educator, reformer, philanthropist as well as a scholar.

Malaviya was the founder of Benares Hindu University, but was also a journalist, political activist and champion of Hindu orthodoxy.

SIR SYED AHMAD KHAN
(1817-1898)

Syed Ahmad Khan was born in Delhi 17 October 1817. He came from the Syed family which had enjoyed prominence under the Mughuls. An ancestor, Syed Hadi, came to India from Herat. Syed Ahmad's paternal grandfather, Syed Jawad Ali Khan, was an army commander under Alamgir II who was given the title Jawad-ud-Daulah, and his maternal grandfather, Khwajah Farid-ud-Din Ahmad, was the prime minister of Akbar II.

Although the Mughul Empire during the time of Alamgir II and Akbar II had lost its vast territories, it retained the pomp of the old days, and Syed Ahmad as a boy used to visit the palace and get robes from the emperor.

Syed Ahmad's father, Syed Muhammad Taqi, was a devout Muslim, and it was undoubtedly from him that the son developed his deep devotion to Islam. The young man received his early education from his mother.

In 1836, his father died, and the following year Syed Ahmad entered the British service as a *serishtadar* (reader in a court). This was contrary to the family's wishes. They expected he would take service with Bahadur Shah II, the Mughul ruler.

After about four years Syed Ahmad Khan was moved up to the position of *munasif* (judicial officer, or sub-judge). While in this position he wrote his first book, *Asar-us-Sanadid; or, The Traces of the Great.* It was about the monuments of ancient Delhi and included notes of some holy men and Urdu and Persian poets. Published originally in 1844, it was reprinted in 1847 and again in 1876. It was translated into French by M. Garcin de Tassy, and it was largely on the strength of this work that Syed Ahmad Khan was elected an honorary member of the Royal Asiatic Society in 1874.

Syed Ahmad was serving at Bijnor at the time of the Revolt of 1857, and he was instrumental in saving the lives of a number of English civilians for which he received a pension for life from the British. He accomplished this by persuading the Nawab, Mahmud Khan, whose 800 men had surrounded the house in which the people were hiding, to let them go in safety to Meerut. Syed Ahmad remained in Bijnor, but was himself forced later to flee to Meerut. He wrote a book on the Revolt in Bijnor entitled *Sarkash-i-Zillah Bijnor.* It was published in 1858 by Mofussilite Press in Agra and was probably the first book ever published on the Great Rebellion of 1857.

After the capture of Delhi by the British in September 1857, Syed Ahmad returned to Delhi and learned that his uncle and a cousin had been killed.

He found his mother and a family servant living in the house of an attendant of their horses. He took his mother to Meerut, but she had been so weakened by the ordeal of the siege of Delhi that she died a month later.

At this point Syed Ahmad Khan started writing his second book on the Revolt: *Asbab-i Sarkash-i Hindustan ka Javab Muzmun*. The English title was *An Essay on the Causes of the Indian Revolt*. The publisher was also Mofussilite Press of Agra. Like *Sarkash-i Zillah Bijnor*, it was written in Urdu; however, the summaries and introduction were in English.

Published in 1859, it was subsequently translated into English by Sir John Colvin, Lord Auckland and Syed Ahmad's friend Colonel (later General) Thomas Graham.

Syed Ahmad Khan was pro-British, and his essay was an effort to prove that Muslims had a minimal role in the Revolt. He listed five causes of the Revolt:

1. Misunderstanding on the part of Indians.
2. The promulgation of objectionable laws and procedures.
3. Ignorance of the Government of the state of the country and their subjects.
4. Neglect of matters which should have received consideration by Government.
5. The insubordinate state of the Indian forces.

Syed Ahmad Khan stated in his book, along with advice for the British, the need to promote education. To this end he opened a school at Moradabad, where he happened to be stationed in 1858, for the study of modern history.

In 1862, he was transferred to Ghazipur where he met and formed a life-long friendship with the Colonel Graham who was mentioned above. (Graham later wrote a biography entitled *The Life and Work of Sir Syed Ahmad Khan* which was published in 1885. A revised and enlarged edition appeared in 1909.) At that time Graham was assistant district superintendent of police, and Syed Ahmad enlisted his help in founding a society for translating English books into Urdu. The society they started, with the support of other Europeans and Indians, eventually came to be known as the Scientific Society of Aligarh.

Syed Ahmad was soon transferred to Aligarh where he made acquaintance with a number of influential Indian families who, like him, were interested in both Western and Eastern learning. In 1866 the viceroy, Lord Lawrence, presented him a gold medal, and later he was transferred to Benares.

In his zeal for Western learning, Syed Ahmad took his sons, Syed Mahmud and Syed Hamid, to England for higher education in 1869. Both of the sons did very well there, and on their return to India, Mahmud was appointed to the bench of the high court in Allahabad, and Hamid went into police work and rose to the rank of district superintendent of police.

Lord Lawrence and Colonel Graham were in England at the same time that Syed Ahmad Khan was there, and both of them introduced him to their influential friends, among whom were Lord Stanley Adderly and

Thomas Carlyle, the Sage of Chelsea. Carlyle and Syed Ahmad talked at some length about Syed Ahmad's book on Muhammad the Prophet.

Syed Ahmad Khan retired from government service in 1876, made Aligarh his home and devoted his efforts to the founding of the Anglo-Oriental College which later came to be known as Aligarh Muslim University and is today one of the leading universities of India. The cornerstone for it was laid 8 January 1877 by the viceroy, Lord Lytton.

Syed Ahmad Khan was a member of legislative council of the Northwestern Provinces and an additional member of the governor-general's legislative council. In 1888, he was knighted.

At one point in his life, the *ulema* (theologians) accused Syed Ahmad of being a *kafir* (infidel) and one of them went all the way to Mecca to have the document signed by the *ulema* there, which he did. When this became known to his friends, they urged Syed Ahmad Khan to publish a rebuttal, but he said he was grateful that a sinful person like himself had caused his opponent to receive virtue by making a pilgrimage to Mecca.

Sir Syed Ahmad Khan died 27 March 1898 and is buried on the campus of the university he founded. In his elegy on Sir Syed, Hali wrote these words:

> To be treated cruelly by your brethren,
>   but to live for their good;
> To be pierced by an arrow, and be fond of the arrow;
> To live anxious to serve your nation,
> And to die with that anxiety in your heart.
> You may aspire to be a Syed Ahmad,
> If you can live up to his ideal of life.

Suggested Further Reading

Nizami, Khaliz Ahmad.
    Sayyid Ahmad Khan. — [Delhi] : Publications Division, Ministry of Information and Broadcasting, [1967]
    184 p. : port. ; 18 cm. — (Builders of modern India)

KRISHNA MOHAN BANERJEE
(1813-1885)

The Rev. Krishna Mohan Banerjee, one of the leading Indian Christians of the nineteenth century, came from a Brahman family of Calcutta. He was the son of Jiban Krishna Banerjee and was born in May 1813 at the home of his maternal grandfather, Ramjay Vidyabhushan, on Bechu Chatterjee Street in Calcutta.

Jiban Krishna was a man of meagre means who lived in Nahagram, 24 Parganas. Krishna Mohan came under the influence of Ramjay and was instilled with the Hindu classics. The boy was educated at David Hare's

Vernacular School at Thanthania, Calcutta, and later at the Calcutta School Society's English School which was managed by Hare and ultimately named after him.

Following a year's study at that school, he enrolled at Hindoo College in 1824 and in 1828 won a scholarship of Rs.16 per month. He left Hindoo College 1 November 1829 and won his certificate of merit 13 March 1830.

In 1829, he got a teaching job at Patalganga School, which was beginning to be called Hare School. Around this time he became associated with Henry Derozio's Young Bengal group and assisted Derozio in editing and publishing his *Hesperus*, an evening paper, and *The East Indian*.

Also around this time he married Bindubasini Devi, the daughter of Radha Mohan Chatterjee of Howrah.

Under the influence of Derozio and Rev. Dr. Alexander Duff he embraced Christianity, being baptised 16 October 1832 in Duff's Scottish Church. However, he felt uneasy in Duff's church, and after three months, transferred to the Anglican Church. A few years later he was ordained a minister and joined Bishop's College as a scholar. He was appointed a minister of Christ Church and became the first Indian clergyman to be entrusted with an Episcopal Church in India.

His career as an author began in 1931 when he published his first play, *The Persecuted*, which was an attack on Hindu society. He then published a number of tracts and papers: *The Nature and Importance of Historical Studies* (1838) and *Reform, Civil and Social, among Hindus* (1840). His prize essay, *The Native Female Education* (1841) had a strong impact on the government's policy on the education of women in India.

One of his greatest publishing efforts was *Vidyákalpadrum Arthát Vividh Vidyávisayak Rachana* ("The Tree of Learning and Various Writings"). The English title was *"Encyclopaedia Bengalensis; or, A Series of Publications in English and Bengali, Compiled from Various Sources on History, Science and Literature."* It was published between 1845 and 1851, and can be considered the earliest Indian language encyclopaedia of the modern period. It borrowed heavily from Western writers like Niebuhr, Gibbon, Isaac Watts, etc., and Henry Scholberg in his *Encyclopedias of India* said of it:

> It could be argued that this was the greatest act of plagiarism in the history of world literature. If this is true, the act was not committed with malice. On the contrary, its purpose was to instruct, and it may have been designed to help Bengalis who were anxious to pass exams for service in the East India Company and to learn about the world beyond.

Banerjee's biographer said of Banerjee's work that "he wrote in Bengali at a time when it was hardly fit to serve as a medium for literary and scientific purposes."

Banerjee was an active member of the Bethune Society and the Bengal Social Science Association, and in 1858 he was elected a fellow of the senate of the University of Calcutta. A prolific writer, he contributed articles to the

Calcutta Intelligencer, the *Bengal Spectator*, *Mookerjee's Magazine* and the *Indian Antiquary*. He also found time to publish two journals in Bengali: *Satyarnava* and *Sambad Sudhanshu*.

His major work was *Dialogues on Hindu Philosophy* (1861) which dealt with the authenticity of Hindu tracts. Another significant work was *Arian Witness* (1875) which sought to discern the living bond between Hinduism and Christianity.

In 1878, he was awarded an LL.D.degree from the University of Calcutta.

Rev. Banerjee was a man of profound insights into both Indian and European culture, and he served as a bridge in India between the East and the West. He died 11 May 1885.

Suggested Further Reading

Ghosh, Ram Chandra.
  A biographical sketch of the Rev. K.M. Banerjee, L.L.D., C.I.E. — Calcutta : Progressive Publishers, 1980.
  72 p. ; 22 cm.
  Originally published in 1893.

SIR RICHARD FRANCIS BURTON
(1821-1890)

Sir Richard Francis Burton, linguist, explorer, scholar, soldier, orientalist, author, translator, wrote that he "was born at 9.30 p.m., 19th March (Feast of St. Joseph in the calendar), 1821, at Barham House, Herts, and I suppose I was baptised in due course at the parish church." He was the eldest child of Colonel Joseph Netteville Burton and Martha Beckwith, the daughter and co-heiress of Barham House, Hertfordshire.

Though he was the author of 50 books, Richard Burton never had a regular education. When he was five, he and his family left England and travelled from city to city in France and Italy for the next three years. In 1829 Richard and his brother, Edward, were put in a preparatory school for a short time, but this did not work out well; so a tutor was hired for the boys, but they treated him badly. In the course of the travels, Richard picked up half a dozen languages and dialects.

In October 1840, he entered Trinity College, Oxford, but was expelled, after five terms, due to his unconventional behaviour, and sent to India where he joined the 18th Regiment of the Bombay Native Army in 1842. He began as a cadet, but was soon promoted to captain. He was stationed at Baroda where he taught himself Indian languages. He would disguise himself as an Indian and circulate in the bazaars, thus learning the languages and the customs of the people.

Late in 1843, his regiment was transferred to Sind where Burton got in the good graces of his hero, Governor Charles James Napier, and was appointed assistant in the Sind survey. As he had done in Baroda, he disguised himself as what his brother officers called, a "white nigger," mingled with people in the bazaars and learned a few more languages. By now he was fluent in Hindustani, Gujarati, Marathi, Punjabi, Sindhi, Arabic and Persian, in addition to the European languages in which he was conversant.

He hoped for active military duty, but it eluded him. In 1846 he rejoined his regiment which was called up for the Anglo-Sikh War of 1845-46, but peace was made before the regiment arrived in the Punjab. Then in October 1848, when the Second Anglo-Sikh War (1848-49) was declared, Burton volunteered his services as interpreter, but his application was rejected.

In the interval between these wars, Burton took sick leave for six months and spent them in the Nilgiris and Goa. This episode provided material for his first book, *Goa and the Blue Mountains; or, Six Months Sick Leave* (1851). He was not impressed with Goa, but in the course of his writing he predicted the Revolt of 1857. He returned to England in 1849, carrying with him bundles of manuscripts and curios.

His historic journey to Mecca began in April 1853 when he disguised himself, first as a Persian *mirza* (prince), then as a dervish and finally as a Pathan *hakim* (doctor) who had been educated at Rangoon. Taking the name "Al-Hajj Abdullah," he went from Cairo to Suez on camel back, from Suez to Yambu by pilgrim ship, and from Yambu to Medina to Mecca by caravan. Because of his familiarity with Muslim customs and forms of worship, he was able to make the trip undetected. He recorded his impressions and adventures in *Personal Narrative of a Journey from El-Medinah to Mecca* (1855) in three volumes. This book and his translation of "The Arabian Nights" in 16 volumes are the works for which Sir Francis is most celebrated.

He returned to India for a brief stay, but in 1854 he was off on another leave, this time to explore Somaliland. He was joined by three other officers, one of whom was Captain J.H. Speke. One night they were attacked by a band of Somalis, and one of the officers was killed and one was uninjured, but both Speke and Burton were wounded, Burton having been pierced from cheek to cheek by a spear. His *First Footsteps in Africa* (1856) told of this adventure.

After Somaliland, Burton tried to see action in the Crimean War, but was stationed at the Dardanelles, far from the fighting.

The rest of Burton's career was outside India. He was involved in the great search for the source of the Nile (which Speke discovered), and he travelled to both North and South America. In 1876 he visited India with his wife, Isabella Arundell, a Roman Catholic woman whom he married in 1861 against her parents' wishes. She was not in favour of Burton's researches in the erotic customs of the east.

From 1872 Burton filled diplomatic posts in Fernando Po in Brazil, Damascus, and finally Trieste, where he died 20 October 1890. After he died, Mrs. Burton burned his diaries and many of his notes and translations in what may have been the worst literary crime in the history of the human race.

Suggested Further Readings

Burton, Isabelle (Arundell), Lady, 1831-1896.
   The life of Captain Sir Richard Burton, K.C.G.M, F.R.G.S. / by his wife Isabel Burton.
   — London : Duckworth, 1898.
   548 p. : ill. ; 23 cm.

Stisted, Georgiana M.
   The true life of Captain Sir Richard F. Burton. — London : Nichols, 1896.
   xv, 419 p. : front. port. ; 19 cm.

JOHANN GEORG BUEHLER
(1837-1898)

Georg Buehler was born in Borstel, Hanover, 19 July 1837 and undertook the study of Arabic, Armenian, German, Greek, Latin, Persian, Sanskrit and Zend at Goettingen University. Sanskrit, however, was the language of most of his subsequent scholarly focus after obtaining his doctorate in 1858.

From 1858 to 1862 he lived in England where, among other duties, he served on the library staff of the Royal Library at Windsor Castle. Thanks to the efforts of Max Mueller, he received the newly-created Sanskrit professorship at Elphinstone College, University of Bombay, in 1862.

He thus joined the ranks of German scholars living or working in India. His rapport with both British authorities and the Indian community of Bombay was excellent. The former, in fact, hired copyists in other parts of India to copy, as well as transcribe into Devanagari, Sanskrit works written in various south Indian scripts, while the latter raised Rs. 5,000 so that his Sanskrit students might have at least the nucleus of a proper library.

In 1864 the government of Bombay appointed him to a commission charged with preparing a digest of Hindu law to assist judges. This work brought him in contact with many segments of Bombay society.

In 1864 he and Franz Kielhorn began the Bombay Sanskrit series, which produced reliable editions of numerous treatises. The government of Bombay asked him in 1866 to undertake the second search for Sanskrit manuscripts within the Presidency. The trip was a huge success and brought 201 manuscripts into what was to become the Bombay Sanskrit Collection, a government-owned library.

In 1866 Buehler accepted the post of educational inspector of the northern districts of Bombay presidency. The position required his constant travel through remote areas to examine students in their educational attainments.

In 1868 thanks to extensive correspondence with Whitley Stocks, secretary of the government of India for legal matters, the government of

India issued an order providing Rs. 25,000 annually to collect and to preserve Sanskrit manuscripts.

Buehler, as one of the two people in Bombay carrying out the order, launched a series of search trips into the northern portion of Bombay Presidency as well as into Rajputana and even Kashmir where he spent a great deal of time looking for manuscripts.

His published reports of his searches and the lists of manuscripts which he thus added to the Bombay Sanskrit Collection attracted worldwide attention and prompted the initiation of an inter-continental inter-library loan programme which lasted until 1913.

His work on the searches for Sanskrit manuscripts led Buehler to the extremely rich manuscript wealth of Gujarat, especially that of the Jain community. His research on the Jains brought recognition in the West of the great contribution of this community to Indian civilization and is one of his great scholarly accomplishments.

Although he was unable to see personally all the Jain temple libraries and sometimes was refused admission to some which he had taken special efforts to get to, subsequent scholarship has been able to survey the rich resources contained in them.

In addition to his purchases of manuscripts for the government collection, the governments of both Bombay and India allowed him to acquire manuscripts for libraries in Europe. His personal library he presented to the India Office Library.

Buehler retired from government service in 1880 because of poor health, and he returned to Vienna where he accepted a position with the Oriental Institute. His chief work in Vienna was editor of the *Grundriss der indoarischen Philologie und Alterumskunde* (Compendium of Indo-Aryan Philology and Archeology), the last of the great German nineteenth century compendia of Indological research.

Buehler tragically died in a boating accident on Lake Constance 8 April 1898.

— **Donald C. Johnson**

Suggested Further Reading

Buehler's contributions to the nineteenth century scholarship on India are vast, and rare indeed is the scholarly series which did not have something by him. Upon his death numerous colleagues wrote tributes or memorial addresses which were published in *The Indian Antiquary*, volume 27 (1898).

KÖRÖSI CSOMA SANDOR
(1784-1842)

Alexander Csoma de Körös, whose Hungarian name forms the title of this sketch, was born 4 April 1784 at Koros in the county of Háromszék in Transylvania to a poverty stricken Calvinist family belonging to the Szekler nobility. (The date given above may be the date of his Baptism.)

His father, a corporal in the Frontier Guard, was András Csoma and his mother Krisztina Getze. They had seven children, of which only four survived: Julianna (1774), Krisztina (1778), Alexander (1784) and Gábor (1788). In later life Csoma added "de Koros" to his name to distinguish his family name from that of his uncle's family name, which was also Csoma.

As a school boy, Alexander was studious and physically tough, a condition which served him well during the days of rigour in the mountains of Tibet. Little else is known of his childhood. His early education was in his village school where the children were taught reading, writing and singing.

In 1799, he was enrolled at the College of Nagy Enyed and completed his course in 1814 but remained another year as a senior collegian.

From 1815-18 he was educated at Goettingen University, where he showed keen interest in the classics as well as Hebrew, Arabic and Turkish literature.

In Search of Magyar Origins

Interested in the origin of the Magyars, he left Budapest 3 January 1820 and headed eastward, believing his ancestors may have come from Central Asia.

He travelled to Constantinople, Alexandria, Syria, Baghdad, Teheran, Mashad, Bokhara, Tibet, Kabul, Lahore, Kashmir and Leh, and finally arrived in Calcutta.

While in Egypt he disguised himself as an Armenian and made his way to Ladakh and Tibet where he studied Tibetan and Buddhist literature. He spent a great deal of time at monasteries in Ladakh, mainly at Yangla, Zanakar, from 1823 to 1826.

He received an allowance of Rs. 50 per month from the government of India and journeyed to Kanum in Kunawar, studying Tibetan at a Buddhist monastery until 1830.

He arrived in Calcutta in April 1831, and in 1834 he published his Tibetan-English dictionary entitled *Dictionary, Tibetan and English* and his Tibetan grammar entitled *Grammar of the Tibetan Language in English*. He also published an analysis of the Buddhist sacred books, the *Kanjur (bKah-hgyur).*

Also in that year he took up the study of Sanskrit and was appointed librarian of the Asiatic Society of Bengal. (By a happy coincidence, the Asiatic Society of Bengal was founded in 1784, the year of Csoma's birth.)

The Hungarian government granted him a pension which he used to buy books for Indian libraries.

From 1836 to 1837 he travelled to Jalpaiguri and Titalya to study other Oriental languages.

He was in Calcutta again from 1837 to 1842. Early in 1842 he decided to renew his quest to learn the origin of the Magyars and set out for Tibet. He reached Darjeeling and died there 11 April 1842.

Csoma was a humble but proud scholar. He knew 17 languages. He was deeply offended when, at one point in his travels, the British authorities detained him on suspicion of espionage. He was in no way ostentatious and was happiest when he was secluded in his room, sitting on his mat, surrounded by his books and manuscripts and doing his research.

He is buried in the Protestant cemetery of Darjeeling. Recently the Hungarian government erected a small memorial over his grave.

He was honoured by the Hungarian Academy and the novelist Jozsef Eotvos delivered an oration.

Suggested Further Readings

Duka, Tiradar.
Life and works of Alexander Csoma de Koros : a biography compiled chiefly from hitherto unpublished data; with a brief notice of each of his published works and essays, as well as of his still extant manuscripts. — London : Truebner & Co., 1885.
234 p. : front. port. ; 22 cm.
Reprinted in 1972 as series II, volume 2 of Bibliotheca himalayica.

Mukherjee, Hirendranath.
Hermit-hero from Hungary : Alexander Csoma de Koros, the great Tibetologist. — New Delhi : Light & Life Publishers, 1981.
viii, 102 p. ; 22 cm.

A two-volume bi-centennial commemorative work honouring Csoma de Koros was published in Budapest in 1984 entitled *Tibetan and Buddhist Studies*. Edited by Louis Ligeti, it forms volume XXIX of Bibliotheca orientalis hungarica.

SIR WILLIAM JONES
(1746-1794)

"If Europeans could be led to understand Indian customs and culture, there would inevitably be improved personal relations between the two people."

So said Sir William Jones, founder of the Asiatic Society of Bengal and one of a number of European scholars who came to love, understand and promote Indian culture.

He was the youngest son of William Jones (1675-1749), the mathematician. He was born 28 September 1746 at Beaufort Buildings, Westminster. His mother looked after his early education, and he was encouraged in his studies by his father's scientific friends.

He enrolled at Harrow and studied there 10 years, excelling in the classics and learning French and Italian. He also picked up some Arabic and Hebrew in his spare time.

His father's friends wanted him to go into law, but he complained that the old law books were written in bad Latin; so he opted for a university degree. He matriculated from Oxford as a commoner of University College in 1764. His mother was too poor to fund his education at Oxford; however, thanks to his reputation at Harrow, he was given a job as tutor to Lord Althorp, the only son of Earl Spencer. This continued for five years during which time he made several trips to Europe and continued his studies at Oxford. By the time he received his B.A. in 1768 and his M.A. in 1773, he had mastered Arabic and Persian as well as Portuguese, Spanish and German.

A rare opportunity came to him in 1768 when King Christian VII of Denmark brought to England a Persian biography of Nadir Shah, *Tárikh-i-Nadiri*. It was proposed that Jones translate it into French. He declined at first, but his friends explained that if he did not do it, the honour of translating it would go to a Frenchman. He translated it, and it was his first book.

During the next few years he was engaged in furious publishing. His *Grammar of the Persian Language* came out in 1771 and was followed by translations of Firdausi's *Shah-namah*, and other Arabic classics. He was elected a fellow of the Royal Society while only 25 years old.

But he discovered that he was not earning a proper living by publishing books; so he decided on a career in law. He was called to the Bar at Middle Temple in 1774 and during the next two years published a number of legal treatises. In 1780, he was a candidate for the House of Commons from the Oxford district. Unfortunately, his opposition to the war in America and to slavery were not well received. He was defeated.

His opposition to the American war also impeded his efforts to be appointed by Lord North to a judgeship in India. However, a coalition ministry in 1783 secured his appointment as judge of the Supreme Court in Calcutta.

The announcement was made 4 March in the *London Gazette*.

He was knighted 19 March.

He proposed to Anna Maria Shipley and married her 8 April.

On 12 April 1783 the happy couple boarded the frigate, "Crocodile" and sailed for India.

"Busy" is hardly the word to describe the activities of Sir William Jones once he was settled in Calcutta. As a judge, he believed it important to learn Sanskrit in order to study Hindu law, but he had trouble finding a teacher. The few Englishmen who might have helped him did not have time to give lessons, and the Brahmans would not deign to teach a foreigner whom they believed unable to master the language. However, he found a Kshatriya to teach him and soon was conversing in Sanskrit with the very Brahmans who had refused to teach him. They became good friends with him and came to call him their "Kshatriya."

Sir William's day began at 7 A.M. He would rise an hour before sunrise and walk three miles to Fort William. After a cold bath and breakfast, his pandit would arrive, and he would study for about an hour. Here is how his day went after that, as told in his own words:

At eight came a Persian and Arab alternately with whom I read till nine except on Saturday, when I gave instructions to my Mogul secretary on my correspondence with the Musalman scholars. At nine came the attorneys with affidavits. I am then robed and ready for court, where I sit on the bench daily for five hours. At three I dress and dine and till near sunset, am at the service of my friends, who choose to dine with me. When the sun is sunk in the Ganges, we drive to the Gardens either in our port-chaise or Anna's phaeton drawn by a pair of beautiful Nepal horses. After tea-time we read, and never sit up, if we can avoid it, after ten.

In January 1784, Jones founded the Asiatic Society of Bengal, and annually he would give his "anniversary discourses" as president of the Society.

During the decade of his service in India, from 1783 till his death in 1794, he published numerous articles and treatises. His main interest was in Oriental philosophy, religion, language and in comparative philology. He was enormously impressed with similarities he found between Sanskrit, Greek and Latin. In his third anniversary discourse he said:

> The Sanskrit language, whatever its antiquity, is of a wonderful structure, more perfect than the Greek, more copious than Latin, and more exquisitely refined than either, yet bearing to both of them a stronger affinity, both in the roots of verbs and in the forms of grammar, than could possibly have been produced by accident. So strong indeed, that no philologer could examine them all three without believing them to have sprung from a common source which, perhaps, no longer exists. There is a similar reason, though not quite so forcible, for supposing that both the Gothik (*i.e.*, Germanic) and the Celtic, though blended with a very different idiom, had the same origin with the Sanskrit, and the old Persian might be added to the same family.

But he was also interested in Hindu chronology, music and chess and in science, particularly botany and zoology. He planned a comprehensive work on the botany of India. In fact, the asoka tree of Indian mythology is known to botanists as *Jonesia asoka*, named by Dr. William Roxburgh in his honour.

After 10 years of hard work, Sir William Jones died 26 April 1794 in Calcutta. He was buried there and these words, composed by himself, are engraved on his tombstone:

Here lies deposited,
the mortal part of a man
who feared God, but not death;
and maintained independence,
but sought not riches;
who thought
None below him, but the base the unjust,
None above him but the wise and courteous;
who loved

his parents, kindred, friends, country,
with an ardour
which was the chief source of
all his pleasure and all his pains;
and who, having devoted
his life to their service,
and to
the improvement of his kind,
wishes peace on earth
and with
good-will to all creatures.

One of his friends paid him a brief tribute in the kind of typical understatement which persons who are not English have come to love:

It is happy for us that this man was born.

Suggested Further Readings

Cannon, Garland Hampton.
  Oriental Jones : a biography of Sir William Jones, 1746-1794. — Bombay : Asia
  Publishing House, 1964.
  x, 215 p. : port. ; 25 cm.

Jones, William, Sir, 1746-1794.
  The works of Sir William Jones / with the life of the author by Lord Teignmouth. —
  Delhi : Agam Prakashan, 1976-80.
  13 v. : ill. ; 22 cm.

Teignmouth, John Shore, 1st Baron, 1751-1834.
  Memoirs of Sir William Jones. — London : Hatchard, 1807.
  xiv, 636 p. ; 22 cm.

MADAN MOHAN MALAVIYA
(1861-1946)

The founder of Banaras Hindu University was born Christmas Day 1861 in Allahabad to a family belonging to the Chaturvedi sub-caste of the Sri Gaud Brahmans. Madan Mohan Malaviya came from a poor family, but one rich in a tradition of scholarship. His grandfather, Pandit Prem Dhar, was famous for his Sanskrit learning, as was his father, Pandit Braj Nath, both of whom were Vaishnavas.

Madan Mohan's formal education began at age five when he was enrolled at Pandit Hardeva's Gyanopadesh Padshala. He left this school when he was eight and entered 3rd class at the *zilla* (district) school. This created an economic problem for the family. Besides Madan Mohan, there were five sons and two daughters, and it was difficult to manage tuition for him on the meagre earnings Braj Nath got from reciting the *Ramayana* and the *Bhagavad Gita*. However, Madan Mohan's mother, Moona Devi, came to the rescue. She mortgaged her gold bangles from month to month to pay for her son's education.

In 1878, he was married to Kundan Devi, the daughter of Pandit Nand Ram, a school teacher at Mirzapur. They had three daughters and four sons. Kundan Devi died in 1942.

He matriculated in 1879 and entered Muir Central College, graduating from the University of Calcutta in 1884. He had hoped to go on for an M.A. degree, but could not do so for lack of funds. He took a teaching job at his alma mater for Rs. 40 per mensem, but he was anxious to get into public life; so in 1886 he attended the second session of the Indian National Congress in Calcutta with his teacher, Pandit Aditya Ram Bhattacharya, whom he greatly revered. He delivered a speech there which won the praise of A.O. Hume, founder of the Congress.

On his return from Calcutta he was offered the editorship of the Hindi weekly, *Hindustan*, with a salary of Rs. 200 a month. He edited the paper from July 1887 until the end of 1889, during which time it was turned into a daily newspaper. He also edited the *Indian Union*, a paper founded by his friend and mentor, Pandit Bhattacharya, from 1885 to 1890.

On the advice of Hume and others Malaviya took up the study of law in 1889 and received his LL.D. degree in 1891.

Malaviya became active in the Congress and attended almost all its sessions from 1886 until 1936. In 1887 and 1892 he invited the Congress to meet in Allahabad. He was rewarded for his services by being elected president four times: in 1909, 1918, 1932 and 1933, but he was unable to preside over the last two sessions named because they had been banned.

Madan Mohan Malaviya is remembered as an educator, a champion of Hindu orthodoxy, a political activist and a journalist. He started the *Adyudaya*, a Hindi weekly in 1907 and made it into a daily in 1915. He started the *Mayada*, a Hindi monthly, in 1910. When issues concerning the peasants of Oudh came to the fore, he started *Kisan*, a Hindi monthly in 1921. In 1909 he started the *Leader*, an English language daily. From 1924 to 1946 he was chairman of the board of directors of the *Hindustan Times*.

In 1906, he founded the Hindu Mahasabha to oppose the British policy of *divide ut regnes*, and he was a strong supporter of *suddhi* (reconversion of Hindus who had strayed from the fold).

He supported the Nehru Report which called for dominion status for India, and he participated in Gandhi's celebrated Salt March of 1930, suffering imprisonment for it.

However, his greatest achievement was the founding of Banaras Hindu University. (The spelling of the city can be rendered "Benares" or "Varanasi," but the University's name is spelled "Banaras".)

He started appealing for funds as early as 1911, hoping to raise a crore.* The Banaras Hindu University Act was passed 1 April 1915, and by the

---

*   1 crore = 10,000,000.

time the cornerstone was laid by Viceroy Lord Hardinge 4 February 1916, Malaviya had collected Rs. 35 lakhs.* Then, 13 December 1921 Banaras Hindu University was declared open by the Prince of Wales.

(By 1939 Malaviya had collected Rs. 125 lakhs* for B.H.U.)

He was the first vice-chancellor, serving until 1938, and was succeeded by Dr. Radhakrishnan.

Malaviya was torn between his conservative, orthodox Hinduism and his desire for social change and improvement. He believed in the caste system and never took food unless it was from the hands of a Brahman. However, he believed strongly in the economic uplift of the depressed classes.

C.F. Andrews said of him:

> In his extreme Hindu outlook lies the main difference between himself and every other leader of first rank in Indian politics today. I do not know any outstanding personality who carries his orthodoxy as far as Malaviya. He is conservative to the last degree in everything where Hinduism is concerned, while at the same time in national affairs he is in many respects an advanced thinker.

In spite of his Hindu orthodoxy, Malaviya had compassion for the poor, regardless of their background. The story is told of a Muslim student who came to him complaining about the bad mess conditions at his hostel.

"My kitchen," Malaviya told him, "is always open to you."

Suggested Further Reading

Chaturvedi, Sitaram.
   Madan Mohan Malaviya. — New Delhi : Publications Division, Ministry of Information and Broadcasting, 1972.
   134 p. : port. ; 21 cm. — (Builders of Modern India).

MAX MUELLER
(1823-1900)

(Friedrich) Max Mueller was the son of Wilhelm Mueller, the noted German poet, and the godson of Felix Mendelssohn, the even more noted German composer. Max was born 3 December 1823 in Dessau where his father was the ducal librarian. Dessau was capital of the small duchy of Anhalt-Dessau.

Mendelssohn persuaded the young boy to forget about music as a career and try something else. The something else he tried was Sanskrit which Hermann Brockhaus of the University of Leipzig induced him to study on his matriculation in 1841.

Interest in Sanskrit at this time was not new in Germany. It had been stimulated in 1791 with the translation of *Shakuntala* as well as dialogues of the *Bhagavad Gita* and the discourses of the *Upanishads*.

---

* 1 lakh = 100,000.

Johann Wolfgang von Goethe gave high praise in particular to *Shakuntala*.

Wilhelm von Humboldt was so impressed with the *Bhagavad Gita* that he said of it: "This episode of the *Mahabharata* is the most beautiful, nay, the only true philosophical poem in all literatures known to us."

Arthur Schopenhauer, the great philosopher, said of the *Upanishads*: "On every page we meet profound, original, sublime thoughts. Everything here breathes Indian air and original existence akin to nature. It is the most recompensing and most elevating reading that (except for the original) is possible in the world. It has been the comfort of my life and will be the comfort of my death."

Mueller studied under Professor Brockhaus at Leipzig and obtained his Ph.D. in 1843 after two years of study, at the age of 20. He studied comparative philology for a couple of years in Berlin before moving to Paris in 1845 to study Sanskrit under Eugène Bernouf.

He finished his studies in Paris in 1846 and resolved to go to England and settle at Oxford. He met and married an Englishwoman, Georgina Adelaide Riversdale Grenfell, and ultimately, he became an English citizen.

On his arrival in England he was commissioned by the East India Company to translate the *Rig Veda* which was published by Oxford. The undertaking had been promoted by Baron von Bunsen and Henry Horace Wilson.

For 25 years Mueller was on the staff at Oxford University in one capacity or another. In 1850, he was appointed deputy Taylorian professor of modern European languages. In 1854, he was made full professor, in 1856 curator of the Bodleian Library and in 1858 was elected a life fellow of All Soul's College.

The prize he really wanted, that of Boden Professorship of Sanskrit, was denied to him, because of his German origin, in 1860. However, the University made amends for this injustice in 1868 when it created for him a professorship of comparative philology.

He resigned the chair in 1875 to undertake the mammoth task of editing *Sacred Books of the East*. This series consists of 51 volumes, and all but three of them were done under his supervision and completed in his life time.

Max Mueller never visited India. This is not to say he did not want to. Rather, he had an idealistic notion of India and feared that to see the real India might shatter that illusion.

"A classical scholar yearns to see Rome or Athens," he once said. "I yearn to see Benares and to bathe in the sacred water of the Ganges."

On another occasion he said:

I feel I am always at Benares. I love to imagine this house as Benares. I do not desire to see the geographical Benares with my physical eye. My idea of that city is so high that I cannot risk a disillusionment... My India was not on the surface, but lay many centuries beneath it; and as to paying a globe-trotter's visit to Calcutta or Bombay, I might as well walk through Oxford Street or Bond Street.

One of the chief aims of Max Mueller was that of interpreting India to the people of the West. To this end he brought out: *History of Ancient Sanskrit Literature, India: What Can It Teach Us?* and *Ramakrishna: His Life and Sayings.*

He also wrote a number of books on religion and philosophy.

He died at Oxford 28 October 1900.

Speaking at a memorial service for him at the English Goethe Society in Calcutta 23 November 1900, Lokamanya Tilak proclaimed:

In him India has lost the warmest friend, the wisest lover, and the most enthusiastic admirer whose place, alas! will be filled we know not when.

In 1957, the German Goethe Institute in New Delhi changed its name to the Max Mueller Bhavan.

Suggested Further Readings

Chaudhuri, Nirad C.
  Scholar extraordinary : the life of professor the Rt. Hon. Friedrich Max Müller, P.C. — New York : Oxford University Press, 1974.
  393 p. [1] leaf of plates : port. ; 22 cm.

Voigt, Johannes H.
  Max Mueller : the man and his ideas. — Calcutta : K.L. Mukhopadhyay, 1967.
  xiii, 101 p. ; 22 cm.

SIR ASUTOSH MUKHERJEE
(1864-1924)

Asutosh Mukherjee was born in Calcutta in June 1864. His father was one of the earliest graduates in arts and medicine at the University of Calcutta. Asutosh was raised under the tutelage of his father, who loved the Bengali language and wrote many books in it on medicine and problems of health. His mother, though not well educated, was a broad-minded, practical, God-fearing woman who had an enormous influence on her son.

Asutosh loved his studies as a child and mastered several languages, both Eastern and Western, as well as literature, philosophy, science, mathematics and law.

He was educated at Presidency College in Calcutta and graduated with an M.A. in mathematics in 1885. In 1888, he became a fellow of the University of Calcutta and was soon elected to the syndicate of the University.

By the time he was 30 years old he had earned a Doctor of Laws degree while still a member of the syndicate of the University. He was subsequently, in 1899 and 1901, elected a representative of the University in the Bengal legislative council.

In 1903, he was elected to represent the University in the corporation of Calcutta, and in the same year chosen to represent the University in the governor-general's legislative council of the non-official members of the Bengal legislative council.

In 1904, he was appointed to the bench of the Calcutta high court, and he held this post for 20 years.

He served as vice-chancellor of the University of Calcutta from 1906 to 1914 and from 1921 to 1923. He had once said:

> It has always been my ambition to be allowed to do something — something great, as I flattered myself in my youthful dreams — for the good and glory of my Alma Mater.

His great achievement was that he transformed the University of Calcutta from a mere examining body to one of the great universities of the East. Lord Lytton, who had served as governor of Bengal, said of him:

> Asutosh, in the eyes of his countrymen and in the eyes of the world, represented the University so completely that for many years Asutosh was in fact the University and the University Asutosh.

When he assumed his duties at the University, enormous obstacles confronted Asutosh Mukherjee. Libraries, laboratories and buildings had to be constructed and scholars and teachers attracted from all parts of India.

He encountered opposition, but he encountered support as well. Sir Rashbehari Ghosh and Sir Tarkanath Palit gave generously towards the establishment of the University College of Science and Technology. Among the scholars hired for this department was Chandrasekhara Venkata Raman, a future Nobel Prize winner in physics.

Another great achievement of Mukherjee was that of giving his mother tongue, Bengali, a more visible place in the University structure. It was made the medium of instruction and important works in Bengali were published by the University.

However, Bengali was not the only subject to receive encouragement. Other Indian languages were taught and departments promoted in literature, philosophy, history, religion, art, archaeology, commerce and pure and applied sciences.

The Earl of Ronaldshay, when he was governor of Bengal in 1921, commented that he saw in Mukherjee's plans for the University of Calcutta "a vision of Nalanda growing up in this the greatest and most populous city of the Indian Empire."

Sir Asutosh died in 1924, but his work survived him. It was the product of his energy, will power and devotion to the cause of improving education in India. His religion was that of Vivekananda: Glory to God and Service to Man.

Sir Michael Sadler said of him that "he was one of the world's commanding personalities who could have ruled an empire."

Suggested Further Readings

Sinha, Narendra Krishna.
  Asutosh Mukerjee : a biographical study. — [Calcutta] : Asutosh Mukerjee Centenary
  Committee, 1966.
  vi, 192 p. : port. ; 22 cm.

Sinha, Sasadhar.
  Asutosh Mukerjee. — [New Delhi] : Publications Division, Ministry of Information and
  Broadcasting, [1970]
  88 p. : port. ; 21 cm. — (Builders of Modern India).

ISHWAR CHANDRA VIDYASAGAR
(1820-1891)

Ishwar Chandra Vidyasagar, Bengali educator, social reformer and writer, was one of the most prominent personalities in the modern cultural history of Bengal. He was born 26 September 1820 in the village of Birsingh in the Midnapore district of Bengal. He died in Calcutta 29 August 1891.

Though born of a family of impoverished rural Brahmans, he rose to become a topmost intellectual in the metropolitan city of Calcutta, a famous man of letters and a renowned (if also controversial) public figure, indeed a legend in his lifetime.

Vidyasagar's life, by now described by many hands, is fairly well documented, but sometimes it reads rather like the *vita* of a saint or legendary hero, full of extraordinary and/or edifying *exempla*. Nevertheless, one can discern in the human dimension of this *vita* the life story of an outstanding man who lived through a time of radical and painful cultural changes and was both their creative agent and, in a way, their victim.

Ishwar Chandra is reported to have begun his education at the age of five at a school in his native village. In 1828, his father brought him to Calcutta on foot, and the boy is said to have learned the English numerals from the figures on the milestones. The father wanted his son to carry on the ancestral profession of teaching Sanskrit at the village school; so in 1829 Ishwar Chandra entered Sanskrit College, founded in 1823 by the famous orientalist, H. H. Wilson.

For more than 12 years, Ishwar Chandra was a diligent student at Sanskrit College and acquired a deep knowledge of Sanskrit and traditional Hindu learning. In 1830 he started learning English, and in 1835 (at 14) he got married. In 1839 he passed the Hindu law committee examination and won the scholarly title *Vidyáságara* which later became his public name (though he himself used to sign his name "Isvara Chandra Sarma".)

In 1841, he finished his studies at the Sanskrit College and entered government service as a teacher in the Bengali department at the College of Fort William. This College was founded in 1800 by Governor-General Marquis Wellesley as the "Oxford of the East" in which future British administrators of India were to be taught Indian languages, both classical and vernacular, as well as to receive solid university education.

In the first decade of the nineteenth century the College of Fort William was an important centre of cross-cultural contacts. It produced, on the one hand, a brilliant group of orientalists (Wilson, James Princep, Brian Hodgson and others) and, on the other hand, the first writers of prose in at least three modern Indian languages: Hindi, Urdu and Bengali.

Vidyasagar must have been influenced by this tradition of cultural and literary ventures. At the College he deepened his knowledge of English and learned Hindi. His first published literary work, *Vetála-pañcavimsati*, "Twenty-five Stories of Vetála" (1847) was a recreation of a Hindi version of the famous book of stories in Sanskrit. Written as a textbook for teaching Bengali at the College, it became, according to Sukumar Sen, "a landmark in the history of Bengali prose."

From 1851 to 1858 Vidyasagar was the principal of his alma mater, Sanskrit College. He proved to be an imaginative and efficient administrator and reformer. The basic idea of his reforms was to combine the classical legacy of Sanskrit and Indian tradition with this modernised culture. His declared aim was "to extend the benefit of education to the mass of people." Before his time only Brahmans and Vaidyas (the two highest caste-groups in Bengal) had been admitted to Sanskrit College. Vidyasagar opened its doors to Kayasthas (though even he was not ready to admit lower castes).

In the late 1850s he worked also as assistant inspector of schools, south Bengal, and contributed substantially to the development of popular education at the grass-roots level. On his initiative and under his supervision many village schools were founded in Bengal. Following the lead of the distinguished British administrator, J.D. Bethune, Vidyasagar in 1857-58 tried to found a network of village schools for girls. But the ambitious project was not approved by Vidyasagar's British supervisors, which must have been one of the reasons for his retirement from government service in 1858.

Nevertheless, he remained an unofficial adviser of the government in matters of education and in later years was connected one way or another with various educational projects.

In 1855, Vidyasagar published two pamphlets on the subject of widow-remarriage. This issue had been already discussed in the 1820s-1840s by Rammohun Roy and other critics of Hindu social traditions, but by the 1850s the prohibition of *sati** must have become an acutely felt social evil. This was especially true among the higher casts, but also among the lower ones for whom it became an index of orthodoxy and status.

According to a contemporary witness, the pamphlets of Vidyasagar "stirred Bengali society to its very depths." A campaign of petitions to the government followed, and in 1856 the Widow-Remarriage Act was passed. Vidyasagar considered his championship of widow-remarriage "the greatest good deed" of his life. But the orthodox Hindus never forgave him for this. He was socially ortracised in many circles and abandoned by many earlier supporters. In 1870, he enthusiastically approved his only son's marriage

---

* Self-immolation of widows on the pyres of their late husbands.

to a widow, which brought about separation from his own wife. He had even to leave forever the parental home in his native village.

Vidyasagar crusaded also against another social evil, that of so-called *Kulinism*, the customs of polygamy (often fictitious) among Kulin Brahmans. This custom must have ruined the lives of many women in Bengal. Vidyasagar wrote several biting pamphlets against *Kulinism* from 1871 to 1886, as well as petitions and letters to the government. But no law was passed on this issue, though estrangement between Vidyasagar and his more orthodox or more conformist compatriots increased. In the later years of his life he used to flee from Calcutta to his house in Markatar in Santhal Parganas to live among the Santhals, the people not spoiled then either by "civilization" or by "sanskritization."

Vidyasagar is remembered now as a social reformer and also as a great philanthropist. In his mature years he was a person of considerable means, the poet Michael Madhusudan Dutt, whom Vidyasagar helped a lot, once wrote of him that he was not only a *Vidyáságara* ("Ocean of Wisdom") but also a *Karunáságara* ("Ocean of Compassion"). In another famous phrase Dutt said that Vidyasagar had "the genius and wisdom of an ancient sage, the energy of an Englishman and the heart of a Bengali mother."

Proverbial and legendary had become the simple traditional dress of Vidyasagar: a coarse *dhoti*, a plain *chadar* and a pair of slippers *chati*. It is said that even the British lieutenant-governor of Bengal allowed Vidyasagar to pay visits in his habitual costume. In fact, Vidyasagar did not lack official recognition. In 1864, he was elected an honorary member of the Royal Asiatic Society in London. In 1880, Queen Victoria conferred on him the title of C.I.E. in recognition of his outstanding work for social reforms. Vidyasagar was a brilliant representative of the new educated middle class, which "dreamt of cooperating with the new rulers in transforming India into a modern nation," though, in the end, it proved rather difficult to realise the dream.

But Vidyasagar's more lasting achievements, perhaps his greatest ones, belong to the realm of Bengali language and literature. Rabindranath Tagore wrote:

Vidyáságara bánlábhásár pratham yathárth s'ilpí chilen.
("Vidyasagar is the first true artist of the Bengali language.")

In 1851 Vidyasagar wrote:

The creation of an enlightened Bengali literature should be the first object of those who are entrusted with the superintendence of education in Bengal.

And he sought to create new Bengali literature, using two sources: Sanskrit and English. Vidyasagar's most valued literary works are based on Sanskrit and English classics: *Shakuntala* (1854), a prose rendering of the famous drama by Kalidasa; *Sítár Vanavás*, "Exile of Sita" (1860), again a prose composition on the theme of the *Ramayana, Bhránti-vilas* (1869), an adaptation, with Indian dramatis personae, of Shakespeare's *Comedy of Errors.*

In 1860, he started translating the *Mahábhárata* into Bengali prose but later entrusted the task to another author, though supervising the whole work.

Last, but not least, Vidyasagar wrote his famous Bengali ABC, *Varna-paricaya* (1855) which was used by several generations of children and was highly praised by Tagore himself.

An unavoidable question (often discussed, but hardly ever answered conclusively) is: What was Vidyasagar's attitude towards religious issues. He himself was rather reticent in this respect, but one cannot help noticing the secular character of his life-style and work. In any case, according to Tagore, "he was not a traditional Hindu." Vidyasagar's contemporary, Ramakrishna Paramahansa, once paid him a visit (5 August 1882) and later remarked:

> *Bhavanagáner ánander ásvád páy nái.*
> ("He does not have the taste of the Lord's bliss.")

Modern authors sometimes called Vidyasagar "humanist," and his faith a "Religion of Man," using the common expression later appropriated by Tagore.

On the whole, Vidyasagar's mentality appears to be strikingly modern and up-to-date, more so than that of some later eminent Indians. His life was a paradigm of cultural activity which still has some lessons to teach both to his compatriots and, perhaps, to humanity at large.

— **Sergei Serebriany**

Suggested Further Readings

Banerjee, Hiramoy.
    Iswar Chandra Vidyasagar. — New Delhi : Sahitya Akademi, [1968]
    88 p. ; 23 cm. — (Makers of Indian literature)

Ghosh, Benoy.
    Iswar Chandra Vidyasagar. — [New Delhi] : Publications Division, Ministry of Information and Broadcasting, [1965]
    174 p. : port. ; 21 cm. — (Builders of modern India)

Haldar, Gopal.
    Vidyasagar : a reassessment. — New Delhi : Peoples Pub. House, [1972]
    ix, 94 p. ; 23 cm.

Tripathi, Amales.
    Vidyasagar : the traditional moderniser. — Bombay : Orient Longmans, c1974.
    x, 112 p. ; 22 cm.

CHAPTER 16

THE MISSIONARIES

St. Thomas	Rev. William Carey
St. Francis Xavier	Rev. John Marshman
Roberto de Nobili, S.J.	Rev. William Butler

$\mathcal{T}$he founder of the Christian religion told his followers:

> Go ye therefore to all nations, baptizing them in the name of the Father, and of the Son, and of the Holy Ghost.

Thousands of men and women, answering this summons, left their homes in the West to bring the message of Christ to India. In the process of "spreading the Gospel," they made contributions to India beyond propagation of the faith.

They built schools and colleges, and many of India's leaders were educated in these schools. Hospitals and agricultural institutes were founded to heal and serve Christian and non-Christian alike.

The first orphanage in India and the first women's hospital in India were founded by Rev. Dr. William Butler, a Methodist missionary.

They standardised languages and brought printing to India. The first book printed in India was published by the College of St. Paul in Goa. The first newspaper printed in an Eastern script was the Bengali *Samachar Darpan*, founded by Rev. John Marshman. Rev. William Carey is called "The Father of Bengali Prose," and Fr. Roberto de Nobili, S.J., is considered "The Father of Tamil Prose."

The works of another Jesuit, Thomas Stephens (Tomás Estêvão) on the Konkani language are classics. The languages of India as the missionaries found them were un-standardised and lacking in proper dictionaries and grammars. The missionaries, of course, had an ulterior motive in working with language: they wanted to translate the Bible into the vernaculars of the people, and thereby spread the Gospel.

Chapter 16 is dedicated to these pioneers who believed it was their duty to bring a new way of life to a faraway country, and who, in the process, left that country richer than when they found it.

Suggested Further Reading

History of Christianity in India. — Bangalore : Theological Publications in India, 1982-
6 v. ; 22 cm.

ST. THOMAS

Thomas was one of the twelve disciples of Jesus. He is known to history as Doubting Thomas because he refused to believe that Christ had
risen from the dead unless he had physical proof to that effect. He is also
known as Judas Thomas, or Didymus (the Twin) because he was a twin.
The identify of his twin is unknown, but some believe it was Jesus.

In the Gospel of John, chapter 20, verses 24-29, is this story:

Now Thomas, one of the twelve, called the Twin, was not with them
when Jesus came. So the other disciples told him, "We have seen the
Lord." But he said to them, "Unless I see in his hands the print of the
nails, and place my finger in the mark of the nails, and place my hand
in his side, I will not believe.

Eight days later, his disciples were again in the house, and Thomas
was with them. The doors were shut, but Jesus came and stood among
them, and said, "Peace be with you." Then he said to Thomas, "Put
your finger here, and see my hands; and put out your hand, and place
it in my side; do not be faithless, but believing." Thomas answered
him, "My Lord and my God!" Jesus said to him, "Have you believed
because you have seen me? Blessed are those who have not seen and
yet believe."

What is known of his activities in the years following the crucifixion of
Jesus is in the realm of conjecture and tradition. That he ventured east gets
virtually unanimous support, but there is some difference of opinion as to
how far east he ventured.

Eusebius has him in Parthia, but St. Augustine and other writers of the
early church say he went to India. There is an abundance of tradition which
supports the India view, and that is of concern here.

According to the tradition of the Syrian Christians of Malabar, Thomas
landed in Muziris on the west coast of India in 52 A.D.

But according to the Acts of Thomas, an apocryphal work of the third
century, after the ascension of Christ Thomas was visited from an agent of
King Gundophoros of Taxila who needed an architect for his new palace.
Thomas accepted the job offer and went to Taxila. The king provided him

with funds for the construction of the palace and departed on a royal visit to foreign lands, leaving the work to Thomas. Six months later he returned and discovered that Thomas had given the money to the poor and had not even begun to build the palace. When asked to explain himself, Thomas assured Gundophoros that he had instead built a palace for him in heaven. The king was not amused and sentenced Thomas to die. That night the king's brother dreamed of going to heaven and seeing that Thomas had indeed built a beautiful palace for Gundophoros in heaven. On hearing this, the king released Thomas and allowed him to continue his more saintly pursuits.

Beyond the *Acts of Thomas* there is no hard evidence that Thomas was ever in north India.

It is not known how Thomas got to south India, but Malabar tradition has him get there by the sea route. Once there, he established churches and Christian communities throughout the south.

There is a delightful tale of one of his first encounters with Hinduism which bears repetition here:

> Some Brahmans were having their morning ablutions in a temple tank when Thomas happened by. They were repeating Vedic incantations and sprinkling water upwards in the palms of their hands. Thomas asked them what they were doing, and they explained that they were making offerings to the gods. Thomas told them that their offerings must not have been accepted, otherwise the water would not have fallen back into the tank. The Brahmans asked him if he could keep the water from falling back into the tank, and he said he would do it if they would accept Jesus Christ as their saviour. They agreed; whereupon he sprinkled some water upward, and it remained glistening in the air.

A Malayalam poet of the sixteenth century wrote a poem based on oral tradition about the martyrdom of Thomas which occurred at the Mount in Mylapore in present day Madras. Thomas was passing by a Kali temple when he was set·upon by the priests there. They forced him to enter the temple, but upon doing so, a light shone, and Kali ran from the temple, which was then consumed by fire. The priests were so infuriated by this that they ran Thomas through with a spear.

It is believed that St. Thomas was buried on the Mount.

When the Portuguese arrived on the Coromandel Coast in the sixteenth century, they built a church over what was believed to be his tomb and named the nearby settlement São Thome'.

Suggested Further Readings

Perumalil, A.C.
  The Apostles in India. — 2d ed. — Patna : Xavier Teachers Training Institute, 1971.
    xvi, 234 p. : ill., maps ; 19 cm.

Thomas, Paul.
   Christians and Christianity in India and Pakistan. — London : Allen & Unwin, 1954.
   260 p. : ill. ; 23 cm.

Wright, William.
   The apocryphal acts of the Apostles. — Amsterdam : Philo Press, 1968.
   2 v. in 1 ; 23 cm.
   See Vol II, pp. 146-298: "The Acts of Judas Thomas (or Twin), the Apostle"

ST. FRANCISCO XAVIER
(1506-1552)

St. Francisco Xavier (Francisco de Yasu y Xavier) was born 7 April 1506 at the Chateau Xavier in the kingdom of Navarre. He was the third son of the president of the Royal Council, Juan de Jassu.

After completion of his preliminary studies at home in 1524 he joined the University of Paris where he studied for the priesthood until 1535, taking the master's degree in philosophy and theology.

In Paris he met Ignatius Loyola and came under his influence. He performed the spiritual exercises under his direction and received sacred ordination with him at Venice 24 June 1537. The following year he went to Rome and assisted at the deliberations which resulted in the foundation of the Society of Jesus.

When D. João III, king of Portugal, learned that members of the new order were prepared to travel to faraway places, he applied to the pope for the benefit of the services of some of their number. The choice fell on Simon Rodrigues, a Portuguese, and Bobadilla, a Castillian. The latter fell ill, and Francis Xavier was substituted for him. He set sail from Lisbon in 1541 on his 35th birthday, arriving in Goa 11 months later.

Before carrying out his missionary work, he spent five months in Goa trying, and apparently succeeding, in raising the moral tone of the city by diligence and example.

From 1542 to 1544 he worked with the Parava pearl fishermen, making numerous converts among them. In 1545 he visited the shrine of St. Thomas in Mylapur (São Thomé) where he became convinced that his call was for kingdoms farther to the east.

From September 1545 until late 1547 he worked in Malacca and the Moluccas during which time he met a Japanese name Anjiro who convinced him that he should attempt to evangelise Japan.

He returned to Goa for a brief stay and sailed with two Jesuit brothers, Cosmo de Torres and João Fernandes, and three Japanese disciples 15 April 1549, arriving exactly four months later at Anjiro's home in Kagoshima in Satsuma Province on the island of Kyushu.

On landing at Kagoshima, Xavier at once went to pay his respects to the daimyo Shimadsu with one of the young men from the college of Goa as his interpreter. Shimadsu was shown an image of Mary with the infant

Jesus before which he prostrated himself, ordering all those present to do likewise. He showed the image to his mother, and she was so impressed with it that she ordered one for herself.

In September Xavier asked for and got from the daimyo permission for himself and his colleagues to preach the Christian doctrine. They made about 100 converts, including members of Shimadsu's family. The daimyo himself, however, never embraced the new faith.

During the next two years Xavier travelled about Japan, learning the language, debating with Buddhist monks and establishing enclaves of Christian proselites.

Finally, in September 1551, a little more than two years after first reaching Japan, Xavier left Japan for the purpose of taking the Christian faith to China. His apostolate in Japan had been a great success.

Xavier was aware that the law interedicting foreigners from entering China was rigorously enforced. He therefore planned to effect a lawful and honourable entry by going in the company of a Portuguese ambassador, if he could persuade the viceroy to dispatch one to the court of Peking. The ambassador could then negotiate with the emperor permission for the missionaries to preach in China.

On his way back to Goa in late 1551 Xavier landed in Malacca and learned that Ignatius of Loyola had appointed him provincial of the province of India and the East.

When he arrived in Cochin 24 January 1552, he set about his new duties there and later went to Goa to gain permission from the viceroy to go to China. Permission was granted, and he sailed for China in April.

He arrived in Malacca, but the Portuguese commandant there, Alvaro do Ataide da Gama, refused him permission to sail to China. He then decided to go on his own, reaching the island of Sancian (St. John) off the coast of China.

While waiting there to obtain passage to China, he became ill and died 3 December 1552.

His body was returned to Goa, and when it arrived there, it was found to be well preserved even though it did not arrive until 15 March 1554.

Inquest was soon instituted in the life of Xavier, and a report was submitted in 1557. Pope Paul V conferred on Xavier the title of Blessed 25 October 1619. He was finally canonised by Gregory 12 March 1622.

The body of Xavier is now enshrined in the Church of Bom Jesus in Old Goa and is viewed daily by tourists of all faiths.

The work of Xavier constitutes not only the foundation but more than half the superstructure that the combined efforts of the evangelical and Catholic sections of the Church have been able to raise, just as Syrian Christianity is largely the result of the apostolate of another saint, Thomas the Apostle.

— **George M. Moraes**

Suggested Further Readings

Bouhours, Dominique, 1628-1702.
   The life of St. Francis Xavier ... apostle of India / from the French of Father Dominique
   Bouhours ... by a Catholic clergyman. — Philadelphia : E. Cumminskey, 1841.
   viii, 464 p. : front., port., facsim. ; 20 cm.

Coleridge, Henry James, 1822-1893.
   Life and letters of St. Francis Xavier ... — London : Burns and Oates, 1881.
   2 v. ; 19 cm. — (Half-title: Quarterly series ; v. 1, 4)

ROBERTO DE NOBILI
(1577-1656)

Jesuit Missionary and Tamil scholar, Roberto de Nobili was born in September 1577 in Rome. His father was Conte Pier Francesco de Nobili, a general in the Papal army, and his mother was Clarice Cioli, a Roman lady. Both were of the nobility, a fact which was useful to Nobili later on.

He was educated at the Roman College and there indicated his intention of becoming a Jesuit missionary. When his father died in 1593, his cousin and guardian, Cardinal Francesco Storza, tried to dissuade him from his plans. In consequence of this Nobili left Rome and put himself under the protection of the Duchessa de Nocera and completed his education in her house.

Then, in 1596, he entered the novitiate in Naples. Four years later he returned to Rome to study theology and in 1603 was ordained.

He sailed for India from Lisbon in April 1604 in a Portuguese carrack. As a non-Portuguese person sailing in a Portuguese ship, he was considered a vassal of the king of Portugal who, by *padroado* (ecclesiastical patronage), was responsible for evangelising India.

Nobili arrived in Goa 20 May 1605 after surviving a shipwreck near Mozambique. He learned Tamil on the Fishery Coast, and was sent by his provincial, Alberto Laerzio, to Madura, an inland town. Here Nobili departed from the custom expected of missionaries and refused to dress like a Portuguese or assume a Portuguese surname.

Missionaries were not welcomed by the Hindu community and were called *feringhis*.* They were looked down upon as beef-eating, wine-drinking outcastes.

Nobili "went native," dressing in saffron clothes, wearing wooden sandals, and adopting the vegetarian diet of a *sannyasi* (ascetic, or holy man). When the people learned that Nobili was of noble birth, they called him a *raja sannyasi*, and he was permitted to associate with Brahmans.

He converted 50 people in his first 18 months in Madura and named his first convert Alberto after his provincial. Among his friends was a Brahman Sanskrit scholar, Sivadarma, who tried to convert Nobili to *Vedanta*,

---

*   A pejorative term meaning "foreigner" — usually applied to Portuguese.

and it was through Sivadarma that Nobili learned about Sanskrit, the *Vedas* and *Vedanta*.

The Brahman community, jealous of Nobili's success, tried to have him expelled as a *feringhi*, but Sivadarma defended him, explaining that, as a scholar-*sannyasi*, he was quite different from the other *feringhis*. In 1609 Nobili succeeded in converting Sivadarma, but a problem presented itself: what to do about the Brahman thread? Should a Brahman, on conversion to Christianity, be required to discard the thread? Nobili argued that he should be allowed to wear it, and Sivadarma was baptized on Whitsunday 1609.

The business about the thread bothered the Jesuit leaders in Goa, and Nobili was censured for permitting this Hindu symbol to be worn by converts. In a brief of 18 February 1618 Pope Paul V ordered Archbishop de Sá and the inquisitors in Goa to hold a conference with Nobili and report the matter back to the Vatican.

The conference was held, and Nobili was outvoted by the inquisitors and priests who questioned him. However, when the report reached Europe, the grand inquisitor of Portugal and the new pope, Gregory XV, sided with Nobili, and Brahman converts would henceforth be allowed to wear the thread.

While this controversy was going on, Nobili was forbidden to baptise; so he devoted his time to writing, mainly in Tamil. Among the works he published during this period were:

1. *Gananpodesam* ("Spiritual Teaching"), a catechism, and considered by *Catholic Encyclopedia* "his most important work, virtually a *Summa theologiae*." Fr. Proença, one of his successors, said that "whoever reads that book will easily judge that it is the best ever written in the Church of God."

2. *Dushana Dhikkaram* was a refutation of attacks against the Christian religion.

3. *Attuma Nirnayam* was a treatise on the origin and end of the human soul and questioned the Hindu doctrine of rebirth.

4. *Janma Akshepam*, like the treatise mentioned above, may have been written first in Sanskrit and later translated into Tamil. It urged its readers to inquire of the author regarding religion.

5. *Nittiya Jivana Saliapam* was a treatise on the importance of accepting religion as revealed by God.

Once the controversy over the thread was settled, Nobili went about south India, baptising and founding new missions.

During the war between the Portuguese and the Nayak of Madura in 1640, Nobili and his fellow-missionaries were imprisoned for about a year.

In 1654 Nobili, with his eye sight failing, retired and lived out his last years in a hut in Mylapore. He died 16 January 1656.

Before he arrived in Madura, there were no Christians there. When he left, there were 4,183.

Suggested Further Readings

Cronin, Vincent.
    A pearl to India : the life of Roberto de Nobili. — New York : Harl-Davis, 1959.
    297 p. ; 21 cm.

Bertrand, Joseph.
    La mission de Madurè d'aprés des documents inédits. — Paris : Librarire Poussilgue-
    Rustand, 1847-54.
    4 v. : facsims. ; 23 cm.

WILLIAM CAREY
(1761-1834)

He was one of the first Protestant missionaries in India, and his name
was William Carey. He was a cobbler. He was born 17 August 1761 in Paulers
Pury, Northamptonshire, the first child of Edmund Carey, a school teacher
and weaver.

Until he was 28, he worked as a shoe-maker, but he spent his spare
time reading travel, history, natural science and adventure books. When he
was 18, he joined a church group at Hackleton and later a Baptist congregation at Moulton, of which he later became pastor.

In 1789, he moved to Leicester and in 1792 published his *An Inquiry
into the Obligation of Christians to Use Means for the Conversion of Heathens*. It
led to the founding of the Baptist Missionary Society.

He embarked for India 13 June 1793 to become a missionary. Arriving
in Calcutta 11 November, he was unnoticed, which was the way he wanted
it. The English clergy had come into such bad repute in India that Governor-General Teignmouth had written to the court of directors of the East
India Company that "our clergy in Bengal, with some exceptions, are not
respectable characters."

(The anti-clerical stand of England was in sharp contrast to that of the
Roman Catholic countries, Portugal and France, which openly supported
and encouraged missionary activity in India as a matter of national policy.)

Carey went into hiding, getting a lowly job in an indigo factory in
Madnabati to keep himself from starving. While there he preached, taught,
built a church and started translating the Bible into Bengali, hoping to set
up a press in order to publish his Bengali Bible.

After six years he moved to Serampore, a Danish settlement on the
Hugli River, where he could enjoy Danish protection under Governor Bie
from East India Company officials.

Of his move to Serampore, he wrote:

At Serampore we can settle as missionaries ... and the great ends of the
mission, particularly in the printing of the scriptures, seem much more
likely to be answered in that situation .... In that part of the country the
inhabitants are far more numerous, and other missionaries may be there

permitted to join us, which here it seems they will not .... Had we stayed at Mudnabutty or its vicinity, it is a great wonder we could have set up our press. Government would have suspected us, though without reason to do so, and would, in all probability, have prevented us from printing; the difficulty of procuring proper materials would also have been almost insuperable.

Carey started out in Serampore by opening a school for children, where they could get a free education and a small dispensary for the treatment of lepers. He completed his translation of the Bible; the New Testament was published in 1801 and the Old Testament between 1802 and 1809. By this time he had established himself as the foremost British scholar of Bengali.

In 1801, Carey was hired to teach Bengali at Fort William College, Calcutta, and in 1807 he was promoted to professor of Bengali. He was also responsible for Marathi and Sanskrit.

Together with Joshua Marshman and William Ward, Carey continued the missionary work in Serampore. Carey was interested in all languages of India, and he translated the Bible into Oriya, Marathi, Assamese, Hindi and Sanskrit, and parts of it into 29 other Indian languages.

With Joshua Marshman, he also translated into English the *Ramayana* in three volumes. As if this were not enough, he published William Roxburgh's *Hortus Bengalensis* (1814) and *Flora Indica* (1832). In 1807, he was awarded a D.D. from Brown University in Rhode Island.

In addition to his teaching duties, Dr. Carey published books in Bengali and helped in the publication of two Bengali journals: *Digdarshan* and *Samachar Darpan*.

Carey was not content to occupy his time solely with teaching, translating, publishing and preaching. He urged the government to take action against such horrors as infanticide and *sati* (self-immolation of widows on their husband's funeral pyres), and he was instrumental in founding the Agricultural Society of India.

Carey's most famous prose works were *Kathopakatan* ("The Dialogues") and *Itihasamala*, a collections of short stories in what Carey called "the beautiful language of Bengali." These works established him as "The Father of Bengali Prose."

He died in Serampore 9 June 1834.

Suggested Further Readings

Carey, Samuel Pearce.
  William Carey, D.D. : fellow of the Linnean Society. — London : Hodder & Stoughton, [1923]
  xvi, 428 p. : front., plates, port., fold. map, facsims. ; 23 cm.

Chatterjee, Sunil Kumar.
  William Carey and Serampore. — Calcutta : Ghosh, 1984.
  xx, 92 p.; 22 cm.

Smith, George.
  The Life of William Carey, D.D. : shoemaker and missionary. — London : Murray, 1885.
  xiii, 463 p. : front. port., ill., plates ; 23 cm.

JOHN CLARK MARSHMAN
(1794-1877)

The man who built the first paper mill in India and founded the first Indian language newspaper in India was John Marshman.

He was born 18 August 1794 in Britain and went out to India with his father, Joshua Marshman, a Baptist missionary and Orientalist, arriving in Calcutta 13 October 1799. They were accompanied by William Ward.

Because the East India Company, which ruled Bengal at this time, looked with a jaundiced eye on missionary activity, the Marshmans were obliged to take refuge in the Danish settlement at Serampore where they had been preceded by William Carey. Carey was at that moment busy translating the Bible into Bengali.

Ultimately, Joshua Marshman, William Ward and William Carey would come to be known as "The Serampore Three."

Beginning in 1818, John took over his father's operations and for 20 years served as a "secular bishop." Much of his time and energy were spent in raising money for mission work.

He built the first paper mill in India and founded, with his father, two newspapers: *Samachar Darpan; or, Mirror of News* and *Digdarshan; Friend of India*. The former, in Bengali, was the first newspaper ever printed in an Eastern language. The latter started out as a monthly magazine, then became quarterly and, finally, on 1 January 1835, weekly.

Digdarshan frequently offended the East India Company officials, and they attempted to shut it down; however, they were prevented from doing so by the king of Denmark who looked favourably on Marshman's efforts in Serampore, which happened to be Danish territory.

Marshman published a series of law books, one of which, *Guide to the Civil Law of the Fort William Presidency*, was for many years the civil code of India.

He attempted to set up a Christian colony in the Sunderbans, but the project failed. But he did not fail in all his projects. He contributed 30,000 pounds sterling to the establishment of Serampore College for the education of Indians, an institution that still exists.

In 1852, he returned to England, but was refused a seat on the Council of India and had to settle for a job as auditor of the East India Railway. He made three unsuccessful attempts for a seat in the House of Commons: Ipswich in 1857, Harwich in 1859 and Marlyebone in 1861.

He wrote histories of Bengal and of India and a biography of Sir Henry Havelock, his brother-in-law. His work in education was finally recognised in 1868 when he was awarded the *Star of India*. He died in London 8 July 1877.

Suggested Further Reading

Marshman, John Clark, 1794-1877.
    The life and times of the Carey, Marshman and Ward, embracing the history of the
    Serampore Mission. — 1859.
    2 v.

WILLIAM BUTLER
(1818-1899)

William Butler, the founder of Methodism in India, was also the founder of Methodism in Mexico.

He was born in Dublin of English parents 30 January 1818 and educated at Hardwick Street Mission Seminary (Wesleyan) in Dublin and at Didsbury College, Manchester, England. Later he earned a D.D. degree. He became a Methodist in 1837, joined the Irish Conference in 1844, and was ordained an elder in 1848.

While in Manchester he married a Miss Lewis who died shortly after bearing him a son. He then married her sister, Julia, by whom he had two more sons.

The family migrated to America in 1850 and the following year Dr. Butler was admitted to the New York East Conference. Later he was transferred to the New England Conference and served several churches in Massachusetts. While at Westfield, MA, Julia Butler died suddenly. Butler later sent for Clementina Rowe of Wexford, Ireland, and they were married 23 November 1854. They had two daughters.

Before coming to America, Butler had been interested in missionary work, and in 1852 his *Compendium of Missions* was published. Finally, in 1856 he was sent to India by Bishop Matthew Simpson.

The Butler family arrived in India during the spring of 1857, just as the Great Revolt of that year was breaking out. Butler picked the area north of the Ganges River for his work, and the mission officially opened in Bareilly in August 1858.

Within three years Butler was able to establish Methodist mission outposts in nine locations.

His career in India lasted only seven years, but in that time he built a printing press and a number of school houses, orphanages and churches. He also founded the first hospital for women in India. He is credited with building the first orphanage in India. It was intended mainly for children who had been orphaned during the Indian Revolt.

In his memoirs Butler wrote:

A few days later Major Golwan, the officer who had so kindly advised me to flee from Bareilly, met me and surprised me by saying he had the first orphan ready for me, a little fellow he had picked up (the son of a sepoy officer who had been killed), who had been found on the back of an elephant in the field of battle.

Butler was not an easy man to get along with, and he had little time for restrictions and regulations imposed by church officials in New York.

He returned to the United States in 1864, served in several New England pastorates and in 1869 was named secretary of the American and Foreign Christian Union.

He was back in the mission field in 1872 when Bishop Simpson sent him to Mexico. During the first year of his work there he organised two English and seven Mexican congregations. Unlike other Protestant missionaries in Mexico, he refused to indulge in attacks on the Roman Catholic Church.

Because of his disregard for orders from the Board of Missions, such as using funds as he saw best and occasionally obligating the church for expenditures beyond what had been appropriated, the Board in April 1878 voted to recall Butler "as soon as possible."

He worked briefly for the Freedmen's Aid Society and took a pastorate in Melrose, MA (1880-1883). He did some travelling, to India, the Holy Land and Mexico and retired in 1891.

He was an invalid the last eight years of his life and died in the Missionary Rest Home in Old Orchard, ME, 18 August 1899.

He published a number of books, in addition to the book on missions which came out in 1852.

In *Land of the Veda* (1872) he wrote about India, and in *From Boston to Bareilly and Back* (1885) he told of his mission work. He also wrote a book on his work "south of the border" entitled *Mexico in Transition*.

Butler was a hard, energetic and headstrong man, but he accomplished what he set out to do, even if he had to break some rules to do it.

"By their works ye shall know them."

Suggested Further Readings

Butler, Clementina.
   William Butler : the founder of two missions of the Methodist Episcopal Church / by his daughter. — New York : Eaton & Mains; Cincinnati : Jennings & Pie, 1902.
   239 p. : front., ill. (incl. music), plates, ports. ; 21 cm.

Butler, Clementina.
   Mrs. William Butler : two empires and the Kingdom of God. — New York : Methodist Book Concern, [1929]
   202 p. : front., ill., plates, ports., facsims. ; 22 cm.

INDEX